Benevolence and Betrayal

FIVE ITALIAN JEWISH FAMILIES UNDER FASCISM

Alexander Stille

SUMMIT BOOKS

New York London Toronto Sydney Tokyo Singapore

Summit Books
Simon & Schuster Building
Rockefeller Center
1230 Avenue of the Americas
New York, New York 10020

Designed by Levavi & Levavi
Manufactured in the United States of America

10 9 8 7 6 5 4 3

Library of Congress Cataloging-in-Publication Data

Stille, Alexander.
Benevolence and betrayal : five Italian Jewish families under fascism / Alexander Stille.
p. cm.
Includes bibliographical references.
1. Jewish families—Italy—History—20th century. 2. Jews—Italy—History—20th century. 3. Holocaust, Jewish (1939–1945)—Italy. 4. World War, 1939–1945—Jews—Rescue—Italy. 5. Holocaust survivors—Italy. 6. Jews—Italy—Genealogy. 7. Italy—Genealogy. 8. Italy—Ethnic relations. I. Title.
DS135.I9A17 1991
945'.004924—dc20 91-28705 CIP

ISBN 0-671-67152-9

Acknowledgments

My greatest debt of thanks is to the families that are the principal focus of this book. They cooperated with a spirit of great generosity, giving me their time and the fruit of their experience, as well as family documents, letters, and photographs. The material they provided me with is the heart of the book. For the first section, I want to thank Carla Ovazza and Franca Ovazza Piperno. For the second, Vittorio Foa, Anna Foa Yona and Giuseppe Foa. For the third section, the late Michele Di Veroli (di Enrico), Gianni and the late Olga Di Veroli; Michele Di Veroli (di Umberto); Silvia and Giuditta Di Veroli. Instrumental to the fourth section were the late Massimo Teglio, Laura and Mario Teglio and Emanuele Pacifici. For the final section, my thanks to Franco and Dory Schönheit.

I would also like to acknowledge the many dozens of other people whom I interviewed in the course of my research. My debt to those who are quoted in the book is clear, while the contribution of those who are not is less obvious but equally great. Their recollections enriched and informed my understanding of the period immeasurably.

I owe a great deal to the help of Michele Sarfatti, Luisella Mortara Ottolenghi, Liliana Picciotto Fargion and Adriana Goldstaub, and their dedicated colleagues at the Centro di Studi Ebraici Contemporaneo in Milan. Equally instrumental in aiding my research were the archivists at the Archivio Centrale dello Stato, in particular, Marina Gennero. Thanks also to historians Renzo De Felice and Mario Toscano for their useful suggestions and to Celeste Pavoncello, who kindly provided me with a copy of her dissertation on the "La Nostra Bandiera" movement.

Other than my family, the person who lived most closely with this book over a period of some five years was my agent, Sallie Gouverneur. I want to thank her for the faith she showed in this project in its embryonic state all the way to its completion and for her tireless efforts on my behalf. Aside from her official duties, she was also a valued friend and reader. At Summit Books, I want to thank Bob Asahina, his assistant Sarah Bayliss and copyeditor Anna Jardine, each of whom did a highly professional job during the editorial process.

I am extremely grateful to Jimmy Finkelstein, publisher of *The National Law Journal,* and to my editors there, Tim Robinson and Doreen Weisenhaus, whose enlightened employment policies gave me the time off I needed to write this book. It is hard to imagine my having been able to complete it without their interest, encouragement, and understanding.

I want to thank my wife and my mother. Aside from providing moral support, their collective talent as professional editors is a resource few authors are lucky enough to have at their disposal.

For Sarah and my family.

Contents

Introduction 11

Fatherland, Faith and Family: the Ovazzas of Turin 17

Commitment and Betrayal: The Foas of Turin 91

A Family of the Ghetto: The Di Verolis of Rome 167

The Rabbi, the Priest and the Aviator: A Story of Rescue in Genoa 223

Ferrara–Buchenwald–Ferrara: The Schönheit Family 279

Epilogue 315

Source Notes 351

Selected Bibliography 363

Introduction

I owe both my name and my existence to Mussolini's racial laws. My father's parents, Elia and Sara Kamenetzki, were Russian Jews who arrived in Italy in 1922. My father and his closest boyhood friend invented the pseudonym "Ugo Stille" when they began writing a magazine column after the racial laws of 1938 prohibited Jews from publishing their writings. *Stille,* meaning silence in German, seemed an appropriate response to fascist censorship.

My father and his family left Italy in 1941, while his friend, Giaime Pintor, who was Catholic, remained behind. The Kamenetzkis were among the last Jewish refugees to escape Europe, taking a boat from Lisbon in September 1941, only six weeks before the Japanese bombing of Pearl Harbor. A year after arriving in New York, my father was drafted, and in 1943 he was sent back to Italy with the U.S. Army during the invasion of Sicily and southern Italy. At the same time, his friend Pintor—the other Ugo Stille—was blown up by a land mine in one of the first actions of the Italian resistance. After the war, my father made Stille his legal name.

Having returned to New York as the U.S. correspondent for an Italian newspaper, my father met my mother, an American woman from Chicago, and they married in 1949. Although my father remained closely tied to Italy, my sister and I grew up in a thoroughly American family.

My father spoke rarely about life before the war and almost never about the period of racial persecution.

My elderly grandparents, however—refugees of czarist Russia and fascist Italy—were a living reminder of the past. Walking with canes and speaking broken English, they seemed to have stepped out of another century into the America of the 1960s. The tragedy of Europe clung to them like the musty smell of their large, dark apartment on West End Avenue, cluttered with the remnants of their life in Rome. They had been wiped out twice already, and were too old to start over again. My grandfather's certifications in dentistry from Russia and Italy were not valid in the United States, so he was reduced to practicing clandestinely, just as he had during the time of racial discrimination in Italy. My family saw them infrequently, and they died before I had a chance to learn much about their lives.

I dimly sensed the presence of important and painful events that had conditioned their (and my father's) lives, but I knew next to nothing about them. Perhaps more than anything else, this almost total ignorance—and the unsatisfied curiosity that sprang from it—led me to write a book about the experience of Italian Jews during fascism.

When I first began to read about the subject in 1984, I found surprising gaps in the literature. The few good books were scholarly histories, concentrating on the larger political and diplomatic scene: the relations between Hitler and Mussolini, and the changing policy of Mussolini toward the Jews. But I was more interested in the experience of ordinary people and the texture of their everyday lives. A number of personal memoirs and autobiographies provided intriguing glimpses into this world but not a total picture. With the exception of Giorgio Bassani's novel *The Garden of the Finzi-Continis,* there was no book that conveyed the paradoxical quality of Jewish life in fascist Italy—a highly tolerant country that suddenly embraced anti-Semitism, the chief ally of Nazi Germany, which had staunchly refused to cooperate with the deportation of Jews.

What distinguished the story of Italian Jews from that of Jews elsewhere in Europe was the long coexistence between Jews and fascists in Mussolini's Italy. Italian fascism was in power for sixteen years before it turned anti-Semitic in 1938. Until then, Jews were as likely to be members of the Fascist Party as were other conservative-minded Italians.

This singular fact altered the entire moral and existential equation for Italy's Jews. In other countries, fascism was the undisguised enemy. But the experience of Italian Jews was far more complex: a strange mixture of benevolence and betrayal, persecution and rescue.

The close bond between fascist Italy and its Jews had a whole series of important consequences—both positive and negative—in the lives of individuals. It changed the Jews' sense of national and religious identity, it affected the decisions they made about whether to stay or emigrate after 1938. During the German occupation, it altered their perceptions of the dangers they faced and the way they reacted to them. After the war, it influenced the decision of most Italian Jews to remain in Italy rather than emigrate to Israel or the United States, as most German and Eastern European Jews did.

It was this world of subjective personal experience—how people lived and thought, what they did and why they did it—that I wanted to explore. Strangely enough, the existing books made little use of a great untapped historical resource, the thousands of Italian Jews who had lived through the period and whose numbers dwindle significantly with every year.

I decided to structure the book around the experience of several different families, on the basis primarily of interviews, letters and diaries. This approach, it seemed to me, would remain close to individual experience while giving a sense of the wide political, socioeconomic and geographic diversity of Italian Jewish experience.

Any choice of families would have been arbitrary. There are, nonetheless, certain characteristic elements of Italian Jewish experience that are reflected in the families I chose to write about.

The first section of the book tells the story of the Ovazzas of Turin, a fascist Jewish family. Their story chronicles the remarkable rise and assimilation of northern Italian Jewish families, who prospered along with the new Italian nation and developed a fiercely patriotic and nationalistic consciousness. The career of Ettore Ovazza—the main focus of this section—is synonymous with the Jewish fascist movement. The experience of his younger relatives typifies the indoctrination of fascist youth in Italian public schools during the 1930s.

The second section is a counterpoint to the first, relating the story of an antifascist Jewish family in the same city. The choices of the three Foa children give an idea of the range of possibilities open to people of antifascist leanings during the period. Vittorio Foa's activities in the antifascist underground provide a window into the netherworld of the Italian secret police and its network of informants. The experience of his older brother, Giuseppe, shows that it was far from unusual for an Italian Jew of antifascist sympathies to be a member of the Fascist Party.

While these first two narratives take place within the highly assimilated, cosmopolitan atmosphere typical of Jewish life in the larger cities of northern Italy, the next one, of the Di Veroli family, describes a radically different but equally characteristic world: the Rome ghetto. Most Jews under fascism belonged to the professional and commercial classes, but more than half of Rome's Jews (the largest community in Italy) still lived in and around the old ghetto area where they had been confined for centuries, dirt poor and barely literate. Their Turinese counterparts participated with passion in the political debates of the day, but the Jews of the Rome ghetto lived in a world apart, locked into a daily struggle for survival. Because of their cultural isolation (and lack of material resources) they were in a particularly vulnerable position after the Germans occupied Rome. Members of the numerous Di Veroli family participated in all the most important moments of the nine-month Nazi occupation of Rome.

The fourth section of the book, set in Genoa, describes the extraordinary cooperation between the Jewish community and the local Catholic Church in hiding and saving Jews. One of the two families that figure prominently in the story, that of Rabbi Riccardo Pacifici, provides an example of that portion of Italian Jewry which remained deeply attached to its religious traditions. The other central character here, Massimo Teglio, is representative of the exceptional efforts made by some Italian Jewish assistance organizations to function clandestinely despite the extreme danger of the German occupation.

Although the book concentrates almost exclusively on what was happening in Italy during the twenty-one years of fascism, I felt it was important to include the experiences of one family that had been deported to Germany. Deportation was, after all, the fate of about one in seven Italian Jews. The Schönheits—the subject of the fifth and final section—were of interest to me for several other reasons as well. First, they were from Ferrara, a city with a rich tradition of Jewish history. Second, they were arrested not by Germans but by Italian neofascists, who played an important role in the Italian phase of the Holocaust. Third, the Schönheits were half Jewish, and the unusual treatment they received at the hands of both the Italian fascists and the German Nazis reveals the interplay between race and religion in Italy. Moreover, while I did not want to repeat the work of the many books about the German concentration camps, I thought it useful to describe the special circumstance of Italian prisoners in German camps.

The book follows a chronological progression as it traces the history of Italian Jews through the various family narratives. The story of the Ovazzas concentrates on the participation of Italian Jews in World War I and in the rise of fascism. The Foa chapters begin in the mid-1930s, when the rise of Hitler stimulated a growing antifascism among many

Italian Jews. The central event of the Di Veroli narrative is the great roundup in the Rome ghetto, on October 16, 1943—the first large-scale action against Italy's Jews. The fourth section begins two weeks later, as the Jews of Genoa brace themselves for the Germans' next move. The story of the Schönheits picks up the thread twelve days later, on the night of November 15, 1943, and describes the final deportations from Italy.

While fairly typical, the people I have chosen to focus on were, however, not chosen as object lessons to prove or disprove a particular historical thesis. A number of writers have tried to use the Holocaust, and the experience in Italy in particular, to make larger points about Italian fascism, Nazi Germany, the Catholic Church, European Jews or human nature itself. Books have been written to prove either that the Church was a silent accomplice to the slaughter of the Jews or that it behaved heroically in saving them. Others have scrutinized the conduct of the Jewish community itself: Were the Jews helpless, "innocent" victims? Or did Jewish leaders, as Robert Katz suggests in *Black Sabbath,* act in their own self-interest rather than to protect the people they represented? Fierce debate has been waged over the role of Italian fascism in the Holocaust: some have stressed the damage done by Italy's racial laws and its alliance with Hitler, others have emphasized the country's later efforts to rescue Jews.

This book does not argue for or against any of these positions, but many passages touch on the issues they raise. Significantly, one can find examples that support or challenge almost every thesis. The answers to questions about the behavior of the Catholic Church or the Italian population vary enormously with individual experience. Some Italian Jews encountered strangers who helped them out of pure compassion; others were turned in by their neighbors for money or spite. (Frequently, the best and worst instincts resided within the same person: members of the Teglio family were hidden by a retired fascist policeman who initially offered them hospitality and later threatened to turn them in to extract more money from them.) It is difficult also to make a blanket judgment about the Catholic Church: centuries of Vatican preaching against the Jews were a critical precondition for the Holocaust, and Pope Pius XII's tepid public response to racial persecution did little to create resistance to the genocide; but it is also true that most Italian Jews who turned for help to individual priests and churches found both material aid and moral comfort. Similarly, the conduct of Italian Jewish leaders was by no means uniform: some were hopelessly naive and myopic while others acted with both courage and foresight.

There was even variety in the behavior of the German occupying troops in Italy: some people I interviewed had their lives spared by German soldiers. This does not mean that one is condemned to moral relativism; the actions of the few do not absolve the conduct of the many. The stark contrast between the behavior of most Italian and German soldiers makes it legitimate to reflect on the cultures in which they were raised. At the same time, the fact that fascist Italy did not exterminate Jews does not spare it responsibility for having persecuted them. Jewish leaders are not above criticism, but they do not deserve to be put on the same moral plane as their persecutors; their errors in judgment, however serious, cannot be meaningfully compared with articulated programs of discrimination or mass murder.

While I was researching this book, several Italian Jews tried to dissuade me from writing about the phenomenon of Jewish fascism, out of a fear of stirring renewed anti-Semitism. Obviously I disagreed. There is no reason Jews should be held to a higher standard than anyone else; they were typical Italians, lived through the same times, were subject to the same forces and passions. As with other Italians, their behavior during fascism ran the full gamut from the foolish and contemptible to the wise and heroic.

If there is a virtue to the collection of individual stories, perhaps it is as an antidote to overbroad generalizations. The complexity of individual experience, with all its rough, solid three-dimensionality, can be a useful touchstone for the abstract, linear theories of history.

Fatherland, Faith and Family

THE OVAZZAS OF TURIN

PRECEDING PAGE–Men of the Ovazza family at the time of World War I. Ernesto Ovazza is seated; standing from left to right are his sons, Ettore, Alfredo and Vittorio.

PRECEDING PAGE–Ettore Ovazza's wife, Nella, and son, Riccardo, before World War II.

A signed photograph of Mussolini dedicated to Ettore Ovazza, dated August of the sixth year of the fascist era, 1928. In the early years of fascism Mussolini favored the topcoat of the parliamentarian; in later years he generally posed in military uniform.

Ovazza
Avv. Ettore
fu Ernesto
abitante
C. Montevecchio 33
di professione Avvocato
è iscritto al Partito dal giorno
15 Marzo 1923

IL FASCISTA

IL SEGRETARIO POLITICO
DEL FASCIO DI COMBATTIMENTO

Ettore Ovazza's Fascist Party card, dated March 15, 1923. Although his membership came after the regime's rise to power, Ettore was granted the much-coveted "certificate" of the March on Rome, for his contribution to the revolution that installed Mussolini in October 1922.

Il barbaro eccidio della famiglia Ovazza rievocato al Tribunale militare

I corpi delle tre vittime bruciati nel termosifone

Contumace il tenente nazista imputato dello sterminio: l'Austria non ha concesso l'estradizione - Il Collegio respinge la richiesta di un rinvio del giudizio - La testimonianza del barone Levi De Veali

A newspaper clipping from 1955, reporting on the trial in absentia of Gottfried Meir for the "Intra massacre."

Chapter One

Before his death in 1926, Ernesto Ovazza asked to have three words carved in marble on his tombstone: FATHERLAND, FAITH and FAMILY. Ovazza had lived by this triple creed. At the age of fifty he had signed up, along with his three sons, to fight in World War I. He had served as president of Turin's Jewish community. And as patriarch of the large Ovazza clan, he had run the family bank and brought together all his relatives for Jewish holidays and summer vacations at his large villa outside the city. By supporting the Fascist Party when it came to power in 1922, Ernesto Ovazza believed he was reinforcing the bonds among his family, the Jewish community and the Italian nation.

All three of his sons shared Ernesto's beliefs, but none more so than his second son, Ettore, who in turn passed them on to the next generation. Moments after his only son, Riccardo, was born, Ettore placed an Italian flag on the cradle above the sleeping infant and next to it a Jewish family heirloom—re-creating symbolically that same trinity: Fatherland, Faith and Family. With great emotion, he recorded the scene in a diary he began keeping for his son:

May 24, 1923

On the crib where my son rests, I have planted a tricolor flag [green, white and red]. Next to the name of God, written in ancient Hebrew script on a silver pendant, this lively "tricolor" note, tied with a blue ribbon, seems to illuminate the room. . . .

While Riccardo was being born, all of Italy was celebrating the eighth anniversary of our declaration of war. May 1915—truly radiant days, a magnificent pulsing of national energies, directed toward the future and a better destiny! . . . On that day our troops crossed the unjust borders.

As Ettore celebrated his son's birth in his Turin apartment and contemplated the convergence between the baby's destiny and that of the nation, he heard a military band march down the street playing the fascist hymn "Giovinezza" (Youth). Ovazza grabbed the baby and took him to the window. "Look, you were born under a lucky star, look at the New Italy passing by!" he said.

The summer after his son was born, Ettore wrote often in his diary while at the family villa in the hills overlooking Turin. It seemed an ideal time to reflect on the past and look toward the future. The terrible war he had welcomed and nearly died in was over. The country had then survived a severe economic convulsion and a "Red scare" in which Italy seemed about to go the way of czarist Russia into a second Bolshevik Revolution. Ettore, along with many former army officers, had joined Mussolini's Blackshirts in order to defend the uniform, the flag and the blood of those who had fought for the Fatherland. In October 1922, along with some 230 Italian Jews, Ettore had participated in the March on Rome that installed Mussolini in power. Now, in place of unruly crowds of striking workers, military bands paraded on the streets of Turin, carrying flags and playing patriotic songs.

With the triumph of fascism, the bloodshed and pain of the war seemed worthwhile. "My son, a grandiose historical cycle has just ended with a gigantic war, and from this appalling struggle, from this crucible of national destinies, Italy has emerged greater and more beautiful," Ettore wrote.

Ettore saw both greatness and struggle for Italy in the years ahead. With Mussolini, the nation would fight to re-create the Empire and restore the Fatherland to its just position in the world. It would no doubt face stiff resistance and possibly other wars, and Ettore hoped that Riccardo would follow his namesake, Richard the Lion-Hearted, and become a great soldier in Italy's imperial destiny.

Although Ettore's enthusiasm for the new regime was considerable, he did have one slight concern. While Mussolini was hardly anti-Semitic, Ettore detected a certain lack of regard for the religious minorities within the fascist movement.

Religion and politics, these great words, will confront you at every turn in the path of your life; they will be like two great tree trunks that will block your path. But you must not try to jump over them, but walk slowly alongside of them and proceed on your way; and just when you think you are free of them, as if by inexorable destiny, you will find them again before you on the path; don't give way to fear or terror, because reason solves every serious obstacle in human existence.

* * *

The inescapable confrontation between religion and politics would come to dominate Ettore Ovazza's life—more than he could have known in 1923. When the first signs of anti-Semitism began to appear in fascist Italy in 1934, Ovazza helped found a militant new Jewish fascist movement. There had always been Jews who were fascists, but it had never been necessary before to emphasize the point. Ettore started the newspaper *La Nostra Bandiera* (Our Flag) in an attempt to make unequivocally clear that the nation's Jews were among the regime's most fiercely loyal followers. During the next four years, he waged a vigorous battle on two fronts: defending the Jews against their anti-Semitic critics while also attacking Zionist and antifascist Jews whose supposed lack of patriotism placed all the others under suspicion.

As war drew closer, and the marriage between Judaism and fascism became increasingly strained, Ovazza raised his voice even louder. Rather than denounce Mussolini's rapprochement with Hitler, he blamed the rising anti-Semitism in Italy on the obstinance of the country's small Zionist movement. At the same time, he and others like him made increasingly extravagant public demonstrations of fascist faith: circulating petitions and loyalty oaths, making open declarations, sending telegrams to the government—all in the hope of warding off persecution.

When this strategy failed and the Italian fascists passed the racial laws of 1938, Ovazza—by now almost alone among Italian Jews—clung to his convictions. In a last, desperate attempt to prove his loyalty to the fascist cause, he and some of his associates burned down the offices of a Zionist newspaper in Florence. Believing that Mussolini's racial laws were a mere tactical maneuver that would be revoked after Italy had won its place in the sun in World War II, Ovazza remained in Italy—with tragic consequences for his entire family.

Within the Italian Jewish community, Ettore Ovazza's name lives in infamy. Considered a traitor to his people, he is an embarrassing family secret, of whom it is better not to speak. In the larger history of the period, he remains little more than a curious footnote, representative of a bizarre, minor phenomenon. But during the years 1934–1938 his brand of militant Jewish fascism was hardly marginal. It was one of the principal currents of opinion competing for the allegiance of Italian Judaism. Although there are instances of Jews making compromises with fascism elsewhere in Europe, these were isolated cases of personal opportunism, of private pacts with the devil. In Italy, Jewish fascism was a real ideological movement, a mass phenomenon, as much as that was possible in Italy's tiny Jewish population of 47,000. In 1938, at the beginning of the racial laws, more than 10,000 Jews—about one out of every three Jewish adults—were members of the Fascist Party.

Unique among the countries of Europe, in Italy Jews and fascism coexisted peacefully and often very harmoniously for nearly twenty years. Before 1938, Italian fascist ideology was free of the anti-Semitism of German national socialism. Mussolini was in power for eleven years before Hitler became chancellor of Germany in 1933. And even afterward, relations between fascist Italy and Nazi Germany were frequently tense. Mussolini publicly ridiculed German racial theories and welcomed German Jewish refugees to Italy. In pointed reference to Hitler, Il Duce declared: "National pride has no need of the delirium of race." The Nazis, in turn, criticized Mussolini for practicing "kosher fascism."

Neither madman nor monster, Ettore Ovazza—at least before 1938—was a rather typical product of the Italian upper middle class for whom patriotism was almost a secular religion. That this intense national feeling should be widely felt among Italy's Jews was natural. While the history of the Jewish community in Italy has been an ebb and flow of tolerance and persecution, its roots there had remained unsevered for two thousand years, making it the oldest in Europe.

The first Jews began settling in Rome in the second century B.C. and may have numbered in the tens of thousands by the time of Julius Caesar, whose death they are said to have sincerely mourned. Their presence increased notably after the sack of Jerusalem in A.D. 70, when the emperor Titus brought thousands of Jewish slaves to Rome to march in his triumphal pageant. During the Middle Ages, Jewish life flourished in Sicily and southern Italy, only to be eliminated after 1492, when the Spanish expelled all Jews from their lands, including their territories in Italy.

As Jews fled Spain and southern Italy, they were welcomed in the Renaissance city-states of northern Italy. The Ovazzas were part of this mass migration, fleeing Spain during the Inquisition, drifting across southern France and settling just over the Italian border in what is now Piedmont. From Spain they brought their name, thought to come from the name of a Spanish town, Ovadia. Piedmont at the time was little more than a French colony, the Duchy of Savoy. But its rulers, determined to expand their small realm, invited Spanish Jewish merchants to settle in their towns, in hopes of stimulating commerce. And for centuries the Savoy relied on Jewish bankers to finance a series of military campaigns designed to extend their territory into a legitimate nation.

This special relationship between the Piedmontese royal family and the Jews continued even after ghettos had been established in most other cities in Italy. Venice created the institution in 1516, when it designated a specific neighborhood for Jews at the site of a former foundry—in Venetian dialect *getto* or *ghetto*. While it became a universal symbol of segregation, the ghetto was regarded initially by the Venetians as a major concession to the Jews, who until then had been excluded entirely from the city.

The ghetto acquired a specifically punitive character only with the infamous papal bull *Cum nimis absurdum* of 1555. Declaring the absurdity of allowing Jews to live freely among Christians, Pope Paul IV confined the Jews of Rome to a single walled area of the city and regulated and restricted almost every aspect of their lives. With the rise of papal power in the seventeenth century, the Vatican gradually enforced ghetto legislation on the other principalities of Italy. One of the last to succumb was Piedmont, which established a ghetto in Turin in 1679. The Jewish families of the city were crowded into a large paupers' hospital in the center of the city; its windows were walled up so that the Jews might not look into Christian houses, and its iron gates closed for the night at nine.

Although highly restrictive, the ghetto rules in Turin were applied with a greater spirit of pragmatism and leniency than in some other cities. In Rome, for example, the Jews were eventually driven out of all businesses other than the repair and sale of old clothes. Turinese Jews were allowed, at least, to continue working in two fields where they had been particularly active: silk manufacturing and banking. Similarly, when the ghetto grew dangerously overcrowded at the beginning of the nineteenth century, the Savoys allowed several of the richer Jewish families to move outside the ghetto.

In the mid–nineteenth century the Piedmontese monarchy became belated champions of the cause of Jewish emancipation. The Savoys had initially resisted the reforms introduced by the French Revolution, but King Carlo Alberto came to realize that his best interest lay in embracing the liberal revolution. By accepting a constitutional monarchy, he shrewdly placed himself at the head of the movement to unify Italy. In 1848, the king signed a decree for the emancipation of the Jews and led his troops into battle against the Austrians, who then occupied Milan.

The star of the Ovazza family and that of the Italian nation rose together on a parallel course. As the war for Italian unification began, Ettore's grandfather, Vitta Ovazza, started his life as a free man. For him, as for all Italian Jews, the processes of national unity and freedom were synonymous: wherever the Piedmontese armies conquered, they extended full equality to the Jews.

Not surprisingly, Jews were fiercely loyal to the Savoy monarchy and supported the drive for unification both financially and militarily. They followed Carlo Alberto and his son King Vittorio Emanuele II into battle. In 1860 the Ovazza family helped raise money in the Jewish community of Turin for Giuseppe Garibaldi's expedition to invade Sicily and unite it with Italy. During the fascist period Ettore Ovazza never tired of pointing out that seven of the legendary thousand men who set sail with Garibaldi were Jews.

Nowhere was the fervent identification with the new Italy stronger than in Piedmont, where Jews considered themselves among the founding fathers of the Italian state. On the death of Carlo Alberto, the Jews of Turin painted the sacred ark holding the Torah scrolls black. Blessings to the Piedmontese royal family became a common part of the liturgy in the Turin synagogue from emancipation through the fascist era.

In return for their sacrifices and contributions, Jews were rewarded by the fullest possible acceptance in the new society. As Italy shifted from a feudal to a capitalist economy, Jews were in a particularly strong position to take advantage of the change. In a rural and largely illiterate country, Jews had managed to maintain an astonishingly high rate of literacy. Despite centuries of discrimination, they were prepared to jump right from the ghetto into the new burgeoning middle class.

For Vitta Ovazza the new Italy was nothing short of miraculous: he was born within the iron gates of the Turin ghetto and died one of the richer and more respected men in the city. Only eighteen years after emancipation, he founded the Banca Ovazza in Piazza Carlina, just outside the walls of the old ghetto. The bank grew into one of the most successful in the city and helped finance growing industries in Piedmont; among its clients were many of Turin's finest noble families. In keeping with his position, Ovazza bought an elegant townhouse in the city and later purchased a beautiful eighteenth-century villa in outlying Moncalieri that had once belonged to a member of the royal family. It was a fitting symbol of the times that the members of the new commercial aristocracy (many of them Jews) began buying up old villas and castles formerly inhabited by the feudal nobility. A number of these Jewish families were in fact awarded noble titles by the monarchy, creating a small Jewish aristocracy.

In the course of one generation, Italy had gone from being one of the most backward and repressive nations of Europe to being one of the most tolerant. Italy was among the last countries to eliminate the ghetto, with the liberation of Rome in 1870; and yet in a few decades Italian Jews achieved a level of acceptance without parallel in any other country. While France was bitterly divided over the fate of Captain Dreyfus, Italian Jews were acting as generals, cabinet ministers and prime ministers. By 1902 six Jewish senators had been appointed by the king, out of a total of 350. By 1920 the number had risen to nineteen. Luigi Luzzatti, a Venetian Jew, became prime minister in 1910. For a tiny population of 47,000 in a nation of 45 million, roughly one in a thousand, clearly there were no impediments.

Given the chance to enter the wider society, the Ovazzas assimilated rapidly, living a life virtually indistinguishable from that of other Italian upper middle class families. The transition was easy: unlike Jews in much of Europe who spoke Yiddish or Ladino, Italian Jews spoke Italian, or more likely the local dialect of the city or town in which they lived. The Ovazzas all spoke Piedmontese at home, and a generation or two out of the ghetto, they dispensed entirely with learning Hebrew. Since both Jews and Italians are Mediterranean peoples, they blended in physically as well as linguistically. Happy to shed the distinctive red strips of cloth they had been forced to wear on their shoulders in the days of the ghetto, the Jews practiced their religion privately and unobtrusively—when they practiced it at all.

The only things that were distinctly Jewish about the Ovazza family were certain formal prohibitions and a powerful patriarchalism. "We knew that we weren't supposed to eat salami or marry a non-Jew," recalls Carla Ovazza, daughter of Ettore's younger brother, Vittorio.

Well into the twentieth century, Jewish marriages were frequently arranged by the couple's parents. Typically, the Ovazza women were entirely obedient to their men. They wore high-necked collars and their hair pinned up. In photographs, the Ovazza men are the picture of bourgeois solidity. They all bear a remarkable family resemblance, fair skin, sharp features, round faces and stocky builds. With age they tended to become rounder and more stolid, taking on a somewhat porcine look.

By the time Ettore and his brothers were growing up, the family had moved out from the old ghetto area into a large apartment building on Corso Re Umberto (named for another Savoy monarch) whose mixture of elegance and solidity conveyed a strong sense of upper-middle-class respectability. Far from the cramped quarters of the ghetto, they lived along a broad, tree-lined avenue, where French doors opened onto balconied terraces and gave Turin some of the look of Parisian boulevards.

"The distinction between Jews and non-Jews didn't exist—that came only later, with the war," says Carla Ovazza, born, like the fascist regime, in 1922. "We were typical bourgeois: we had beautiful houses, governesses, servants. Most of our friends were Catholic; we celebrated Passover, they celebrated Easter—that was it. We followed the formal, material traditions of religion, but there was no moral substance to it. My father never once explained a passage of the Bible to me or said a kiddush before we left for America. We knew no Hebrew. There were some religious Jews, but they tended to be poorer, closer to the roots."

In searching to explain the tragedy of his Jewish fascist family, Vittorio Segre, whose father was a cousin of Ettore Ovazza, suggests its origin in a loss of moral and religious values. "In the thirty years that followed [the emancipation of 1848] they forgot most of the rites and values of their ancestral faith," he wrote in his autobiography, *Memoirs of a Fortunate Jew.* "My grandfathers were already unable to read Hebrew, still a language of current knowledge in the preceding generation." Segre tells the story of his grandmother who, throughout her long life, said her prayers in Hebrew every morning without understanding them. "For over seventy years she apparently recited in Hebrew the morning blessing in which a Jew thanks the Lord 'for having made me a male.' "

According to Segre, the Jews of this period, especially in Piedmont, forgot their origins and their God and, as in the Book of Exodus, went chasing after the golden calf of assimilation. "To the extent they enriched themselves monetarily, they impoverished themselves religiously, losing contact with the roots of their collective identity, expressing their new existence with grandiose temples, making their services externally imitative of the Christian service, profoundly different from the atmosphere of sacred learning of the small ghetto synagogues. In Turin they reached the point of conceiving, for a tiny community of 3,000 [sic] people, a gigantic temple that would rival the Eiffel Tower."

The skyline of Turin is to this day dominated by the incredible building that the newly emancipated Jews of the city intended as their temple. Known as the Mole Antonelliana (Antonelli's Pile), it is a bizarre triumph of engineering that features a pointed granite spire reaching five hundred feet in the air. In 1863, three years before Vitta Ovazza started his bank, the Jews of Turin—although they were a mere 1,500 at the time—commissioned the city's most famous architect, Alessandro Antonelli, to build their new temple. So grandiose and complex was the project that it took thirty-four years to complete. By the time it was finished in 1897, the Jews had long abandoned it for a simpler and less expensive temple.

Traditionalists claim that the Mole Antonelliana never became the Jewish synagogue only because the Turinese Jews ran out of money—a fittingly ironic end to their blasphemous dream of self-aggrandizement. They see the story of Antonelli's Pile almost as that of a modern-day Tower of Babel, a parable of the overweening, shallow pride of the "nouveau-riche" city Jews.

Others say that the Turinese Jews backed out because they themselves recognized the absurdity of using a skyscraper as a temple. "My grandfather, who was rabbi at the time, went and told Antonelli in good Piedmontese dialect: 'We need a place to pray to God in and not a tower to go up and see him,' " says Maria Vittoria Malvano, who lives within sight of the current Turin synagogue.

Whatever the case, the Mole is certainly symbolic of the burst of energy, pride and ambition that followed the Jewish emancipation. The synagogues of little towns of Piedmont are small and unobtrusive, with no external decoration to betray their function. Exercises in architectural camouflage, these buildings are the expression of a small, endangered species, the ghetto Jews, who meant to call as little attention to themselves as possible. In contrast, the city synagogues built after emancipation in Turin, Florence and Rome are lavish and monumental, the work of people eager to celebrate their new status and make a mark on the landscape of their cities.

For assimilated families like the Ovazzas, Jewish identity was more a matter of family tradition and honor than of spiritual commitment. Not to follow tradition would be to insult one's ancestors. They were proud of being Jewish the way they were proud of being Italian and Piedmontese—and for the Ovazzas these identities were all interconnected.

For Ettore Ovazza and his two brothers, all born in the last decade of the nineteenth century, the Risorgimento—the unification of Italy—was a very recent and tangible reality. The streets of Turin bear the names of Risorgimento heroes; their statues and monuments dominate almost every piazza. Ettore was born in 1892, only twenty-two years after the war of unification ended and the Rome ghetto was dismantled.

Throughout his youth, he met many people with firsthand recollections of the founders of the nation—King Vittorio Emanuele II, Prime Minister Camillo Cavour, and others. The school he attended was named after Massimo D'Azeglio, the Piedmontese patriot who had written a famous tract advocating the emancipation of the Jews. Each day he went to work at the bank founded by his grandfather in Piazza Carlina, right next to the old ghetto. In the middle of the square was a statue of the great Piedmontese statesman Cavour, who had supported Jewish emancipation and whom the Jews, in turn, had helped elect to parliament. Such were the bonds of mutual obligation that tied the city and its Jews.

Turin at the turn of the century still had much of the grandeur of a national capital. From 1861 to 1865 it had been the first capital of Italy, before the government moved to Florence and later Rome. But Turin remained the heart of Italy's royal family. The painter Giorgio de Chirico called Turin a "monarchical and fluvial city." Fluvial because of the Po River that winds through the city, monarchical because of its countless reminders of the Savoy. Many of De Chirico's surreal cityscapes, with their long empty boulevards and grand heroic monuments, are paintings of Turin. The huge early Renaissance Savoy castle dominates the center of the city. And court life continued in Turin throughout the fascist period. The prince of Savoy, heir to the throne, lived with his princess in the royal palace next to the castle, as well as in the spectacular royal hunting lodge just outside of town at Stupinigi—Italy's version of Versailles. The Ovazzas, like many Jews, were invited to court and personally knew members of the royal family. Ettore's brother Vittorio attended the same military academy as the duke of Bergamo and the duke of Pistoia, nephews of the king, and they used to come to the Ovazza house for dinner. Ettore and his wife were invited to the wedding of the prince of Savoy in 1928. Three years earlier, Ettore had been granted a personal audience with the crown prince. He recorded the visit with appropriate awe in his diary, calling the future monarch a model for Italian youth, although his conversation did not stray far from the topic of his favorite winter sports.

Despite losing its position as capital, Turin became, along with Milan, one of the two great centers of Italian industry. In 1865, Turin had a population of about 200,000, but by World War I it had become a city of half a million, with more than 5,000 companies and about 200,000 factory workers. With this large industrial proletariat, it became one of the most politically radical cities in Italy, a stronghold of socialism and anarchism. But, as the home of the monarchy and the Risorgimento, it was also one of the most conservative of Italian cities. As the region that had led the drive for unification, with its strong military tradition and national culture, Piedmont was in a sense the Prussia of Italy. Piedmontese Jews participated fully in this tradition. While a military career was either impossible or unlikely for Jews in most of Europe, it was common for "good" Turinese Jewish families to send their children to military academies to prepare them for the army or the navy.

Ernesto Ovazza took time out from his duties at the bank to become a colonel in the army. He sent his youngest son, Vittorio, to three different military academies in preparation for a career in the cavalry. To fail in one's patriotic duty toward a nation that had been so generous and open would have seemed the height of ingratitude. In 1911, when Italy invaded Libya with plans of making it a colony, Alfredo Ovazza signed up to fight. Ettore accompanied his older brother to the train station in Turin, stood in the excited, jubilant crowd and watched—no doubt with pangs of envy—as Alfredo and the other soldiers headed off into the distance. A few years later, when Italy entered World War I, Ettore would have his own chance to fight for the nation.

* * *

Like the fascist movement itself, Ettore Ovazza's political commitment was molded in the crucible of World War I, a war of such unexpectedly catastrophic dimensions that it shook the whole social order of Europe and helped create the Soviet revolution in Russia, the rise of Hitler in Germany and the emergence of fascism in Italy.

At its outbreak in 1914, the conflict between the Central Powers (Germany and Austria-Hungary) and the Alliance (France, Great Britain and czarist Russia) provoked intense debate in Italy over whether to intervene in the war. And the divisions formed by the question of intervention helped prepare the future battle lines between fascism and antifascism. Italy had, in fact, been allied to Germany and Austria-Hungary, but many Italian nationalists saw the war as the country's chance to complete its unification. By attacking Austria, Italy might recover Trieste, Trento and Gorizia in the northeast, as well as the segment of the Adriatic coast (the Istrian peninsula and Dalmatia, now part of Yugoslavia) that had once belonged to the Republic of Venice.

Above all, the interventionists saw the war as a call to national greatness. History appeared to offer Italy an opportunity to resume its place among the great nations of Europe. To shrink before the challenge, the nationalists felt, would condemn Italy to the status of a second-class power for the rest of the century. War, they recognized, would exact a terrible human price, but they believed that greatness was always forged through blood and sacrifice.

Ettore Ovazza, as a law student at the University of Turin, argued in favor of Italian intervention in his graduating thesis, titled "International Law and the European Conflagration." He was puzzled and hurt by the fact that not all Italians were as eager to fight for the glory of the Fatherland. The ruling Liberal Party favored neutrality, and the socialists—unlike their counterparts in France and Germany—staunchly opposed intervention from the beginning. They saw the conflict as a capitalist war in which workingmen were being forced to butcher one another for the greater profits of weapons manufacturers and plutocrats eager for colonial expansion. In Turin, the factory workers struck to protest the war.

Fascism was born out of this struggle. Benito Mussolini, who had been editor of the socialist newspaper *Avanti!* and the leader of the most radical faction of the party, suddenly broke ranks and came out in favor of intervention. He founded his own newspaper, *Il Popolo d'Italia,* which he used as a pulpit to advocate the cause of war. His unusual mixture of socialist-influenced populism and fervent nationalism became the basis of the fascist movement.

When Italy finally entered the war, on the side of the Alliance, in May 1915, Ernesto Ovazza and his three sons instantly volunteered. The family celebrated the occasion with a photograph that shows the four officers in uniform—an image that became a kind of family icon. They were joined by a disproportionate number of their fellow Jews. No fewer than fifty Jewish generals served in the Italian army in World War I, many of them Piedmontese. More than a thousand Jews won medals of valor. Both the youngest and the eldest volunteers to win Italy's highest military honor, the Gold Medal, were Jews.

These expressions of patriotic sacrifice not only reflect the profound assimilation of Italian Jews but also suggest that their sense of belonging was more tenuous than they liked to profess. By signing up in record numbers for the war, the Jews acted like citizens on probation. Rather than see themselves as having the same rights and duties as everyone else, they felt a special obligation to show their gratitude, to prove their patriotism, to be more Italian than other Italians. Their overemphatic expressions of *italianità,* Italianness, reveal a trace of insecurity, an unspoken fear that if they fell short in their national duties, the gates of the ghetto might again swing shut on them.

Chapter Two

The earliest photographs of Ettore Ovazza show him with long, flowing blond curls, wearing a frilly collar and a hat with a ribbon—his mother's darling. Into his twenties, he retained his fine features, steel-blue eyes and handsome, open gaze.

Within the family he was regarded as something of a dreamer. When he was in high school his father wrote him stern admonitions about ignoring his schoolwork for his own "confused and stupid ideas." Ernesto Ovazza—the hardworking and highly successful banker—was a rigid disciplinarian who placed considerable pressure on his three sons to follow him into the family business.

Alfredo, the classic eldest child, presented little trouble. He immediately began work for his father and later became one of the most important brokers at the Turin stock exchange. Vittorio, the baby of the family, was attracted by the glamour of the cavalry. Instead of going to university like his two older brothers, he went to three different military academies and became an officer in an elite cavalry regiment. But after he married, he gave in to family pressure to enter the Ovazza bank. Throughout his life he kept a horse, and he rode every morning.

Of the three brothers, Ettore appears to have had the greatest yearning to branch out. After getting his law degree, he went to study foreign affairs in Freiburg, Germany, with the intention of pursuing a diplomatic career. At the same time, he nursed ambitions of being a poet, writing melancholy, crepuscular verse in an ornate nineteenth-century style. In one poem, dated July 23, 1915, Ettore wrote:

> We pined together
> for a rose-colored world,
> a life of lovers and poets,
> full of sweet dawns and beauty.

While this seems like the standard inventory of callow adolescent love poetry, Ettore's sighing and pining may have alarmed his family. In January 1916, his hardheaded banker brother Alfredo wrote him a letter expressing concern for his state of mind.

> Dearest Ettore,
> Your very sad and melancholy letter worried me greatly. I don't know what goes on in your head. You are always on the dark side of the moon. You don't have a positive concept of the reality of life.

Alfredo goes on to complain about being the only one of the three sons working in the bank and warns Ettore against considering any other career. A strange mix of bossiness and affection, the letter ends with an interesting insight into Ettore's character: "The more I know your sweet and profoundly emotional nature, I realize that you will never seriously dedicate yourself to anything unless you feel loved."

Ettore's early poetry suggests a young man waiting impatiently and somewhat unhappily for the romantic adventure of life to begin. On July 25, 1916, while waiting at a military academy to be sent to the Austrian front, he wrote:

> I am searching for a good that has not bloomed,
> I am waiting for a dawn that has not flowered,
> I love a woman I have not yet found.

The "dawn" he was waiting for appears to have been war. For Ettore, the war matched romance with reality. Suddenly he was living grand, historic events like the ones he had read about in his school books on the Risorgimento; he was marching in the footsteps of Garibaldi, Mazzini, Cavour.

After several months at the military academy, training to be an artillery officer, Ettore was finally sent to the front at the end of 1916 or the beginning of 1917. He now turned his literary talents to the glories of battle and began writing a series of letters home that greatly impressed his rather unliterary family. In a letter to Ettore, Alfredo Ovazza wrote: "Papà greatly enjoys repeating your 'literary flowers.' You give him, as well as Mamma, great pleasure when you describe your thoughts and impressions with such beautiful style."

Published in 1928, Ettore Ovazza's *Letters from the Field* are much more striking for what they omit than for what they contain. To read them, one would never guess that 7 million men—the flower of European youth—had been slaughtered in a brutal war of attrition. One would never know that Ettore had participated in the most humiliating defeat on the Italian front, the battle of Caporetto, in which 300,000 soldiers were taken prisoner after the Italian army scattered in panic during an Austro-German offensive.

Ovazza's descriptions of war are surprisingly empty and insipid, full of lofty, formulaic expressions of patriotic sentiment with virtually no description, no sense of tragedy, seemingly no consciousness of the war's brutal cost. They appear to describe some picturesque nineteenth-century military adventure he had read of in history books rather than the horrifying reality that was World War I.

> I hope you are satisfied with our magnificent army. We will win and perhaps we will have decided the destiny of the world! . . . With the vision of our Fatherland made greater, despite its enemies, not with wordy rhetoric but with the blood of its best sons, I shout to you: "Long live Italy!"

At home in Turin, Ettore's mother, Celeste, also became fully involved in the war effort, spending her days preparing care packages for soldiers at the front. Ettore's description of his mother casts her as a latter-day mother of the Gracchi, one of the stoic matriarchs found in schoolboy histories of ancient Rome who were proud to sacrifice their sons in the defense of the Republic.

> I remember after the misfortune of Caporetto, when she saw me again after having no news of me for a month, my mother said: "I was afraid you had been taken prisoner. I would have preferred to see you wounded than taken prisoner." This was my mother!

Despite his triumphal tone, the war must have been traumatic for Ettore. After several years had passed, he allowed some of the pain and humiliation of Caporetto to come through, in one of the few passages in his writing that have any ring of authenticity:

> The ground of all the valleys and mountains was ravaged, almost broken apart by explosions; the vegetation had ceased to exist entirely. . . . How many men were left in that tragic, fatal land!

The path from Piave to Tagliamento, crossing that tragic and bloody sea, under a deluge of rain, surrounded by the weeping population, by ox carts dragging the moaning wounded, is a terrible memory that is carved into my mind.

In the heart of the night, we reached a godforsaken little town near Tagliamento. We stopped near a little church lit by burning torches. Wounded men from the hospital were lying under the colonnade, out of the pouring rain. Near the jerry-built cots, women were crying quietly. Nearby military storehouses were burning, set afire by our own men. I was riding at the head of a column of my own brigade on horseback, covered by a cape which, soaked by the continuous rain, weighed like lead. My head bowed, almost stupefied with anguish, I held myself in the saddle only with difficulty. My attendant came along beside me, weeping, and asked me: "Where are we going, Lieutenant, sir?"

My jaw tightened and I broke out in tears . . . and so we retreated, we who would have given our life, our blood, everything, in order to advance for Italy, toward victory.

Clearly, Caporetto challenged all of Ovazza's notions of war and patriotism. The widespread panic, the chaotic retreat, the fields full of corpses and broken bodies contradicted his idea of the war as a chance to "crown Italy with roses in the garden of the Veneto," as he put it poetically. What must have been even more disturbing to Ovazza was that Caporetto was as much a mutiny as a military defeat. Tens of thousands of infantrymen threw down their rifles and refused to "go over the top" into waves of machine-gun fire.

Because it ran contrary to his idea of a valiant, united Italy marching inexorably toward glory, Ovazza regarded the defeat at Caporetto as a "mystery" or a "betrayal," ignoring both the serious military mistakes and the subversive, revolutionary quality of the mass desertions. He never solved the mystery, but Caporetto and Italy's response to it taught him another lesson. The defeat finally shocked Italy into unified support of the war. Seeing its territory invaded and its cities threatened, the scattered army managed to pull itself together and, despite exhaustion, held the Austro-German troops at bay. The government rallied public support by promising better conditions for the soldiers and economic reform at home.

Italy "rediscovered in its pain the force and the reason for its salvation," Ovazza wrote. "Caporetto was lost because of a lack of discipline and the war was won through discipline." This veneration of discipline is one of the things that attracted Ettore to fascism and Mussolini.

DISCIPLINE: Here is a great word that the Italian people must learn and repeat like a magic incantation. . . . If necessary we should create a goddess Discipline; let us raise our altars and learn to venerate her, because she alone is the secret of our certain destiny, that of yesterday and that of tomorrow.

When Ettore Ovazza returned from the war, he had a second, equally hard blow awaiting him: unlike his feelings of jubilation and euphoria over the outcome of the war, the mood of the nation was bitter, cynical, full of anger and grief. Millions of families mourning their dead found the offerings of the goddess Discipline cold comfort.

At war's end the country fell into a deep economic crisis, marked by inflation and devaluation of the lira. As the cost of living rose in 1919, riots broke out and people looted food shops. When the government failed to deliver the land reforms it had promised after Caporetto, peasants occupied the fields. Workers and trade unions, which had never supported the war effort, began an aggressive campaign of strikes. They looked with excitement to the Bolshevik Revolution that had taken place in Russia and talked about duplicating it in Italy.

In Turin socialists and communists seemed to have taken over the city; they shut down the trains and the postal and telegraph service, and occupied the factories. While the Socialist Party had no serious intention of overthrowing the government, it paid lip service to the idea of revolution.

"The party did not have a plan," acknowledged Pietro Nenni, a former head of the Italian Socialist Party, in 1946. "It did not even bother to explain what it meant by dictatorship of the proletariat. In Italy the industrial proletariat is a minority. Did it want a dictatorship of this minority? Certainly not. But then it should have reassured the other classes—the petit bourgeoisie, the small landowners, the tradesmen, and the returning soldiers, for their interests were not in contrast with those of the proletariat. The party never reassured them."

Not only did the left terrify the middle classes, it went out of its way to alienate the millions of soldiers returning from the front. Along with excoriating the war effort, the socialists actually prevented war veterans from joining their party. Members of the radical left insulted and jeered at returning soldiers. Unionized streetcar drivers in some instances stopped their vehicles if a man in uniform came on board.

In the face of the mounting crisis, the Liberal government of Giovanni Giolitti seemed weak and vacillating. When workers occupied the factories in Turin, Giolitti refused to call in troops to expel them. At the same time, the Italian government was having trouble at the Versailles Peace Treaty meetings. The French and British were able to deliver only a portion of the territory they had originally promised when Italy entered the war. Italy did win Trieste, Trento and the rest of Trentino–

Alto Adige north of the Veneto, and part of the Istrian peninsula—but was denied the city of Fiume and the Dalmatian coast, which became part of newly created Yugoslavia.

The betrayed hopes of the Versailles Treaty were immediately denounced by the poet Gabriele D'Annunzio as "the Mutilated Victory" —a phrase that became the rallying cry of injured Italian nationalism.

For Ettore Ovazza, as for many returning veterans, the period immediately after the war was among the most bitter of his life. Everything he had fought for seemed to turn into a kind of mockery. "Occupation of the factories, the abandonment of Valona [in Albania], giving Porto Baros to Yugoslavia . . . Where was our Italy, for whom we were ready to offer our lives as we would to the most beautiful of all things we loved?" he wrote several years later. Turin, the royal city of the Savoy, was now the Leningrad of Italy. With more than 200,000 factory workers making up nearly half of its population, the cradle of the Risorgimento had become the capital of Italian communism.

The revolutionary fervor among workers and peasants (like the desertions at Caporetto) was completely incomprehensible to Ovazza. Having led a sheltered, privileged life, he had always assumed that admiration for the Fatherland and belief in the established order were virtually universal. He blamed the turmoil in Italy on an obscure, mysterious conspiracy rather than on any injustices in Italy's rigid class society:

> In the nation, political hatred spread like wildfire. From the poisoned cities, intriguers spread out to plant the seed of class war in the countryside; and the clear, serene eyes of our peasants—used to studying the heavens—became clouded over with sudden resentments. The young returning home, proud of having fought with honor, many with their brave bodies wounded, were downcast and alone, shoved aside as if guilty. No friendly or understanding voice comforted their soul. . . . Instead suspicion, hostility, inexplicable feelings had developed against those who had, with clear conscience, served their country. Ideal values, the spiritual heritage of our dead, were spurned . . . all national passion denied. Everything seemed to lose its fascination, nature, life itself. . . .
>
> This cry of anguish was heard by a man who was fully worthy of it, by Benito Mussolini.

A counterrevolutionary movement rose up parallel to the growing socialist and communist parties. On March 23, 1919, Mussolini founded the *fasci di combattimento,* which later became the Partito Nazionale Fascista, the National Fascist Party. The party took its name from the ancient Roman symbol of imperial authority, the *fasces*—a bundle of wheat with an axe emerging from the top. In the same year D'Annunzio, acting independently of both Mussolini and the government, led an expedition of former soldiers to occupy Fiume, the ancient Roman and, later, Venetian city that had been awarded to Yugoslavia. The occupation, meant to vindicate the "Mutilated Victory," became the opening shot of the fascist revolution. The fascist militia that Mussolini established wore the black shirts of the *arditi,* the ardent army stormtroopers who formed the nucleus of D'Annunzio's legionnaires.

Initially the fascist program was highly radical, with a nationalist spin applied to an essentially socialist platform, but Mussolini quickly adapted it to the exigencies of power, accepting free enterprise, the Italian monarchy and the Catholic Church.

Excluded by the socialists, many of the 5 million recent veterans were attracted to the new party. With the aggressive and sometimes violent tactics of the left, many thought it natural they should take up arms against the bands of workers who appeared to have taken over the major cities. At a veterans' meeting in Turin, Ettore Ovazza joined the cause.

The early days of fascism in Turin, as in most Italian cities, involved violent demonstrations as well as punitive raids against workers' organizations. It is not clear what role, if any, Ettore played in Turin's violent squads. But from his description of the meeting at which he joined the party, it would seem his support was more moral and financial than military: while others passed out revolvers, Ettore stood up to ask for "greater responsibility in the area of propaganda and intellectual activity against the poisonous theories of Communism."

Since squad violence was a badge of honor during the fascist period, Ettore probably would have mentioned specific episodes if he had participated in them. Violence was an integral part of the fascist program, and the *santo manganello,* or "holy cudgel," with which the fascists beat their opponents was a proud icon of fascist power. Between 1920 and 1922 fascists killed some six hundred antifascists in street fighting. They are estimated to have lost about half that many of their own men, who were enshrined as "fascist martyrs." Ettore does mention participating in an attack on the Turin Camera di Lavoro in which fascists occupied the workers' principal union hall, ransacked its offices and then set the building on fire. But he never explained what part he took in the attack.

He did, however, help found and finance an early fascist newspaper in Turin, *Eco d'Italia,* which lasted for several months in 1922. That same year a play he had written celebrating the rise of Mussolini, *L'Uomo e i fantocci* (The Man and the Marionettes), was produced in Milan. Describing a performance of the play, Ettore offers a portrait of himself in the role of fascist propaganda warrior and of Italy on the eve of the fascist revolution. In an arrogant show of strength, fascists put on the play in the heart of a communist Milan neighborhood.

> I reached the hall by evening. There was much electricity in the air, and the police were on hand. There was much enthusiasm in the strong chests of the Blackshirts. The police surrounded the theater, keeping guard. Mario, the protagonist—a wounded war hero—received the applause of the audience, while Ettore Vanni, the draft-dodger, earned its antipathy. I was called on stage. . . . I thanked the public and left by the proscenium door. At the end of the play, the fascist squad lined up outside the theater shouted out its *"Eià, eià, alalà"* [the fascist battle cry] in my honor.

Ten days later, Mussolini became prime minister after the so-called March on Rome. Mussolini was always proud of the fact that he came to power through violent and illegal means, unlike Hitler, who slipped into office through the parliamentary system they both despised. While the phrase "March on Rome" evoked images of Julius Caesar's crossing of the Rubicon with his troops to end the Roman Republic, it was hardly an accurate description of the fascist seizure of power.

On October 28, 1922, fascist squads across Italy occupied various public buildings. In most cities they were quickly ousted by government troops; in Milan an order was given for Mussolini's arrest. But after agreeing to put down the rebellion, King Vittorio Emanuele III changed his mind and invited Mussolini to form a new government as prime minister. The Italian army would have had little difficulty in putting down this putsch; instead, because of the king's sudden about-face, it succeeded with hardly a shot being fired. Along with many members of the government, Vittorio Emanuele thought that inviting Mussolini into the government would end this period of anarchy and parliamentary paralysis. Rather than march to Rome at the head of a popular army, Mussolini and the fascists traveled to the capital by train, unopposed.

Ettore's dramatization of the March on Rome, which became the new ending to "The Man and the Marionettes," shows his own continuing preference for romance over realism. It seems less a description of Italy in 1922 than a copy of the many nineteenth-century illustrations of Garibaldi's ragged troops. It does, however, provide a window into Ettore's mental universe and his fantasy version of fascism.

> *Scene 1*
>
> *A road in the Roman countryside. The shadows of night begin to fall. The lights of Rome burn in the distance. It is the night of October 28, 1922.*

Distant cries are heard:

To Rome! To Rome!

To whom Rome? To Us!—To whom Italy? To Us!

Young men run along the road dressed in the strangest costumes, some in uniform, armed with rifles, swords, muskets. They wave their weapons and pass through.

Several young men ride by on horseback, holding torches in their fists.

Distant church bells announce the day that is born.

Mario enters in a gray-green uniform, accompanied by Folco, who holds him up. . . .

MARIO: I am tired, so tired, and the Eternal City is near. Look how it glows on the horizon.

Let us stop a moment: a while ago, when those legionnaires passed by, I thought my heart would give out. In a few hours we will enter the Rome of my dreams.

The words of Il Duce return to my mind:

—O Rome! O ship launched toward World Empire that emerges from the flux of time!—O, Rome, which awaits the luminous hours to come!—Greetings, Goddess Rome! Greetings for those that were, that are and will be your sons, ready to suffer and die for your power and your glory! . . .

At dawn we will pass the Milvian Bridge and Rome will be ours. (*He looks at the sky with his arms raised.*) O comrades of war, comrades buried in the snow and the valleys, descend and come with me, let me accompany you to the glory of the Capital!

Chapter Three

The years of the fascist revolution were particularly active and fruitful for Ettore Ovazza. In fact, during the two years after returning from the war, he settled all the important questions of his life: he entered the family bank, published a book of poetry, wrote a play, joined the fascist movement, started a newspaper and married.

His marriage, as in many Jewish families, was arranged by his parents. His wife, Nella Sacerdote, who was eighteen, was a first cousin and, like Ettore, came from a rich Turinese Jewish family.

"Nella was nice, far from beautiful, rather fat," says Franca Ovazza Piperno, daughter of Vittorio Ovazza. "It was an organized marriage, which they accepted. She was rather simple. I think she admired her husband very much. Wives were the devoted servants of their husbands; it was in the tradition of the old Jewish family."

The fascist revolution did little to disturb the tranquil flow of the Ovazzas' family life. "Nothing in their lives changed," says Carla Ovazza, Franca's younger sister. "Before fascism they went to the theater and to concerts, they had servants and beautiful houses, and with fascism none of that changed. Shamefully, the fact that there was no more freedom of the press or freedom of ideas didn't matter a bit to them. We were all fascist and all our friends were fascists. You just took it for granted." Carla was born in 1922, quite literally a child of fascist culture, particularly in the Ovazza household.

"We were raised to obey, to respect and to belong to this big family clan," says Franca. "As a family we stood together. The whole Ovazza gang was considered fascist. We still lived in medieval times up through fascism. Traditions were carried on. You didn't think about whether there should be a monarchy or a republic. It was a duty to follow the leader. You didn't discuss it. The prince and the king were always there."

Franca and Carla and their parents lived for several years with Vittorio's mother and father; the two girls were used to the same family atmosphere in which Ettore had grown up. Their maternal grandparents, the Fubinis, lived upstairs in the same building. The two sets of grandparents were friends; Celeste Ovazza and Alessandro Fubini played the piano together often. Vittorio Ovazza and Olga Fubini had been childhood playmates and were engaged when he was twenty-two and she only sixteen. Her father, honorary consul to Greece, participated frequently in the pomp of Savoy court life.

"My grandfather [Alessandro Fubini] was always invited to court, so he had to wear a uniform, and this funny hat, '*la fellucca,*' " says Franca. With her hand she describes a long thin hat, its bill several inches long and tapering to a sharp point. "I was attracted by the brilliance of the uniforms, the veils and dresses. They would say, 'Children, behave, so you can grow up and watch your grandfather and grandmother go to court.'

"The Savoy were very open to the Jews and the Jews were very loyal to them. My father had been at the cavalry school at Pinerolo with the duke of Bergamo and the duke of Pistoia, first cousins of the prince. Once a year, they would come to the house for dinner. We were trained to bow in a certain way and had to get all dressed up. It was fun for us. When the duke of Pistoia got married, my parents were invited to the wedding. I still have the dress and the veil my mother wore."

During the first years of his marriage, Vittorio Ovazza was still in the cavalry and, like all officers at that time, had a military attendant who lived with the family and served as his personal valet. "My father gave us a military education," Franca says. "We had to stand up straight in front of the table, and if we put our wrists on the table, we'd be spanked." She and her sister had to hold napkins under their armpits as they ate so that they would keep their elbows in, their wrists up, their backs straight. "One day, my father even made me eat with a stick behind my back going from one arm to the other so that my back would be perfectly straight," she recalls. "I think that his strictness was a kind of hidden weakness. He had this way of commanding that made him feel strong, also because he was the youngest of the three sons and the others suffocated him. It was always Ettore, Alfredo. And the way Alfredo behaved toward him . . . I'd better not talk."

The Ovazza grandparents were affectionate but equally strict. "My grandmother Celeste was very ladylike, very nineteenth-century, small, elegant but simple," Franca says. "She was very severe but very loving. She was a highly reserved person, she hardly went out. She was dedicated to her family completely. She would have me build something out of wooden sticks, and then she would blow the whole thing down and make me redo it as a kind of training, do it over and over again. She observed all the Jewish holidays and gave her sons a profound sense of belonging to Judaism."

Although most of the family's friends and business acquaintances were Catholic, the center of their life was the family. While formal religion was not particularly important, the Ovazzas' Judaism manifested itself in its extreme clannishness.

"It was a whole gang," Franca says of the family. "We always went to the villa at Moncalieri, grandparents, parents, aunts, uncles and children. There were usually twenty-two people staying there in the summer. My grandfather and grandmother, the three brothers and their families. All the women were together; they were very close. All the men were ugly. My uncle Ettore bought another villa nearby, the Rizzoglio, a very beautiful eighteenth-century villa. There was a huge house, with a park and a lake in back. We took one floor and Ettore's family took the other. There was a fence surrounding the grounds, and we used to put chestnuts on the sharp pointed stakes. We danced and played games. We had a lovely, simple life. We didn't have to look for other friends because we had this huge family."

By the time Ernesto Ovazza's three sons reached adulthood, each had his own villa. When Ernesto died in 1926, Vittorio took the family villa at Moncalieri; Ettore kept his villa nearby at Rizzoglio, while Alfredo had a villa that belonged to his wife's family.

Despite the Ovazzas' strong political affiliations, their home life was extremely apolitical; social issues and current events were rarely mentioned. Fascism, among Jews and non-Jews, thrived in an atmosphere in which ideas were accepted and not discussed. Jewish patriarchalism and Piedmontese military tradition blended naturally and imperceptibly with the new blind obedience to fascism.

The children were not allowed to sit with the adults in the living room after dinner and listen to their conversation. They were packed off to be with maids and nurses; when they were ready for bed they were brought back to be kissed good night. "A girl at sixteen then was much less mature than a girl at sixteen today," says Carla. "We were extremely ignorant, we traveled with our governesses. We were given no real cultural preparation by our families. We had no idea that freedom is a good thing and that the lack of it is bad. There was no discussion of fascism or antifascism. We simply didn't frequent people who were antifascists or who were Zionists. We were ordinary bourgeois."

The Ovazzas were relatively well educated but in no way intellectual. They played musical instruments and attended concerts but read little and discussed less. This mental passivity and political obedience left the children open to the steady diet of fascist propaganda they received at school.

"The professors all wore black shirts, but that didn't interest us," Carla says. "To us fascism meant parades on Via Roma and free skiing. We were happy when Mussolini came to Turin, because it meant we could skip school. There were maybe two or three Jews to a class. And there was absolutely no difference between us and non-Jews except that we left the class during the hour of religion. In history class they taught that the Jews killed Christ. But we just accepted it."

"I was a great fascist when I was a kid," Franca recalls. "I loved the parades, the drills, the uniforms and the songs. I really was fascist. I used to drag my friends to all the assemblies. I could go skiing without paying, we could march in parades and do exercises instead of going to school. For a kid it was marvelous. Then there were the uniforms. The girls had three kinds [depending on their age]: The Piccole Italiane [Little Italians] wore a black pleated skirt, a white piqué blouse, long white stockings, and a black cape and beret. The Giovani Italiane [Young Italians] had the same uniform, but their stockings were black. And I don't remember how the Giovani Fasciste [Young Fascists] dressed, because I never got that far. In school we wore black, but for parades and holidays we wore the special uniforms. And I remember all the songs:

Noi siamo l'alba d'oro,
Vispe cresciamo all'aria e al sol,
Siamo d'Italia bimbe.

We are the golden dawn,
Lively we grow in the light and air,
We are young Italy.

"It's crazy," Franca says, then pauses, drifts back to her youth. She cannot resist another song.

Siamo l'eterna gioventù
Che conquista l'avvenire
Di ferro armato di pensier.
Per le vie del Nuovo Impero
Che si dilunga nel mar,
Marceremo come Duce vuole,
Come Roma già chiamò.

We are the eternal youth
That conquers the future
Armed with iron thought.
We will march where Duce wants
Through the paths of the New Empire
Which stretch along the sea,
Where Rome once called.

She laughs with momentary embarrassment at having given way to nostalgia for her fascist youth.

* * *

Ernesto Ovazza's presidency of the Turin Jewish community during the first years of fascism was largely symbolic, a recognition more of his social standing than of his religious observance. No one found it strange that the head of the community should be a member of the Fascist Party. Indeed, it would have been difficult to hold such a quasi-public position without party standing.

To some, faith in fascism seemed incompatible with religious belief. Fascism demanded the subordination of the individual to the national cause, and many sensitive Jews and Catholics saw this as inconsistent with true religious freedom. But more often than not, the praises of Mussolini were sung in churches and synagogues alike.

Mussolini's religious politics were, as almost all his politics, contradictory and highly expedient. He had begun his career as a fire-breathing anti-Catholic, but during his drive for power he reversed himself shamelessly and proposed to make Catholicism the official state religion. With respect to the Jews, Mussolini tailored his statements to suit the needs of the moment; in his writings and speeches one can find almost every possible stand—and its opposite. In 1917, Mussolini briefly blamed the Russian Revolution on "Jewish vengeance" against Christianity: "Race does not betray race. . . . Bolshevism is being defended by the international plutocracy. That is the real truth." A few weeks later, he did a 180-degree turn: "Bolshevism is not, as people believe, a Jewish phenomenon," he wrote. "The truth is that Bolshevism is leading to the utter ruin of the Jews of Eastern Europe."

Even when he was later allied with Hitler, Mussolini was never a Nazi-styled biological racist. A great believer in national traits, Mussolini did, however, make sweeping generalizations about the Jews as a people: they were unusually intelligent, drawn to money, tendentially subversive and democratic. With an alternating mix of resentment and admiration, Mussolini frequently used the terms "Jewish finance," "Jewish International" and "international plutocracy" to refer to a vaguely defined cabal of Jewish interests. Because he believed more in the idea of Nation than that of Race, he regarded Italian Jews as Italian; but he was suspicious of Zionism because of its connections to the "Jewish International." Mussolini's anti-Jewish sentiments resembled his opposition to Freemasonry; like Judaism, it implied a secret loyalty independent of fascism.

During the first months of fascism, Ernesto Ovazza publicly rejected an appeal to aid the growing cause of Zionism.

> As President of this Community I have received your . . . petition in favor of creating a Jewish national homeland in Palestine. While I consider with faith and sincere pleasure every effort and every generous act toward . . . the suffering and persecuted Jewish masses, I must with equal sincerity affirm that I cannot as an Italian participate in a program of such extreme consequences, particularly now in this moment, when we have a greater duty to participate in the front lines of the reconstruction of our country. In few nations in the world does the Jew enjoy such consideration as in Italy. . . . We do not believe that in order to feel intimately connected to our fellow Jews suffering unjust persecutions it is necessary to create a second Fatherland. It is not selfishness that stimulates my firm stand on this point, it is the higher sentiment of the Fatherland which, from the ranks of the Thousand [Garibaldi's troops] to the soldiers of Vittorio Veneto [the last Italian victory of World War I], so many of the purest heroes of Jewish blood have died for.

The same sentiments would echo many times in Ettore's battles with Italian Zionism.

Despite his feverish commitment to fascism, Ettore was acutely sensitive to potential conflicts between his new faith and the religion of his fathers. He constantly combed the newspapers trying to gauge the shifting attitudes of Mussolini and his followers toward the Jews. In one of his few articles on religion written during the 1920s, Ettore criticized both the excessive violence of the fascist squads and fascism's insensitivity toward religious minorities.

Despite these initial reservations, Ettore was quickly reassured by Mussolini's behavior in office. While courting the Catholic Church, fascism did not infringe on the rights of Jews or Protestants. His occasional remarks about the "Jewish International" notwithstanding, Mussolini had warm relations with Jews at various levels. His first cabinet included Aldo Finzi, an early Jewish supporter who became undersecretary of the interior. His mistress and official biographer in that period, Margherita Sarfatti, was also Jewish. The status of Jews in the country or abroad was simply not an issue of importance in fascist Italy during the 1920s and early 1930s.

Ettore settled into the more prosaic life of banker, husband and father. With the elimination of all opposition parties, political life in the conventional sense ceased to exist. The entire Italian people, as it seemed to Ettore and fascist propagandists, were united "in one granitelike block" in support of Il Duce. Ettore occasionally took time out from his routine at the bank to write newspaper articles and publish his writings in book form, often at his own expense. In 1923 he wrote a short book about the battle of Caporetto, *In the Margin of History*; there followed *Diary for My Son* (1928); a collection of his letters written home during World War I, *Letters from the Field* (1932); and a collection of newspaper articles, *Fascist Politics* (1933). He was an active philanthropist and along with his brothers founded an orphanage for indigent Jewish children in the name of his parents.

Although he enjoyed a position of wealth and prestige, Ettore sometimes found his civilian life rather flat: "Life has buried and suffocated me in its heavy mediocrity," he wrote in his diary on August 31, 1925.

> Now I must take up my city life again. Bourgeois life, life as a family man. It is what I do but not what I prefer. Nonetheless it is my current existence, not very heroic, but perhaps it will be a rest that precedes a more lively period.
>
> Meanwhile time passes; I am thirty-four. Do I live or only imagine that I live? I don't know. I have a lot of patience and great faith in myself. I try to do things for others as well as for myself; perhaps I work more for others than for myself; and that at least is something.

On national holidays he put on his old artillery lieutenant's uniform with the fascist black shirt and marched in military parades. In one rather comic scene he describes, he exultantly dragged his young son through the streets of Turin on the fifty-sixth anniversary of Italian unification. And after lecturing Riccardo about the Fatherland, liberty, Mazzini and Mussolini, he realizes at the end that the child is completely uninterested.

> We returned home. His mother greeted us at the door and with a sweet smile asked Riccardo: "So did you have fun with Papà?" I looked at my

son with a moment of apprehension. Riccardo, poor thing, didn't answer, but made a face that I can't describe, that meant to say what he dared not: "Mamma, I was very bored." Then he ran to his room in order not to give himself away.

In 1929, Ettore was rewarded for his patriotism—an audience with Mussolini. He came at the head of a delegation of decorated Jewish war veterans, and orphans and widows of fallen Jewish soldiers. Dressed in uniforms, draped in medals and widows' weeds, the group had come to express their gratitude at the regime's beneficent tolerance toward the Jews. Ettore described the encounter several years later with the reverential tone common to Mussolinian hagiography.

> He welcomes us affably with a slight smile. He is serene, seated at his desk. He motions to us to advance as we stand hesitantly on the threshold. It was the first time I was to see the face of Il Duce up close. . . .
>
> His Excellency Mussolini remembers having read a book of mine, *Diary for My Son,* and asks me: "And your son?" I answer: "He is six years old, Excellency!". . . But when he learns that Il Duce asked me about him! Marvelous faculty of a Man so absorbed by the important affairs of State, to remember so clearly and follow the needs of his faithful!
>
> Il Duce's question moves me. I am unable to speak, I don't know what to say in front of him. I have come from my city, accompanied by a woman in black mourning clothes, a war widow, by valiant young men wearing the Silver Medal of War, and by an *avanguardista* who is wearing on his chest the medals of valor belonging to his uncle who was killed at the front. We have come to express our gratitude for the fascist laws that recognize the love of country and the sacrifices of those who belong to religious minorities.
>
> On hearing my affirmation of the unshakable loyalty of Italian Jews to the Fatherland, His Excellency Mussolini looks me straight in the eye and says with a voice that penetrates straight down to my heart: "I have never doubted it." When Il Duce bids us farewell with a Roman salute, I feel an urge to embrace him, as a fascist, as an Italian, but I can't; and approaching him at his desk I say: "Excellency, I would like to shake your hand." It is not a fascist gesture, but it is a cry from the heart. . . .
>
> Such is The Man that Providence has given to Italy.

Although it occurred years before the time of persecution, this show of Jewish loyalty—complete with uniforms, medals and widows' weeds—was a kind of dress rehearsal of a scene that would repeat itself many times in many forms when the first rumblings of anti-Semitism began to be heard in Italy.

Chapter Four

The turning point in relations between Mussolini and the Italian Jews was the election of Adolf Hitler as chancellor of Germany in 1933; this was by no means apparent at the time, however. Mussolini greeted Hitler's victory with mixed emotions. He considered it a personal triumph but could not help expressing certain reservations. In August 1933, in an editorial in *Il Popolo d'Italia,* he wrote:

> Behold another great country creating a unitary, authoritarian, totalitarian, that is to say, Fascist State, with certain accentuations that Fascism has spared itself, acting in a different historical milieu.

The "certain accentuations" to which Mussolini referred were its virulent anti-Semitism and its hostility to the Catholic Church.

During the rise of Nazism, Mussolini had gone to considerable lengths to distinguish himself from his German counterpart. In his widely publicized conversations with the German Jewish journalist Emil Ludwig, Mussolini made a stinging criticism of Nazi racial theories:

> Race! It's a feeling, not a reality; ninety-five percent, at least, is a feeling. Nothing will ever make me believe that biologically pure races can be shown to exist today. . . . National pride has no need of the delirium of race.

Although they were both fascist dictators, an alliance between Hitler and Mussolini hardly seemed inevitable to most Italians, including Il Duce himself. Germany had been Italy's enemy in World War I and many Italians were nervous about Pan-German expansionism. Hitler's ambitions to annex Austria would place the Third Reich at Italy's northeastern border and threaten the parts of Italy with substantial German-speaking populations.

Mussolini placed himself in an independent position between the European democracies and the Third Reich, gaining leverage for Italy by pitting the two sides against one another. In this role of Statesman of Europe, Mussolini also attempted to mediate between Germany and the Jews, encouraging international Jewish leaders to soften their criticism of Hitler and trying to convince the Nazis to modify their racial policies.

At home, his policy toward the Jews was equally ambiguous. On the one hand he opened Italy's borders to several thousand German Jewish refugees, on condition they kept their noses out of politics. On the other he allowed fanatical right-wing fascists to start a small but insistent anti-Jewish campaign. Their attacks appeared in minor but influential fascist papers that Mussolini often used as a forum to test new ideas without having to take responsibility for them. Thinking that he perhaps might have to align his racial policies with those of Hitler, Mussolini permitted a debate on Jews and Zionism to play itself out while he watched silently from the sidelines. The new anti-Semitic rhetoric fell largely on deaf ears: several prominent fascists came out strongly in the Jews' defense, while most of the larger newspapers ignored the debate entirely.

The majority of Italian Jews dismissed these early anti-Semitic voices as isolated and marginal, but they were seized by genuine panic when news that police had uncovered a "Jewish antifascist plot" appeared on the front page of Italian papers on March 31, 1934. The incident itself was minor. Two young Jews from Turin (one of whom was actually only half Jewish) were caught at Ponte Tresa, a town southwest of Lugano, trying to smuggle antifascist literature from Switzerland into Italy. Subsequently fifteen of their Turinese friends and acquaintances (nine of them Jewish) were arrested for antifascist activities.

Many non-Jews might well have missed the news entirely. In most newspapers the account of the arrests was limited to a short, factual government news release that did not even mention the religion of most of the alleged conspirators, although many of the headlines accompanying the story did. Most mainstream papers dropped the story quickly, but the right-wing fringe seized on it as proof of the Jews' inherently disloyal, subversive, internationalist tendencies. The Jews felt that an old, unspoken covenant between Mussolini and themselves had been broken. The fact that the incident was reported at all in a society where news of dissent was generally suppressed and that many newspapers picked up the anti-Jewish theme was an alarming signal to a Jewish public already nervously scanning the controlled fascist press for signs of Hitler's influence.

For Ettore Ovazza the idea of a Jewish antifascist plot in his own city was a violation of everything he held sacred. From the day he heard of the incident, his life changed dramatically. After only minimal involvement in Jewish affairs during the first forty-two years of his life, the cause of Jewish fascism suddenly became his personal crusade.

Ettore learned of the arrests the day before they were made public, and fired off a message to Mussolini in choppy, telegraphic style.

> Turin, March 30, 1934
> In this most sad hour for the Jews of Turin, while handful of renegades go to well-deserved, severe punishment, I recall sacrifice Italian Jews for greatness of Italy and send to our great and most beloved Duce expression profound pain and scorn confirming unshakable devotion to cause of Fascist Fatherland.

Although some Jews had the self-possession to protest the fact that a single incident was being exploited to tar an entire people, a large number, including Ettore, felt that it was necessary to make a show of public penitence. In a flood of petitions, open letters to newspapers, and telegrams to Mussolini, prominent Jews throughout Italy expressed shock, outrage and anger at the so-called antifascist elements within their community and begged the dictator not to blame the great majority of loyal Jews for the sins of a few. A number of local Jewish communities (in Turin, Milan and Verona, for example) went so far as to make generous donations, as if to expiate some collective guilt.

The sudden reappearance of anti-Semitism clearly struck a raw nerve, awakening deeply atavistic behavior, ancestral reflexes developed over centuries in the ghetto. Payments of tribute money, lavish gifts, demonstrations of remorse and loyalty, delegations of Jewish elders bowing humbly before the local ruler—these were all defenses that the ghetto Jews had used countless times before when faced with danger, in the form of accusations of ritual murder and deicide, or threats of expulsion.

After all, the Jews had enjoyed only seventy-five years of equality after almost two thousand years of living precariously as a barely tolerated guest people always one false move from expulsion. Faced with arbitrary power in its many forms, they learned to keep their heads down and let the storm pass. When faced with a crisis, rather than protest, they redoubled their efforts to remain exemplary, law-abiding citizens, stressing their long-standing service to the ruler and increasing their contributions to his coffers.

The Jews' public breast-beating did not mollify the extremist pro-German wing of the Fascist Party, which adopted a new menacing and inquisitorial tone. A month after the arrests, the right-wing newspaper *Il Regime Fascista,* run by Roberto Farinacci, a powerful former squad leader from Cremona, led the attack:

> The editorial we published days ago . . . has stimulated a number of letters from Jews who want to separate themselves from those in Italy who support Zionism. We do not exclude the possibility that there are good Jews, but it is also our right to demand clarity.
>
> Does there or does there not exist a Zionist movement in Italy?
>
> To deny it would be to lie. The existence of a newspaper in Florence [*Israel*] should cut short any discussion. And so these others who claim to be anti-Zionists, what are they doing to fight the other Jews who believe they have another Fatherland that is not Italy?
>
> So far, nothing.
>
> Therefore, it is necessary to decide. We have reached a point at which everyone must take a position. Because he who declares himself Zionist has no right to hold any responsibilities or honors in our country.

The editors of *Israel* responded in an unruffled, dignified manner:

> With all due respect to *Regime Fascista,* we must ask, for example, Are you sure you know why "we have reached a point at which everyone must take a position"? . . . What new has happened to make something that up until yesterday, until today, was perfectly acceptable suddenly intolerable and prohibited?
>
> *Regime Fascista* gives the impression of having discovered that there exists a Zionist movement in Italy, stating rhetorically, "to deny it would be to lie." Who ever denied it?

While the Zionists of *Israel* had the presence not to be drawn into this specious debate, Ettore and many of his friends in Turin felt that they had to meet Farinacci's challenge, by fighting "the other Jews who believe they have another Fatherland that is not Italy." He and other patriots led a coup in the government of Turin's Jewish community; the old administration resigned en masse (as if somehow responsible for the incident), and Ettore became acting administrator until a new council could be elected. At the same time, he founded a Jewish fascist newspaper, *La Nostra Bandiera* (Our Flag) as a show of loyalty.

Prominently displayed at the top of the front page of the inaugural issue was a quotation from Il Duce: "The blood sacrifice of the Italian Jews in war has been vast, ample and generous." Below that was a large photograph of a funeral monument in the Turin synagogue for Jews who had died in World War I. Ettore's front-page editorial announcing the birth and purpose of the paper was a strident call to arms entitled "An End to Ambiguity."

> We are soldiers, we are fascists. We feel equal to all other citizens, especially in our duties toward the Fatherland. Members of the same family, in peace and in war, we want to kiss the tricolor flag for which we are always ready to fight and die; we want to pray to the God of our fathers in good conscience.
>
> Whoever takes a sacrilegious hand against our country or disturbs our religious peace will find us ready to defend and attack. . . . The Italian Jews have always guarded jealously the perfect spiritual unity between love of religion and love of Fatherland.

Ettore alluded to the arrests of the so-called Jewish antifascists, but the incident was so unspeakable that, like many Jews at the time, he referred to it only indirectly, as "a very painful event." Instead, the bulk of his polemical energies was spent attacking the members of Italy's small Zionist movement—despite the fact that they were completely extraneous to the arrests. *La Nostra Bandiera* was needed, Ettore explained, to balance the negative and unpatriotic image of Jews created by the Zionist newspaper *Israel.*

> The attitude of a group of Zionist-nationalist intellectuals who, strangers in Italy, make much noise because they have a newspaper of their own, made it necessary, we thought, [for us] to have one of our own.
>
> Otherwise our prolonged silence might be interpreted as either indifference or tacit consent.

Interestingly enough, Ettore did not condemn "philanthropic" Zionism, charitable aid to Jewish settlers in Palestine who were escaping persecution in Europe; what he rejected was political Zionism, the creation of an independent Jewish state. He felt that it was unpatriotic for Jews living in a condition of equality in the Diaspora to dream of creating a second fatherland. "We clearly reject the Zionists, who live

. . . with one eye looking to Rome and the other to Jerusalem." He called Zionism "the greatest ally of racist policy."

Following the logic of Farinacci, Ettore demanded that all Italian Jews clarify their position and declare their "full and absolute adhesion to the Fatherland." Finally, he insisted that whoever did "not feel the sacred and obligatory love for the Fatherland where he is born should remove himself from his own country." This extreme position—almost advocating the expulsion of Zionist Jews from Italy—went far beyond anything fascism had ever articulated. Ettore and the Bandieristi—as the anti-Zionists came to be called—divided Italian Jews into bitterly warring camps precisely at a time when they faced an extremely dangerous common threat.

Although based in Turin, the Bandiera movement had prominent followers throughout Italy. As Ettore noted, the governing councils of numerous cities—Rome, Verona, Ancona, Modena, Livorno—all sent messages of solidarity to the newspaper after its first issues. During its early months, the paper had a weekly circulation of about 2,800 and some 1,100 regular subscribers. If its actual readership was somewhere between the two figures, one can infer that roughly 2,000, more than fifteen percent, of Italy's 12,000 Jewish households received the paper.

While most contributors were highly assimilated middle- and upper-middle-class Jews like the Ovazzas, a number of Italian rabbis also wrote for the paper.

A sermon given by Rabbi Gino Bolaffio of Turin on May 20, 1934, shows that the panic of the arrests there was felt strongly within the synagogues. Bolaffio tried to blend Judaism and fascism by weaving Mussolini into Jewish theology, depicting him as a providential, semi-divine figure.

> We live in the twelfth year of the Fascist Era. On Italy's horizon, a bright star has appeared, meant to illuminate the country and the entire civilized world. He is a man of great genius, a spiritual heir of the prophets of Israel. . . . We Jews, educated, as I have said, in a school of duty and discipline, and not unaware of our Nation's history, remain struck with admiration by the noble figure of Il Duce, powerful, gifted with amazing, I would almost say divine, qualities. No, the true Jew does not follow fascism out of duty, out of opportunism. . . . The true Jew considers fascism as a providential phenomenon, meant to take him back to God and his forefathers.

Bolaffio's sermon also contained a clear warning to the Zionists: "The prophets of Israel talk often of a distant Messianic era, but never of a

Zionist problem. . . . Let us not delude ourselves, my dearest friends; that day is far, very far away."

In June 1934, Ettore organized special elections to form a new governing council for Turin's Jewish Community. In true fascist style there was only one electoral list, composed of prominent Jewish fascists, who were elected almost unanimously (733 out of 741 votes in their favor, with fifty-seven percent of eligible members voting). The new president of the community was General Guido Liuzzi, a highly decorated soldier who headed Italy's principal military college. Like Ettore, he had only the remotest interest in religion but felt it was his duty to both Italy and his family tradition to bring Judaism and fascism back into perfect harmony. Also on the new governing council was Alfredo Ovazza, Ettore's older brother.

On the day of the elections, Ettore sent a telegram to Mussolini declaring triumphantly: "Turinese Jews thus reaffirm their intention to humbly serve Fascist Fatherland and Duce."

A number of Jewish communities in other cities—Rome, Genoa, Ancona and Livorno—followed Turin's lead and elected fascist administrations in tune with the Bandieristi.

In this phase of aggressive growth, the Jewish fascist movement attempted to lay siege to the Union of Italian Jewish Communities, the official governing council that had been created during fascism to set national policy for the various local communities. *La Nostra Bandiera* kept up a drumbeat of attacks on the Union to pressure it into publicly renouncing political Zionism.

The official leaders of Italian Judaism were in a difficult quandary: a failure to embrace the Bandiera initiative could be interpreted as coolness toward fascism, while a condemnation of the Zionists would split Italian Judaism in two and unjustly brand the Zionists as disloyal. Either move could further fan the flames of anti-Semitism. But just as external events—the rise of Hitler—had created the crisis, they acted again to dissipate it, if only momentarily.

When Ettore telegraphed Mussolini in June to announce the triumph of the militant fascists in the Turin elections, the dictator was still reeling from his first encounter with Hitler, which he described as a "collision." Mussolini had been forced to listen to Hitler's endless, ranting monologues—partly because he had insisted on conducting their talks without an interpreter in order to impress the Führer with his command of German. Hitler, Mussolini commented, "was a gramophone with just seven tunes, and once he had finished playing them he started all over again."

A few days later Il Duce was shocked to hear that Hitler had arranged the murder of several hundred of his closest followers in the infamous "Night of the Long Knives"—a criminal act that went far beyond anything ever contemplated by Mussolini's Blackshirts. The next month Italy and Germany almost went to war over a Nazi attempt to take power in Austria. At the time Austria was virtually an Italian protectorate and its premier, Engelbert Dollfuss, Mussolini's protégé. On July 24, while Mussolini was entertaining the Austrian premier's family in Italy, pro-Nazi conspirators assassinated Dollfuss in an attempted coup d'état. Mussolini was beside himself with rage and immediately sent Italian troops to the Austrian border at the Brenner Pass, prepared to attack if Germany should move on Vienna.

Mussolini now regarded Hitler as his greatest menace. "It would mean the end of European civilization if this country of murderers and pederasts were to overrun Europe," he told one foreign diplomat at the time. "Hitler is the murderer of Dollfuss . . . a horrible sexual degenerate, a dangerous fool." Mussolini saw his own dictatorship in very different terms. "Fascism is a regime that is rooted in the great cultural traditions of the Italian people; fascism recognizes the right of the individual, it recognizes religion and family. National Socialism, on the other hand, is savage barbarism. . . . Murder and killing, loot and pillage and blackmail are all it can produce."

With this souring of German–Italian relations, the polemical debate over Jews, Zionism and fascism quickly evaporated. In fact, Mussolini began actively courting the leaders of the international Zionist movement. "I am a Zionist myself," he told Nahum Goldmann, a leader of the World Jewish Congress.

For a time, Mussolini believed the Zionists might serve as his beachhead in the Middle East and as a useful ally in Italy's plans to wrest control of the Mediterranean from the British. In his meetings with Goldmann he actively tried to outbid the British for the Zionists' loyalties. "You must have a real state, not the ridiculous National Home that the British have offered you. I shall help you create a Jewish state."

This courtship was based, however, on Mussolini's distorted view of the Zionist movement as a kind of all-powerful Jewish cabal with much greater influence than the Third Reich. Mussolini told Goldmann:

> I know Herr Hitler. . . . He is an idiot, a rascal, a fanatical rascal, an insufferable talker. It is torture to listen to him. You are much stronger than Herr Hitler. When there is no trace left of Hitler, the Jews will still

be a great people. We [the Italians and the Jews] are great historical powers. Herr Hitler is a joke.

Ironically, the sudden reflowering of relations between Mussolini and the Jews took the wind out of the sails of the Jewish fascist movement. In fact, the government began leaning on Ettore Ovazza to close down *La Nostra Bandiera* in November 1934, the same month Mussolini met with Goldmann.

Both Ettore and General Liuzzi, the president of the Turin Jewish Community, had to lobby heavily to find a face-saving way out of the situation. Ettore wrote a formal appeal to the government:

The newspaper . . . has already achieved many of its objectives leading to a clarification and almost totalitarian affirmation of the Jews' traditional attachment to the Fatherland and of their adherence to the ideals of the Fascist regime.

The abolition of this newspaper at this moment would create serious problems compromising the results already obtained. Shutting down this paper while allowing the weekly paper *Israel* in Florence to continue, would allow the (fortunately) small groups of anti-nationalist and Zionist-nationalist Jews to regain their breath and cry victory.

Ettore offered instead to transform his paper from a political weekly into a biweekly that would deal mostly with Jewish culture. Because he and Liuzzi were about to enter the national council of the Union of Italian Jewish Communities, the muting of the paper's political tone could be presented as a gracious compromise rather than a stinging slap in the face from the government.

The fact that Jewish fascists were being muzzled by the government while the Zionists continued to publish freely never caused Ettore or any of his chief associates to rethink their relation to fascism. They never grasped the fact that Mussolini's policy toward the Jews was purely expedient: it depended on larger political interests and not on the loyalty or disloyalty of Italian Jews. The crisis over Zionism and the Jews' supposed double loyalty had been manufactured for political purposes and for the same reasons had been made to disappear. Now that Mussolini had decided the Zionists could be useful, the government regarded the ideological fervor of the Bandieristi as an embarrassing nuisance.

But Ettore Ovazza continued to see himself as a soldier in the front lines of fascism rather than as a pawn in a larger game, a pawn the regime would have no qualms about sacrificing when the occasion demanded.

Chapter Five

For most of 1935, relations between Italy and Germany remained cool. Mussolini signed a military treaty with France, and the "Jewish Question" disappeared from the Italian press. The Italian invasion of Ethiopia on October 2, 1935—Mussolini's first step in the fatal march toward world war—changed the equation again. France and Great Britain, already colonial powers in Africa, condemned the invasion with loud rhetoric but comparatively mild economic sanctions; Mussolini effectively exploited the sanctions to rally the Italian masses around the threatened Fatherland.

Like their Catholic counterparts, Jewish leaders throughout the country staged elaborate displays of patriotic solidarity. Mussolini declared a national "Day of Faith," on which all the women of Italy were expected to give up their gold wedding rings to raise money for the Fatherland. Jewish communities responded with a religious blessing, turning the Day of Faith into a kind of wedding ceremony, marrying the Jewish community with the regime.

On December 18, 1935, in virtually every synagogue in Italy, the Day of Faith was celebrated in ceremonies that began with the playing of the Royal March (the Savoy hymn) and the fascist song "Giovinezza." A patriotic sermon followed and then the women of the community came forward to perform their act of sacrifice. Typical of the Day of Faith sermons was that given by Rabbi Rosenberg of Ancona:

> Today is the sacred Day of Faith. Today is the thirty-first day of the economic siege, ordered to humiliate the Italian people and stop its march to victory.
>
> But Italy is demonstrating today to the entire world its firm will to defeat the ignoble siege . . . and you, wives and mothers, are in the vanguard.
>
> Following the august example of the Queen of Italy you have today placed on the altar of the Fatherland the most precious object you possess. . . . More than a gift of gold, it is a gift of the soul.

The rabbi emphasized that the Jews had an extra reason for giving: "for the honor of your religion." Rabbi Aldo Lattes of Rome made the point quite explicit in his sermon.

> Just as during the war of unification the Jews did not lag behind in their sacrifice of blood, so today they should be second to none in the resistance to the iniquitous sanctions.
>
> Brothers and Sisters!
>
> Falling short today in the duty we owe the Fatherland would be a betrayal not only before mankind but also before the Lord! . . . Strip from your houses all foreign products, make every possible economy, and give, give gold to the Fatherland!

A number of Jewish communities, including that of Turin, went beyond the official request and offered the most precious gold and silver religious objects from their synagogues to be melted down for the Fatherland. The Union of Italian Jewish Communities tried to check this enthusiasm and ensure that the synagogues were not mindlessly stripped. Rabbis consulted Talmudic texts and drew up lists specifying which objects could and could not be destroyed for their metallic value.

This was the ideal fusion of religion and nationalism that Ettore Ovazza and the Bandieristi envisioned. And so, for a time, all levels of Italian Judaism were in perfect harmony.

Only the more perceptive among Italian Jews understood that the Ethiopian conflict increased rather than decreased the danger to them. By pitting Italy against its former allies, France and Great Britain, the war pushed Mussolini into the arms of Hitler and polarized Europe into fascist and antifascist blocks.

Just two days after the Italian invasion, Hitler made a rather sinister prophesy: "The Italian people too will recognize at the end of this struggle that there is a Jewish question. Let us leave it to the future to reveal how the Jew has had his finger in this pie."

Certainly with the imposition of economic sanctions the fascist regime turned up the heat of its antidemocratic rhetoric and gave legitimacy to various paranoid conspiracy theories. Any Italian setbacks were explained in terms of the insidious efforts of its enemies: plutocratic democracies, international capitalism and so on. Because the Zionist colony in Palestine operated under the aegis of the British Empire, "international Jewry" was now portrayed in the fascist press as a British agent harmful to Italian interests. It was only a matter of time before the old Judeo-Masonic and Judeo-Bolshevik conspiracy theories would be taken out of mothballs and dusted off by the right-wing press. And indeed, by January 1936 the hook-nosed caricature of the Jew reappeared in Italian vignettes side by side with the octopus of International Plutocracy and the Masonic-Bolshevik hydra, both shown wrapping their tentacles around the Italian nation.

These attacks were published, however, with standard disclaimers. "We have received complaints from Italian Jews about some of the vignettes we have published," the newspaper *Marc'Aurelio* explained, "but these vignettes are not directed against the Italian Jews whose patriotism and Italian faith we recognize; rather, they are against the Zionists, allies of Free Masonry, Democracy and Bolshevism which are plotting to damage our Nation."

Once again these instances of anti-Semitism seemed isolated and unofficial. Mussolini himself expressed great satisfaction with the Jews' solidarity: "In these great days for the Italian nation I declare that Italian and Jewish ideals are fully merged into one," *La Nostra Bandiera* proudly quoted him as saying in December 1935. And the Italian Foreign Ministry, in an attempt to combat the international condemnation of the Ethiopian invasion, published a pamphlet called *The Jews of Italy* advertising Italy's liberal treatment of Jews.

Mussolini even enlisted the help of Italian Zionists to try to reverse the negative international reaction to the Italian invasion. At the behest of the fascist government, Dante Lattes, editor of *Israel* (the bête noire of Ovazza's newspaper) flew to London to plead with Zionist leaders to intercede on Italy's behalf with the British government. "But since Jewish influence on world politics was a mere fable," Lattes later wrote, "our efforts . . . had no concrete result whatever."

Initially Mussolini saw the Ethiopian war as a new opportunity to strike a deal with Zionism for control of the Mediterranean. He secretly offered to create a Zionist settlement in Ethiopia, the first step toward a Jewish state in Palestine. When the fascists took over the Middle East, the Jews would get Israel and the Italians would keep Iraq and Syria. The leaders of the Zionist movement were justifiably skeptical of this plan, and it never acquired any concrete reality.

For Ettore Ovazza and other Jewish fascists, the conquest of Ethiopia was the fulfillment of a long-standing dream of Empire. In January 1936, at age forty-three, Ovazza wrote to Il Duce, offering his services as a volunteer in Africa. He received a polite reply from a party official gratefully declining his patriotic offer—probably because of his age.

Because Ethiopia had an ancient Jewish community, Italian Jews felt they had a special civilizing mission of their own, parallel to that of fascism. The Falasha descended from Jews who had migrated to Africa several centuries before the Christian era and lived cut off from the rest of the Jewish world since then. *La Nostra Bandiera* saw the invasion of Ethiopia as a war of liberation. After a series of Italian victories during the spring of 1936, the Italian Jewish community was encouraged to send rabbis to establish contacts with the Falasha.

Italian Jews greeted Mussolini's Declaration of Empire with the same kind of patriotic fanfare that had accompanied the invasion. But the climate surrounding the Jews had changed in the intervening seven months. The attacks against the alleged Jewish International and Judeo-Masonic conspiracy cast a shadow over their jubilation. *La Nostra Bandiera* published an anguished letter from a young woman describing an anti-Semitic incident at one of the imperial celebrations.

> On the evening of May 9, what should have been for me, as for every Italian, a moment of serene joy became instead one of pain and indignation. . . .
>
> Just as my heart palpitated with the most ardent love and pride, when my eyes wept tears of joy, when my soul echoed the sublime words of Il Duce, and I felt myself more than ever bound by a solemn vow to forever serve the cause of Italy as my ancestors before me, in silence and humility, at that precise moment a little voice next to me, called out the ignoble phrase . . . "Damn the Jews!"

With the return of anti-Semitism, the rift among the Jews widened again. In the same issues in which *La Nostra Bandiera* welcomed the Italian triumph, the paper also renewed its assault on the Union of Italian Jewish communities. In typically schizophrenic fashion, Jewish Fascists alternately criticized growing anti-Semitism and denounced the leaders of the Italian Jewish establishment for their suspect loyalty and their ties to international Jewry.

Ettore Ovazza and his newspaper did not ignore the danger of anti-Semitism. They paid close attention to developments in Germany and Eastern Europe, and answered anti-Semitic critics within Italy. One of the sad ironies of Ettore's life is that while he was more acutely sensitive than most to the dangers of anti-Semitism, his blind attachment to fascism prevented him from attributing the anti-Jewish attacks to their true source. More often than not, he blamed the growth of anti-Semitism in Italy on the Jews themselves rather than on fascism's growing alliance with Hitler.

The situation, however, was very confusing. Publicly Mussolini and the regime never uttered a word against the Jews, and occasionally expressed words of support; those who attacked them appeared to act on their own. This barrage of conflicting messages put Italy's Jews in something akin to what psychological studies call a double bind. Researchers have noted that the parents of schizophrenics often place their children in an emotional double bind: demanding affection with their words, but pushing the children away with their body language or tone of voice. Similarly, Italian Jews became increasingly disoriented by a society that simultaneously reassured and attacked them.

Like children with a difficult parent, fascist Jews tried everything to please Mussolini, giving increasingly large sums of money to help develop new Italian colonies and renouncing all ties to the international Jewish community. Fascist Jews in Turin began a second major offensive against the Jewish establishment. General Guido Liuzzi prepared a booklet, published and warmly endorsed by *La Nostra Bandiera,* called *For the Fulfillment of Jewish Duty in Fascist Italy,* which proposed a radical reform of Italian Judaism along fascist lines. Liuzzi wanted to oust the current leadership, set up a new centralized governing body with authoritarian power, prohibit contact with Jewish groups overseas and limit religious observance to its purely ritual functions. Absorbing much of the rhetoric of anti-Semitism, Liuzzi even accused the official Jewish leadership of "old Masonic roots" and "international links" with subversive, anti-Italian elements.

Despite the climate of intimidation, the Union of Italian Jewish Communities did not back down. Its old president, Felice Ravenna, who had tried desperately to hold Italian Judaism together in this period of profound crisis, replied to Liuzzi with a characteristic sense of dignity, laced with a certain bitter irony.

> It is strange that these lessons [on the problems of Judaism] should be offered to men of Jewish and Italian faith, as we are, by someone who began only yesterday to show an interest in Jewish life. . . . We are happy to listen to criticism from any quarter as long as it comes from competent people motivated by a desire to build rather than destroy Jewish unity . . . and as long as that criticism does not insult our honesty, morality, idealism or our feelings as Italians which are no less than those of General Liuzzi.

Once again, the Jewish fascists' aggressive attack on the Union did not win them praise from the regime. Instead, the Ministry of the Interior privately rebuked the editors of *La Nostra Bandiera.* A May 1, 1936, dispatch from the ministry to the prefect of Turin read:

> *La Nostra Bandiera* in its latest issues has published articles criticizing the delegation from the Union of Italian Jewish Communities for having participated in the Conference of the World Jewish Congress, held in Paris in February.
>
> Since the Union was able to use that conference to inform Jewish public opinion about Italy and make it appreciate the attitude of our country toward its Jewish citizens, we ask Your Excellency to explain to the editors of *La Nostra Bandiera* the inappropriateness of these kinds of articles.

Only a few months later, the Bandieristi found themselves being whipsawed from the other side. After Mussolini joined Hitler in sending troops to fight in the Spanish Civil War, Farinacci's right-wing *Regime Fascista* attacked Jewish fascists viciously for failing to act against their subversive Zionist brethren.

> Why do they do nothing concrete to disassociate themselves from all other Jews in the world, the ones whose only goal is the triumph of the Jewish International? Why have they not yet risen against their fellow Jews who are perpetrators of massacres, destroyers of churches, sowers of discord, audacious and evil killers of Christians? . . . There is a growing feeling that all Europe will soon be the scene of a war of religion. Are they not aware of this? We are certain that many will proclaim: We are Jewish fascists. That is not enough. They must prove with facts that they are fascists first and Jews second.

Rather than shake their fascist faith, the attacks simply hardened the determination of Ettore and his colleagues to show that they were "fascists first and Jews second." While he was more concerned than most about anti-Jewish rumblings in Italy, like most Jews Ettore appears not to have regarded discrimination as a possibility. Aside from the editorials in certain fascist newspapers there was little stirring of anti-Semitism among the Italian people. Italian anti-Semitism seemed an entirely unreal phenomenon.

A more skeptical and perspicacious observer might have concluded that since there was no popular pressure fueling anti-Semitism, it was the government keeping this artificial phenomenon alive. But the whole grain of Ettore's experience contradicted the growing signs of anti-Semitism. His non-Jewish fascist friends continued to treat him with esteem and admiration. In 1935 the government made him a Knight of the Colonial Order of the Star of Italy for his generous contributions to the development of the Italian colony in Libya. And just as the anti-Semitic press campaign started up again in early 1936, Ettore received an invitation to participate in the honor guard that stood watch outside the tomb of Italy's royal family in Turin. This was obviously an important recognition of his patriotism, and he kept the invitation carefully preserved along with his army identification papers and his fascist membership card among his most important possessions.

Ettore Ovazza and Benito Mussolini were both fond of recalling the story in Suetonius that the Jews of ancient Rome had asked permission to weep on the funeral casket of Julius Caesar and had kept watch over his tomb for several days and nights in gratitude for the emperor's religious tolerance. The clear implication of the tale in fascist Italy was not hard to divine: Mussolini, who considered himself the modern Caesar, was being cast in the role of the first emperor in the hopes of reinforcing his own commitment to religious freedom.

One can imagine Ovazza, dressed in his artillery captain's uniform and fascist black shirt, with his war medal and Fascist Party pin, standing at attention before the royal tomb and recalling his Roman Jewish ancestors at the grave of Caesar. As he felt the weight of two thousand years of history tying the Jews to the Fatherland, from the first Roman emperor to the creation of the new Italian Empire, the recent flurry of anti-Semitism in the newspapers must have seemed to Ettore a small and insignificant misunderstanding.

* * *

On February 25, 1936, just a few days after he had stood guard at the Savoy family tomb, Ettore was nearly killed in an automobile accident while returning home from a wedding in Milan. The family chauffeur, momentarily blinded by the headlights of an oncoming car, rammed into a truck in front of him. Ettore was hit on the head by a metal pole, which left a deep gash over one eye and shattered part of his skull.

After a series of operations and several months of recuperation, Ettore returned to an active life in both business and politics. But he lived with a scarred face and a patched eye. Some of his political opponents referred to him as "Platinum Head" because of the metal plate used to repair his skull. And the image of Ettore that has been passed on to posterity is influenced partly by his rather terrifying appearance after the accident and lends to his reputation as an abnormal, deranged fanatic.

While it is tempting to blame the severe blow to his head for his extreme political views, Ettore's writings after the accident show no change from those before. Nevertheless, there is a tendency within the family to paint Ettore retrospectively as a crank, as someone who was always a little strange. Maria Ovazza, the widow of Alfredo, recalls nothing distinct about her brother-in-law, but she has the impression that her husband looked askance at Ettore's militant fascism: "My husband used to say, 'Since the accident Ettore isn't the same.' " Alfredo himself sat on the governing council of the Turin Jewish Community from 1934 until 1938 and actively supported the Jewish fascist movement in all its initiatives.

Franca Ovazza Piperno acknowledges the family's fascism and at the same time tries to disassociate her father from Ettore. She attributes Vittorio's fascism to a vow he supposedly made to his mother on her deathbed rather than to poor political judgment. "My grandmother told him, 'You have to watch out for your brother, even though he's older than you.' She told him to look after Ettore because he was hot-tempered. And my father would have gone through hell to keep his promise to his mother. He went through years of hating and fighting, but he just had to do it, which was quite courageous. He was rather proud of his intellectual brother."

But this account also has too much of the wisdom of hindsight. Celeste Ovazza died in 1926, when the entire family, including Franca's father, was already fascist. Moreover, at that point fascism was hardly a courageous choice: Mussolini was in power and there were many advantages to be gained from belonging to the party.

"They were all fascist," says Vittorio Segre, Franca's second cousin. "Ettore, like my father, was a genuine enthusiast, the others less so. I would say there was a scale among the three brothers. At the bottom would be Vittorio, who was an officer in the cavalry, patriotic, a nationalist, but more of a monarchist than a fascist. The army went along with fascism but considered its first allegiance to the king. In the middle was Alfredo: he was more interested in money than in politics but was still a fascist. Ettore really believed. He was sufficiently rich that he had no particular need to be fascist. If there's one thing I'm sure of, it is that he was completely in good faith."

Franca's portrait of Ettore as someone who needed looking after is inconsistent with the rest of her account. Before 1938, Ettore was the most prominent member of the family, honored repeatedly by the government, invited to audiences by both Mussolini and the prince of Savoy, a published author and respected banker. "My uncle was very cultured and intelligent, and he could also be very pleasant," Franca says. "He could tell stories. He thought Mussolini would be the savior of Italy, that he would bring dignity to Italy, that it would become one of the leading nations of Europe again. No one would spit at us, the way England used to do. He hated England. But he was a very quiet person, he wasn't a shouting person."

Rather than look after Ettore, Vittorio Ovazza looked up to him. When Ettore bought his own villa after getting married, Vittorio and his family spent the summers with him. In 1928, Vittorio and Ettore together wrote a waltz, "Attesa" (Anticipation), whose romantic lyrics Franca remembers well. *"O fanciulla, sei fuggita, e ti vedo dileguare nella nebbia . . . che svanisce al primo sol. Torna ancora, mio tesoro. . . .* (O girl, you've fled, and I see you disappear into the mist . . . which vanishes with the morning sun. Come back, my treasure.)

Neither his militant political activity nor his car accident eclipsed the sentimental side of Ettore's personality. In 1937, the year after the accident, he published a long narrative poem meant to serve as the libretto to an opera. A love story set in India between a princess and a shepherd, *Sita* is pure romantic fantasy, with Oriental skies "begemmed like diadems," exotic dancers, lute players, sage Brahmans, a wise king and a faithful populace. Perhaps this flight of utopian fantasy was a welcome escape for Ettore at a time when he was recovering from the accident and Europe seemed to move closer to war with each passing day.

While love and happiness triumphed in Sita's land of Vindia, the situation in Italy grew increasingly tense. In May 1937, as fascist and Nazi officials shuttled between Rome and Berlin preparing a German–Italian alliance, anti-Jewish propaganda took a quantum leap forward. An important fascist publicist, Paolo Orano—a member of parliament and rector of the University of Perugia—published an attack on Italian Jews thinly disguised as a disinterested scholarly analysis. More disturbing was the fact that virtually all Italian newspapers, including Mussolini's own *Popolo d'Italia,* used Orano's book, *The Jews in Italy,* as a pretext to raise the so-called Jewish Question.

The book helped create a specifically Italian fascist brand of anti-Semitism, based not on biology and eugenics but on historical, religious and national considerations. Orano, while speaking warmly of several individual Jews (particularly Ettore Ovazza), argued that the Jews were a fundamentally subversive, revolutionary people who inevitably sought to control and undermine the nations in which they settled. He dedicated an entire chapter to Ettore, incorporating his critique of Zionism and then extending it to apply to all Jews. While calling Ettore "the most frank" of the Italian Jews, Orano accused him of suffering from some of the worst traits endemic to his race: "vanity, pride, sense of superiority . . . presumption of belonging to a chosen people."

For Ettore, the book's publication must have been particularly painful. Orano was a good friend, with whom he corresponded regularly. After learning of Ettore's accident, Orano had remained in almost daily contact with the Ovazza family and sent them numerous solicitations and prayers for his recovery. That a leader of the Jewish community should be on close personal terms with one of the country's leading anti-Semites is emblematic of the paradoxical nature of the relationship between Jews and fascist Italy.

Orano's letters (there is no trace of Ettore's side of the correspondence) tell a strange story of betrayal and support. Even as he was preparing the psychological terrain for the Jewish persecutions, Orano never failed to demonstrate affection and respect for Ettore and his family. More incredibly, their friendship survived the publication of Orano's book with no loss in cordiality. During the subsequent racial campaign Orano worked diligently to help the Ovazzas.

In May 1937, after the book had come out, Orano wrote to Ettore:

> Dear and noble friend,
>
> Your position in relation to the Zionism of the Italian "fascists" of the Jewish faith is the clearest, the most precise, the true and necessary one. In this we are in complete agreement: that Palestinian Zionism is a British expedient. . . . You should be proud and happy that your position earns you the esteem of all Italian fascists, regardless of whether they are Jews or Christians. . . .
>
> Cordially and fascistically yours.

By the last months of the year, Ettore had obviously communicated his growing preoccupation over the increasing rapprochement between Italy and Nazi Germany. Orano responded blending sympathy and anti-Semitism. "Your letter is tinged by a not unjustified worry," he wrote, and then launched into a diatribe about the Zionist conspiracy against Italy. "The British minister of war is a Jew—the news has been made public today, I have known it for some time—and he sees only according to the feeling of race." The letter ended, characteristically, with affectionate greetings: "Let's try to arrange a meeting in Rome. . . . My best to your *signora.*"

Their friendship did not prevent Ettore from returning Orano's fire in his own book, *The Jewish Problem: Response to Paolo Orano.* Perhaps the most interesting of Ettore's works on the Jews, it is a cry of desperation written in the shadow of the impending persecutions, a strange mix of blindness and insight.

Some of his comments on Zionism sound like anti-Semitic tracts: "An openly Zionist movement operates in Italy which, while headed by organizations established in Italy, is in fact dependent on the headquarters in London and Palestine. This Zionist activity . . . is hostile to the interests of Italy and extraneous to the soul of the Nation."

At the same time, Ettore offered a passionate and heartfelt defense of the Jews and adopted a tone that distinguished his response to Paolo Orano from his earlier writings: hurt and moral indignation took precedence over his anti-Zionist polemic. His was a blistering attack on the cynicism and intellectual dishonesty of the new Italian anti-Semitism.

> We are the masters of Europe? So why are we having so much difficulty resolving the Zionist question in Palestine? Why are the Jews in Russia oppressed and tyrannized? (Aren't they supposed to be in charge?) Why is Poland trying to send its three million Jews into exile? Why is the Jew in Germany no longer a citizen? Why in many of the Balkan states are the Jews shoved aside and treated like animals? . . . All of this is tragic and . . . the fruit of that infamous and ghastly propaganda that has made the Jew across the centuries an object of hatred to the world. . . . My anguish about Zionism is nothing when compared with the gratuitous and continuous insults that offend our patriotic and civic feelings.

Ettore repeated his usual rhetoric about the spiritual unity between the Italian Jews and Italian fascism, but he also mentioned some of the darker corners of Italian history—the centuries in the ghetto for example—and pointed out the grotesque logic of Orano's complaint that the Jews had contributed only modestly to Italian history until very recently.

> Let's speak frankly: In what conditions did the Jews of Italy live before 1848? How can a plant grow without sun? If you lock a child in a room for several years and then let him out and expect him to run a race, he won't be ready for the marathon. . . . On the one hand we are supposed to be the dominators of Europe, taking control of society's nerve centers, millionaires and communists; on the other [we are] "incapable of creating, lacking in initiative and modest in synthetic thinking." I would like to say to . . . the prosecutors and . . . judges: If you want to put Judaism and the Jews on trial, get together and decide what the charges are.

Ultimately, however, Ettore accepted Orano's premise that it was reasonable for the regime to distinguish between good Jews and bad Jews, fascists and Zionists: "Congressman Orano, I am an Italian fascist, without reservation, Mussolinian and totalitarian." Ettore's book unwittingly played into the hands of the propagandists of anti-Semitism: its title alone gave credibility to the notion that there was in fact a "Jewish problem." Ettore's publisher, Pinciana, was also Orano's and helped orchestrate the "debate" on the Jews. Indeed, Pinciana marketed the two books together, offering a special price to the reader who bought both.

* * *

Despite the intense debate over Orano's book, few people understood its gravity. A British envoy in Rome, William McClure, in May 1937 described the sudden burst of anti-Semitism as something that flared up and died down periodically in Italy during moments of crisis: the Risorgimento, the Libyan war, World War I, the Russian Revolution.

Even as they began to see signs of trouble, fascist Jews found them easy to ignore. Vittorio Segre describes an incident that captures the strange atmosphere of both menace and false security:

> On Yom Kippur in 1937, when the cantor started singing the Kol Nidre prayer for the third time, three bareheaded youths entered our synagogue with the obvious intention of disturbing the service. There was a moment of tension even though the cantor continued singing the prayer. My father looked around, and when he saw that nobody reacted, he left the bench on which I was sitting and with his prayer shawl wrapped around his shoulders went straight to the intruders. Without a word, very slowly, he withdrew his wallet from his inner pocket and pulled out a document showing his position in the Fascist Party. The three youngsters jerked to attention and left the synagogue. The incident confirmed, more than anything else, my feeling of total security.

Like their cousin Segre, Carla and Franca Ovazza had only the dimmest idea of the ideological debate in the fascist press. "Every Jewish family would invite a German boy or girl to the house, and they would tell us of the terrible things going on in Germany," Carla recalls. "We started to think: What a terrible thing—but it will never happen in Italy."

Franca had her first unpleasant brush with anti-Semitism under particularly strange circumstances when a fascist official, infected by freshly imported German racial theories, mistook her for a member of the master race. "I was with my mother skiing at Sestriere in the Italian Alps, and this disgusting little old man kept telling me, 'You are the perfect Aryan beauty, with your blue eyes and blond hair.' One evening he asked me to dance. As a teenager, I was never allowed to dance. So I looked over at my mother, thinking that she would never let me dance. But she nodded her approval and I had to dance with this creature. Afterward I said to her, 'How could you let me dance with that disgusting little man?' And she just told me, 'Behave yourself; he's one of the heads of OVRA [the Italian secret police].' "

Perhaps because of the climate of growing insecurity, Franca's father tried to marry her off to a Jewish war hero, Bruno Jesi, who had lost a leg fighting in Ethiopia. At a time when storm clouds were gathering, Jesi's valor and sacrifice made him a hero in the community, a living symbol of the unity between the regime and its Jews.

"I think Jesi wanted to marry me to get my father's money," Franca says. "He thought that marrying Vittorio Ovazza's daughter would settle him for life. He was a very unpleasant man: tall, and with this missing leg. My friends told me, 'And when you go to bed, he'll unscrew his wooden leg.' My father was rather keen on the idea because he was a national hero. Thank God my mother intervened and put an end to the whole thing." Jesi eventually became engaged to one of Franca's cousins, who then left him at the altar the day they were supposed to wed.

Franca herself began to experience her first doubts about fascism—and these led to a showdown with Uncle Ettore. "My family sent me for a couple of months to a Swiss pension, where I lived with some Hungarian and Czech girls. The world opened up for me. I was very proud of being from Italy, this great country that had become even greater with the African war. And in Switzerland I suddenly realized that this was not how the world saw it. Other people had freedom, they weren't grouped in uniforms. They saw Mussolini not as a great man but as an oppressor. When I came back home I started talking in school. My uncle Ettore called me up to his villa one day and said, 'Franca, you are the troublemaker of the family. And if you don't watch yourself I'm going to teach you a lesson you will never forget.' Sure enough, one morning some men came and rang my doorbell. They were OVRA people. They took me away to a hotel and beat the hell out of me, then left me in a corner. It was my uncle's doing. After that I kept my big mouth shut."

Oddly, Franca appears not to have told her family about the incident at the time. Nor did she talk about it with her uncle, and their dealings remained superficial but pleasant. "He was nice when we went to his house," Franca says. "They had this beautiful villa. They were just uncle and aunt."

* * *

"I was at the seaside with my cousin during the summer of 1938," Franca recalls. "We were sitting there listening to the radio. When they announced that Jewish children would not be allowed to go to school again, we started crying and crying. That was the end of our world. We had just graduated from high school, and all our friends would be going on to university and we would be left outside."

When the regime finally initiated the racial campaign that summer, the news—despite two years of growing debate in the press—came as a total shock to most Italians, Jews and non-Jews alike.

On July 14, 1938, Italian newspapers published "The Manifesto of the Racist Scientists." A pseudo-scientific document, commissioned by Mussolini but signed by a group of so-called racial experts, the Manifesto announced the discovery of an Italian race (something Mussolini had previously declared did not exist) and laid out a series of racial precepts:

1. Human races exist.
2. There are great and small races.
3. The concept of race is purely biological.
4. The population of modern Italy is of Aryan origin and its civilization is Aryan.
5. It is a myth that other peoples have mingled with the Italian population during the modern era.
6. There now exists an Italian race.
7. The time has come for Italians frankly to proclaim themselves racists.
8. It is necessary to distinguish between European Mediterranean people and Africans and Orientals.
9. Jews do not belong to the Italian race.
10. The European physical and psychological traits of Italians must not be altered in any way.

Several days later, as if in response to this "independent initiative," the government expressed its approval of the Manifesto and its intention to enact laws "in defense" of the Italian race.

"We never believed that there would be something like the racial laws," Carla recalls. "Suddenly you felt different, you became aware of reality, and you felt that something very bad was going to happen." Carla, like all Jewish children, had to leave public school that fall. When she returned in October to take an exam for a course she had flunked the previous spring, she suddenly found herself an outcast. "The instructor said to me: 'Ovazza, you're Jewish, sit in the last row.' I did very well in the exam, but she gave me the lowest possible grade that would allow me to pass."

The Jewish community had to scramble quickly to set up its own secondary school. "It was wonderful creating the school," Carla says. "We had fantastic teachers—all the [Jewish] professors from the universities who were not allowed to teach there anymore. They would always tell us to be careful of what we said when we went out into the street. You couldn't talk when you were out of school. One day people threw stones at the windows of the school. That didn't happen before the racial campaign."

Before now most of Carla's and Franca's friends had been Catholic, and while the majority remained loyal to them, the two girls suffered a few bitter shocks. Franca remembers bumping into a friend, Paolo, who turned, spat on the sidewalk, and said, *"Porco sangue di ebreo"*—"Blood of a Jewish pig." "Right after the war I met him again, almost exactly in the same spot, and I said, 'Paolo, I'm alive, I've come back, and this time it's me who's going to spit.' And I spat on his face. I was shaking. Aside from that, most of our friends were marvelous."

Because Franca was not allowed to attend university in Italy, the Ovazzas sent her to Switzerland for the 1938 academic year. "At the pension where I lived there was a German girl who kept Hitler's photograph on the wall. One day when we were having lunch she started screaming 'Heil Hitler. . . . We Germans . . . you dirty Jews.' and so on. We told the lady who ran the pension. She said, 'We are here to study at the university and to learn to live in peace together. Politics has no place here.' And the German girl was sent away."

Chapter Six

Logic would seem to dictate that as soon as the fascist regime openly embraced anti-Semitism during the summer of 1938, Jews would have automatically turned against the regime.

They did not.

Despite the devastating impact of the campaign, Ettore Ovazza continued to maintain an outward attitude of fascist devotion. "We remain silent today before the public with our pain," he wrote on July 15, 1938, the day after the publication of the Manifesto of the Racial Scientists. Curiously, this letter—the only known expression of Ovazza's private torment and even anger toward the regime—was sent to none other than Mussolini himself. Overcome by emotion, he writes, at one point: "I write poorly because my hand is trembling."

> It is the end of a reality: that of our feeling one with the Italian people. Was this really inevitable? I don't think so . . . how many starting in 1919 and up until today, have followed You with love, through so many battles, wars, living Your life.
>
> Is all this over? Was it all a dream we nurtured? I can't believe it. I cannot consider changing religion, because this would be a betrayal—and we are fascists. And so? I turn to You—DUCE—so that in this period—so important for our revolution, and you do not exclude that

> healthy Italian part from the destiny of our Nation. . . . We took our machinegun fire and cannon fire along with the Jews from other countries between 1915 and 1918. Where was the Jewish International?

Along with its expression of pain, the letter also attempts to justify and accept the new fascist position. At one point, he writes: "Have the needs of the Nation and the tenacious, infamous anti-Fascist campaign of the pluto-democracies—in which, unfortunately, there are many Jews—forced the government to assume a position so cruel for us Italian Jews? The answer is clear. I bow down before the necessary sacrifice; but I ask You to allow us our proud and integral Italianness. . . . Don't tell us we never integrated with our country." He seems to be prepared to accept persecution as long as the government makes some formal recognition of the patriotism of Italian Jews. And in the end, old loyalties win out over his recent shock. He concludes: "If my soul is in pain—and with how many others—I give you a Roman salute and wish Your High Mission a glorious triumph."

Ettore's decision to publicly accept the racial laws as a "necessary sacrifice" soon prevailed as the official position of the Turin Jewish Community. Its governing council voted, after much agonized debate, to maintain its position of unqualified support for the government. The leaders of the Community held a rare public meeting to explain its decision.

The council of the Turin Jewish Community, after much agonized debate, voted to maintain its position of unqualified support for the government. The council held a rare public meeting to explain its decision.

One member of the audience that night, Sion Segre, later described the thinking of the crowd as they waited for the arrival of the council: "Let us not raise our voices! Let us instead regain our ancient wisdom: blend in. The tempest will pass, peaceful days will return. Let us keep our faith in Mussolini." Confusing rumors circulated in the room. According to one, a prominent Jewish fascist had been to see Mussolini, and Il Duce had reassured him that "no one will touch a hair on the head of the Italian Jews, as long as they keep quiet and don't create any more problems than they already have."

Finally, General Guido Liuzzi, president of the Community, spoke.

> Inexorable exigencies of an international nature, whose recondite motivations are beyond our immediate perception, require us to make a sacrifice for the common good. We accept them with a strong spirit, out of that sense of duty that has always animated our conduct. Moreover,

> we have been assured from highly authoritative sources that if we respect the law—as has always been our honor and our pride . . . no new measures of a harsher sort will be adopted aside from those that the ineluctable course of history has made necessary.

The speech was greeted by "frenetic applause in the first rows, more tepid clapping in the next several rows, and whistling and shouting" from the back of the room, according to Segre, a well-known opponent of the regime who had been arrested after the alleged "Jewish antifascist plot" of 1934. Ettore (whom Segre referred to as "Platinum Head") then stepped up to the podium and gave a speech blasting antifascist and Zionist Jews for having helped bring about the current wave of anti-Semitism. The meeting then degenerated into a fracas with members of the audience pushing, shoving, shouting and calling each other names.

The leaders of the Turin community were not alone in their unswerving loyalty. In October 1938, eight Milanese Jews sent a telegram to Il Duce attacking American Jews who had protested Italy's new racial laws. "Certain of speaking for the majority of Italian Jews," the signatories denounced the "unheard-of, provocative interference of American Jews" and insisted they did not "feel bound to any community beyond the Alps or beyond the seas."

In December, five months after the publication of the Manifesto, a group of Florentine Jews publicly reaffirmed their loyalty to the regime and attacked the Union of Italian Jewish Communities as a puppet of the international Jewish conspiracy:

> We want to place a wall between Italian Fascists of the Jewish religion and international, Masonic, democratic Judaism . . . because the political activity of the Union of Italian Jewish Communities has always been inspired to support arbitrarily that international Zionism which is absolutely antithetical to Mussolinian and Fascist Italy.

The continuing split between Italian Jews was in a sense natural: it reflected divisions established by the laws themselves. The first racial legislation, passed in September and October 1938, reinforced the difference between "loyal" and "disloyal" Jews by creating a special category of patriotic Jews who were exempted from some provisions. Those who had been wounded or who had received medals in World War I, those who had participated in the March on Rome or in D'Annunzio's occupation of Fiume, and those who had joined the Fascist Party in its first years were termed, rather ironically, *discriminati,* because they were discriminated from discrimination.

The racial laws were instituted gradually through a steady turning of the screw. In the first, sketchy laws, there was a great difference between the treatment of *discriminati* and the treatment of the rest. While thousands of Jews were expelled from the Fascist Party, and all public employment, and were forbidden from owning large businesses and substantial tracts of land, and from marrying non-Jews, the only provision that initially affected the *discriminati* was the one regarding public education. For the moment they were allowed to keep their jobs and businesses, and even their membership in the Fascist Party.

For a brief time, until a second, sweeping series of decrees was passed in November 1938, the racial laws in fact accentuated the division between fascist and nonfascist Jews. For the Bandieristi these early racial laws were a terrible betrayal but also a confirmation of the logic of their movement.

The discrimination clause was a distinctive feature of Italian anti-Semitic legislation, reflecting the degree of improvisation and opportunism as well as the fundamental lack of conviction of the Italian racial persecution. From a theoretical standpoint, the concept of discrimination made a mockery of Mussolini's newly espoused doctrine of biological racism by creating a loophole based on patriotic standing. It was a classical political compromise, tacked onto the racial laws at the insistence of moderate fascist leaders who were uneasy about betraying their Jewish friends and fellow party members.

Although little more than a public-relations gimmick, the discrimination clause had surprising psychological weight. Playing shrewdly on the mentality of fascist Jews, it was a nod of recognition to them that their faithful service had not been forgotten and an indication that, despite everything, there was still a difference between Nazi Germany and fascist Italy. It left a small window of hope for those eager to delude themselves about the good intentions of the regime.

"Naturally, we were *discriminati,*" Carla Ovazza recalls. "Ignorant as we were, we were delighted. When I think back, it's absolutely scandalous that we fought for that, but it's true."

During the fall of 1938, Italian Jews held their breath to see how far the regime would go. Some still hoped that they might move Mussolini to leniency. Ettore and some of his followers devised a desperate plan to grab Mussolini's attention and remind him of the Jews' unswerving loyalty. Ettore proposed leading a squad of Jewish fascists to burn down the offices of the Zionist paper *Israel* in Florence. Vittorio Segre, who was sixteen at the time, later recalled Ettore's effort to enlist his father (Ettore's cousin) in the assault.

> On a cold, gray, autumn day, Ettore Ovazza arrived at my parents' home on my mother's farm near Turin, accompanied by two or three people. . . . He explained his plan in great detail. . . . Devoted and reliable friends who had direct access to Il Duce had told my cousin that Mussolini was irritated and sad at having to follow Hitler along the path of anti-Semitism. He had to do it for higher political reasons, but it was against his better nature and the very tradition of Italian fascism. . . .
>
> However, the anti-Fascist Jews as well as the Zionists played into the hands of their enemies in the Fascist hierarchy . . . by offering a reason to attack them, and through them the whole of Italian Jewry. One had to be honest and recognize that the Jews of Italy had made themselves too prominent. . . . How right—said [Ettore]—were our forefathers who preached to their sons not to show off, not to boast of their new privileged status outside the ghetto. However, since it was no longer possible to go back in history, it was necessary to make a clear distinction between the Jews who had always been faithful to the Fascist regime and wanted to remain so, and all the rest. . . . It was therefore important to show on which side the Fascist Jews, the patriots, stood. A punitive action . . . could be an act more useful to the Jews of Italy than a thousand written polemics. The operation would also remind Mussolini of the heroic days prior to the March on Rome, during which the Jews had so ardently supported him.

Ettore's proposal both shocked and attracted Segre's sixteen-year-old mind: the feeling of total helplessness created by the racial laws gave the idea of action (even self-destructive action) a certain appeal. But Vittorio Segre's father, who had previously shared Ettore's ultrafascist politics, staunchly rejected the proposal: "To attack other Jews in such hard times . . . in order to ingratiate ourselves with a regime that had betrayed us [is] to act as slaves, not as free men."

This bizarre paramilitary adventure was Ettore's final political act. As monstrous as it seems, in a way the attack was a natural—if extreme—extension of the logic of the Bandiera movement. For years fascist hard-liners, as represented by *Il Regime Fascista,* for instance, had been goading Jewish fascists to rise up "against their fellow Jews," to do something "concrete" in order to "prove with facts that they are fascists first and Jews second." Fascism had always stressed the importance of action over words and had risen to power by taking to the streets in rebellion against the impotence of parliamentary democracy. The action against *Israel* was a deliberate echo of the early revolutionary days of fascism, when black-shirted squads had sacked the offices of opposition newspapers. Although it was carried out, the attack seems to have elicited no official response.

What finally killed off what little was left of the Jewish fascist movement was the second series of racial laws, passed on November 17, 1938, which pulled the rug out from under the loyal *discriminati.* The laws were amplified considerably, reducing fascist Jews to the same second-class status as other Jews. They were fired from all public jobs, as well as from the army, navy and air force, and were expelled from the Fascist Party. They were forbidden from owning businesses with more than a hundred employees, and banks or businesses related to national defense. They were no longer allowed to have non-Jewish domestic help.

Later the screw was twisted even tighter. In June 1939 all Jews were banned from the skilled professions; some 2,500 Jewish doctors, lawyers, architects, journalists, dentists, engineers, accountants and others were stripped of their right to practice. The category of discriminated Jews had been reduced to little more than symbolism.

The laws now hit the Ovazzas in full force. Not only were they expelled from the party and the army reserve, they were forced to sell the family bank that Grandfather Vitta had founded only a little over seventy years earlier, in the jubilant days of Jewish emancipation. "For my father it was a great shock," Franca recalls. "He said: 'I fought in the war and was wounded, and now they tell me I'm not an Italian.' The Catholic maids who had lived with us since I was born had to be kicked out. They were part of our family. My father was not able to work. My sister and I were not able to go to school. Those things were shattering to us. Everywhere you went you felt like a fly. It was only then that I realized I was different from everybody else. For Uncle Ettore it was the crumbling of all his beliefs and hopes. It must have been terrible."

Carla remembers the shock of walking past the Caffé Romana e Bass, a fashionable café in downtown Turin where she and her friends used to go, and seeing a sign in the window: "No Jews Allowed." "Jesi, the war hero with one leg, saw the sign and took his crutch and broke the window. Never in a million years would you have thought we would arrive at that."

If the material effects of the racial campaign were catastrophic for most Italian Jews, the psychological effects were even more devastating. A Jewish army colonel from Turin, stripped of his command, called his troops to attention a final time, took his pistol from his holster and shot himself. In protest and despair, the prominent Jewish publisher Angelo

Formiggini jumped to his death from the bell tower of the Modena cathedral. On hearing the news, Achille Starace, secretary of the Fascist Party, commented: "He died like a Jew—he jumped from the tower in order to save the cost of a bullet."

The trauma of being disenfranchised as Italians was so great that some 5,706 Italian Jews converted to Catholicism. (Children of mixed marriages who rejected Judaism remained citizens.) The Jewish community was rife with stories of friends and acquaintances whose mothers had signed affidavits stating that their children were the products of extramarital affairs with Catholics so that their children might obtain Aryan status. Other Jews converted first to Protestantism and then to Catholicism in order to get around fascist laws against conversions of convenience. Acquaintances of the Ovazzas even dragged their dead from the Jewish cemetery in Turin and buried them a second time as Christians. A sordid traffic in "Aryanization" certificates began, to the profit of fascist bureaucrats. Although most conversions were purely opportunistic, aimed at keeping jobs or property, they indicate a powerful urge among Italian Jews to cling at all cost to their Italian identity.

After the harsh racial laws of November, the remnants of the Bandiera movement were swept from positions of leadership in Turin. Earlier in the fall General Liuzzi had stepped down as president of the community, and Alfredo Ovazza formally resigned from its governing council in December. Ettore went a step further, actually severing all connections with organized Judaism. The community seemed to be falling apart. Ettore was one of 247 people (out of 5,000) who formally withdrew by the end of 1938. While virtually all of these apostates were converting to Catholicism, Ettore left for his own reasons, protesting what he perceived as the Jewish community's insufficient fascist rigor.

Ettore's letter of withdrawal was so inflammatory that the Turin council felt it necessary to register an indignant response in the minutes of its December 23 meeting:

> The council . . . deplores that [Ettore Ovazza] would connect his withdrawal with a desire to separate himself from international, Masonic, democratic, antifascist Judaism, forgetting that it was this Council that in 1934 publicly affirmed the Italian and Fascist faith of the Turinese Jews and its clear opposition to Zionism or any internationalism hostile to Italy or Fascism.

By then Ettore was politically out of tune not only with the Jewish community but with the rest of his family as well.

Alfredo left Italy for South America in 1939. Vittorio, while broken and embittered by the laws, was still unsure whether to leave or not. "He was very reluctant," says Carla. "He saw his eldest brother going to South America, while Ettore was trying to persuade him to remain. We forced him to leave. He never did understand."

"I had to fight with my father to persuade him," Franca remembers. "He did not want to [leave] because he had promised his mother that [he and Ettore] would always stick together. He didn't want to leave his house or his position. I think that secretly my father felt everything might pass."

When Vittorio and his family finally sailed from Genoa in the summer of 1940, Ettore was furious. "He wouldn't even say good-bye to us. He thought we were traitors," Franca says. " 'There is nothing to fear,' he said. In spite of everything he acted as if all they did to us was nothing."

Vittorio Ovazza's family entered the United States with only a tourist visa because there was no room within the Italian immigrant quota. By the middle of June 1940, Italy had entered the war beside Nazi Germany against Britain and France.

Once in America, Vittorio began to understand the tragedy that awaited Europe, and he wrote to Ettore telling him and his family to come. Ettore angrily refused. "My father then begged him at least to send his children," Carla says. Ettore "replied that his children were much safer in fascist Italy than in any of those 'plutocratic democracies.' " Ettore's angry letters denouncing the United States caught the attention of immigration officials and delayed the Ovazzas' entry into the country.

"In order to obtain an immigrant visa that would allow us to work, we had to go out of the country and come back again," Carla explains. "We couldn't go to Canada because we were considered 'enemy aliens.' So we went to Cuba. We had to stay in Cuba six weeks because of those letters my uncle was writing to my father. My father's mail was under surveillance; they had to check whether he was like my uncle. They found out he had no particular role in the Fascist Party."

As insane as Ettore Ovazza's continuing belief in fascism appears, it is perhaps not surprising when one considers his past experience. For his brothers and most of his friends, fascism was important but hardly central; in contrast, political activity had been the core of Ettore's life for twenty years. To have rejected fascism would have been to deny everything he had stood for, fought for, to erase virtually every word he had ever written. He had gone to war, he had been among the Italian troops at the horrible disaster of Caporetto and at the great victory of Vittorio Veneto. He had been among the first to support the fascist cause, and he had given his time and money. He had donated funds for orphanages and libraries. He had consecrated war monuments, marched in endless parades, founded and financed fascist publications, contributed endless books and articles, brought up his son under the tricolor flag in ardent fascist faith. He had stood watch over the dead of Il Italian royal family. Moreover, he had been received personally by Il Duce, who had looked him straight in the eye and told him that he never for a moment doubted the loyalty of Italian Jews.

What was loyalty if it could not survive the hardest of tests? And clearly this was the ultimate test. War in Europe was inevitable. Germany would win. It was in Italy's best interest to align itself with Hitler. Obviously, anti-Jewish measures were necessary to placate the Nazis. Through the war Italy would become a great power and regain the empire that was her destiny. And when the war was over, life would return to normal and the laws against the Jews would be repealed. A few years of sacrifice for a mere 47,000 people was a small price to pay for an empire. When the war was over, the regime would remember who had broken rank and who had stood his ground. Then the regime would remember Ettore Ovazza, Knight of the Colonial Order of the Star of Italy, regional president of the Association of Fascist Bankers, Captain of the artillery in the Great War, decorated with the Cross of War. . . .

While Ettore lost many Jewish friends because of his continued support of fascism, his resolve was undoubtedly strengthened by the unqualified support he received from his old non-Jewish fascist friends. In fact, the person who appears to have worked hardest on his behalf was Paolo Orano, harbinger of the racial campaign and author of the Jew-baiting book *The Jews in Italy*.

In their correspondence, Orano attempted to reassure Ettore and nourish his illusions. Through either cynicism or monumental insensitivity, he minimized the importance of the racial campaign and noted that the new laws stopped short of Nazi racial persecution. After Ettore wrote him in alarm over the race manifesto, Orano wrote back suggesting that the Jews could simply convert to Catholicism.

July, 20, 1938

Dear Friend,

What you wrote me about [the Manifesto] seems excessive. Above all, Ettore Ovazza has given ample proof of having married the Fascist cause with such enthusiasm that he should not feel himself in any way inferior to any other Italian citizen. It seems to me that the purpose of the publication . . . is to push toward assimilation. Don't you think so? All the other original races of Italy—the document says—have assimilated over time. The Jews have not; and this is true. Therefore it seems natural to conclude that assimilation would solve the Jewish problem.

When the racial laws were passed a few months later, Orano used his considerable influence in Rome to help Ettore with the bureaucratic complications of obtaining discriminated status. Even though Ettore would seem to have qualified on several grounds, the process appears to have been surprisingly difficult. For nearly a year they wrote back and forth discussing bureaucratic roadblocks.

In mid-April 1939, on learning that the "certificate of discrimination" had finally come through, Orano wrote Ettore in a jubilant mood.

My dearest friend,

I can't think of any news that I could receive that would give me greater pleasure than that which your wife gave me by phone in Florence. . . . I am extremely happy, my friend. You know how much I admire you, and the sincerity of my friendship. I thought it impossible that the request wouldn't eventually be resolved. But to know the happy ending gives me a profound consolation. Please give your wife all my respects and to your dear children a warm greeting from your friend.

* * *

Little is known about the last phase of Ettore's life. Because his brothers and their families left the country they can provide no direct testimony. And because all public life was closed off to him and he could no longer publish, Ettore left few written traces of his thoughts. There are, however, a few surviving documents among his personal papers that provide glimpses into what must have been the darkest period of his life.

Perhaps the most important is a letter Ettore sent in November 1941 to his lawyer, announcing triumphantly that after two years of work he had finally succeeded in obtaining certificates of discrimination for his mother-in-law and sister-in-law. Even after three years of racial persecution, Ettore clung desperately to this now useless privilege. For him it was obviously a symbolic vindication of his patriotic career, a sign that someone somewhere in the government had not forgotten his contribution to fascism.

It is with great and genuine—not merely rhetorical—pleasure that I send you the two discrimination certificates.

In order to obtain this result I have worked for two years in the face of some enormous difficulties.

It remains a satisfaction for the moral recognition of the patriotic and nationalist tradition of my Family.

By now Ettore appears to have parted company entirely with reality. It is not that he had descended into a state of madness; rather, he remained frozen in a posture of patriotic rectitude while the world around him had changed utterly. In late 1941, when Italy's ally, Hitler, was busy rounding up the Jews of Europe, Ettore spent his empty days writing letter after letter to innumerable bureaucratic offices, struggling to obtain a meaningless recognition from a government that had taken away his business, robbed his children of their education and reduced him to the status of a pariah.

Ettore's dogged pursuit of discrimination certificates seems all the more pathetic in light of the demeaning restrictions imposed on him during this period. He was forced to go cup in hand to the Turin police department to request permission for the most banal privileges. With Italy's entrance into the war in June 1940, Jews, seen as potential spies, were not allowed to visit the seaside or own radios. But because Ettore was a discriminated Jew, the prefect of Turin sought the advice of his superiors in Rome.

To the Minister of the Interior

July 10, 1941

The discriminated Jew, Ovazza Ettore . . . born in Turin March, 21, 1892, lawyer, has made a request to be authorized to take his family to Rapallo, since they need a seaside cure, as is indicated in the medical certificates here attached. . . .

They all appear to be of regular moral conduct and politically have not given rise, so far, to any problems.

In pursuance to the clauses contained in circular number 41050 of June 6, 1941, since Rapallo is classified as a luxury resort, I would appreciate having the Minister's determination on the merits of this case.

A few days later, the ministry replied.

In relation to the attached note please communicate to the Jew in question that he is not, repeat, not, authorized to go to Rapallo, since it is a luxury seaside resort. The subject can, however, choose another, non-luxury beach.

A year later a similar exchange occurred after Ettore asked to be allowed to have a radio. The prefect of Turin made a long appeal to Rome, listing in great detail all of Ettore's patriotic credentials. The reply from Rome allowed Ettore a radio but insisted that it be adjusted so that it could receive only one local station.

* * *

The last words either of his brothers had from Ettore were in a telegram to Alfredo in Montevideo shortly after the fall of fascism in July 1943: "Finally free." By then the Allies had invaded Sicily and King Vittorio Emanuele III and most fascist leaders were convinced that the war was lost. The fascist Grand Council, which previously had been a mere rubber stamp for Il Duce, suddenly voted him out of power. The king then had Mussolini arrested and appointed as Prime Minister Marshal Pietro Badoglio, chief of the Italian armed forces.

Although Badoglio declared that Italy would continue fighting alongside Germany, most Italians (and particularly the Jews) were in a state of euphoria, believing the war would end in a matter of weeks. Badoglio did not abrogate the racial laws, but privately he let it be known that he would do so at the earliest opportunity. Meanwhile the new government was negotiating a separate armistice with the Allies. The Germans understood Badoglio's double game and sent a stream of troops into Italy in order to hold the country. Alarmed by the massive flow of German troops and by Badoglio's failure to prepare a defense for Italy, the Allies suddenly announced the armistice on September 8, 1943. Badoglio and the king fled Rome, leaving no clear instructions to the Italian army. Within little more than forty-eight hours the Nazis had taken control of most of Italy and captured entire divisions of well-armed Italian troops.

The sudden presence of Nazi troops in Italian cities was obviously a particular threat to the country's Jews, and many went immediately into hiding, but most were far from clear about the extent of the danger. They knew that the Nazis persecuted Jews in Germany and Eastern Europe, but few imagined an organized mass extermination. Under fascism any such news had been carefully suppressed. Many Italians listened secretly to BBC radio reports of the slaughter of Jews in German-occupied Europe, but after twenty years of fascist propaganda they viewed all government news with skepticism. During World War I there had also been vivid tales of German atrocities that afterward had proven to be greatly exaggerated.

In fact, the experience of Italian Jews so far in the war gave reason for cautious optimism. Mussolini had kept his promise not to harm Italy's Jewish citizens. Because Italy and Germany had been allies, Hitler had never even raised the question of deporting Italian Jews. Moreover, although few Italians knew this, the Italian army had steadfastly refused to hand over foreign Jews in Italian-occupied territory in southern France, Yugoslavia and Greece. Some Italian Jews hoped that despite the armistice the old policy of noninterference might continue—particularly since Mussolini had been reinstated as head of a new Italian government after the Germans rescued him from prison on September 12. Although by now the Jews despised Mussolini, they hoped he might at least act as a moderating force on the Germans. Others placed great faith in the power of the Vatican: it was inconceivable to them that the Nazis would round up and slaughter innocent civilians directly under the nose of the pope.

Those in most immediate danger appeared to be Italian soldiers and young men of military age who were ordered to report to Mussolini's German-dominated puppet government. If they failed to obey, they were arrested and sent as slave labor to Germany. The Nazis were too busy with this and other problems in the first few weeks of the Occupation to worry about the Jews.

Two of Ettore's relatives, a cousin who lived in Milan and his brother-in-law, came to visit him in this period and tried to persuade him to flee with them to neutral Switzerland. But Ettore felt their fears were exaggerated: "They'll never touch me, I've done too much for fascism," he said. Nonetheless Ettore did at least leave Turin. He liquidated a good portion of his property, selling two houses and converting at least 6 million lire (a considerable fortune at the time) into precious jewels, gold, cash and foreign currency. In late September 1943 he took his family to a hotel in Gressoney, a ski resort in the Italian Alps where they had often vacationed, so that they could flee to Switzerland if it became necessary.

From the time the Ovazzas left their villa in Moncalieri their story is documented to an extraordinary degree by a nearly unbroken chain of eyewitnesses. The recollections are exceptionally precise and detailed, as if the witnesses were haunted for years by what they had seen.

The region of the Italian Alps along the Swiss border to which the Ovazzas fled, became a theatre of intense drama during the German occupation. Simultaneously, it was the seat of Mussolini's new puppet government, the magnet for thousands of refugees hoping to flee to Switzerland; and the base of partisan bands using the mountainous terrain for protection. A busy traffic in human lives flourished among the thousands of people on the run: Jews, deserters, escaped prisoners of war, antifascists and collaborators. Mountain guides conducted a lucrative but risky business leading groups of refugees through Alpine passes and around Nazi patrols into Swiss territory. Some, however, robbed and killed their charges and left their bodies in deserted mountain passes while others sold Jews to the Nazis for the price on their heads. And there was the added uncertainty of the Swiss government's ever-changing policies: sometimes refugees were welcomed, other times they were sent back across the border.

The hotels of the area were filled to capacity with people carrying crudely forged identification papers and suitcases full of money and jewels. Innkeepers could overlook the false documents or bring them to the attention of the German authorities. Guests feigned the nonchalance of vacationing tourists in this macabre atmosphere in which the luxurious surroundings contrasted with the daily presence of suspicion, fear, blackmail, betrayal and death. The extreme pressures and temptations produced heroes of rare courage and villains of unsurpassed cruelty, as well as a variety of gray figures in the middle, who played double and triple games, shifting nervously with each change in the political wind, alternately committing acts of cowardice and compassion.

This was the world Ettore Ovazza (fifty-one), and his wife, Nella (forty-one), their son, Riccardo (twenty), and daughter, Elena (fifteen) entered during the last days of September 1943.

They left Moncalieri at about seven-thirty in the morning. One of the women who worked for the Ovazzas noted that when someone offered to take a small leather suitcase from Ettore and put it in the trunk of the car, Ettore declined, saying he would keep it with him. She could tell from the way Ettore held the bag that it must have been very heavy and inferred (correctly) that it "contained jewels or other objects of value."

The drive went smoothly except for a frightening moment when a German army vehicle scraped the Ovazzas' car, tearing off its license plate. Having sensed that Ettore was quite nervous, the driver asked him if he was sure that the place they were going was safe. Ettore assured him that it was and that the hotelkeeper was informed about the movements of German troops. The family arrived in time for lunch at the Hotel Lyskamm in Gressoney. "Commendatore Ovazza was visibly pleased with the trip . . . and insisted on paying me two thousand lire for the trip instead of the fifteen hundred we had agreed on in advance," the driver recalled later. He also remembered that Ettore gave the hotel owner two very thick stacks of thousand-lire bills to deposit in the hotel safe.

Unlike many of the guests at the Lyskamm, the Ovazzas registered under their real names—a sign that they did not understand the full danger they were in. The man in whose hands they placed themselves, the hotelkeeper Arnaldo Cochis, was described later by other guests in almost universally unflattering terms. Virginia Faccio del Mastro, who was staying there at the time, testified that "Cochis was very hesitant to help anyone, while he was generally . . . very obsequious toward the Germans and the fascists."

A local doctor described the innkeeper as a "pro-German fascist" and noted that while everyone else in the town had his guns confiscated during the German occupation, Cochis was supplied with a hunting rifle for his own protection. He also claimed that Cochis denounced a local woman who had expressed joy when she heard the news that the Germans had retreated from Rome. A Jewish guest at the hotel, Franca Vernikoff, of Bologna, said she never revealed her identity to Cochis until after the end of the war because she suspected him of collaboration.

The Ovazzas stayed at Lyskamm about fifteen days and, according to another guest, Giulio degli Esposti, Ettore was sociable, pleasant and apparently relaxed: "During several walks we took together he always seemed rather calm because he claimed to have in his possession a signed photograph of Mussolini dedicated to him."

While Ettore did not believe that he, his wife and Elena were in any immediate danger, he did fear for his son, who was of military age. Ettore arranged for Riccardo to escape to Switzerland with a guide and a group of Yugoslavian refugees, probably in the first days of October. According to some observers, Ettore tore a sheet of paper with a Hebrew prayer in half and gave one piece to Riccardo, for him to give to the guide once he reached Switzerland. Apparently the guide returned to the hotel with Riccardo's half of the prayer and announced that the border crossing had gone as planned. But if Riccardo Ovazza made it to Switzerland he did not remain there long.

There are two versions of what happened to him. According to one, a guide named Rudy Lercoz, who was later shot for having collaborated with the SS, robbed Riccardo of the 50,000 Swiss francs and the gold he was carrying and then turned the rest of the family in to the Germans. The second version suggests that after successfully crossing the border, Riccardo was sent back to Italy by Swiss authorities and arrested in the train station at Domodossola. From documents in Riccardo's possession and possibly through torture, the SS was able to find out where his family was hiding.

What is certain is that on the evening of Saturday, October 9, at about eight-thirty, three members of the SS entered the dining room of the Lyskamm, gave a Nazi salute to the assorted company and sat down to eat at a table next to the Ovazzas. Although the officers wore civilian clothes, everyone guessed immediately who they were. Two of them, tall and blond, were "unmistakably German"; the other, a dark-skinned man who spoke both Italian and German, was described as "a mulatto." It was the evening of Yom Kippur and the Ovazzas had observed the twenty-four-hour fast preceding the evening meal. The hotel cook later remembered "having prepared the dinner ordered by the Ovazzas to celebrate the breaking of the Jewish fast and having received a generous tip from Commendatore Ovazza for the excellent preparation of the food."

The three officers said nothing about the reason for their visit. The Ovazzas nervously finished their meal in silence.

After dinner the officers asked the hotelkeeper to call over Ettore Ovazza. A guest noticed that Ettore was forced to pay the Germans' bill before they went to speak privately with him in an adjacent room. Apparently the Germans told Ettore that they had arrested his son, and that Riccardo was charged with possession of foreign currency, a serious crime. They indicated that Ettore would have to go with them the next morning and that the family should prepare their bags for an early departure.

Another guest at the hotel, named Ruffino, was in the game room, where Nella and Elena Ovazza were playing cards. The two watched nervously as Ettore was led upstairs by the officers. "Signor Ovazza came back down to get his wife and daughter and, in order not to frighten them, turned toward the others in the room and said: 'We'll finish the game a little later,' " Ruffino reported. "But then, turning to Signor Storero, Ovazza quickly implored him under his breath to call his lawyer in Turin, to inform him about what was happening."

The family then disappeared upstairs with the Germans. Ruffino's mother, who had the room next to the Ovazzas', "could hear very well that the wife and daughter were crying and that one of the Germans was there with them. She also heard a loud discussion and an insistent slamming of the dresser drawers." Later that night the Germans got drunk and in their stupor banged on Ruffino's door, mistaking it for the Ovazzas'.

At one point during the evening, two local antifascists appeared at the hotel to try a rescue operation. Having heard of the arrival of the SS, a certain Dr. Raggi, a medical doctor in the town, and a fellow partisan ("one Mario Rossi, later executed by the Germans") went to the Lyskamm to see what could be done. The Ovazzas were locked in their room, the Germans were drunk and the hotelkeeper had the key. Raggi and Rossi begged Cochis to give it to them, insisting that they would take full responsibility for the Ovazzas' escape, but according to Raggi,

"Cochis flew into a rage and then assumed a menacing tone, saying: 'Enough! I don't want any trouble, and if you don't get out of here there will be trouble for you.' " A similar scene repeated itself a few weeks later, when another Jewish family at the hotel was arrested. Cochis again refused to cooperate, saying "It's better to get these Jews out of our hair."

As he lay in bed on the night of October 9, 1943, Giulio degli Esposti, whose room was directly beneath the Ovazzas, could hear Ettore "walking continuously up and down the room."

By the time most of the guests awoke the next morning, the Ovazzas were gone. Arnaldo Cochis, who saw them leave, later said that Nella and Elena could have stayed behind but insisted on going with Ettore. The Ovazzas "left most of what they had brought with them at the hotel, saying that they would be back and that it wasn't worth the trouble to bring all those suitcases with them."

Cochis later told Ruffino that, with Ettore's connivance, he attempted to bribe the SS officers with money Ettore had given him for safekeeping. He claimed the SS refused the money, but as Ruffino pointed out, Cochis "never explained where or with whom those thousand-lire bills ended up." Neither did he account for a handsome gold ring with a large ruby and two diamonds that Ovazza reportedly gave him to put in the hotel safe.

From Gressoney the Ovazzas were driven to the SS command in the town of Intra, near Lake Maggiore. The driver, Doardo Targhetta, recalled that after he left the Ovazzas at SS headquarters, he noticed that they had forgotten their umbrella in the car. When he returned to give it to them, the Nazi guard "threw it into a corner with a visible gesture of contempt" and said, in pidgin Italian: 'German soldier not use umbrella, and Jews not need anymore.' "

The SS command at Intra was based in a girls' elementary school that the Germans had commandeered. The custodian of the school, Ida Rusconi, lived on the grounds and saw much of what went on during the day of October 10. She recalled the arrival of the three SS men and the family of husband, wife and daughter. Although she did not learn their names, her description fitted the Ovazzas: "A man about fifty with a scar above one eye . . . dressed in sports clothes, with brown Zouave pants and a brick-colored checked jacket . . . A lady about forty and a young woman about twenty [*sic*], each rather plump but elegantly dressed in furs, speaking in Piedmontese dialect."

For much of the day the Ovazzas were kept in a military truck, apparently, with the intention of transferring them somewhere else. But at about six in the evening, the Germans asked Rusconi to light the furnace in the basement of the school—"a rather strange thing, given the warm day and the scarcity of fuel," she testified. From her window she saw the Germans force the man toward the school building with a pistol pointed at the back of his neck. "Let me live! Have pity! Let me live!" he cried. After the man disappeared into the building, Rusconi head the soldiers of the garrison making an enormous racket, yelling, singing, and banging on pots and pans. Then, despite the din, she distinctly heard a gunshot.

About fifteen minutes later she saw German soldiers leading the two women toward the school building. She recalled they were "calm and smiling," and concluded that the Germans had told them some reassuring lie in order to avoid the kind of desperate pleas for mercy that had preceded the man's disappearance. Again she heard the soldiers making an infernal racket, and then two or three gunshots.

Later in the evening she heard a dull cracking sound, as if wood were being chopped, and began to suspect that the Germans were cutting up the bodies in order to burn them in the furnace. She asked the Germans' Italian interpreter: "He confirmed my fears about the burning of the bodies with the words, 'Be quiet, be quiet, pretend you don't notice a thing.' "

Getting rid of the bodies proved no simple matter; for three days the furnaces burned, and people in nearby houses complained of the odor. "Even the Germans themselves," Rusconi testified, "appeared horrified by what had happened."

A few days later the workman who repaired the school's furnace (and also operated the crematorium at the local cemetery) came to examine the school basement. "When I cleaned the furnace," he later testified, "the characteristic odor of burnt flesh did not escape me . . . and I noticed small fragments of calcified bones." While playing in the basement a few months later, Ida Rusconi's child found a tooth.

Commitment and Betrayal

THE FOAS

OF TURIN

PRECEDING PAGE–The Foa family circa 1918. From left to right, with their parents, Ettore and Lelia, are ten-year-old Anna, nine-year-old Beppe and eight-year-old Vittorio.

Giuseppe Foa, chief rabbi of Turin, and grandfather of Anna, Beppe and Vittorio.

Pitigrilli; in Paris in 1935, the year of his greatest activity as an OVRA spy.

Prison photograph of Vittorio Foa taken during the summer of 1935.

A portrait of Vittorio Foa by Carlo Levi painted in the spring of 1935. Fellow members of Giustizia e Libertà often posed for Levi, thus creating a mask for their underground antifascist activity.

Piaggio employees in front of the plane designed by Beppe Foa that set a record for continuous flight in 1938, just as the racial campaign was getting under way in Italy.

Beppe Foa at the Piaggio factory in Finalmarina circa 1934. Behind him is an airplane he designed.

Chapter One

Police Station of Turin, August 25, 1935

Subject: Vittorio Foa, son of Ettore and of Lelia Della Torre, born in Turin, Sept. 18, 1910

political affiliation: antifascist
height: 5′7″
hair: black, thick
face: oval
coloring: olive
forehead: high
eyebrows: large, black and curved
eyes: black
nose: long
beard: clean-shaven
chin: round
movements: quick
facial expression: serious

Subject was part of the Turinese group Giustizia e Libertà, together with the notorious Mario Levi. After Levi fled the country (March 1934), he took on the direction of the movement, maintained communications with headquarters, received and distributed the newspaper and pamphlets of GL.

Contributed to the revolutionary propaganda of the group with articles published in . . . the newspaper *Giustizia e Libertà,* which were shipped clandestinely into the country . . . As a result he has been denounced before the Special Tribunal for the Defense of the State for the crime of political conspiracy. . . . He is a lawyer, practices in the firm of lawyer Abello. He is of lively intelligence. . . .

Like most Piedmontese Jews, the Foas migrated to Italy from Spain after the expulsion order of 1492. Along the way, passing through southern France, they picked up their last name, from the town of Foix. They crossed the French border into Piedmont where they worked in the manufacture and trade of silk. They settled in the small provincial towns of Piedmont—Casale Monferrato, Moncalvo, Cuneo, Saluzzo, Asti and Ivrea.

Unlike the Ovazzas, who were in Turin before the Jewish emancipation of 1848, the Foas did not assimilate into the cosmopolitan life of the city until much later, after Vittorio's grandfather, Rabbi Giuseppe Foa, brought his family from Asti around 1885. Entering Turinese life almost two generations after the Ovazzas meant that the Foas were a rung or two further down the economic ladder and much closer to the religious roots of the small ghetto communities of provincial Piedmont. The family's move was part of the great migration that drained the smaller Jewish communities of Piedmont: by the 1920s about eighty percent of Piedmont's 5,000 Jews lived in Turin.

The Foas quickly joined the city's growing professional class. Vittorio's father, Ettore, studied law at the University of Turin and then entered a business that imported coal from England. While not rich, Ettore and his family lived comfortably, with a cook and a housekeeper, on an elegant tree-lined boulevard in one of the city's fashionable new neighborhoods. Although they moved in different circles, the Foas were just a few blocks from the Ovazzas.

In coming to the city, the Foas shifted rapidly from strict Orthodoxy to almost total assimilation. As long as Rabbi Foa was alive, the family followed all the religious rules and customs. After his father's death in 1916, Ettore kept up the traditions, but with steadily decreasing rigor. Rather than enroll his children in Jewish primary schools, he sent them to public schools, where most of their friends were, naturally, not Jewish. The Foa children had little to do with organized religion after age thirteen.

"My father would bless the wine on Friday nights, and bless his children," Vittorio, the youngest, recalls. "He would go to temple at

Passover, put on his prayer shawl and say a few prayers. My brother and I were given a religious education. We studied Hebrew and learned to recite a psalm in the temple. But the strange thing is that as soon as we had our Bar Mitzvahs, we forgot everything and lost all connection to religion. We removed it from our lives, as if we had completed our religious duty. It's pretty strange when you think about it: You learn Hebrew, you learn Jewish history and Jewish ritual, and then at age thirteen, it just disappears from your life. My grandfather died when I was six. He had had a paralytic stroke a couple of years before, so my memories of him are ones of terror. I was profoundly assimilated, a son of the French Revolution, which had assimilated the Jews."

Jews in Italy had enjoyed their first period of political freedom during Napoleon's brief reign in Italy, from 1796 to 1815. Under the banner of *Liberté, égalité, fraternité,* French troops knocked down the ghetto walls of each city they occupied and replaced them with a tree of liberty. When the French troops withdrew, Jews in all but a few pockets of Italy were forced back into the ghettos. It is not surprising that many Jews remained faithful to the ideals of the French Revolution. A large number joined in the many secret societies that plotted to bring about a unified, liberal Italy.

Vittorio owes his name, and possibly more, to events of the Risorgimento. "I was named after my maternal grandfather, who was born in 1850 and named after King Vittorio Emanuele. I am convinced that if, after the battle of Novara and the armistice of Salasco, King Vittorio II had not confirmed the emancipation of the Jews, I would have been named Samuele or Abramo and not Vittorio."

Unlike the Jewish fascists, who saw the Risorgimento as the triumph of national aspirations, the Foas identified with its liberal democratic and Jacobin roots. In fact, there are traces of this revolutionary tradition in the family. Vittorio says, "There were several arrests in my father's family. He had a cousin, Florio Foa, who was sent into exile on an island. A cousin of ours, Umberto Segre, a journalist and university professor from Trento, was arrested for political activity."

Another great influence on Vittorio was Natale Della Torre, a relative of his mother's whom he never met but who grew into a kind of childhood legend. "My mother had an uncle whom she spoke of with great affection, a tall, handsome young man with blond hair and blue eyes, who had trained as a painter at the Brera Academy in Milan. He was an internationalist, a revolutionary, and he would be sent to prison from time to time because he kept starting newspapers and printing articles. In him, action and thought were melded in an extraordinary way, and his thinking was dominated by the problem of poverty. All that he had, he gave away. If he was given a coat with a fur collar in the morning, by that evening he would have given it away to someone who was cold. When he was supposed to be put on trial for crimes against the state, he put on workers' clothes and fled to France. He became an engraver. In Paris he became a legendary, Tolstoyan figure, with a long white beard. He died there at a very old age in 1936. I never met him, but the idea of this middle-class Jewish intellectual who chose to live among the poor made a great impression on me."

Vittorio's father was a liberal, which in Italy at the time meant a supporter of free trade, a free press and parliamentary democracy. "My father had an enormous political influence on me. He was an antifascist, but without rhetoric or emphasis. He educated me in the love of democracy and liberty."

Vittorio had a precocious knowledge of politics and a passionate dislike of fascism. His earliest political memories are attached to Italy's entrance into World War I, when he was not yet five. As the family sat down to dinner one evening in 1915, Vittorio's father turned to an Austrian girl who was a guest that day and said: "You will have to return home: Italy and Austria are at war!" She immediately burst out crying. "And so I associated war with tears," Vittorio says.

The Foa children witnessed the violent battles between workers and fascists after World War I, leading to the triumph of fascism. There were sharp clashes too between Vittorio and his older brother, Giuseppe, known as Beppe. "At the start of fascism, in 1922, I was thirteen," says Beppe. "I remember afternoons when suddenly the shopkeepers would close their stores and shut the metal blinds on the storefronts. You would see crowds of workers protesting, and fascist rallies, and continual strikes; there was a sense of impending violence. I was, at that point, in favor of fascism and Mussolini. No one in my family had given me that idea, they were all antifascist. Vittorio and I would fight constantly. At bottom, I was a little simpleminded. I had the impression that Mussolini would straighten things out and end this time of uncertainty and violence."

Vittorio remembers watching the sack of the Camera di Lavoro, the big union hall in the center of Turin; papers and typewriters were flung from the upper windows, and the building was set on fire. He and his sister, Anna, stood outside as a cordon of young fascists surrounded the building and workers watched, talking softly under their breath so as not to be overheard, realizing they had been defeated.

Another event that made a great impression on the entire family was the murder of socialist leader Giacomo Matteotti in 1924. The uproar over the killing nearly toppled fascism, but it served, in the end, to help Mussolini snuff out Italian democracy.

"At the time of the Matteotti affair, Vittorio was only fourteen, but he wanted at all costs to get the newspapers and find out what was going on," says Anna, the oldest of the three Foa children. "We were on vacation, and we children were home alone and forbidden to go out for any reason. The house had a garden with a high fence around it, and we didn't have the key to the gate. Vittorio climbed over the fence and went into town so he could read the news about the killing. When my mother and father came home, they punished him for going out, but he was already so consumed by politics he didn't care."

By the time he was a teenager, Vittorio had developed what his close friend Sion Segre describes as a classic "revolutionary's face": intense and very serious, with a huge, granitelike chin, his trademark since childhood. His friends from adolescence referred to him jokingly—and not in his presence—as "Rifle Butt," because of his prominent chin. Foa has a large, magisterial head placed on a medium-sized body. When he is silent, his face is long and mournful, with a triangular shape recalling a Modigliani portrait. But when he begins to speak his face loses its melancholy, granitic quality and becomes highly animated, with a playful, amused light in the eyes.

Despite its dry, telegraphic style, the description in the police report of 1935 is essentially accurate: the dark eyes, round chin, oval face and high forehead are present from Vittorio's earliest photographs. Police Commissioner Finucci correctly noticed his characteristic mixture of "serious" expression and "lively" intelligence.

Vittorio did brilliantly in school, graduating from the *ginnasio* in four years instead of five, the *liceo* in two years instead of four, and earning his law degree with the highest honors without attending classes. Instead he went to work, first at a bank in Paris and then at a law office in Turin; he studied on his own and showed up at the university only to take his exams.

In high school he became good friends with Giancarlo Pajetta, eventually one of the most important leaders of the Italian Communist Party. Even in his teens, Pajetta was a dedicated communist, and was arrested for passing out leaflets.

"Pajetta frequently tried to persuade me to join the communists, but I was never convinced," Vittorio recalls. "When he was expelled from school it made a great impression on me. I admired him very much for his political commitment, even though I never shared his ideas. It created a sense of frustration in me, so that after the *liceo* I went to work as soon as I could. I felt in some way inadequate to the task of political action. I didn't have the strength at that moment."

But only a few years later, in 1933, at age twenty-two, Vittorio joined the ranks of Giustizia e Libertà, which was developing into Italy's principal non-Marxist antifascist organization. "I think one of the overwhelming factors for me [in my decision to join the group] was boredom," Vittorio says. "Italian fascism was a fairly mild dictatorship. It had suppressed civil liberties, but apart from the killings that took place during the drive to power, physical elimination of opponents was not a normal instrument of power."

Italian fascism in 1933 was at perhaps one of the strongest positions in its history, what some have called "the years of consensus." The previous year, the regime celebrated its tenth anniversary with an orgy of rallies and speeches. Mussolini, elevated to the status of a demigod, appeared no longer in civilian clothes, but always in uniform. The man Benito Mussolini was replaced by Il Duce, the name printed in newspapers in capital letters, "DUCE." Articles portrayed him as the master of all pursuits: a world-class economist; an unrivaled scholar of Roman history, statesman, aviator and horseman; a virile Don Giovanni; and a devoted family man. As Mussolini pursued his pretentious dream of re-creating the glory of ancient Rome, the regime's chest-thumping oratory became more insistent. Public life under fascism became a string of interminable military parades, with everyone from kindergarteners to doddering old veterans marching and singing fascist hymns. But beneath the public pageantry was a nasty underside. Any protests by workers or peasants were brutally suppressed; public officials from top to bottom were notoriously corrupt; university professors were forced to sign loyalty oaths; squalid opportunism was rampant among party members who used politics to obtain jobs and favors for friends and relatives or to punish enemies and rivals. It was hard for an inquisitive young intellectual to respect a regime whose central credo was "Mussolini is always right!"

"I remember feeling this terrible boredom with the crudity and stupidity of the regime," Vittorio says. "The only way you could survive within a world that was so stupid and boring was to become stupid yourself. I made the choice to become politically active when I realized I would become an idiot too, unless I did something to maintain my integrity." Although Vittorio had a promising career as a lawyer, he joined GL (as Giustizia e Libertà was called by its members), fully aware that it would probably lead to arrest and imprisonment.

The group had few illusions about overthrowing the government; its purpose was to keep independent antifascist thinking alive until the day when fascism would stumble. Its primary tool was its newspaper, published in Paris. Since GL's leaders were in exile, they depended heavily on a network of sources within the country to cut through the smokescreen of official news. Operatives collected information about fascist economic and military policy, about working conditions, unauthorized factory strikes and peasant uprisings. Much of Vittorio's activity for the group was gathering information, smuggling it out of the country and then smuggling copies of the paper back into Italy.

It was a source of both amusement and embarrassment to the leaders of GL that the group attracted a high number of Jews. When Vittorio told Carlo Levi, a leader of the Turin branch, in early 1934 that his friend Sion Segre wanted to join, Levi replied: "Oh no, another Jew!" Clearly Levi did not want the group, which was very much an Italian movement, to be pigeonholed as Jewish. "You wouldn't want me to be a fascist just because I'm a Jew? Or should I become a Catholic in order to be an antifascist?" Segre asked Levi, jokingly. The group decided to admit him.

Because Segre was one of the few members of the group with a car of his own, Vittorio asked him to drive to Switzerland with another GL member, Mario Levi (no relation to Carlo), to pick up a collection of the group's pamphlets being smuggled in from Paris. When they entered Italy at Ponte Tresa, fascist police stopped them and began searching the car. Realizing they were caught, Levi bolted free, dove into Lake Lugano and swam for the Swiss shore.

The police arrested Segre and, along with the GL material, confiscated a leaflet with a Hebrew name on it, Oneg Sciabbath. The flyer was only the announcement of a small Jewish study group in Turin, and Segre had not even thought of hiding it, because it had nothing to do with politics; but the police believed they had found the linchpin of a Zionist conspiracy. Further proof was the identity of the two suspected conspirators: Levi and Segre are both common Italian Jewish names, and Sion is, in fact, the Italian for "Zion." (Levi, son of a Jewish father and a Catholic mother, was not officially Jewish. But the border police were not interested in subtle religious distinctions.)

Vittorio waited for them on the evening of March 11. When they didn't arrive, he felt certain they had been arrested. Preparing for the possibility of his own arrest, he got rid of any compromising documents. But, while the police rounded up a number of his friends, they never came for him.

The Foa family had some notion that Vittorio was involved in clandestine political activity, but they had no idea in what way or to what extent. During the past year he had kept odd hours and was evasive about his comings and goings; but his family suspected a romantic rather than a political intrigue.

During the next few weeks the family held its breath, waiting for news of the arrests, but nothing happened. Then, on the last Saturday of the month, March 31, the news broke. The Foas were sitting down to Passover dinner at the house of relatives when the maid arrived with the newspaper. The front-page headline of Turin's *La Stampa* read: "Arrest of Jewish Antifascists Working with Exiles Abroad."

> On the eleventh of this month, a foreign-made automobile coming from Switzerland, driven by its owner, Sion Segre, son of Emanuele, of Turin, together with Mario Levi, son of Giuseppe, of Ivrea, was stopped for a normal border check at Ponte Tresa, and found carrying a large number of leaflets and antifascist libels. . . . Levi, realizing that he had been caught, fled to Swiss territory, where he shouted anti-Italian invective: "Cowardly Italian dogs!"
>
> On the basis of the initial statements made by Sion Segre and the documents found on him and in the house and offices of Mario Levi in Ivrea, OVRA [Operazione di Vigilanza per la Repressione dell' Antifascismo] immediately began an investigation that has led to the arrest of other people, who, together with Mario Levi and Sion Segre, constituted an antifascist network operating within the Realm and working in tandem with foreign exile antifascists.

Accompanying the story was a list of names of people arrested for complicity in the plot; it read like a page out of a Who's Who of Turin's respectable Jewish upper middle class. (Eleven of the seventeen people were Jewish, and virtually all were prominent intellectuals and professionals.) Especially disturbing for the Foas was that many of them were good friends of Vittorio's, while others were social acquaintances who sometimes came to the family's house on Friday evenings for the meetings of Oneg Sciabbath, the study group, which Anna Foa and her husband were involved in.

As shocking as it was to see family friends branded in the newspapers as criminals, perhaps, even more so was the pointed reference to the religion of the malefactors and the use of the term "Jewish antifascists" in the headline. Coming the year after Hitler's rise to power in Germany, the article suggested that the tacit pact between Mussolini and the Jews had been broken. The account of Mario Levi's hurling "anti-Italian invective" and shouting "Cowardly Italian dogs!" had the decided air of a frame-up: no Italian Jew—fascist or antifascist—would think of himself as anything other than Italian. The fact that the news was released for dramatic effect on Passover was not lost on Jews or non-Jews. The virulently right-wing fascist paper *Il Tevere* ran its headline half in Hebrew, half in Italian: "Next Year in Jerusalem, This Year in Court," making a maliciously witty play on the prayer that concludes the Passover meal. "This year we are captives in the land of Egypt, next year in Jerusalem."

After this news, the mood at the dinner became decidedly strained. The Foas detected a chilly note of irritation from some of their cousins, several of whom were members of the Fascist Party. While these relatives had joined more out of convenience than conviction, they appeared irritated that Vittorio's hotheaded antifascist friends had jeopardized the well-being of all Italian Jews, whose patriotism was suddenly under attack.

Although the Foas and their relatives celebrated Passover each year, none of them was particularly religious or placed special importance on being Jewish. They rarely attended temple, they followed few of the religious rules and prohibitions, and they participated passionately in the mainstream of Italian life. Most at the Passover seder thought more about the delicious food than about the Hebrew ceremony few of them could remember or understand.

For these highly integrated, completely Italian citizens, the verses read at Passover—telling of the Jews' captivity in the land of Egypt, of plagues, of rivers running red with blood, of flight from the armies of the pharaoh—seemed a quaint and infinitely distant legend of long-forgotten troubles. Now the words acquired an uncomfortably contemporary feeling. Again and again the ceremony posed the question: "How is this night different from all other nights?"

Not only was the Ponte Tresa incident the catalyst for Ettore Ovazza to start *La Nostra Bandiera*—it was also a pivotal event for the antifascist element in the Jewish community.

The Foas had always seen themselves as antifascists, but as spectators in the distant battle between the regime and its opponents. Now, with friends and acquaintances in jail and the eyes of the nation briefly trained on the "antifascist Jews of Turin," they had suddenly become involuntary protagonists of the drama. "We knew that something in our lives had changed," Anna Foa wrote many years later. The family had never thought there was any connection between their being antifascists and their being Jews, but the arrests of 1934 forced them to consider the question.

"Let us remember that the best of antifascism past and present belongs to the Jewish race," thundered *Il Tevere*. "From Treves to Modigliani, from Rosselli to Morgari, the organizers of subversive antifascism have been and are members of the 'chosen people.'" The paper's attack on Italian Jews as a fundamentally antifascist segment of society was belied by the presence of many Jews in the Fascist Party. And yet there was a grain of truth in the accusation: Claudio Treves and Renato Modigliani, both Jews, were among the principal leaders of the Socialist Party. Umberto Terracini, a Jew, was one of the heads of the Italian Communist Party. The founder of Giustizia e Libertà, Carlo Rosselli, was Jewish, as were its leaders in Turin: Leone Ginzburg, Carlo Levi, Vittorio Foa and his friends.

Then, most of them would have resented the implication that their religious or ethnic background had any influence on their political ideas, but now they recognize that it may have played a role. "I've asked myself many times why in the universe of the struggle against fascism there was such a high number of Jews," Vittorio says. "I do not have a strong sense of Jewish identity, and yet the people who initiated me into political life, Leone Ginzburg and Carlo Levi, were Jewish, although both totally assimilated." Ginzburg, a Jew of Russian origin whose family had moved to Italy, was a literary critic and scholar of Russian literature. Levi, already well-known in the 1930s as a painter, became famous as a writer with the publication of *Christ Stopped at Eboli.*

The early leaders of GL in Turin were not Jewish; but when they were wiped out by a police crackdown in 1933, Ginzburg and Carlo Levi began rebuilding the group, and a preponderance of the new recruits were Jewish. Interestingly, the influx of Jewish members coincided with the rise of Nazism in Germany.

"Hitler had come to power and one sensed a greater threat facing the Jews," Vittorio says, although he insists it had nothing to do with his own decision to join GL. "There is another factor: Giustizia e Libertà was composed almost entirely of people from the bourgeoisie, and virtually all Italian Jews, with the exception of the communities in Rome and Livorno, were members of the middle class. Of course, there were plenty of fascist Jews. The Jews are no different from anyone else—good and bad, intelligent and stupid. But beyond that, I think there was a certain link between the Jews' affinity for antifascism and their democratic roots. They were liberated by the process of democracy in Italy."

While not a material threat to the regime, GL had great symbolic importance because of the prestige and cultural sophistication of its members and the writers and readers of its paper. Composed mainly of intellectuals and professionals of the upper middle class, the group was not easily penetrated by the secret police, whose agents were mostly underpaid and without university educations. While it was relatively simple to plant an informant into a communist cell made up of factory workers, the members of GL moved in tightly knit, respectable circles, bound closely by friendship, blood and, sometimes, religion. Tracking their movements did not automatically reveal who the leaders were; unlike the full-time revolutionaries of other groups, they went on with their normal lives. One scholar has called GL's method "conspiracy by the light of day." It was hard to distinguish social life from conspiracy. If members of the group went to the movies, the police had no way of knowing whether they discussed Gary Cooper or politics.

Carlo Levi used his artistic pursuits as a cover for conspiracy, having Vittorio Foa and other GL members sit for portraits while discussing political plans. Levi used trips to exhibitions in Paris as a pretext to consult with GL leaders there.

GL in Turin was also a family conspiracy whose members were intimately connected. Vittorio Foa asked an aunt of his who traveled often to France to carry packages for him. Although he told her nothing about the contents of the packages, she understood perfectly well what was going on. Leone Ginzburg was the fiancé and later husband of Natalia Levi, sister of GL members Mario and Alberto Levi. When police agents questioned him about his frequent visits to the Levi house, Ginzburg insisted they were for the purpose of courtship. (After their marriage, Natalia began writing under her married name, Natalia Ginzburg.) Mario Levi had almost become engaged to Anna Foa, and Vittorio was a close friend of Alberto's.

To break up this family conspiracy, OVRA needed an insider. The Ponte Tresa incident created the first crack in this tight circle and provided the perfect opening for someone prepared to betray friends and relatives.

Chapter Two

The atmosphere of anti-Semitism that accompanied the arrests of the so-called Jewish antifascists of Turin dissipated within a few months. It was chased from the front page of newspapers during the spring and summer of 1934 by the mounting tensions between Hitler and Mussolini over the fate of Austria, which Germany hoped to annex. In July, Nazi agents attempted a coup in Vienna, assassinating the premier Engelbert Dollfuss. Mussolini responded by sending Italian troops to the Brenner Pass, and the two dictators were on the brink of war. Overnight, Mussolini was again the ally of France and Britain and the paladin of world peace.

Almost as suddenly as it had started, the public debate about the Jews in Italy evaporated. Mussolini publicly ridiculed Hitler's theories of Nordic superiority. "Thirty centuries of history allow us to regard with sovereign pity certain doctrines from beyond the Alps, proposed by the progeny of people who were illiterate . . . in the age when Rome had Caesar, Virgil and Augustus."

Perhaps because of the changed international situation, or because of the lack of evidence, OVRA radically scaled back its prosecution of the alleged Jewish antifascist plot. After interrogating the seventeen people arrested and searching more than fifty homes, the secret police began to suspect they had caught few real fish in their net. Most of the detainees appeared to be exactly what they said they were, social acquaintances of Sion Segre and Mario Levi. The Jewish study group Oneg Sciabbath was in fact only a study group. Finally, charges were dropped against all but Segre and Leone Ginzburg, who were given much lighter prison sentences (one and two years, respectively) than expected.

A secret police memorandum written sometime in 1935 explained OVRA's dilemma and mapped out a new strategy:

> The arrests made in Turin on March 13 after the Ponte Tresa episode . . . considerably decimated the Turin group of GL.
>
> We had the immediate impression, however, that the operation had not achieved the result we desired, that of wiping out all the major leaders. . . .
>
> It was therefore necessary to reexamine the Turin situation and repair the broken threads of our network of informants, which had been compromised during some of the interrogations, and to reconstruct a web of informants capable of bringing the movement under control.
>
> As a result we brought into action agents 373 and 282, as well as number 353 in Paris.

Over the next several months, as reports from the informants poured in, it quickly became apparent that confidential agent 373 was the star. The other two filed reports only occasionally, offering mostly scraps of secondhand information and banal speculation; clearly, number 373 had penetrated the core of Giustizia e Libertà in both Turin and Paris. He worked himself into a position of confidence and became the principal courier between Vittorio Foa in Turin and Carlo Rosselli in Paris. Taking to his new job with great gusto, agent 373 wrote to his handlers in Rome two, three, four, sometimes five times a day with minute details of the group's daily activities. The quick style of his reports, their dialogue, color and humor, reveal the hand of a natural writer.

Agent 373 was known throughout Italy by his pen name, Pitigrilli. His real name was Dino Segre, and he was Sion's first cousin—a perfect Trojan horse to introduce into GL's closed world.

In 1920, when he was only twenty-seven, Pitigrilli achieved instant fame and scandal with his first book of stories, *Luxurious Beasts.* This was followed by the novel *Cocaine* and the collections of stories, *The Chastity Belt* and *Outrage to Decency.* In respectable and, at least superficially, prudish Italian society, Pitigrilli was branded a pornographer, but his books became immediate best-sellers and spawned a host of imitators. In reality, there is virtually nothing pornographic about his books. They contain deeply cynical, amoral satire of the Roaring Twenties in Italy, where lip service was still paid to Victorian morality, but where premarital sex, prostitution, adultery and illegitimate children abounded. Rather than scenes of wild eroticism, Pitigrilli's readers found corrosive aphorisms about love, sex, marriage, politics and friendship, such as these from *The Chastity Belt*:

> Do not covet thy neighbor's wife, but if you do, take her quickly. In bed, one must behave as in the theater or on the tram: if there is a free place, take it before someone else does.

> Do not believe in a woman's friendship. When a woman tells you she is your friend, it means either that she has started to love you or that she no longer loves you.

When Pitigrilli's early books were attacked, Mussolini himself came to his defense: "Pitigrilli is right. . . . He photographs the times. If society is corrupt, it's not his fault."

During the twenties, Pitigrilli was translated into more than a dozen languages; he was a celebrity from Buenos Aires to Warsaw. He lectured throughout Europe and started three different magazines, all of them highly successful, in particular the literary journal *Le Grandi Firme* (literally, "the big signatures"; figuratively, the great writers).

His life was no less a source of scandal than his books. While in his early twenties, he became the lover of Turin's leading poetess, Amalia Guglielminetti, a literary femme fatale who dressed like a flapper and puffed on a long cigarette holder. He experimented with narcotics, participated in occult séances and was rumored to have gambled away large sums of money at roulette.

As if from nothing, the young writer had created an exciting and exotic new character, Pitigrilli, into whose skin he slipped as into a new life. In becoming Pitigrilli, he may have been anxious to leave behind the more prosaic and unhappy existence he had led as Dino Segre. Indeed, after his literary self-creation even his friends and relatives called him "Piti," not Dino.

Like one of his own characters, Dino Segre was "a mistake," an illegitimate child and the cause of a forced, unhappy marriage. ("With few exceptions . . . each of our lives is the result of a broken rubber or the failure of some neo-Malthusian device," he wrote. "If the serpent, instead of giving Adam and Eve an apple, had hung a good contraceptive on the tree of good and evil, the human race would never have existed. One is born almost always by mistake.") His father was from a well-to-do Jewish family, while his mother was a poor Catholic girl. As the bastard child of an undistinguished mixed match, young Dino's arrival was a Segre family scandal. His parents did not marry until he was eight. His descriptions of childhood are universally bitter, reflecting the ostracism he suffered.

> I was eight years old when my father and mother married and all the Jewry descended on my house: my grandmother, my aunt, my crazy uncle, my cousins. My mother opened her living room to a flock of petulant, know-it-all parrots related to my grandmother, my aunt and uncle, who tolerated my mother from a distance, and bent over me with their disdainful nostrils, asking me to name the capital of Sweden, in order to show that if one didn't have the benefit of circumcision one could not know what their sons knew.

Pitigrilli's treatment of the Jewish half of his family is savage.

> I grew up without religious education. My mother, from an old family of Catholic peasants, was a simple and mild woman, tormented by two old crones of the Jewish race. Her brother was too young to take up her defense. My father, an indifferent and atheistic Jew, was attached enough to tradition to eat certain herbs and foods at Passover, but not enough to be a Jew according to scripture all year. My coming into the world was not greeted with "wine and lute and lyre and drum and trumpet," and if I had remained where I was I would have pleased everyone except my mother. The older of the two crones [his grandmother] tried to facilitate my rapid return while my mother was sick in the other room, when she suddenly woke up, as if jolted by a supernatural warning, and arrived in time to stop her and save me.
>
> Luckily I was baptized in secret, at the age of four, in the Parish of Sts. Peter and Paul in Turin. At Christmas, I received gifts from my mother's family, but in front of my father I was not supposed to mention Baby Jesus. A letter I wrote to him on pink stationery with a crèche in the corner was not well received. To silence the two crones, I was allowed to skip religion classes in school, but I secretly attended mass with the Capuchin monks. My father told me that God did not exist, that Jesus Christ was a kind of Garibaldi, that all religions are a cheat, except the Jewish one, and that all priests are clowns, except for rabbis. My cousins gave [the familiar] *tu* to my grandmother, I gave her [the formal] *Lei*: and I didn't understand why. Because I was a goy. They recited their prayers in Hebrew, and if I asked for explanations, they responded: "What's it to you?" I languished under their crushing privilege of being Jewish.

* * *

The cousins under the weight of whose Jewishness young Dino claims to have languished were Sion Segre, his brother, Nello, and their sister, Ilda. One has to read his account of childhood with some caution. Sion, who still lives in Turin, dismisses as a self-justifying invention Pitigrilli's statement that his grandmother tried to suffocate him in his cradle, and doubts very much that the young Dino would have addressed his grandmother with the formal *Lei.* Sion recalls his cousin as an adolescent composing verses for the family; Pitigrilli, who was seventeen at the time, even composed a poem on the day of his young cousin's birth. A few years later, Sion, Nello and Ilda performed a little skit Pitigrilli wrote for a family occasion. And Sion still has a copy of a humorous poem Pitigrilli wrote in honor of Sion's father's birthday. (Interestingly enough, the poem touches with affectionate humor on a Jewish theme. Emanuele Segre's birthday fell that year on Yom Kippur, and the poem is based on the conceit that the children are looking forward to a delicious feast, only to discover that they must observe the fast of atonement.) Unlike the majority of Piedmontese Jews, the Segres took their Judaism seriously: Emanuele's wife, Margherita Amar, was an early Zionist, and her cousin Alfonso Pacifici was a leader of the nascent movement in Italy.

To make things even more uncomfortable for young Pitigrilli, his father, also named Dino, lived in the shadow of his younger brother, Emanuele. Dino senior—as a dashing young man with a large handlebar mustache—attended military school, but he gave up his army career, probably because of the unexpected need to support a family. Emanuele, meanwhile, had begun a career in agriculture in their hometown of Saluzzo. He expanded into real estate so successfully that by age forty he had moved to Turin and owned a medieval castle in the hills outside the city. Emanuele supported his older brother, giving him a job as an accountant in his business.

Even when Pitigrilli reached adolescence his parents' marriage was still a delicate subject in the Segre family. "My uncle Dino came to the house almost every day to see my grandmother, but his wife never came," Sion recalls. "At a certain point—Pitigrilli must have been in his twenties—he got involved in some scandal, which my parents never discussed in front of me, for which he was never again allowed into our house. I believe it was a love affair; probably he had gotten a girl pregnant and abandoned her, the kind of thing that caused a great scandal then. After that we never spoke of him in our house."

After the ostracism Pitigrilli suffered at the hands of his respectable Jewish family, he spent most of his literary career thumbing his nose at the moralistic values by which he had been judged and rejected. Although he later tried to disassociate himself from Judaism, Pitigrilli did not have the comfort of belonging to the Catholic world either. In school he was listed as Jewish and skipped the obligatory Catholic religion classes. His first marriage, in 1932 (it too was a mistake, resulting from an unwanted pregnancy), was with a Jewish woman. A natural gadfly, Pitigrilli was an outsider in all worlds, a half-Jew considered Catholic by his Jewish relatives, Jewish by the Catholics, immoral by everyone. In fact, in one of his stories he says that being an outcast bastard is the best training for true enlightenment. "Bastards should be considered as an elect, privileged caste . . . like the Japanese samurai. . . . All men should be bastards so that they care for no one and are attached to nothing. The bastard! What in the world could be more beautiful than to be a bastard so that one can despise everything, without making an exception for one's own father and mother?!"

Although he had never showed much interest in politics, Pitigrilli regarded the patriotic rhetoric that flourished in Italy during World War I as another of society's lies:

> The Spartan mother who gladly sacrificed a son to the Fatherland must have been a common whore looking to get rid of him in order to practice her trade more conveniently. A mother who loved her son wouldn't care less about Victory or Fatherland . . . She'd help her son desert.

With the coming of fascism, Pitigrilli's cynical desecration of all accepted pieties made him automatically an object of suspicion. In 1926 he was prosecuted for obscenity and escaped narrowly with an acquittal. Although he later bragged about never having curried the favor of fascism, his confidential police file in Rome indicates otherwise. He sent copies of his books to Mussolini, including one in 1931 with the dedication: "To Benito Mussolini, the man above all adjectives." In 1927 and 1928 he tried frantically but unsuccessfully to become a member of the Fascist Party. Nonetheless, his courtship of fascism did not keep him out of trouble. Pitigrilli was someone to whom rumors stuck like flypaper. Every time a good joke about fascism circulated in Turin, people attributed it to him. A grainy photograph taken in the twenties shows Pitigrilli fighting a duel with a young Blackshirt over some disparaging remarks about fascism the writer was thought to have made.

One day in 1928, Pitigrilli descended from a train in a Turin railway station and was met by Pietro Brandimarte, the fascist consul of Turin, who slapped him across the face and dragged him off to jail for antifascist activities. Brandimarte's name struck a chord of terror in the hearts of many Turinese: he had led the infamous "Turin Massacre," in which twenty-one antifascists were murdered on the night of December 22, 1922.

The case against Pitigrilli was a frame-up, a product of greed and a love affair turned sour. Several people who wanted to take over Pitigrilli's magazine *Le Grandi Firme* had convinced his former lover Amalia Guglielminetti to compromise him politically. Guglielminetti, who had subsequently become Brandimarte's lover, supplied them with personal letters from Pitigrilli to which they added crudely forged passages insulting Mussolini and fascism. As in a scene from one of his own novels, Pitigrilli turned the tables on his enemies at his trial. The forgeries were so poor that they were easily exposed. Guglielminetti broke down in the courtroom and confessed her role. Pitigrilli was freed and his tormentors led off to jail.

Some believe that at this time Pitigrilli sought the protection of the secret police, by offering his services as an informant. His position as a Jew, and as an "immoral writer" in danger of having his books banned, may have contributed to his sense of vulnerability and his need for protection. This theory is bolstered by the fact that he first crops up as an OVRA informant in a police document in 1930. It was not until March 1934, however—the month his cousin Sion was arrested—that Pitigrilli's letters began to fill the police files. An OVRA memorandum notes that his earlier trial for antifascist activities would prove useful in allowing the "well-known informant" to penetrate Giustizia e Libertà.

Indeed it did. Natalia Ginzburg, at the time Natalia Levi, recalls that her family consulted Pitigrilli, as a veteran of fascist jails, when her father and brother Gino were arrested after Mario Levi escaped to Switzerland. "I remember my mother said: 'I'd like to talk to somebody who's been in prison who can explain how we should take laundry to them and so on.' I suggested that we could telephone him, this cousin of Sion's who had been in prison. So my mother called him and he came. He explained how you should bring food to people in jail. You had to remove the pits from the fruit."

A letter in the police files records Pitigrilli's visit to the Levi household:

> Turin, March 27, 1934
>
> Signora Levi, wife of the arrested professor [Giuseppe Levi] cannot communicate with her husband through his doctors because the doctor is now accompanied by two guards. . . .
>
> Before [his arrest] Giuseppe Levi . . . was able to warn his family. They burned many letters in a fireplace. Since not all were burned entirely an attentive examination would probably reveal some letters from [Carlo] Rosselli. . . .

> Mario Levi, who managed to escape to Switzerland . . . is now probably in Paris and with the Rossellis [Carlo and Nello, his brother]. With the excuse of going to take him clothing and money from his family, I think I can learn much from him. Now that he is free he should talk very openly.

Natalia Ginzburg recalls that just as Pitigrilli was concluding his visit to the Levis', her brother Alberto came in with his good friend Vittorio Foa. "And Pitigrilli said, 'Walk with me a bit.' That's when the trouble started." As the cousin of one of the arrested members and as someone who had been prosecuted (albeit wrongly) for antifascist sentiments, Pitigrilli immediately won their trust.

"Sion Segre used to talk all the time about this cousin of his," says Vittorio Foa. "When he came to us we were happy because it seemed he might be able to help Sion. This is how he acquired our trust. He told us he could be very useful to us because he traveled constantly between Turin and Paris. We used him as a courier to take the material from Italy to the headquarters in Paris. When he would cross the border, the guards would ask for his autograph instead of searching his luggage. His books were extremely popular.

"The only one who opposed his becoming a member of the group was Michele Giua, who said we shouldn't associate with him because he was an 'immoral writer.' We thought that was very funny at the time, but maybe he was right. Pitigrilli was not an appealing character."

Vittorio often wonders what pushed him into spying. Money may have been an inducement. Pitigrilli received a princely sum for his spying work, 6,000 lire a month at a time when a standard middle-class wage was 1,000 lire a month. "I think he gambled—otherwise it's hard to explain where all the money went," Vittorio says. "He also earned a lot from his books and yet he led a very modest life." But Vittorio believes that something other than money also must have motivated Pitigrilli. "I think he had a kind of taste for the perverse, that is, a pleasure in doing harm to others, a certain sadism."

The emotional fuel for this "pleasure in doing harm" was very likely the keen resentment he felt for the Jewish half of his family that had snubbed him from birth. His career, as both writer and spy, can be read as an elaborate exercise in revenge. "Hate your neighbor as you love yourself: and don't forget that revenge is a great safety valve for our pain," he wrote.

Writing after the war, Emilio Lussu, a member of GL in Paris, said that Pitigrilli was a perfect emblem of the regime he served. If Hitler's Germany produced the ideologically fervent stormtrooper who exterminated with conviction, and Japan the self-sacrificing kamikaze, the typical product of Mussolini's fascism was the cynical opportunist, who served whoever paid the most and who happily changed sides with each shift of the political wind.

Pitigrilli celebrated this spirit of amorality in his books. "What could be more relative than an idea? A man is a traitor or a martyr, depending on whether you look at him from one side of the border or another," he wrote in the story "The Serene Pessimist." Although Vittorio Foa laughed at Michele Giua's prudish distrust of Pitigrilli as an immoral writer, Giua was closer to the truth than he realized.

What Vittorio calls a "taste for the perverse" perhaps also explains the pleasure Pitigrilli took in sometimes double-crossing his own fascist paymasters. According to various GL members, he liked to write anonymous pieces mocking fascism for their newspaper. (Of course, the real joke was on GL.) A lover of intrigue and irony, Pitigrilli must have enjoyed the many levels of this multiple betrayal.

His spy reports show some extremely curious entries, including the latest Mussolini jokes current among antifascists. On June 10, 1934, he recounted this one in his dispatch:

> Mussolini visits an insane asylum. All of the patients have been instructed, with the help of sedatives and straitjackets, to shout "DUCE! DUCE!" when the leader arrives.
>
> One man is silent.
>
> "And why don't you shout *'Viva Il Duce!'*?" Mussolini asks him.
>
> "I'm not a mental patient. I'm a doctor."

It is difficult to understand what intelligence value this might have had. One suspects that Pitigrilli was thumbing his nose at the regime even as it was paying him to spy.

Pitigrilli fooled many in Giustizia e Libertà because he spoke with the same kind of cynical irony antifascists used in putting down fascism. While some of this may have been a cover, some of it may have been sincere. Pitigrilli had many affinities with the people he was betraying. They were intellectuals and nonconformists like him, and his letters show that he enjoyed engaging in discussion and argument with them.

Yet Pitigrilli may also have wanted revenge against these respectable Jewish intellectual families, to which he belonged but from which he was generally excluded. Natalia Ginzburg remembers her father's explosion of rage when he discovered she had published her first short story in one of Pitigrilli's magazines. Pitigrilli may well have had idealistic Turinese antifascists in mind when he wrote:

> I am afraid of incorruptible people. They are the easiest to corrupt. Corruptible people have their price: it's only a question of the amount.

> Sometimes, luckily, the price is so high that no one reaches it. But incorruptible people are really dangerous, because they . . . are corrupted not by money but by words.

Vittorio believes Pitigrilli loved spying and was very proud of his ability. He recalls going once to an appointment with Pitigrilli and having the distinct feeling there was someone observing them. "I think he wanted to show them how good he was."

During the 1930s, the Foas lived on Via Legnano, not far from Pitigrilli. When Vittorio and Alberto Levi, who lived a few doors down, would meet and walk along the tree-lined promenade of Corso Re Umberto, Pitigrilli would use the excuse of walking his dog to come and join them.

Whether by chance or clever design, Pitigrilli adopted an attitude that completely fooled GL members. "He behaved exactly like a spy," Vittorio says. "He would ask us questions about our organization. He behaved so much like a spy that we didn't think he was one. Alberto Levi and I would joke between ourselves: 'Have you seen our *agent provocateur* lately?' "

Through his constant probing and seemingly ingenuous questions, Pitigrilli was taking measure of the group, identifying its members, assessing their roles and weaving, letter by letter, the net into which Vittorio and the others would eventually fall.

> Turin, June 1, 1934
>
> Vittorio Foa told me something rather important, although vague and without details: that OVRA, although it stopped the distribution of [the GL] newspaper and arrested a few people and conducted searches, failed to find the three or four people who really matter. This is not a person given to bragging or idle chatter. He is very reserved, uses his words carefully and is very precise in his expressions. As a result, I have the definite impression that there's more to this. He is convinced that the Turin group will slowly re-form.

While he himself may have behaved like a spy, Pitigrilli was careful to keep all other OVRA surveillance away from Vittorio and his friends, in order to avoid creating any suspicions.

> Paris, June 21, 1934
>
> I beg you, within the limits of the possible, to leave Vittorio Foa and the Giua family alone: if not, you will deprive me of two important sources of information. Vittorio Foa is the one who will keep me abreast of what

> is happening in the Turin group, and it is he who will know what I should say to [Carlo] Rosselli, and it is to him that Rosselli will send me with the most important news of the movement.

In some instances, Pitigrilli let his writer's imagination run away with him, finding elaborate plots in the most ordinary circumstances. When he noticed Vittorio holding a number of secret meetings with another antifascist and delivering letters to an apartment building on Corso Sommeiller, he alerted the police that something big was afoot. In fact, Vittorio was acting as a go-between in a love affair between a friend and a girl who lived in the building. Since her parents disapproved of the romance, the couple's correspondence had to be conducted secretly. At Pitigrilli's suggestion, fascist agents kept the building under constant surveillance. There are at least a dozen different police reports dedicated to solving the mystery at Corso Sommeiller 2b.

Frequently Pitigrilli would "intuit" nonexistent conspiracies in order to confirm his value to his fascist employers. He often discerned assassination plots against Mussolini in ambiguous phrases.

Vittorio recalls that Pitigrilli encouraged him to use terrorist tactics on behalf of GL. "He invented many things and had an active imagination, as his letters show. He thought we knew everything about what was going on at the Brenner Pass, along the Austrian border. There's a letter in which he asks me: 'Why don't you do something really big?' By which he meant plant bombs. And I answered him that it wasn't something we would even consider. That was against the principles of the Turinese group. We were more socialists and we believed in mass action. Pitigrilli wrote in his letter [to OVRA] that because I was so pale, any emotion of mine was immediately registered on my face for him to read. And when he saw that the question didn't elicit any emotion, he knew I was telling the truth. He was right. He was very intelligent, but a very unpleasant character."

Pitigrilli's reports, for all their exaggeration and fantasy, contain an accurate portrait of Vittorio: "I think his activities extend only to propaganda. . . . I can see him turning the pages of a book, not handling a bomb; I can see him engaged in discussion in the salon of the publisher [Giulio] Einaudi, but not lurking in the shadows like a terrorist."

* * *

Pitigrilli appears initially to have considered the possibility of a Zionist conspiracy. In an early letter to OVRA he writes that Alfonso Pacifici, a relative of Sion Segre's and a Zionist leader from Florence, might be in on the plot. But any notions of such a conspiracy were quickly deflated. Almost immediately after the Ponte Tresa incident, the governing body of Turin's Jewish community resigned and the fascist group led by Ettore Ovazza took control.

Pitigrilli, taking stock of the changed atmosphere, wrote OVRA on May 24, 1934: "I don't think the Zionists are up to much; for the moment they are completely demoralized." At the same time, he noted that the Jewish fascist movement did not seem to have impressed the more intellectual antifascist Jews he frequented. "Nobody," he said, "takes *La Nostra Bandiera* seriously."

Writing immediately after the trial of Segre and Ginzburg, agent 373 describes the changing moods of the Turinese Jewish community during the preceding months.

> The sentence of Sion Segre-Leone Ginzburg trial was greeted with relief in the Jewish world of Turin. I have conducted a vast inquiry and I can describe with an approximateness approaching exactitude the state of mind of this Community. In the days after the arrests last March, a real panic was unleashed. One Friday evening, at the beginning of the Sabbath, the Jews were afraid there would be a demonstration in front of or within the Synagogue. Rumors were flying that only a rapid police intervention had prevented it. The OVRA dispatch, published with a title that highlighted the word "Jews," the violent attacks of "Tevere" . . . and the recrudescence of sarcastic caricatures in the humor magazines, had created an atmosphere of "pogrom." People were saying that Italy was about to adopt methods used in other countries and at other times by Princes who, when they wanted money, got it from rich Jewish merchants by threatening persecutions. The little Jewish shopkeepers of Turin began to tremble for the crystal of their poor shop windows and to worry about whether their Catholic clientele would abandon them.
>
> But the situation . . . faded in a few days: a few people sent off to internal exile [*confino*], a few slaps on the wrist, many people released from jail. At bottom—people said—it's right that that ingrate Ginzburg and that cretin Sion should remain in jail. Of Ginzburg they said: "That Russian should have stayed in his own country." Of Segre they said: "He went too far . . . When your name is Segre—and Sion to boot—and you live in a country where the Jews are granted all possible rights, you have a duty to keep still and not compromise with foolish gestures all the other Jews, who mind their own business, are good Italians . . . and don't give a hoot about Zionism or other sterile abstractions . . ."
>
> And finally the sentence: nobody can believe that Sion Segre got such a mild sentence . . . Even the antifascists of Turin are amazed by the lightness of Sion's sentence. Signorina Natalia Levi, daughter of the anatomy professor, her sister [Mrs. Olivetti] and Olivetti himself all told me: "We were expecting double for Sion . . ."

By the beginning of 1935, the attention of both the Italian government and the antifascist movement focused increasingly on the prospect of war with Ethiopia. In anticipation, Italian papers sounded a daily drumbeat of bellicose propaganda to prepare public opinion for Mussolini's imperial adventure.

Dissent in Turin began to expand beyond the small band of intellectuals gathered around Carlo Levi, Leone Ginzburg and Vittorio Foa. As Pitigrilli noted in his reports, students made fun of the contradiction between Mussolini's campaign to increase Italy's population and his determination to send them off to die in war.

> Turin, Feb. 20, 1935
>
> Foa tells me that the African campaign is not very popular among the young university students, who repeat the following phrase: "The regime wants to increase the population and so it sends off young Italians to get their balls cut off by the blacks!"

The same day, Pitigrilli filed a second report on the same theme:

> I ran into Alberto Levi today [who] . . . said there was a big increase in new recruits. . . . "A lot of them are not Jews or sons of old liberals, and yet they are starting to react to the state of things. . . . Because they know my father [Giuseppe Levi] has been in prison for political reasons, they approach him in order to hear a word of freedom. A paradoxical situation has arisen: that my father, who underneath is an antifascist, in reacting to their extremism must play the fascist."

Moreover, Pitigrilli reported, Vittorio Foa had gathered fairly sensitive information about Mussolini's military preparations for the war in Ethiopia: "His brother [Beppe], who is employed . . . at the Piaggio factory in Finalmarina, has learned that they are making numerous airplanes with the Letters A.O. (Africa Orientale) [East Africa]."

With war imminent, the regime was anxious to nip any dissent in the bud. Armed with reams of evidence provided by agent 373, OVRA decided it was time to act against the Turinese section of GL. An unsigned secret police memorandum of May 6, 1935, advocated moving ahead with a new series of arrests.

> We retain that it is necessary to proceed with the simultaneous arrest of all [GL's] elements. . . .
>
> The reasons for this necessity are as follows:
>
> 1. The most active and dangerous elements of the group (lawyer Vittorio Foa, Massimo Mila, Michele Giua, Norberto Bobbio, Prof.

Mario Carrara, Prof. Giandomenico Cosmo . . . etc. etc.) have passports with which they can leave the country. . . .

2. As we can see, the principal, almost maniacal objective of the leaders in Paris is an assassination attempt against our Leader or, where possible, terrorist acts aimed at sowing alarm and discouragement in the Country. . . .

3. It is clear that the Turinese group is the most important for the underground circulation of antifascist libels and negative propaganda. . . .

4. The leaders of GL in Paris have decided to unleash within our Realm a campaign against the Abyssinian War meant to demoralize the nation, and will no doubt make use of their friends in Turin.

All this induces us to believe that it would be imprudent and dangerous to allow the Turinese group to continue to live and grow.

Chapter Three

Anna Foa sensed something was wrong when the phone did not ring at seven o'clock on the morning of May 15, 1935. Every day at seven sharp her father would call to say good morning. She waited until about ten past the hour and then decided to phone her parents. A man with a strong southern Italian accent answered and told her to wait a minute. After a long wait, she heard her father's voice.

"Papà, who was that on the phone just now?" she asked.

There was a pause and then he replied, uncertainly: "It was the milkman, he was here in the study and picked up the phone. We are fine, good-bye, my dear." And then he hung up.

Anna was five months pregnant with her first child; she had been sick in bed for the first three months. With the arrival of spring she had begun to feel better, and that day, a gray, rainy Wednesday, she had planned on going shopping.

Although she was more puzzled than worried by her conversation with her father, Anna decided to stop by her parents' apartment, which was just across the street, before running her errands. When she arrived at the third floor, she noticed that the door of their apartment was ajar. As soon as she entered, she was surrounded by OVRA agents.

She recalls Vittorio dressed in pink pajamas, her father very pale and still unshaven, and her mother clenching her lips tightly from tension.

Six agents were there, all with southern accents, arrogantly ordering her family about. The books in the study were scattered everywhere as the agents searched for documents. The mattresses in the bedrooms were slit open. After five hours the agents told Vittorio and his father to get dressed and took them to police headquarters.

Anna decided to go there as well, to plead with the authorities to release her father on account of his weak heart. When she arrived she saw a number of Vittorio's friends handcuffed together. Some hours later, to her amazement, she saw her brother Beppe, who had always kept his distance from politics, arriving in handcuffs. Before the police could drag him away, she whispered to him the names of the other people she had seen arrested.

Lelia Foa had not yet grasped the magnitude of the situation, and she expected that her son and husband would be released quickly after questioning. But when she heard that Beppe, who was not even living in Turin, had been arrested too, she suddenly broke down and wept. It was the only time Anna can recall her mother losing her composure.

More than fifty people were arrested in Turin that day, and about two hundred homes were searched for compromising material. Rumors of mass arrests swept quickly through the Turinese upper-middle-class families of lawyers, businessmen, doctors and professors. A terrible silence came over the Foa apartment, unbroken by a single visit or phone call. Anna remembers eating dinner in silence that evening with her husband and her mother, until finally a cousin, Eugenio Fubini, came to find out how the family was. After about a week Ettore Foa was released, but Vittorio and Beppe remained in solitary confinement.

Anna and her mother were not allowed to visit the prisoners but were able to bring them food and clean laundry. The waiting room at the police station turned into a kind of social club for wives, mothers and girlfriends of prisoners; they spent hours talking, joking and complaining. Anna remembers in particular a remark made by Lidia Levi (Mario, Alberto, and Natalia's mother) that struck her as especially prescient. "She complained that one day the government would open all the safe-deposit boxes belonging to the Jews. 'Do you know what I am going to do?' she said. 'I'll put a chamber pot in my safe-deposit box.' "

Unlike the Ponte Tresa incident, the May 1935 arrests were followed by a news blackout. There were no articles about Jewish antifascist plots, but some members of the fascist regime were privately concerned about the high quotient of Jews among the people arrested; some Jews feared the arrests would provoke wider racial persecutions.

Four days after the arrests, OVRA informant 433 wrote from Turin to his bosses in Rome: "The news circulates of the arrests of about fifteen young Israelites for spreading subversive propaganda in the factories." The rumors this informant reported were largely incorrect—there were far more than fifteen people arrested, only a minority of them Jewish—but it clearly reflects a popular view that Giustizia e Libertà was a Jewish group.

A dispatch sent the next month from Milan by OVRA agent 374 told of the great anxiety among Milanese Jews about the arrests:

> I was talking about it yesterday with a Jew who is very well known and respected in the Jewish community, a Mr. Coen, a rich fur merchant. He said there is much ferment among the Jews living in Milan about the Turin arrests and general condemnation for the work of these Jews who, if actually guilty of actions against Italy, not only are deserving of the most serious punishment but are violating completely the spirit of the Jewish class, the great majority of which is devoted to the Regime and is truly grateful to the Government of Mussolini for all he has done and does for the Jews in Italy, and especially for allowing those from Germany to work in peace. . . . Such, concluded Coen, is the conviction of the Jewish community, which would be greatly pained if it were looked upon with suspicion because of a few misguided souls.

This same fear of being confused with the Jewish troublemakers was shared by many Turinese Jews. Anna Foa recalls the family felt abandoned by friends. The Foas' shock, isolation and uncertainty over where to turn set the stage for Pitigrilli, who reappeared in the disguise of a guardian angel. About two weeks after the arrests, Anna received an anonymous phone call from a man saying he wanted to see her; he would not give his name. This was understandable, since it was fair to assume her phone was tapped. Later that day Pitigrilli arrived at her house, saying he wanted to try to win the release of Vittorio and Beppe. Angry at the desertion of many of their friends, Anna and her mother regarded this sudden offer of help as a godsend. The only one who was suspicious of Pitigrilli was her husband, Davide Jona, but Anna discounted this as male jealousy.

Pitigrilli, after all, she says, "was a handsome man with a marvelous way of talking; he was a man of great appeal. He came with a little notebook. He always came in the afternoon, when my husband was at work. But he was so nice, so kind and thoughtful. I was delighted, because all of my friends either were in prison or were afraid to be seen with us.

"Once he called me and said, 'This is Pitigrilli. I am going to send you a letter, and after you read it I want you to rip it into small pieces and flush it down the toilet.' Now, anybody else with a minimum of sense would have understood that this was the behavior of a spy, because clearly our phone was tapped, but I didn't suspect a thing. This letter arrived, and it said: 'I am leaving shortly for the mountains, and my lover is also the lover of Judge Ingrao'—this was the judge at Vittorio's trial—'and I will try to use my influence to help Vittorio.' So here I was, ripping up this letter and flushing it down the toilet. I suspect it was all a fantasy, because he had a fervid imagination. I fell for it completely, thinking, How wonderful this person is! He continued to come, and he would have his little notebook out and would ask me questions about all the people I knew."

Although Pitigrilli exploited the Foas' desperation, he did serve them one good turn, protecting them from another vulture who had started to hover. Nello Segre, Sion's brother (and Pitigrilli's cousin), had approached the family with a plan to win the release of Vittorio and Beppe. He claimed to have connections with powerful fascists and assured the Foas that his friends could have the charges dropped if the family would pay substantial bribes: 100,000 lire for Vittorio and 50,000 for Beppe. Although these were enormous sums at the time, the Foas were seriously considering the proposal. Nello had told them not to discuss the offer with anyone outside the family, but they decided to consult the family confidant. "And for once Pitigrilli told us the truth, urging us not to give Nello a penny, because he was flat broke and simply out for money."

* * *

Some three weeks after the May 15 arrests, Beppe and Vittorio were transferred to Regina Coeli prison in Rome. The police interrogated about two hundred people, and the list included the cream of the Turin intelligentsia: Luigi Einaudi, an economist of world renown and future president of the Italian Republic; his son Giulio, head of the Einaudi publishing company; the writer Cesare Pavese; the philosopher Norberto Bobbio; the biologist Giuseppe Levi and his sons; the chemist Michele Giua; the literary critic Leone Ginzburg; and the painter Carlo Levi. The police had swept with a wide net, picking up many people only peripherally involved with Giustizia e Libertà in order to get them to implicate the leaders.

While the regime made no public comment about the fact that many of those arrested were Jewish, records of the interrogations show that the police noted with interest that many of the prisoners had attended the Friday-night meetings of Oneg Sciabbath. Although hardly a political conspiracy, the group did reflect a growing spirit of both Zionism and antifascism among Turinese Jews. There was little political unanimity in the study group, and sharp conflicts often developed between the

Zionists and antifascists such as Vittorio, who, according to Davide Jona, looked on the Jewish group with superior detachment. But the police viewed this mixing of the two movements as dangerous.

Relying on Pitigrilli's reports, OVRA had decided Vittorio was the head of the Turin GL. Many others tried to exculpate themselves by putting the blame on him. The police report on the interrogation of a doctor named Giulio Muggia, dated June 17, 1935, noted:

> He admits that he spoke on more than one occasion at the Friday Jewish meetings, but about Spinosa [*sic*]. . . . He admits knowing that [Vittorio] Foa was a friend of [Leone] Ginzburg, and says he might have supposed, "if I had been more alert, that they shared a program of political ideas and aims. I recognize that it was my error to continue seeing Foa and his circle of friends, and find it logical, unfortunately, that suspicion has fallen on me of belonging to the conspiratorial group Giustizia e Libertà. I deny, however, ever having participated in the criminal activity of the group."

Another acquaintance of Vittorio's, Leo Levi, appears to have criticized him to police inspectors for not being a good Jew.

> I used to see Foa sometimes at Jewish get-togethers held on Friday evenings. . . . Foa seemed to participate in these evenings more than anything else to pass the time, rather than out of any profound spiritual conviction. . . . I knew that Foa was an antifascist . . . given that he spoke quite openly against Fascism and the Police.
>
> Vittorio Foa appeared to me to be a person of frank, open and impulsive character; I would not hesitate to call him a revolutionary. I remember during one of these Jewish evenings, in the course of an exposition on the personality of Christ from a Jewish viewpoint, he insisted on the social revolution brought by Christianity in the ancient world and on the phrase from the Gospel: "I come to bring war, not peace." . . . I could tell you many anecdotes of that kind, but I repeat that I knew nothing of any conspiratorial activity of his.

While he was held in Regina Coeli along with the other suspected antifascists, Leo Levi wrote a letter to Mussolini begging for mercy. The letter is a model of the servile and adulatory rhetoric common during fascism and an example of the depths to which people routinely sank to survive under the regime.

> DUCE!

> Confiding in Your Excellency's paternal benevolence, I dare to supplicate myself before your magnanimity, certain of not being disappointed.
>
> For the last eighteen days I have been detained in prison for a suspicion, I believe, of a political nature, of what I know not, nor can I imagine. I know only that I have been a loyal citizen and a fascist of fervent faith. . . . I was awarded the Mussolini Prize for Piedmont, in Rome on April 21, 1933, by Your Excellency, whose inspiring words I can still hear now, heard in those moments of supreme emotion for the high honor I enjoyed. . . .
>
> Duce!
>
> I am certain I am the victim of a mistake: and I beg You to remove from my fascist heart the weight of these tears that I weep for the shame of this unbearable accusation. . . .
>
> But above all I confide in the goodness of Your paternal heart, since I myself have no father. Not only does my mother await anxiously my release, but so does a young woman whom I was about to marry when I was arrested, and who will soon be a mother, because she already carries my child in her womb. What will happen to the poor girl if these proceedings drag out?!
>
> Duce!
>
> Act, so that this new family and this new Italian who is about to be born do not carry this badge of shame; act, so that I be returned soon to my family, to work for the glory of Italy; act, so that I and my son can walk with honor, build and fight for Fascist Italy!

This lachrymose plea had the desired effect of obtaining Levi's release, and thus made an impression on the families of other prisoners. Lelia Foa began pressuring her sons to write letters to Mussolini asking for clemency. Vittorio staunchly refused. But Beppe, since he was not part of the GL, wrote in mid-August.

* * *

That Beppe Foa decided to ask for clemency, while his brother refused, was quite natural. Beppe was far more interested in engineering and science than politics. He was perhaps the furthest removed from the family orbit; in 1930 he had gone to study aeronautical engineering in Rome and then had taken a job with the airplane manufacturer Piaggio near Genoa. Taciturn even by Piedmontese standards, Beppe was known among Anna's friends as "the mysterious brother" because of his terse replies to their questions. "Every time he came home for a weekend, when we asked him about his work and his life, his answers were always monosyllabic," Anna wrote many years later.

Beppe and Anna were, and are, opposites in many ways. She is passionately engaged and anxious to express herself; he keeps an ironic distance and is highly reserved. Beppe was his mother's favorite, perhaps because of the remarkable resemblance between the two: both of them fair, fine-featured and strikingly attractive. Anna was like her father, with dark eyes and complexion, and a volatile temperament, easily moved to pity or anger. Vittorio appears to have drawn from both parents, having a passionate moral commitment and an ironic, detached ability to laugh at himself and others.

Beppe describes himself as the "most mediocre" of the three Foa children because he was the least politically active. He was certainly not mediocre in his intellectual or professional accomplishments. But he was probably the most typical member of the family in his relative indifference to politics. Like many Italians, Jews and non-Jews alike, he joined the Fascist Party in order to be able to get a job, although he was privately against fascism.

"I must say that two years after the killing of Matteotti, I became rather indifferent to politics," Beppe says. "At the end of 1926, when I was seventeen, I entered the Polytechnic Institute to become an engineer. At that moment my world changed completely, even though I was still living at home in Turin. I became much more interested in mathematics, physics and engineering. I wanted to live in this world of students who came from all over the world. And in 1928, in my third year of engineering, I did something I shouldn't have: I joined the fascist university student group. Students who belonged could travel anywhere in Italy virtually free. My closest friends and I went to Venice, Trieste, Trento, Rome, Naples. I signed up without really taking stock of the fact that I had joined the party. I didn't wear a black shirt or have anything to do with party activities. One day in 1930 all the members of the student group were ordered to join a patrol to maintain order on the streets of Turin. And suddenly I, and many of my friends, realized what being a party member meant, and we decided not to go on this patrol. We no longer took advantage of the things that being a member offered, without, however, resigning from it."

Beppe won a fellowship to do graduate work in Rome in 1930 in aeronautical engineering. For his thesis, he designed a new kind of plane, capable of setting a world record for continuous flight. The design met with such success that he was approached by the director of Piaggio, who wanted to hire him and build his new plane. But in order to work in an industry closely tied to the government through military contracts, it was necessary to be a member of the Fascist Party.

Beppe recalls going to talk the problem over with Vittorio, who had a surprisingly undogmatic view. "He said, 'The problem comes down to this: if you don't join you can't practice your profession. You absolutely have to join.' Coming from him, it made it very easy for me to decide. So I joined, but I never gave the fascist salute or wore the black shirt."

Although everyone working at Piaggio was a party member, Beppe remembers that the atmosphere there was antifascist. He in fact gave Vittorio information that he learned on the job, about an attempted strike at the Piaggio factory in Finalmarina and about new airplanes being manufactured with the initials AO, for "Africa Orientale," which suggested the war that Mussolini would soon declare against Ethiopia. Pitigrilli, acting as courier for Vittorio's dispatches to Paris, had surmised correctly in his police reports that the information came from Beppe.

Virtually all of Beppe's friends at the factory in Finalmarina were non-Jews. As a result Beppe felt out of place among his sister's friends in Turin, where antifascism and Jewishness were combined in the Friday-evening meetings held frequently at the Foa house. "I found these meetings a little strange," he says. "I couldn't understand why these young Jews would get together and talk about politics. It bothered me as an antifascist that they would separate themselves as Jews from other antifascists. And this was interpreted by others, as I learned later, as arrogance on my part."

Thirty-five years later, Davide Jona wrote about their disagreements with some heat. Beppe and Vittorio "affected the most detached attitude toward anything smelling of Judaism, starting from the Synagogue to the friendly meetings of the activist members of the Association. . . . Both of them used to leave hurriedly . . . when the group was expected: and indeed [Beppe] was prone to express his disdain addressing that activity with half-joking, disparaging remarks." Anna remembers that Beppe used to call the crowd of Jewish friends who would descend on the Foa household on Friday nights the *kinim,* meaning lice in Hebrew, reference to one of the biblical plagues that struck Pharaoh's Egypt.

Anna's husband explained the link between antifascist and Jewish activity as an indirect result of the repression of fascist life. The Zionist group provided one of the few sanctioned forums for open discussion of any kind. It was, Davide Jona wrote, "a sort of escape from the frustration of Italian political life. . . . Fascism succeeded in creating an atmosphere . . . in which nobody was sure if his friend was really trustworthy, or an agent of the police." In this world of fear and suspicion, the small Jewish community seemed a safe harbor, where the risk of betrayal was greatly reduced.

Because these Turinese Jewish antifascists operated in such a tight-knit, literally familiar world, they were stunned by the arrests of May 1935. "It was a total surprise for all of us," Beppe says. "I knew Vittorio was involved in some political activity. I knew he wrote for Giustizia e Libertà's newspaper. But he talked very little about it. Sometimes I gave him information that might have been useful. But I didn't know about all his activity with Carlo Levi and so on."

Beppe recalls the morning of his arrest: "At six o'clock, five or six men suddenly arrived in my bedroom and told me to get up and began emptying my drawers. The first thing I thought was that they were looking for American cigarettes, because American cigarettes were prohibited in Italy at that time. They took me to Savona and then to Turin, never telling me a thing about what they were arresting me for and not letting me eat anything. At about nine in the evening, when I arrived at the police station in Turin, I heard my sister's voice yelling 'Beppe.' I turned and saw her, and she told me that my father and brother had been arrested as well. At that point I understood that it was something political. Up until then I thought I had been arrested alone."

The conditions in the Turin jail were squalid and primitive. "There were lice everywhere. There was a light on over you all night. I was alone; I had no cigarettes; I wanted to read, and the only thing they gave me were children's books. And the only thing to eat all day was this terrible thin soup that they would give you in the morning. My initial idea was to drink half in the morning and then leave the rest till evening, but I quickly learned this was a bad idea. This stuff was so foul and full of grease that a whole layer of fat would form and it would become undrinkable after a couple of hours. So I drank it all right away.

"After the twentieth day in the cell, they came to get me, still without telling me anything. They put me in a car and started toward the train station. I thought they were taking me home. So when they turned to the left, toward the station, I said, 'No, you've got to turn right.' They said nothing and kept going toward the station. I was put in a railroad car with little cells, a cattle car with tiny spaces for each prisoner, and I could hear the voices of other prisoners, of people I knew. I didn't know they had been arrested or why. But then, after ten days in Rome, they finally interrogated me. They asked me mainly about my relationship with Vittorio. In 1924, Vittorio had gone to Paris for a while; this was the time of the first—and last—elections after the rise of fascism. Vittorio had written me from Paris that Mussolini would be defeated in the elections. I wrote him back a postcard saying that Mussolini's government 'would not fall as long as he was alive.' What I meant was—I was still profascist at the time—that Mussolini would win the elections and remain in power indefinitely. They wanted to know about my relations with workers at Piaggio. I couldn't understand what the accusations were. After quite a while, someone—perhaps through my mother—told me to write a letter to Mussolini asking him to let me go. It was the advice of Pitigrilli, whom my family still considered a person to trust. I wrote the letter."

* * *

Vittorio says that he might have won his brother's release much earlier if he had taken a different tack during his own interrogations. "If I had simply admitted that Beppe had given me the information without knowing what use I would make of it, he would have been let go right away. And it was true; he didn't know anything about my political activity. Instead, we both denied everything." At the time, the Italian courts still managed to retain a small margin of independence and the government needed some corroborating evidence to win convictions. "Theoretically, you could win an acquittal if you denied everything," Vittorio says. "They couldn't use the information provided by their spies at the trial, because they would expose the informants. In court they would have to present other evidence that would confirm what the spies had told them." They would, however, skillfully use the information from the spies to frighten prisoners into admitting things in interrogations, and then use the testimony of one prisoner to incriminate others. The strategy of denial worked only if prisoners could maintain a united front.

Vittorio experienced no brutality in his interrogations. The police officials, he said, were old-fashioned bureaucrats who had grown up under Italy's old liberal regime. They seemed to treat GL members almost as worthy adversaries rather than enemies to be despised. Vittorio remembers the rather gentle smile that the Turin police commissioner, Fulvio Finucci, gave him on the morning of his arrest when Finucci noticed a photograph of Leone Ginzburg on Vittorio's bedside table. "That photograph was the only indiscretion, contrary to the norms of conspiratorial life, that I allowed myself, and Finucci noticed it and gave what seemed to me a smile of comprehension."

When Vittorio was still in jail in Turin, he asked the police why they had arrested his father. "If you cooperate with us, we will release him," they told him. "No, that's blackmail!" Vittorio responded, and the police abandoned the strategy and let his father go. Although fascist Italy was very much a police state, there was a residue of fair play.

Because he and his co-conspirators were university graduates from good upper-middle-class families, a certain deference to them held up even behind bars. The police "might have beaten a peasant, but not a bourgeois," Vittorio says. "My friend Mario Andreis, who was arrested in 1932, told me that they started to beat him and he shouted, 'But I'm an official in the Alpine division,' and they stopped hitting him. The police then were still very Giolittian [Giovanni Giolitti was the principal liberal leader before fascism]. Their rule was: 'Respect the bourgeois, tolerate the worker, beat the peasant.' "

Police officials took an interest in the romantic life of one of the arrested antifascists, Tina Pizzardo. In searching her house they had found numerous letters from three well-known antifascists: Cesare Pavese, Bruno Maffi, and Enik Rieser, a Polish communist. (Pizzardo is described in Pavese's poetry as *"la donna dalla voce rauca"* [the woman with the deep voice].) In defending herself against accusations of antifascism, Pizzardo explained that since she had turned thirty she had decided to marry and these three were her suitors. Vittorio recalls that Mambrini of OVRA's political division liked talking and joking with Vittorio about other GL members. " 'What kind of people you frequent!' he would tell me. 'Listen to this letter from Bruno Maffi to Dottoressa Pizzardo. "My love, I will come to you on a white horse!" How can anyone write such drivel?' When she was finally released, the police took her aside and told her: 'As for your various admirers, marry the Pole, he's the best of the lot.' She did. And they were right. Pavese was something of a madman, Bruno Maffi was a fanatical Trotskyite, and Enik Rieser was an extremely sweet person. There was something very human about these police officials."

It did not take Vittorio long to realize that Pitigrilli had betrayed them. Again and again, the questions the police asked referred to conversations and events that only he and Pitigrilli knew about. Moreover, one of the OVRA agents interrogating Vittorio was a man Pitigrilli had introduced him to, referring to him as a friend—Pitigrilli would have enjoyed the irony.

Since Vittorio was kept in solitary confinement for five months before his trial, he had no chance to warn his friends or family about Pitigrilli. "The only real opportunity would have been at my trial. I could have shouted out in court that Pitigrilli was a spy, but that would have been an admission of guilt. I had chosen the route of denying everything."

By the time the trial came around, in February 1936, the vast majority of the people arrested in May had been released, the charges against them dismissed. OVRA had identified the leaders of the movement, and the trial itself was largely pro forma.

The only unusual thing Vittorio remembers about it is a letter that the prosecution read aloud as evidence, sent to his co-defendant Vindice

Cavalera from Nicola Chiaromonte, a well-known antifascist living in Paris. "The letter read: 'Remember, Vindice, that revenge is the food of the Gods and that it can also be eaten cold.' They read it to show how dangerous these people were, but I found it very comforting. It made me think: 'We only have to wait, our day will come.' "

Vittorio Foa and Michele Giua were each sentenced to fifteen years in prison. Two others received sentences of eight and seven years. Several others were sent *al confino,* to a kind of house arrest in southern Italy—a device the fascists used to keep political enemies out of circulation. One of them, Carlo Levi, turned his exile in a malaria-stricken town into his famous memoir *Christ Stopped at Eboli.*

Just before the trial, Pitigrilli disappeared from the Foa family orbit. He never acknowledged the expensive ceramic bowl Anna and her mother (against Ettore Foa's advice) had sent him as a Christmas gift in thanks for his efforts on Vittorio's behalf. "And then," Anna recalls, "one day when we were walking through the center of Turin, in Piazza Castello, we saw Pitigrilli coming our way. Instead of saying hello he turned the other way. We simply thought he hadn't seen us. It turns out the agents of OVRA had told him to stop seeing us."

Soon after the trial, when his parents were able to visit him in prison, Vittorio managed to warn them about Pitigrilli. "Then we understood his behavior," says Anna.

After the trial, Vittorio's months of solitary confinement ended; he was reunited with friends and fellow conspirators. There were Massimo Mila and Vindice Cavalera, who had been arrested and tried with him, and a pair of older GL leaders, Ernesto Rossi, an economist and leading antifascist thinker, and Riccardo Bauer, who had both been arrested six years before.

Vittorio, with his usual seriousness, turned his imprisonment into a prolonged graduate course in politics, economics, history and literature. His prison dossier consists almost entirely of interminable lists of books that he requested to buy and bureaucratic arguments with the prison censors over which books they would allow him to read.

The authorities were strangely arbitrary in what they would and would not allow. In one instance he was denied a book that had been the bible of fascist economics, *The New Economy* by Walther Rathenau. "It's extraordinary," Vittorio says, "because he was in fact the theorist of corporativism, on which all the economic theories of fascism were based. All the hammering propaganda we had been hearing for years was taken from Rathenau's book, which the police then kept from me as dangerous. Crazy. Typical of the imbecility of fascism."

Foa, Rossi and Bauer studied economics in their cell, writing formulas on walls with bars of soap because they were not allowed pen and paper. The prisoners supplied the friendship and humor necessary to tolerate the unbearable aspects of incarceration. Rossi was known for his motto about the prison soup: "After the third worm, stop."

"I remember at one time we became aware that a microphone had been placed in our cell," Vittorio says. "We were at first uncertain about what to do: we could keep silent and not say anything compromising, or make a tremendous racket. We decided to swear and insult the head of the police and Mussolini until they decided to remove the microphone."

Although the company of like-minded souls kept Vittorio's spirits up, prison took a rather heavy toll on his body. "When he was in prison, he was allowed one visit a month," Anna says. "My parents would go one month, and then I would go the next. Once I saw that his hands trembled, his neck and face were so swollen he couldn't button the collar of his shirt, and his eyes bulged out. Luckily, he couldn't see himself, because there was no mirror in prison. During his years there his physiognomy changed completely. He had been a good-looking young man. He courted many girls in Turin. Then in prison he got this terrible disease, Basedow's disease. They took out all of his teeth. His features were completely changed. He doesn't talk about it.

"I was very upset. I went to the Ministry of Justice in Rome; I went down on a night train, arrived in the morning and returned to Turin that night because I hated Rome in that period. I got to the Ministry at eleven and they made me wait until three. I asked the minister to let us consult someone other than the prison doctor. He said: 'The political prisoners do not need another doctor, the prison doctor will do.' I was furious and said, 'I thought I was in the Ministry of Justice,' and then his assistant wrote out the permission. My parents chose a doctor named Frugoni, who was the personal doctor of the king himself and of Mussolini. Frugoni went to the prison to visit Vittorio and then wrote to my mother and father. He said that the disease Vittorio was suffering from was impossible to treat while he was in prison and that he would have it as long as he was there. He needed a normal life to be cured. My father wrote to thank Frugoni, and the doctor wrote back saying that he was honored to have had the opportunity to help such a great young mind. This was the doctor of Mussolini."

Although his health was permanently affected by his years in prison, Vittorio nonetheless remembers with amusement his mother's first visit after he contracted Basedow's disease. She looked at his eyes bulging out of his head and, instead of reacting with shock and pity, said to him jokingly: "You've lost the only good-looking feature you had!" That was typical of her, Vittorio says. "The members of her family all have a characteristic smile, a slightly ambiguous and ironic, mocking smile, a little like the Mona Lisa. Imagine a person sick and in prison and her saying that . . . but knowing my mother, it made me happy to see that her spirit and sense of humor were unaffected by the unfavorable circumstances."

Chapter Four

The roundup of the Turinese branch of Giustizia e Libertà should have been the crowning achievement of Pitigrilli's career as a secret agent, but in fact it was the beginning of new troubles. Since his principal contacts within the group were now in jail, his usefulness was greatly diminished. And having "escaped" arrest himself, he was terrified of being fingered as a spy. This not only would endanger him in Italy but also would destroy his reputation as a writer abroad.

He managed to be conveniently in Paris at the time of the roundup. Carlo Rosselli and the members of GL in Paris appear not to have suspected him initially. Pitigrilli played on his previous arrest in the Guglielminetti–Brandimarte case to deflect suspicions.

Paris, Saturday, June 8, 1935

> [Carlo Rosselli] advised me strongly against returning to Italy until it becomes clear what direction things take after the Turin arrests. . . . "You are too visible a personality; if they arrest you it could mean trouble for the others and would serve beautifully to magnify the whole *affaire.*" I told him that my political troubles of several years ago, which ended with a clear demonstration that I was the victim of a campaign of falsehoods and forgeries, has vaccinated me for life against the danger of political trials. But Carlo answered: "Don't kid yourself."

While it was relatively easy to fool people in Paris, the danger of being identified as a spy in Turin was much more serious. Pitigrilli attempted to get around the problem by making a bold but impractical proposal, suggesting that OVRA arrest him and keep him in jail for a short time. "Rosselli does not seem to suspect me, but the people with whom I was in contact, Foa and his Professor Giua, could point suspicion my way, if not now, later," he wrote his bosses in Rome. "Logically, if I weren't working for you, I should be arrested."

Amusingly enough, Pitigrilli asked to be arrested in Rome rather than Turin in order to avoid the unpleasant experience of riding in one of the jail wagons used to transport prisoners.

> I don't mind the idea of spending a couple of days at Regina Coeli [the Roman prison where Vittorio Foa and the others were held], but I would not enjoy traveling from Turin to Rome in such uncomfortable conditions.
>
> So this is what I propose.
>
> On [June 23, 1935], I arrive in Turin. The same day you arrest Nello Segre or Sion Segre. You transfer them to Rome. Three days later, my father tells me to go to Rome to bring them fresh laundry and money. . . . With a little play-acting (a two-day beard, no tie, no shoelaces) I can pretend I've been arrested too. If that's not enough I can spend a couple of days at Regina Coeli.

* * *

Sion Segre began to see a lot of his famous cousin when he left prison in March 1935, about a year after his arrest at Ponte Tresa. Sion's mother, who had banished Pitigrilli from their house, was now dead. Pitigrilli had become a good friend of Sion's wild and reckless brother, Nello. And he had written Sion solicitous letters when he was in prison, recommending books for him to read. Besides, Pitigrilli was good company: "He was very amusing: he spoke the way he wrote," Sion says. Moreover, Pitigrilli didn't have a "bedbug" in his lapel—the antifascists' term for the Fascist Party insignia, which many members wore in their lapel and whose ubiquity recalled an infestation.

In addition, when Sion returned home he learned that Pitigrilli and Nello had paid a substantial bribe to the lover of the head of OVRA, Arturo Bocchini, in order to fix his trial. This explained the otherwise mysterious presence of this woman in court. (Women were normally not allowed to attend the hearings of the *Tribunale Speciale,* the special tribunal for political crimes, except as witnesses.) Sion had also noticed Bocchini pacing up and down in the gallery above the courtroom during the proceedings. The bribe, Sion believes, may have had something to do with his surprisingly mild sentence.

Pitigrilli, of course, may have had an ulterior motive: out of prison, Sion was a valuable source for his spying activities. Indeed, almost as soon as Sion was released, Pitigrilli began filing reports on him that might have sent him back to prison for a much longer time.

Sion did not prove an especially valuable contact. Knowing he would be under close surveillance, he kept his distance from his old GL friends. Then, only two months after his release, they were all arrested in the May 1935 roundup. As both antifascist and Jew, Sion began to feel as if he had no future in fascist Italy. He thought seriously, as a number of antifascist Jews did, of emigrating to Palestine.

Pitigrilli was thus stranded, with no real sources inside what little remained of Giustizia e Libertà in Turin after May 1935. Both the quantity and the quality of his reports dropped off noticeably. He was forced to collect gossip, repeat generic antifascist comments, speculate about possible political activity and hint of possible plots and conspiracies in order to justify his paycheck. He continually tried to arouse suspicion about Sion and frequently fanned the flames of anti-Semitism—something that was beginning to acquire respectability in Italy in late 1935 and early 1936.

Turin, Jan. 2, 1936

> The salon of Paolo Olivetti [wife of the industrialist Adriano Olivetti and sister of Natalia Ginzburg] is frequented by people who move continuously, like those groups of gamblers who meet first in this house, then in that one, in order not to arouse the suspicion of the police. Sion Segre is in the group; so is Colonel Sacerdote, Beppe Foa (all the Jews are here) and a certain number of non-Jews, whose names I don't know.

A few days later, he wrote: "It is my conviction that Signora Olivetti, with diabolical ability, is holding antifascist meetings that grow stronger every day." He then conceded that his conviction was based on "imponderable proof." Obviously Pitigrilli was not invited to these parties, and was forced to reconstruct the conversations by buttonholing unsuspecting people, such as his cousin Sion, who were.

At another point Pitigrilli hinted at the possibility of a Jewish cabal to kill Mussolini, reporting a conversation in a kind of Jewish code language to give it more flavor of conspiracy. "The young Malvano told Sion Segre: The success of Italy in Africa will force our friends to modify their policies (probably he means their propaganda). Unless someone blows out the brains of the Aluf (in Hebrew Aluf means leader), there's no way out."

In a letter of July 1936, Pitigrilli described the increasingly confused state of the Jewish community, divided between feelings of patriotism and fear of Italy's increased proximity to Hitler. In light of the war in Africa and renewed rapprochement with Hitler, some Jews had emigrated to Palestine, while others tried to protect themselves by cleaving more closely to fascism. The letter also contains a revealing self-portrait of Pitigrilli as a spy in his later phase, reduced to hanging around the post office trying to pick up odds and ends of information.

> Signora Valabrega (the wife of that Leo Levi who was arrested and let go, who went to Vienna two years ago and is now in Palestine . . .) was here in Turin recently. I met her in the Post Office, introduced to me by Signora Bolaffi (wife of the engineer) who lives at Via Toselli 1. Signora Levi was looking for various people who would sign money orders to send to Palestine. . . . I lent myself to the scheme in order to find out what was going on. . . .
>
> What was interesting was what she had to say about the political sentiments of Italian Jews who are now living in Palestine. She said they all have a great admiration for Il Duce, and that the victories in Africa were followed with great passion. People are wrong, she said, to think that the Jews are indifferent to patriotic sentiments. I've seen people who left ten years ago to live in Palestine homesick for Italy. Despite that bit of irony in the soul of the Jews, the political and military successes of Mussolini have made a great impression on everyone. . . . Because of the almost messianic appeal of Mussolini, because of the infallibility of his predictions, many Jews would like to return from Palestine to Italy. Those who remain antifascists do so because Mussolini had the misfortune of inventing Fascism, which in the hands of Hitler has been turned into persecution of the Jews. Or rather just out of stubbornness, like Wardi (the husband of Ilda; the brother-in-law of Nello and Sion Segre) which is more on the surface than in reality. "What I don't understand," said Signora Levi-Valabrega, with the approval of Signora Bolaffi, "is the pigheaded antifascism of Sion. If there's anyone who should thank the regime, which acted with an unheard-of indulgence toward him, it's he. If you think of the heavy sentence they inflicted on that poor Vittorio Foa, Sion Segre ought to kiss the ground every time he walks by the courthouse. Instead he says he wants to go to Palestine, not to live in the Land of the Ancestors but to get away from the Fascist Regime."
>
> To these words Signora Bolaffi added: "The next time they arrest him, he's not going to get off so cheap!"
>
> I (Pericles) [one of Pitigrilli's code names] answered: "They're not

going to arrest him again, because he's not involved in politics anymore. He's got a grain of sense now."

"He may not be distributing leaflets or books, but he talks, talks, talks. He's involved in verbal propaganda. The Russian method," Signora Bolaffi said.

Since this interested me, I came up with a pretext to get Signora Bolaffi to come back to my house. I tried to get her to tell me what she meant by "the Russian method." "Do you think Sion is a communist?"

"No, I wouldn't say a communist," she replied, "but in the antifascist ranks the categories are not so clear and schematic. What's happening here is what's happening in Germany. I have a governess I brought from Berlin. She explained to me what the underground struggle against Hitler is like: the same as the underground struggle against Mussolini is what Sion and these others are up to. You should tell him to be careful, because even if they are more clever than the devil, one day or another they are going to fall into a trap. Sion and the others have formed into . . . into . . . how do you call them . . . you know, into the little groups with only a few members, independent in appearance from one another, but in fact tied together by links of which they themselves are not even aware."

"Are they all Jews?"

"No. In fact only a small minority is Jewish. The . . . of Sion is composed entirely of Jews, however."

I believe the word she was searching for but couldn't recall was "cell." I didn't suggest it to her because I didn't want to give the impression that I knew anything about these things or that they interested me. But does there really exist a cell of which Sion is the nucleus?

* * *

For all his speculation and exaggeration, Pitigrilli was correct in detecting increased agitation among Turinese Jews, caught between lingering loyalty to Italy and growing concern about the ties of fascism to Hitler's Germany. "The years 1935 to 1937 were crucial for fascism's policy toward the Jews, as [for] all aspects of fascist policy," Italian historian Renzo De Felice has written. "On the one hand, for the vast majority of Jews, these were years of peaceful work, of hope, trust and participation in the spirit of national life; on the other, for that small group of Jews who understood toward what disaster Italy and the Jews were now heading, these were years of intense anxiety, anxiety that became increasingly spasmodic as fascism systematically forged the links that would bind Italy solidly to Germany."

In the short time between his arrest in May and his release from prison in August 1935, Beppe Foa noticed a difference. When he returned to Turin after his imprisonment, he did not find himself isolated and shunned by friends, as Anna found herself immediately after the arrests in May. The reason, he believes, was the growing uneasiness over war with Abyssinia, which was clearly imminent. "There was a growing sense of antifascism not only among Jews, but outside the Jewish community too. In the north, antifascism was much stronger than in the south, and I think in Piedmont and in Emilia-Romagna it was stronger than elsewhere. There, being antifascist was quite normal."

Each week more troops sailed to Africa to "protect" the border of Italy's colony in Somalia against Ethiopian "aggression." Each week Mussolini's rhetoric became more bellicose. "If the Regime of the Blackshirts calls the youth of Italy to arms, it is because it is strict necessity, because it finds itself faced with a supreme duty," Mussolini declared in June 1935. "The entire Italian people feels it, and the people are ready to spring into action like a single man, when the power and glory of the Homeland are at stake."

On September 9, Anna gave birth to her first child, Eva. Three weeks later, on October 2, Mussolini declared war on Abyssinia. A nationwide mass rally was held, with loudspeakers set up in the central square of every Italian town to broadcast Mussolini's speech. Every citizen was expected to attend in uniform. Twenty-seven million Italians turned out for what was said to be the largest staged event in history. The Foas registered their quiet dissent by staying home and listening to the declaration of war on the radio. Anna recalls hearing Mussolini's speech while looking down at Corso Re Umberto. The long, majestic avenue, completely deserted in the middle of the day, took on, she thought, the surreal quality of many of de Chirico's paintings of Turin.

"A solemn hour in the history of our Homeland is about to strike," Mussolini proclaimed from the balcony overlooking Piazza Venezia in Rome, and over loudspeakers and radios throughout the peninsula. "Twenty million men in this very moment fill the streets of Italy . . . twenty million men with one heart, one will and one determination. . . . For many months the wheel of destiny, under the impulse of our calm determination, has been moving toward its goal: in these hours its rhythm has quickened and become unstoppable!" Italy, he announced, was ready to seize its "place in the sun."

When Mussolini called for all Italian women to donate their gold wedding rings to support the war, Anna refused, and continued to wear hers openly. Her friends were scandalized; some avoided her, after telling her she was crazy and would be arrested. Anna's mother and mother-in-law did not want trouble but resented having to donate their rings to the cause of fascism. Eventually, they handed in cheap gold rings and kept their actual wedding rings hidden at home—a common ruse at the time.

The Ethiopian war, paradoxically, gave the family hope that Vittorio might be released soon. "If the war ended with a sound Italian defeat, Mussolini might fall," Beppe says. "If it ended with an Italian victory or a half-defeat, it would be very bad for Vittorio. There was hope that Italy wouldn't make it." This was strongly reinforced by the difference Beppe immediately noticed when he was recalled briefly for military service in 1936.

"When I did my military service in 1931, the army was very poor, but the troops with whom I served were highly disciplined." When he spent a month in the army at the beginning of the Ethiopian war, however, he was shocked to find the troops in a state of near mutiny. "Before joining my regiment, some officers at headquarters warned me I would find the soldiers very undisciplined and in fact quite dangerous. One day a major was walking in the courtyard of the barracks and a soldier threw a pail of dirty water on him. The major did nothing and pretended that nothing had happened, because he knew he couldn't do anything to punish this soldier. In the morning I woke up when I heard the bugle, and went outside my tent: the only people who had bothered to get up were the captain and a couple of officers and me. The captain was yelling, 'Get up! Wake up, please!' And no one moved. So it seemed impossible that Italy would win a war, even against Abyssinia. At that point, one began to feel that fascism would not last forever."

For many Italians called up to serve in the Ethiopian conflict, the experience was a shocking revelation. While the state-controlled press reported that the spirited fascist troops were moving from victory to victory, the reality was different. The poorly trained and equipped Italian troops encountered serious difficulties in Africa, although they were fighting against an even more underprepared army. The key to Italy's ultimate victory was not the spirit of its fighting men but mustard gas, against which the Abyssinians had no defense—and this fact went unreported in the Italian press. The hollow triumph in Africa nonetheless left Mussolini and many fascists exhilarated and eager for new horizons to conquer.

In many ways, the war in Ethiopia set in motion the forces that would lead to both World War II and the racial laws in Italy. Mussolini's imperial thrust placed Italy in conflict with Britain and France, and aligned him firmly with Hitler's Germany. The extensive contacts between Italian soldiers and African women raised the delicate questions of miscegenation and intermarriage, and brought Italian fascism to set down strict racial guidelines. In grabbing for his imperial dream, Mussolini first embraced the concept of race. Thrilled with his victory in Ethiopia, Mussolini sent Italian troops and planes to fight alongside Franco and Hitler in Spain in 1936. He began to speak frequently of the need to mold the undisciplined Italian people into a warrior nation and to view war as a form of education for the soft bourgeois class. The war in Spain, Il Duce said, would give the middle class "a sound kick in the shins . . . and when that's done, I'll invent something else so that the character of the Italians forms itself through war."

These efforts reached comical proportions, as middle-aged fascist bureaucrats were forced to jump through rings of fire meant to transform them into empire builders. Government officials were required to run to and from their desks in order to increase their physical prowess. Citizens were forbidden from using foreign words and phrases branded as un-Italian. The handshake was officially banned and was replaced by the "Roman salute." The handshake, Mussolini maintained, was an effete bourgeois custom which through its physical, human contact made people softer and friendlier, while the Roman salute (lifting the right hand in the air at a seventy-five-degree angle) promoted the bellicose virtues of the second Roman Empire.

The militarization of the Italian schools, already extensive, now became complete. Even the smallest elementary school children were organized into military cadres and dressed in tiny fascist uniforms. Saturdays (a normal school day) was set aside for military parades and exercises, in which all schoolchildren were expected to participate. Although the Italian military was poorly organized and technologically backward, Mussolini bragged about having 8 million bayonets ready to respond to his call at a moment's notice.

The increasingly militaristic tone of government propaganda, the closer ties with Germany and the first use of racial ideas increased uneasiness among the Italian middle class. They had admired Mussolini for ending strikes and disorder, but were highly apprehensive about the prospect of being dragged into a series of military adventures.

Already in 1936, Beppe sensed that Italy was heading irrevocably toward an alliance with Hitler and the institution of racial persecution. "I felt it very much. I spoke about it to the director of Caproni [an aircraft manufacturing company in Reggio Emilia for which he worked at the time]. I told him that what was happening in Germany could happen soon in Italy too. He said that was ridiculous, as did many of my Catholic friends."

For the moment, Beppe had to worry more about being persecuted for his antifascist connections. When he was first released from prison, he was rehired by his old employer, Piaggio. The company directors had been putting pressure on the government to free Beppe because they were eager to complete production of an airplane that would fly nonstop from Rome to San Francisco, which he had designed. While Beppe was in prison, the plane was tested without one of the features he had introduced, and it crashed into the side of a mountain. "Although it was not a military plane, it was supposed to set a world record, and Mussolini had this great passion for world records," Beppe says. "The project was of interest to him and the fascist regime."

But a week after his return to the Piaggio plant, the local fascist authorities ordered the company to fire him. Beppe spent the next three months in Turin, unemployed. He was then hired by Caproni, but after only six months in his new job, fascist authorities in Reggio Emilia forced Beppe's new employer to dismiss him. Six months later the company rehired him. "But I left shortly thereafter to return to Piaggio, because I was still interested in that airplane project I had started several years before," Beppe says. "It had been in limbo since I left."

As Beppe worked on a plane that would stand for the greater glory of fascist Italy, the country was moving perceptibly closer to racial persecution and to a European war. Throughout 1937, meetings between high-ranking German and Italian officials became more and more frequent, culminating in Mussolini's famous Rome–Berlin Axis speech on August 20.

While Mussolini had once courted the international Zionist movement in an attempt to rival British interests in the Middle East, he now excoriated it as a pawn of British imperialism. With much public fanfare, Mussolini flew to the Italian colony of Libya, mounted a white horse and, holding aloft the "Sword of Islam," proclaimed himself the protector of the Arab people. Attacks on "international Jewry" in Italy began to extend beyond the usual right-wing fringe newspapers. Even the respected magazine of the Jesuit order, *La Civiltà Cattolica,* denounced Jewish attempts at world domination and, without fear of contradiction, labeled the Jews as heading both capitalist and communist worldwide conspiracies. And 1937 saw the publication of Paolo Orano's anti-Semitic tract, *The Jews in Italy,* which received wide and respectful attention throughout the Italian press. While this orchestrated propaganda campaign was meant to prepare the psychological terrain for racial persecution, most Italian Jews wanted to believe Mussolini when he announced in March 1938 that the regime was not planning any discrimination against Jews.

"I authorize you to let the Jews of America know," Mussolini told Generoso Pope, publisher of New York's Italian-language newspaper *Il*

Progresso, "that their worries for their brothers living in Italy are entirely unfounded and are the fruit of malicious information. I authorize you to specify that the Jews in Italy have received, are receiving and will continue to receive the same treatment accorded any Italian citizen and that I am not contemplating any kind of racial or religious discrimination."

And so, despite the many warning signs, Beppe, like most Italians, was shocked to pick up the newspaper on July 14, 1938, and read the "Manifesto of the Racist Scientists." The news came out while Beppe was in Turin. When he returned to Finalmarina by train the next morning, he found a crowd of his colleagues awaiting him at the station. "They were all there waiting for me, and the first thing they said to me was, 'We're ashamed to be Italians today.' They came to tell me this. The atmosphere surrounding me was far from anti-Semitic."

The new racist propaganda, while adopted by the party and the servile Italian press, never convinced the larger public, to whom it seemed an unnatural Nordic import, foreign to the experience of the Italian people, itself a mix of dozens of nationalities. Nor could they forget that Mussolini himself had inveighed against German racial doctrine for years and described Italy as a healthy blend of different races. Moreover, the Jewish population of Italy was so small that it was very difficult to argue convincingly that a Jewish conspiracy dominated the nation.

In a letter Beppe sent his parents in August 1938—intercepted by OVRA and preserved in the state archives—he ridicules the racist propaganda of the paper *Il Tevere.*

> I don't think they will apply discrimination to one in a thousand [the rough proportion of Jews to the total population]; if they did, forty-nine out of fifty Jewish professionals would have to go plant potatoes. Have you read *Il Tevere*? Up until now, each of us, including Manuela [Anna's second child], has succeeded in imposing our thinking, our interests and our goals on one thousand Aryans, who, it would seem, do little other than allow themselves to be persecuted by the Jews. I am so flattered, that if I weren't Jewish, I'd be ashamed.

It is not an exaggeration to say that many Italians had no idea who or what Jews were. Because most Jews lived in only a few dozen cities and towns in the central and northern regions of the country, many Italians had never met one, as Beppe had discovered earlier that year.

"I lived in a little hotel in Finalmarina. One rainy evening in winter I was alone in the dining room when a fellow entered, a traveling salesman, a southerner. Because we were the only ones in the dining room, we decided to eat together. At a certain point he started saying something against Jews. And I said, 'Look, I'm Jewish.' He said, 'You're Jewish? That's impossible, Jews are black.' The southerners had no idea of what Jews were, since the Jews had been expelled from southern Italy centuries before."

Despite Beppe's skepticism that the regime would really make "forty-nine out of fifty Jewish professionals . . . go plant potatoes," in September the fascist government began handing down decree after decree that quickly stripped the country's Jews of virtually all their civil and economic rights.

For Beppe, the racial laws had no immediate practical effect. As an employee in private industry, he was able to keep his job. In fact, in the summer of 1939, his airplane was finally ready to attempt a world record for uninterrupted flight. King Vittorio Emanuele was to come to the air base in Guidonia, near Rome, to watch the takeoff. The day before, Beppe was called into the office of the base commander and told not to show up at the takeoff because they did not want any Jews on hand.

Beppe still has a photograph album that his mother prepared, documenting the plane's accomplishments. Underneath the picture of the plane ready to take off that day at Guidonia, Lelia Foa wrote: "Not a Jew on the field."

Beppe enjoyed a small, private revenge on the people who had excluded him. On the side of the plane the letters PF are clearly visible. "Originally the plane had no insignia, other than the letter P for 'Piaggio,' but without telling me the workers put the letters PF on it, for 'Piaggio Foa,' " he says.

In July 1939, a year after the publication of the race manifesto, Beppe left Piaggio. He was not fired, but documents in the state archives indicate that he was about to be: with the country preparing for war, there was no place for an antifascist Jew in a company that built fighter planes for fascist Italy.

Even though the racial campaign was in full swing, his colleagues at Piaggio never turned against him, Beppe remembers. "In fact, when I finally left Piaggio, there was another demonstration of affection that was even more moving to me than the one my friends showed me after the publication of the race manifesto. I had already said good-bye to my colleagues at the factory, but when I went to catch my train, there must have been, without exaggeration, 250 or 300 workers at the station. As I waited for the train, they were just lined up in silence, not saying a word. I didn't understand why. Then one of the workers slipped from the crowd and came to me and said under his breath: 'We can't say anything, but we wish you every possible good.' They had come to the station just to see me off. I was so moved I didn't know what to say. And when I got on the train, I leaned out of the window and waved as the train went off."

* * *

Ironically, the one member of the family not directly affected by the racial laws was Vittorio. Having already persecuted them for their political activity, the regime made no such distinctions among political prisoners. Although he was cut off from what was happening, clearly the racial persecutions had a deep emotional effect on Vittorio. He reflected often on the problem in his cell in Regina Coeli, as the letters he wrote to his family show. "He never complained," says Anna, "and although he had never read Thoreau, he often said that he was more free in prison than we were outside."

Prisoners were allowed pen and paper only once a week, to write their families. Having no other outlet, Vittorio used these letters for many purposes, from making comments on his extensive reading in history, politics and philosophy to expressing his most private thoughts. His more personal letters show a tenderness, sensitivity and good humor that are remarkable in light of the depressing and isolated circumstances of his life. Equally striking is his clairvoyance regarding the direction of Italian politics.

In a letter of October 8, 1937, a year before the institution of the racial laws, he warned his family about the inevitability of the persecutions. The letter was written in response to news that Anna was pregnant with her second child, and in it he tried to quell her doubts about bringing a child into the world at such a desperate time. Surprisingly, Vittorio invoked the millennial resilience and strength of the Jewish family, while warning her to expect the worst.

> Dearest Anna,
>
> Yesterday I received Papà's letter in which he told me that you and Davide had returned precipitately home from a trip because you realized that you were ready to produce another nephew or niece for me. . . . Let us hope that there are no more family cataclysms that accompanied your pregnancy in 1935 [a reference to his, Beppe's and their father's arrest]; nonetheless I am afraid there will be cataclysms occurring in a sphere far more vast than our family. Now I want to recommend something: Try with your will to create an interior state of calm and serenity. . . . Live for yourself and don't give a thought to the world, imitate the egotism of those pretty friends of yours and let the professionals of redemption take the pains of the world onto their shoulders; there are always enough of them in the world to ensure the progress of civilization. As a practical

> man, I think you do well to have another child. . . . I can't stand the . . . argument one hears from even rather intelligent people, about the responsibilities of parents bearing offspring in calamitous times. . . . If you scratch a little, underneath a certain cynical posturing there is a noble if unreflective concern in the viewpoint . . . that it is vile and shameful to bring into the world a race of slaves. But these deterministic ideas . . . lose all meaning in the face of our Jewish family life, which in its unifying and cohesive force survives every assimilation and, against rational argument, continues to see in each new child the blessing of the Lord. If a shadow of doubt had overcome them, in the centuries of infinite suffering, how would they have survived? Not long ago I read in *La Civiltà Cattolica* that the good Jesuit fathers would like to close us up in ghettos again and deprive us of our rights, although they stop short of advocating that we be annihilated and erased from the face of the earth: not so much out of the goodness of their hearts, but due to the consideration that if we have remained intact through all these unheard-of persecutions it is a sign that God willed it and that He wants our survival.

For someone who had previously "affected the most detached attitude toward anything smelling of Judaism," as his brother-in-law put it, the impending sense of racial persecution seems to have worked a profound change on Vittorio.

In another letter, written at the beginning of 1938, some seven months before the publication of the race manifesto, Vittorio warned his parents: "I can tell from your letters you are angry about the spreading anti-Semitism. You will see much worse, so be prepared."

In September of that year, after the first anti-Jewish provisions (affecting Jewish schoolchildren and foreign-born Jews) Vittorio foresaw the more devastating economic restrictions and urged Anna and the rest of his family to leave the country.

> So far I've had news about the expulsion of the foreign-born Jews and the exclusion [of Jewish children] from the schools. Although these provisions do not touch you directly, do not delude yourselves, your turn will come, so prepare yourselves spiritually for the fact that it will soon be necessary to pack your bags. Luckily you are young and full of spirit, and Mamma and Papà have enough youthful spirit to get through this storm, but how much pain of others it will fall to you to know and share. I am completely in the dark, in the thickest shadows, and yet I am able to see that suffering and feel disdain and bitterness.

The racial campaign, Vittorio wrote, reminded him of the smug certainty of the Turinese Jews who were convinced that the regime would never turn its back on them.

> But you would be totally wrong, Anna, if you thought that I feel a sense of triumph over these people, that I am thinking: "I told you so," or "They deserve it," the feeling of a prophet who enjoys watching those who didn't believe him suffer. Not at all. I take no pleasure in seeing those professors who [acted] in bad faith laid low, or in watching opportunists for whom I had little respect ruined. . . . Instead I have a deep feeling of pity and commiseration . . . because between myself and them there is this difference: I lost my professional career as a direct result of a fully conscious act. . . . You might ask me: "What's this? Wouldn't you have liked to see the likes of Fano, Foà [no relation] and Arias tossed out of their positions?" I would answer yes, and with a swift kick too . . . but not as the result of a blind, arbitrary criterion such as race . . . which offends the mind, no matter who the victim is. Injustice is never a healing virtue. . . . I received Papà's letter of August 30, but to my great disappointment it was heavily censored. . . . Dear Anna, please write me and give news of the particular fate of our relatives and friends hit by the racial campaign.

One of the most touching elements of Vittorio's letters is his preoccupation for his two nieces, whom he had never seen. Eva was born just after Vittorio's arrest, and on the occasion of her third birthday he wrote: "She is a living calendar synchronized with this strange life of mine; when I want to know how long I have been here, all I have to do is remember Eva's age."

Vittorio was extremely worried about being used in his absence as an educational tool to persuade Eva to do all the things she didn't want to do.

> I am thankful that Eva's respect and affection for this invisible uncle of hers grow, but one thing troubles me. Apparently you find it convenient to use my situation for educational ends with phrases such as: If only Vittorio could eat this soup, or take this walk, or drink this medicine! In this way, Eva's affection will be bent to utilitarian ends and turned into its opposite and in her mind my image will be irrevocably linked with foul-tasting soups and medicinal syrups. When I used to refuse to eat something, Mamma would say, "Go to the Dogali barracks," to which I owe my aversion to the infantry, which is linked in my mind to this day with cabbage soup and rice pudding. . . . In any event I would not like to become a scarecrow for the children, an involuntary pain in the neck.

The meeting between Vittorio and little Eva finally occurred in 1940, just before Anna and Davide set sail with their children for the United States. Anna had bought a little bottle of carnation-scented perfume for Eva to give to Vittorio. She had chosen perfume because the prison guards would not rip it apart looking for concealed objects and because perfume was always welcome to counteract the stench of the prison. Eva was standing in the visitors' room clutching the bottle when Vittorio entered in a striped prison uniform, his face swollen and disfigured from his confinement. "Eva paled with fright," Anna recalls in her memoirs. "Vittorio with a sweet smile moved a step forward to her." Eva dropped the bottle, which shattered and filled the room with a powerful odor of carnation. "For years Eva could not stand the scent of carnations because it reminded her of that visit."

* * *

For Anna and Davide the racial campaign had a direct and immediate effect. The laws passed in October 1938 banning Jews from all public employment cost him his job as an architect for the City of Turin. In December he became seriously ill with a ruptured hernia; the hospitals would no longer accept Jews. Through the efforts of a family friend, Davide was admitted to a children's hospital and operated on there. Anna recalls her husband's feet sticking out over the end of the child's bed in which he lay recuperating.

To save money the couple moved in with Anna's parents. Davide decided to work in his family's small metalworking business, in which he invested much of his savings. A couple of months later, the regime passed laws forbidding Jews from owning businesses with more than a handful of employees. To try to get around the laws, many Jewish businessmen handed over legal ownership of their companies to Gentile friends. Usually these titular owners allowed the real owners to continue operating the businesses and promised to give them back when the racial persecutions ended. Many Jewish businesses survived the entire war period in this fashion, but their success depended on the good faith of those who agreed to help them. In the case of Davide's family, the "friend" took advantage of the situation, fired his Jewish "employees" (Davide and his brother) and confiscated the company for his own profit.

This last blow left Anna and Davide little choice but to leave Italy. By 1939, Beppe had reached the same conclusion. Other friends had already left. Sion Segre and his sister had left for Palestine. Several of the Foas' cousins had gone to America, where Anna and Beppe also hoped to go. Vittorio, from prison, tried to convince his parents to go with them but they kept refusing. "At a certain point," he says, "Beppe wrote me a very stern letter saying, 'Stop telling them to leave; you know very well why they won't." Meaning that they wouldn't because they didn't want to leave me alone in prison in Italy. So I stopped."

"It was a terrible time, especially for my mother," Beppe says. "She had a son in prison. She had a son who could no longer work in Italy and a daughter who also wanted to leave the country. But my mother and father didn't want to leave Vittorio in prison alone. It was a very sad situation."

Obtaining passports was no easy matter. Beppe had first requested one in 1935, after he got out of prison and then lost his job, in order to go to the United States. Naturally, the authorities didn't grant him one, he says. Three years later, during the racial campaign, mysteriously, without his even asking for it again, two police officers appeared at his office with a passport. But the passport they had brought granted him permission to go to Germany or Britain, not the United States. "Certainly I didn't want to go to Germany," he recalls. "And to go to England you needed a transit visa to go through France, and I had heard it was difficult to get. But I decided I'd try for England."

Later that day, the same two police officers came and asked Beppe to return the passport they had given him. "It was like the cat playing with the mouse. I had asked for a passport for the United States in 1935, I never heard a word, and then in 1938 they bring me a passport for Germany and England. And then take it away. Why they came then and why it was for Germany or England I have no idea." A letter in the state archives indicates that the fascist government was reluctant to allow Beppe to leave the country because of his knowledge of the Italian aircraft industry.

"I went to see the head of the Genoa newspaper [*Il Secolo XX*], which was one of the less enthusiastically fascist newspapers of Italy. He was a very decent person. He looked at me and said that what was happening with the Jews was the intellectual hemorrhaging of Italy. He was very moved. . . . He told me I should ask for a weeklong visa to go to Switzerland for reasons of health, and then leave from there. So that's what I did, in the summer of 1939. I left Piaggio in July. After that I kept my suitcase packed so that I could leave at any moment once the visa came through. I received it on July 31 and left immediately for Switzerland." Before leaving, Beppe went to the French consulate to see whether he could obtain a transit visa to go through France to get to England. But the French required a baptismal certificate, making it impossible for Jews to enter France.

After arriving in Switzerland, Beppe applied at once for permission to go to the United States. "The American consul in Zurich asked me if I had a passport. 'No, I don't,' I told him. 'Good, that means you're not a fascist spy,' he said. Then he asked me if I had a job there. I was convinced that having a job was a condition for being allowed to emigrate, so with great trepidation I told him I didn't. It turned out it was just the opposite: when I told him I didn't have a job, he said, 'Good.' I then sent a telegram to my cousins, who were already in the United States, to procure me an affidavit. It arrived on August 21 or 22, and it's a good thing it did, because I remember going to the station around that time and picking up a newspaper and seeing that the nonaggression pact between Hitler and Stalin had been signed, which indicated that the war would begin shortly. I went to one shipping line and asked if there were boats leaving by the end of the month; there was one leaving on August 31, the *Athenia.* The ticket cost $175 and I had only $250, which didn't leave me much for when I arrived in America. So I went across the street to the Holland-America Line to see if it had anything cheaper. There was space on a Dutch boat and the ticket cost $155, but the boat wouldn't leave until September 2. I thought that the difference between August 31 and September 2 could mean the difference between getting out and not getting out, but it was also a difference of twenty dollars that I needed. I decided to risk it and save the money. Then as soon as I had done so, I thought: What an idiot to risk being stuck in Europe during the war! When I arrived at the port in Genoa, I went to see the boat I was to sail on. It was an old beat-up freighter that had been converted into a passenger ship, all rusty. By the time we departed, on September 2, the war had started. We were 750 passengers, the maximum number. When we made it out onto the Atlantic, I went up on deck and noticed that the boat was going around and around in circles instead of going straight. When I asked why, an officer told me our boat was searching for survivors from the *Athenia,* the ship that had left two days earlier but cost twenty dollars more. It was the first passenger boat hit by the Germans. They didn't find anyone."

* * *

Anna and Davide had to wait several months longer before they were ready to leave, scratching together a living while they waited for visas. Anna tried to get work as a nurse, since she had taken nursing courses at the Red Cross, but the new racial laws forbade it. She and a friend taught themselves to weave so that they could sell clothing. Anna used the wool stuffing from two mattresses to weave cloth. Soon their apartment was full of looms and yarns. Aside from the clothing for sale, Anna made coats for the entire family.

Anna and Davide wanted to follow Beppe's lead in going to Switzerland to obtain visas for the United States, but they had to have Italian passports and special border passes to do so. These passes were hard to come by, since the Italian government tried to discourage contact between Italian citizens and foreigners. Anna and her husband learned that a certain police official might be willing to grant the permit if one "visited him at home"—implying that a bribe was necessary. Two thousand lire was said to be the going rate.

The couple climbed several dingy flights of stairs to the policeman's apartment. A short, poorly dressed woman appeared at the door, surrounded by several children. The apartment was small and poorly furnished. The bribe had to be handled delicately in order not to offend the man's dignity. When Davide finally raised the possibility of getting a border pass for Switzerland, with perfect synchronization he handed over an envelope with 2,000 lire. The policeman looked in the envelope, took out the four 500-lire bills and handed three of them back to Davide. The incident was a lesson in Italian corruption, which involved a certain honor among thieves. The man had clearly sized up the Jonas' situation and ability to pay, and calculated his bribe accordingly.

Chapter Five

With his keen sense of shifting political winds, Pitigrilli must have felt the racial campaign coming; four months before its start, he initiated another strenuous campaign to join the Fascist Party, including a personal appeal to Mussolini himself.

Turin, March 19, 1938

Duce!

For too many years, calumny, misunderstanding and errors have gathered around me. In the summer of 1924, when the fascist insignia disappeared from many lapels [as a result of the murder of Matteotti], I asked for the party card. I still haven't received it to this day, even though his Excellency Galeazzo Ciano [foreign minister and son-in-law of Mussolini] promised it to me. I will paint the picture of all the injustices of which I am victim. But allow me to present my case to someone in Rome who can hear it with friendly serenity and then explain it to you.

If his letter is to be believed, Pitigrilli had already fallen on hard times; "calumny" and "injustices" mentioned may refer to the fact that in 1936 the fascist government began to ban the reprinting of some of his books, on moral grounds. At the same time, his work as an informant dwindled to almost nothing. He does not appear to have been formally dismissed, however, until 1939, when he was exposed as a spy in France. Acting on a tip, French police raided the apartment of Vincenzo Bellavia, head of OVRA operations in Paris. Among his papers they found Pitigrilli's code name, with his address in Turin. Pitigrilli was later stopped by the French police and under questioning admitted giving some information to Bellavia but denied being a paid spy. A 1939 note from OVRA told him: "We thank you for all you've done until now for us, but given the present situation we are compelled to renounce your further collaboration." Pitigrilli went from being the author of OVRA reports to being an object of OVRA study. His next appearance in the files comes as "the well-known Jewish writer Dino Segre, alias Pitigrilli."

Since he was the product of a mixed marriage and had been baptized a Catholic, theoretically Pitigrilli should have been able to avoid the force of the racial laws. Despite his serving ably as a fascist spy and betraying many of his Jewish friends and relatives, Pitigrilli suddenly found himself in the position of being persecuted as a Jew. He was unable to write for Italian newspapers; his books, along with those of all other Jewish authors, were taken out of circulation. What seems to have bothered the new arbiters of racial purity was his marriage to a Jewish woman. The couple had not lived together for years, but since there was no divorce in Italy at the time, he and his wife were still legally married.

In his efforts to escape from this bureaucratic dilemma, Pitigrilli turned to a prominent lawyer in Turin, Lina Furlan, who claims to be Italy's first woman lawyer. She recalls that in her first meeting with Pitigrilli, in the summer of 1938, he asked her: "Is there anything I can do? Not for myself, but for my son?" (This account of Pitigrilli's altruistic concern for Giovanni Segre, the son he had abandoned, is not reflected in his many letters to the government, which are concerned exclusively with exempting himself from the racial laws.)

Rather than rely on the legal process, which she regarded as useless under the circumstances, Avvocatessa Furlan (as she likes to be called) seems to have directed her energies toward the Vatican, where she had powerful friends of the highest rank. Of particular help, she says, was Monsignor Giovanni Battista Montini, the future Pope Paul VI. After the attorney-client relationship between Avvocatessa Furlan and Pitigrilli turned romantic, her entreaties to the Vatican focused on Pitigrilli's need for an annulment in order to remarry.

Because Pitigrilli and his wife had been married outside the Catholic Church, Furlan's friends told her an annulment would not be necessary. "Montini told me, 'As far as we're concerned there has never been a marriage [between Pitigrilli and his first wife]; it was only *concubinaggio* [living in sin].' We were married in the Church of San Lorenzo in Genoa, on July 26, 1940. Piti was forty-seven, I was ten years younger. . . . Piti was the only man in my life."

Avvocatessa Furlan must have been truly devoted to Pitigrilli: July 1940 was hardly a propitious time for a wedding. Marrying someone officially considered Jewish was a clear violation of the fascist racial laws. To make matters worse, on June 10, 1940, Italy had entered World War II on the side of Hitler's Germany. After much delay and hesitation, Mussolini had decided impulsively—now that England was in retreat and France on the verge of surrender—to jump into the war, to ensure himself a seat at the peace table when Hitler carved up Europe.

With the declaration of war, Pitigrilli's name was placed on the list of dangerous Jews to be interned in the remote southern region of Apulia—to northern Italians, being sent to the South was generally considered a fate worse than death. "The well-known Jewish writer Dino Segre, alias Pitigrilli . . . has always maintained an ambiguous attitude toward the regime, which has made us doubt his true sentiments," the Turin police chief wrote in ordering his arrest. "Wiretaps of his telephone conversations revealed him unleashing harsh criticism of the regime. Therefore we believe his detention would be prudent."

Pitigrilli and the Avvocatessa managed to soften the blow by having his destination changed from Apulia to a small town on the Riviera, Uscio, just outside Genoa and only two hours by train from Turin. The terms of his confinement were not especially onerous: he would live in private lodgings and would be required to appear once a day at the local police station to show he had not escaped. Apparently it did not prevent Pitigrilli from going into Genoa to get married.

During this period, according to his own spiritual autobiography *La piscina di Siloe* (The Pool of Siloe), Pitigrilli took the first steps toward embracing to Catholicism—by dabbling in occult séances.

> There was a medium living in a city about an hour and a half away and I decided to invite her over. Twenty years of disappointment hadn't entirely discouraged me. . . . The medium knew no one in our group, and introducing myself to her I let her believe that I was a comic actor whom I vaguely resemble. . . . After an inspired prayer asking to communicate with the dead, she fell into a trance and began to write generic phrases that I no longer remember, but whose contents seemed more or less the same as I had heard in all the séances I had attended for twenty years. I got up from the table, thinking: the usual nonsense. But before I had time to say to myself, "Another disappointment," I heard the person reading the medium's writing say out loud: "I am speaking to

you . . ." and she spoke my name. And then a string of advice, warning and criticism, with a detailed description of my personality, a reference to characters of a forgotten novel of mine . . . to episodes of my life of which I alone knew. . . .

In that meeting and the ones that followed, the medium transcribed messages from people who had long since disappeared, known to only one of us, and not invoked by us.

During the séances, according to Pitigrilli, he was contacted by the spirit of Angelo Formiggini, the Jewish publisher who jumped from the cathedral bell tower in Modena after the passage of the racial laws. The poet Amalia Guglielminetti, Pitigrilli's former lover, dictated elaborate verses in her own unmistakable style through the medium. Pitigrilli suddenly became a believer in the spirit world.

At the end of the summer, Pitigrilli was released from his exile, after continuously petitioning the government. By 1941 he was in Rome, living in the Hotel Esperia, eking out an existence writing dialogue for a movie production company (anonymously, and in violation of the racial laws), and trying to qualify for Aryan status.

During this bitter period Pitigrilli poured out his soul to another OVRA informant; at the same time he suggested that his status as a persecuted Jew would make him a particularly useful informant for the secret police. The informant quoted Pitigrilli in a report of November 6, 1941:

"Naturally, despite being baptized forty-two years ago, I have had to suffer the fate of the non-Aryans, because of which I have not attempted to reestablish my contact with our friends [OVRA]. However, I can tell you that I would like to, if only to find out why I was fired. What I can assure you is that being considered in disgrace, I would have access to information that they couldn't even imagine. I know about fascist groups who would like to attempt a second March on Rome."

[OVRA informant:] "I know about that too, people are talking about it here." . . .

"But I know the names, I know all, I know with precision what they are planning and what they want to do and what they will do if they are not stopped in time."

A letter from the same informant dated February 9, 1942, tells of Pitigrilli's continuing preoccupation with his racial status:

Pitigrilli is very worried about not being recognized as an Aryan. Acknowledgment that he expects, since he is the son of a woman of the

Aryan race, baptized forty-two years ago, at age seven. . . . Except that a passing adventure, that is, a brief relation with a young woman he met at the seaside, put him in the position of having to marry the woman he had made a mother. This woman has never lived with him, according to Pitigrilli, and from 1932 on, the time of their marriage, he has hardly seen her. This young woman was Jewish. Pitigrilli, however, is anxious to demonstrate, in almost comic fashion, that this was not in order to reaffirm his Hebrew faith, but because the woman was attractive. He is prepared to annul this marriage, which has basically ruined him, in order to obtain his Aryan status so that he can work on his novels. [He feels] bitter and depressed at having to write dialogue anonymously for films. . . .

Recently he remembered that he knew Count [Galeazzo] Ciano, to whom he has turned for help with his problem. . . . "He received me like a friend, he said he would do everything possible to straighten it out, and [told me] to return to work, saying, 'You're the only one in Italy who knows how to write.' "

Pitigrilli was never rehired by OVRA. And the last entries in his personal dossier in the state archives are a couple of pitiful letters to Mussolini in which he begged for Aryan status.

Rome, March 25 XX [1942]

Duce,

I understand that my little personal troubles are irrelevant to the great historical drama of the moment. But since you, with a word, can resolve my situation. . . . I ask you to consider it: you will see at first sight that my request for recognition of belonging to the Aryan race is legitimate, since I have all prerequisites stipulated by the law.

Remove me, Duce, from this unjust, degrading and paradoxical situation, in which I am forced to work in secret, to suffer the pettiness of rivals and to continue boring you with my tedious tale.

In March of the next year, with fascism only months from collapse, Pitigrilli approached Mussolini again, this time sending him a photograph of the ruins of his house in Turin, which had been hit in a bombardment.

Duce,

This was my house. I have lost everything: furniture, art objects, books, letters, notes. I no longer have a photograph of my father, of my dog or of the women who have embittered my life for years or sweetened it for an hour.

You know I am not an immoral writer. You liked my *Experimento di Pott* [Pott's Experiment].

You know I am not a Jew, even if some bureaucratic formality maintains this unfounded error.

I can't work in the movies or in journalism. The Ministry of Public Culture prevents me, with ferocious surveillance, from making five lire.

Your Excellency is inflexible in punishing the guilty but is equally rigid in restoring justice. Your genius encompasses the universe, but your heart bends down to small misfortunes. For this you are exalted and loved. Let me have an interview of a few minutes. When you look me in the eyes, you will see I am not unworthy of your gaze.

In the middle of 1943, Pitigrilli and Avvocatessa Furlan had a child, Pier Maria. They were in Turin on July 25, 1943, when Mussolini and his fascist regime were removed from power by King Vittorio Emanuele III. Shifting with the prevailing winds, Pitigrilli is said to have participated very visibly in one of the city's jubilant celebrations of the fall of fascism. Six weeks later, when the Germans occupied Italy, Pitigrilli knew enough of the world to flee quickly to Switzerland. Since his new wife and child, as Catholics, could travel openly without fear of arrest, he went separately, through an underground railroad organized and financed by the Olivetti family of Ivrea. Thus Pitigrilli's life was saved by one of the families he had spied on for the fascists several years before.

* * *

Anna Foa and Davide Jona and their two small daughters had very little with which to start their new life in America. There were strict laws against taking money out of Italy, but people were allowed to take household goods with them. The Jonas set sail from Genoa with furniture they hoped to sell in the United States, and with four diamonds belonging to Davide's mother that Anna had sewn into her dress. A wealthy Jewish friend gave them a painting to sell in New York, a portrait of Martin Luther attributed to Lucas Cranach.

The Jonas entered a rough struggle for survival in Depression America. For several months Davide was unable to find work of any kind. Neither he nor Anna spoke English. The entire family was crammed into one room of an apartment they shared with another Italian refugee family. Anna worked feverishly at home making gloves, scarves and lingerie for boutiques and department stores. In her account of their initial years in New York, the children seem to have been laid low with one illness after another. Finally Davide landed a job sorting metal in a junkyard in New Jersey, but it paid so badly that little was left over after the commute. For a time he worked in a chicken farm in Pennsylvania set up to help Jewish refugees. Eating chicken morning, noon and night, the job left Davide with a permanent dislike of poultry. Anna went about New York hawking the furniture they had brought, but her English was so uncertain that she never knew if she was getting a good price or not.

Since it was illegal to export works of art, the family never mentioned the Cranach painting of Luther directly, referring to it as "Zio Martino"—Uncle Martin. They discussed the progress of the sale in a kind of code, using terms of health and sickness to indicate the success or lack thereof in finding an interested buyer—"Uncle Martin isn't well today," "Uncle Martin is feeling better," and so on. In the end, an antique dealer paid Anna a few hundred dollars for the picture; she and Davide had hoped it would fetch tens of thousands.

For stretches of time Anna had to maintain the family on her own, as Davide traveled in search of work. He enrolled in a course in structural engineering at MIT while hunting for jobs in Boston. As difficult as this period was, it was also an important and exhilarating time for Anna, in which she discovered her own considerable powers. In many ways the catastrophic events that befell the Foas—from the arrest of Sion Segre at Ponte Tresa in 1934 to the racial persecutions in 1938 and the decision to emigrate—had a progressively liberating effect on her. The struggle for survival in the United States and the separation from her family in Italy brought out a resilience and competence that were not required or encouraged in the society in which she was raised. It is not easy to recognize the timid, conventional woman Anna claims to have been during the 1930s in the strong-willed, independent-minded woman she became. Perhaps in reaction to her upbringing, Anna developed into a person of fiercely held, passionate convictions, warm and generous with her friends, unforgiving toward her enemies.

Her husband, in his memoirs, admitted amazement at Anna's tenacity and resourcefulness: "How courageous and spirited she was in her quest for work, how steady in the defense of our family. To tell the truth, when I got married, I could not even have imagined that I had acquired such a companion . . . hidden under the crust of conventional gentility and propriety characteristic of . . . the Jewish upper middle class."

In Italy, Anna had been stifled by social custom and convention. She recalls, with severe self-reproach, that she had often walked away from her daughter Eva when the child cried in public, pretending not to know her in order to avoid embarrassment.

The Jona family's fortunes turned when Davide landed a job as an engineer in Boston. They settled in Cambridge, and there Anna came into her own. She helped prepare an hourlong Italian-language radio broadcast and translated wire-service dispatches, and during the war was eventually called on to produce and direct the program, since all the men had been drafted into the army.

Away from the society in which she grew up, Anna learned to act on her feelings and beliefs rather than blindly follow convention. "We learned many American customs," she wrote in her memoirs. "We learned that one never airs the bedsheets out of the windows, and one throws out everything which is not of immediate use. . . . I learned to shop once or twice a week, while in Italy I shopped twice a day. I learned to call by their first name people I barely knew, while in Italy I used to call people Mr. and Mrs. although I knew them for years and years. I learned also to choose my friends according to my opinions and ideas, and not according to what was good to have as friends."

* * *

Anna saw little of Beppe, who shortly after his arrival had left New York for a job in a factory in New Castle, Delaware, owned by an Italian businessman. "I know the reason he hired me was that I was Jewish. Old Mr. Belanca, G. M. Belanca, was not Jewish, he was Sicilian, but he felt the horror of what was happening in Europe. He was very intelligent and very good. He hired not only me, but also Leone Ginzburg's brother, Nicola, and a third Jew, named Pozniak, a Yugoslav who had lived in Italy for a long time. But many of the other employees were southern Italians who were extremely profascist, which was very unpleasant." Beppe, like Anna, was surprised at the amount of open anti-Semitism in the United States at the time. "When I began to understand English I heard people making anti-Semitic cracks. They called New York 'Jew York' and Roosevelt 'Jewsevelt.' In Italy you would never hear things like that. There was much more anti-Semitism here than in Italy."

Beppe was offered a teaching position at the University of Minnesota in 1941. "The students were marvelous, even though my English was terrible," he says. "And nothing changed after Italy and America went to war."

Not long after moving to Minnesota Beppe shocked his family with a sudden announcement. " 'I'm thinking of getting married,' he told Anna," Vittorio says. " 'I have three choices. One is very beautiful. One is very intelligent. And one is very nice.' My sister was scandalized that Beppe could think this way. But they are so different. My brother always maintains a certain critical distance from things, including himself. My sister throws herself completely into whatever she does. He has irony and self-irony. She is full of passion and enormously generous with people. Beppe has a kind of reserve and a dry wit that seem very English to me. When I saw him after the war I asked him, 'So which one of the three did you marry?' 'The nice one,' he said.

"My parents were very worried about the fact that Beppe might marry a non-Jew. He wrote them a letter that is a perfect example of his detached, offhand manner. He said he was moving to Seattle to build airplanes, and talked of various other things, and at the end of the letter he added a P.S.: 'By the way, I have gotten married. My wife's name is Lucy. She is twenty-three, and her eyes are the shapes of almonds.' And that was it. My parents were beside themselves over this letter. 'A woman named Lucy. Who can she be?' they said. There was still a residue of the old terror of mixed marriages, although the racial campaign did a lot to cure them of that. I wrote back to them from prison, very angry. 'How can you carry on this way? I'm full of joy for my brother. I know Beppe and I'm sure if he's decided to marry someone she's a wonderful person. That letter is just his way of doing things. He never talks about his life, and when he does, he does it in just this deadpan way to tease you.' "

* * *

For Vittorio, the war years were the hardest he spent in prison. Immediately after Italy entered the war, he felt the effects of the racial laws that had transformed the world outside the prison. "I was the only Jew in Regina Coeli, and I think they were uncertain what to do with me. I was left alone in a cell for two terrible months when France fell, one month at Regina Coeli and then a month at Civitavecchia. I protested in order to have some company."

At Civitavecchia he was finally reunited with other antifascists. Prison food, which had been poor but adequate before, now became extremely scarce. Sometimes Vittorio felt weak from hunger. And the news that reached his cell was uniformly disheartening. "The outside world was an uninterrupted series of defeats," Vittorio says. "Fascism had grabbed up piece by piece almost all of Europe. We tried very hard to maintain a kind of double commitment: to see things as they were, with cold-eyed realism, and at the same time to keep our hopes up. My letters to my parents were always full of questions about what was happening: What is happening to the Jews of Hungary? What is happening in America? What is happening in Palestine?"

In the course of the defeats, some of Vittorio's friends were themselves killed. While rallying Italian antifascist forces against Franco, Carlo

Rosselli, head of Giustizia e Libertà, was assassinated along with his brother, Nello, on orders from Rome. Renzo Giua, a friend of Vittorio's and son of his prisonmate Michele Giua, was killed fighting in Spain.

Although he kept up regular correspondence with his parents, at a certain point during the war Vittorio asked them to stop visiting him. "These prison visits were incredibly difficult. Imagine, you have an hour after not having seen each other for two months, with a guard there listening and a microphone recording you. We were breathless with all the things to say and no time to say them. I told my parents it was just too painful for me."

With the fall of fascism, on July 25, 1943, Vittorio and his companions expected to be released immediately. But Italy was in a strange state of limbo; the new government, headed by Marshal Pietro Badoglio, was still nominally fighting side by side with Nazi Germany. In reality, as virtually everyone knew, the Italians were secretly negotiating an armistice with the Allies in order to withdraw from the war. In this uncertain period, the government didn't know quite what to do with its antifascist prisoners, so it did nothing. In protest, Vittorio and his prisonmates went on a hunger strike, until they were finally released on August 23.

Vittorio and the others were met at the prison gates by a group of antifascists, who took them to have sandwiches and wine. As they celebrated their release, they were treated to a sobering spectacle. "We saw a huge motorized German division, the Hermann Göring division, heading south. The soldiers were all very young—the Germans were at the bottom of the barrel—but it was a very powerful division. So this moment of liberation was accompanied by an impressive show of German military might. That tended to make us very realistic. It was clear that the exit from the war was going to be extremely difficult."

Vittorio headed north by train to Turin; he had directions on how to reach his parents, who were at a villa outside Turin that belonged to a cousin who had left for America. The first person he saw was his maternal grandmother, Emilia, sitting in the garden reading a book. She greeted him as if she had last seen him only the day before. " 'Ah, you've arrived,' she said. And then I saw my mother, who said in the same way, 'Ah, you're here. We've been expecting you.' Without a tear. My mother even wanted to play a joke on my father and surprise him, and I said absolutely not. I could hear hammering. My father loved to fix things up around the house, and the sound of his hammering was enormously comforting and familiar. I felt this great, pleasant sense of continuity; while the whole world was falling apart, here everything went on as before. Then my father, hearing voices, came over and saw me. He broke down and wept."

The end of the summer of 1943 was a strange time of violently conflicting emotions. The weather was lovely, the family was staying in a beautiful villa in the country, fascism had fallen, and Vittorio was free for the first time in eight years. But amid the jubilant celebrations over the imminent end of the war, Vittorio and other antifascists prepared for what they suspected would be the last and hardest part of the struggle. Almost immediately after his return his old friends Leone Ginzburg and Norberto Bobbio and other antifascists came to see him. They were all struggling with what to do in the event of German occupation.

Although Vittorio wanted to take up his political activities, he first had to recover from profound mental and physical exhaustion. "Ginzburg took me to Milan for a political meeting. I could barely understand what they were talking about." A distant cousin, Anna Maria Levi (sister of the writer Primo Levi), recalls that in the first days after his release Vittorio was so conditioned by prison life that he couldn't eat at a table and would take his plate or bowl and hold it on his knees. "There were a number of strange things I suffered from," he remembers. "I wasn't able to grasp the idea that I could go into a store and buy things. I thought people were supposed to bring them to me. If my shoes were too tight and hurt, it quite literally didn't enter my head that I could just go and buy a new pair."

In the last days of August, he had a visit from a young woman, Lisetta Giua. Although he barely knew her, he felt as if they had a special bond. Her father, Michele, had been with him in prison the past eight years and her brother, Renzo, had also been a member of Giustizia e Libertà. In prison in 1937, Vittorio had had a terrible dream in which Lisetta appeared to him, weeping. To his astonishment, he learned that he had had the dream on the day Renzo had been killed fighting in Spain. Vittorio remembered having met Lisetta only once before, when he had gone to meet Renzo, who was then living in exile in France; she was a pretty girl of about twelve then. Fixed in his mind was the image of her slowly pouring him a glass of water during lunch; and over the long years in prison this small, thoughtful gesture had acquired a certain symbolic importance for him.

Now Lisetta was a woman of twenty. And in the fall of 1943—with their world seemingly gone to hell under the German occupation—she and Vittorio decided to start a life together. Under the circumstances marriage was impossible, but the war had swept away many of the old conventions. Vittorio's parents, who had complained vociferously when Beppe had married a non-Jew, uttered not a word of protest.

Lisetta soon became pregnant with their first child. "It's strange, but as in all periods of war and death, there is an enormous desire to bring forth life," Vittorio says. "We both felt it. The day we decided to live together I remember telling Lisetta: 'I want to have six children!' "

* * *

With the arrival of the Germans on September 8, Vittorio headed for the mountains north of Turin, near the Swiss border, and joined the ranks of the Partito d'Azione (Action Party), the partisan group formed from the remnants of Giustizia e Libertà. Vittorio and Lisetta began an exciting but dangerous life in the Resistance. First they were in the mountain valley north of Turin; when Lisetta advanced in her pregnancy, they moved to Milan, where he worked as one of the group's political leaders. One day, when Lisetta was about six months pregnant, she was captured by fascist soldiers. "She had gone to see a friend, who was also pregnant, and they were arrested along with her friend's husband," Vittorio says. "I missed being arrested by the skin of my teeth. When she didn't come home or call, I fled."

Lisetta was arrested by a semi-independent Italian fascist band headed by the infamous Pietro Koch. The Koch band often outstripped the Gestapo for acts of extreme cruelty and gratuitous violence, including torture, murder of civilians and the hunting down of Jews. Their base of operations was a villa in Milan that came to be known as Villa Triste (Sad Villa) because of the tragic end many people met there. With the band was a pair of famous Italian actors, Luisa Ferida and Osvaldo Valenti—the Fred Astaire and Ginger Rogers of torture, who lent a macabre, surreal quality to Villa Triste that has made it a symbol of the decadent twilight of fascism.

One day Koch decided to release two prisoners temporarily, in order to negotiate a deal with the partisans. "They had been badly beaten and were in terrible shape," Vittorio says. "Koch had told them that if they didn't return that evening, all the other prisoners would be shot. And one of the men had left his wife there. Koch proposed releasing the prisoners if we agreed to suspend all military actions in Milan. Obviously, this was unacceptable to us. One of the worst moral dilemmas I faced during the war was to have to tell these two men that we were refusing the offer and that they had to go back. Most of Koch's prisoners wound up in German camps like Mauthausen and never returned. For me, the dilemma was even worse because Lisetta was a prisoner at the time. Fortunately, I didn't have to make the decision alone; the whole leadership of our group was in agreement. We couldn't make a deal with a person like Koch.

"Even the Germans were horrified by the Koch band," Vittorio recalls. "And the archbishop of Milan, Ildefonso Schuster, prevailed on the Nazis to inspect Villa Triste. And so, strangely, the first touch of humanity Lisetta saw there was in the form of an official of the Wehrmacht. Because the Germans didn't like Koch, they had the women transferred to an ordinary prison. With Lisetta was a well-known woman gynecologist who explained to her how to fake labor pains." Luckily, one of the chief doctors at the prison was working secretly for the Resistance. "He told Lisetta, 'The Germans have told us not to allow any more people into the hospital, but the partisan committee has told me you are to go to the hospital, and you shall go.' The doctor then telephoned me and said in a kind of code, 'Your wife's operation will be this afternoon.' We sent a partisan squad to the hospital, and they disarmed the guards and took away Lisetta and her friend, who ran off in their nightgowns, waving as they left."

Lisetta joined Vittorio in Turin, traveling by train disguised as a Red Cross nurse. Because she had no idea about the uniform, she wore the cap backward; no one noticed. "This whole episode shook me, very deeply," Vittorio says. "And I never fully recovered the same sense of security. We missed being arrested in Turin by a hair's breadth. The police came to search the apartment where we were staying. I was out, but Lisetta realized what was happening, and hid. She was excellent. She stayed and waited for them to leave, without moving a muscle or making a sound. Then, when she heard them descend the stairs, she went up to the roof and found a way out of the building. We led a very lively, turbulent life, constantly on the move, but I felt much better doing things and moving around. In 1944 we went to live in a little apartment where we led a more quiet, bourgeois life. That's where the baby, Anna, was born."

* * *

Immediately after the German occupation in September, Lelia and Ettore Foa were still living in the villa outside Turin. Like most Italian Jews, they did not consider themselves in immediate danger. They did not flee, even when a platoon of German soldiers arrived at the door and announced they were requisitioning part of the villa as a dormitory. The Germans, not realizing they were Jews, allowed the couple to remain there, and keep their bedroom and use the living room, dining room and kitchen. For several weeks the Foas and the German soldiers lived peacefully side by side in the house. The troops were headed by a very well-mannered, cultivated German officer who treated the Foas with great respect and insisted that his men do likewise. If the soldiers came in late they took off their shoes and tiptoed into bed in order not to wake the couple. The Foas would sit in the living room after dinner and discuss subjects of common interest with the officer. Although they never let on about being Jewish, they suspected that somehow he knew.

One day in November, they listened to a speech on the radio about the Jews. Now that the Germans had occupied the country, Mussolini had been freed from prison and placed in charge of a new fascist government. The Republic of Salò, as it was known (it was named after the small town in Lombardy where it had its headquarters), was little more than a puppet government taking orders from Hitler. If Mussolini had previously protected Jews in Italian territory from German demands for deportation, this radio speech indicated a clear change. The new government announced that all Jews were now considered enemy aliens and were to be rounded up and kept in concentration camps in Italy until the end of the war. The Foas told the Germans that they had to go to Turin for a doctor's appointment. Although winter was coming on and they could carry only a few belongings, they set off into the Piedmontese countryside, a pair of elderly fugitives.

They moved from house to house for several months. For a time they stayed with a former housekeeper, a Catholic woman, but as they ran out of acquaintances, they threw themselves on the generosity of strangers, mostly poor farmers and peasants. Hiding Jews was punishable by death during the Occupation, but the Foas found a surprising willingness to help. In the second winter of the Occupation, worn down by this life of wandering, the couple returned to Turin and rented a room in a private house that had been turned into a pension of sorts. They slept on two sofas in a parlor. The circumstances were hardly ideal: the house was full of people, some of them fascists, and the owner's pet hen had free run of the place and left its droppings everywhere. The Foas hid their identities with false documents Vittorio had obtained for them. But frequently Ettore forgot to use his wife's new, Christian name, Teresa, kept calling her Lelia, and then had to correct himself. It didn't take the owner of the house long to grasp their predicament, but she said nothing until the war was over.

In the last months of World War II, Lelia's mother, then in her eighties, fell ill. Lelia would sneak through the city to nurse her, and both of them were terrified that every sound might be the arrival of the Germans. After her mother died in March, Lelia was unable to attend the funeral; SS soldiers followed the hearse hoping to catch relatives—anyone who might appear to be paying his respects to the dead.

German forces in Italy surrendered in April 1945, and the following month Anna received a letter from her mother. Written as if in a single stroke, punctuated mostly by dashes, it seems the prolonged gasp of someone finally coming up for air.

May 21, 1945

My Darling, the joy of these weeks has been completed by receiving your dear, dear letters, Anna, Davide and children! They have lifted our hearts from the devastating toll of these years of misfortune. We are alive! My dear, beloved grandchild, thank our Lord, who has heard your prayers. I have too many things to tell you, Anna, whom I have thought of so often, that I hardly know where to begin. And there is a great need to forget: one feels an enormous desire to live, to breathe (with four lungs, if one had them!), to move about freely, without suspicion or terror, to enjoy this life that has been oppressed for so many years . . . and a great need also to forgive—although this last thought has generated much protest from friends . . . So be it: I need to feel at peace—And what consolation I find in your letters and in the epistolary rediscovery of my granddaughters. Has my Beppe had a new daughter? Vittorio's little daughter is fine, and so dear! . . . Vittorio lives like a gypsy and, thank God, is well—after eighteen months of dangerous and tumultuous living; of struggle, work, dangers—crowned by many satisfactions despite many difficulties and unknowns. We don't see him very often—but he is so good and sweet—even handsome—in his disorderly way—I could write volumes about his and Lisetta's adventures: I'll tell you about them a bit at a time . . . We felt a terrible pain for the death of dear Angelo, as do all who know him! How many are missing, unable to enjoy the day of resurrection! On December 10 my poor unhappy brother Fausto breathed his last, reduced to a skeleton—racked by pains, consumed by hypochondria and maniacal cures! My poor wretched mother had her heart worn out by it and by the deepening of the winter cold virtually without heating—she took to her bed on the first of January—and died on March 27—also reduced to mere skin and bones—but she was totally lucid in her final weeks—thinking of all of you—with unforgettable words for you and me. My poor mother! I would stay with her every afternoon—with both of us terrified—that with every noise—the German SS had arrived—they had already come to look for her—and Fausto—at the moment of her burial—I had to follow her coffin from a distance—because not even that was safe. Another month and she would have seen the moment of liberation and had the prospect of seeing you again—A month later Aunt Adelina followed her to the grave—right during the days of jubilation—after finally being reunited with her children—whom she hadn't seen for months! I saw her again only in her coffin. . . . Here the [Jewish] Community is trying with great difficulty to rebuild . . . but so many capable young people have been lost to emigration, death or deportation—the Temple was completely destroyed in the fire of November 28, 1942—along with schools, offices, archives—its treasures, like the sacred Torah scrolls (from the seventeenth century and of inestimable value), buried by [Rabbi] Disegni—all lost or stolen—What little escaped the fire (doorways and lamps etc.) stolen—The hospital was also destroyed—In the temple we lost the three prayer shawls including that beautiful one in which both your father and Davide were married . . . As for Elena and Ida—still no certain news: they were buried by a bombardment during the autumn of 1943; unfortunately this date coincides with the date of a massive deportation of Jews from Rome—this supposition leaves their aunt in Rome a small vain, glimmer of hope that they may return: but in what condition? Also the Bassanis, Anna Maria's parents, were deported along with many other people we know from Turin, and unfortunately the descriptions we have heard so far about the camps do not leave us with much doubt about their long, painful end! We certainly have to consider ourselves very lucky, my dear children! I know how you must have worried—And now it is all over . . . knock on wood—after so many escapes and peregrinations—We found much help and assistance: we missed only one thing in the most critical moments: a little bottle of poison to swallow at the arrival of the SS—the lack of which caused me real terror—Let's not think of it anymore! I will think instead about my lovely granddaughters.

A Family of the Ghetto

THE DI VEROLIS OF

ROME

PRECEDING PAGE–Di Verolis gathered in front of the Rome synagogue for a family wedding before World War II. Later Giacomo Di Veroli's daughter Silvia placed dots on the photograph on the faces of those who were deported during the war.

LEFT–Giacomo Di Veroli (1885–1944), the second oldest of the four Di Veroli brothers. CENTER–Angela Funaro Di Veroli (born Rome, 1881; died Auschwitz, 1944), Giacomo's wife. RIGHT–Giacomo and Angela's daughters, Silvia (*left*) and Giuditta (*right*), with a friend in Rome before the German occupation.

Michele (born Rome, 1919; died Auschwitz, 1944), son of Giacomo and Angela, and brother of Silvia and Giuditta.

LEFT–Umberto Di Veroli (Monsieur Macaroni) and his wife, Elena Frascati, circa 1915, when they were twenty-eight and twenty-six, respectively. RIGHT–Michele, son of Umberto and Elena, before the war. At the time a bicycle was a rare luxury for a child of the ghetto.

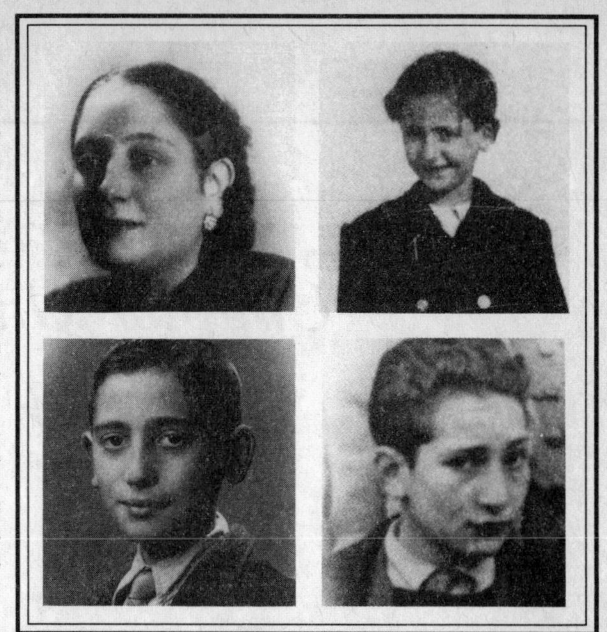

TOP LEFT–Silvia (born 1909), Enrico and Grazia Di Veroli's eldest daughter. She was arrested with her husband and their three children on October 16, 1943, and deported two days later. TOP RIGHT–Rina Calò, daughter of Silvia Di Veroli and Romolo Calò. She was seven when she and her family were deported. BOTTOM LEFT–Marco Calò, Rina's brother. He was ten when he and his family were deported. BOTTOM RIGHT–Michele, son of Attilio and Costanza Di Veroli, circa 1941. On March 24, 1944, at age fifteen, he was the youngest of the 335 victims of the Ardeatine Caves massacre near Rome.

TOP LEFT–Michele Di Veroli, son of Umberto, with Attilio's daughter, Silvia shortly after the war. Because she had lost her father and brother, her cousin accompanied her to the altar for her wedding at the Rome synagogue. TOP CENTER–Monsieur Macaroni leading his niece Ita to the altar. FAR RIGHT–A Di Veroli wedding in the Rome synagogue. At the altar are Vilma, fifth of Umberto and Elena's eleven children, and her husband, Aldo Di Consiglio. To the right of the altar, in the white prayer shawl, is her father. BOTTOM LEFT–Di Verolis gathered for a family wedding just after the war. In the back row, in front of the left-hand column, is Enrico and Grazia's son Michele. Just below him and to the right is his sister Olga; to the right and above her is their brother, Gianni. In the front row, holding a baby, is their sister Fernanda; to the left and above her, in the fur, is another sister, Flora. The older man in the hat, to the left of the right-hand column, is Umberto Di Veroli. The bride, holding flowers in the middle, is Elia, the eighth of Umberto and Elena's eleven children.

Chapter One

At the end of Via del Portico d'Ottavia, a busy street of shops and houses, stand the ruins of the splendid public arcade the Roman emperor Augustus built for his sister, Octavia, in 23 B.C. The magnificent marble columns—some still standing, others lying neglected on the ground—are not as old as the Jewish community of Rome, the oldest in the Western world.

Although the buildings that line the street are mostly from the Middle Ages and Renaissance, they incorporate portions of an old Roman wall. Latin inscriptions and ancient decorative fragments are embedded in the building façades of the block where Umberto Di Veroli had his clothing store (still run by his eldest son), and the white marble faces of a Roman couple, part of an ancient sarcophagus, stare out from the surface of the wall.

The first known link between the Portico d'Ottavia and the Jews is ancient, and highly significant. In A.D. 70 it was the site of a victory pageant the emperor Vespasian held for his son Titus's conquest of Israel and the destruction of Jerusalem. Titus arrived in Rome dragging hundreds of Jewish slaves behind his chariot and carrying the rich spoils of the Temple of Solomon, including several silver trumpets and a golden menorah. The scene was recorded for posterity on the triumphal arch built for Titus in the Roman Forum. Because of its painful associations, the Jews of Rome traditionally refused to walk under the Arch of Titus.

The procession was also described by the Roman Jewish historian Josephus Flavius:

> At the break of dawn Vespasian and Titus issued forth, crowned with laurel and clad in the traditional purple robes, and proceeded to the Octavian walks. . . . A tribunal had been erected in front of the porticos with chairs of ivory placed for them upon it; to these they mounted and took their seats. Instantly acclamations rose from the troops . . . and, having donned their triumphal robes and sacrificed to the gods whose statues stood beside the gate, they sent the pageant on its way driving off through the theaters in order to give the crowds an easier view.

It is unclear how long the Jews of Rome have lived in the Portico d'Ottavia neighborhood. But it was already a predominantly Jewish area in the mid–sixteenth century, when Pope Paul IV made it the site of the Jewish ghetto. Situated in a dank, low-lying part of the city on the banks of the Tiber, the ghetto has been, historically, a place of frequent flooding and intermittent outbreaks of plague. Although its external walls were torn down before emancipation in 1870, the interior of the ghetto remains as it has been for centuries: a cramped, humid labyrinth of narrow, twisting alleys that seem dark even at midday.

Because the popes were always reluctant to expand the territory of the ghetto, in a short time it became one of the most overcrowded parts of the city: initially the home of 2,000 Jews, by the late seventeenth century the ghetto crammed nearly 7,000 souls into its seven and a half acres. The families of the ghetto were generally poor and numerous, often living six or seven people to a room. Because of severe overcrowding much of the life went on out of doors: the women sitting on stools, mending clothes and talking; the children playing at their feet; the men pushing their carts and hawking goods in a high nasal tone intended to rise above the general din. The noise of the ghetto was such that the expression *fare un ghetto* (literally "to make a ghetto") became a colloquial way to refer to making a commotion.

Although most Jewish communities in other cities melted with astonishing rapidity into the growing Italian middle class after emancipation, life in the Rome ghetto went on much as before—crowded, bustling and desperately poor. Rome too had its educated, middle-class Jews, who, as they prospered, moved out of the area into newer and more elegant sections of the city. But the majority of the city's Jews remained rooted in or near the old ghetto and continued to scratch out a living as itinerant peddlers, rag pickers, salesmen, tailors and shopkeepers. In 1938, when the fascist government took a survey of the city's 12,000 Jews, it found that more than half of them lived either within the confines of the ghetto or just across the Tiber in the working-class section of Trastevere. While most Jews in northern Italy were cosmopolitan, highly assimilated and far from religious Orthodoxy, the Jews of the Rome ghetto were barely literate, deeply religious and powerfully linked to the life and traditions of their community.

That the Roman Jews should be the poorest, the least educated and the most insular in Italy is a direct result of their long and tragic history. In many northern communities, the ghetto was relatively short-lived; in much of Piedmont, for example, it was not instituted until around 1700 and it lasted only about 150 years. In Rome the ghetto was started in 1555 and ended with the defeat of Vatican forces in 1870 and the incorporation of the Papal States into a newly unified Italy. While many other Italian city-states had applied ghetto laws with a certain spirit of pragmatism and leniency, in Rome they had been enforced with a punitive ferocity that actually increased over time.

Before 1555 the Jewish community of Rome had been as free and flourishing as any that existed in Europe. While some occupations were closed off to Roman Jews, they were active as bankers, doctors and silk merchants; they were able to own real estate and live where they chose. The city's Jewish doctors were world-famous during the Middle Ages and Renaissance and often acted as attending physicians to the popes. During the sixteenth century, however, the Catholic Church responded to the Protestant Reformation by lashing out furiously against religious heterodoxy in all forms. Although the popes were powerless to halt the spread of Lutheranism in northern Europe, within their own territory they could force the Jews to knuckle under to the most rigid conformity.

The scope of the ghetto system in Rome went far beyond insulating Christian society from the pernicious influence of the Jews. As the wayward people whose conversion to Christianity would crown the Last Judgment, the Jews occupied an important place within Catholic theology. The ghetto was to be a theater for the great drama of Christian redemption. In Rome, Jews were forced to attend weekly sermons meant to convert them to the true faith. Indeed, it was a form of popular entertainment for the rabble to jeer and throw objects as they watched Jews file off to church. Jews were forced to participate in public footraces at Carnival time; the practice ended only when the Jewish community agreed to pay a tribute of 300 scudi to the pope, to be delivered each year in the capitol above the Roman Forum. With the crowning of each new pope, elders of the community were compelled to pay tribute, kissing the pontiff's foot before the symbol of their humiliation, the Arch of Titus. "In the seventeenth century," notes historian Cecil Roth, "Pope Urban VIII added a new and hardly credible humiliation to the ceremonial; henceforth, at such audiences, the Jews might no longer kiss the foot of the Pope, but only the spot where it had stood."

Lest the populace think that the wages of sin were high, the Jews of Rome were systematically stripped of all their resources. Forced to sell whatever real estate they owned, saddled with all manner of taxes and tributes, they were also gradually excluded from all but the most humble and degrading occupations. Banned from practicing medicine, banned from lending money, banned even from selling new clothing, they were eventually permitted no other livelihood than repairing and selling secondhand clothes. Per capita income in the Rome community, which had been a fairly florid 250 scudi a year before the institution of the ghetto, had shrunk to a paltry 15 scudi a year by the year 1800. In the last decades of the ghetto, a third of Rome's Jews depended almost entirely on the charity of their fellow Jews.

* * *

The arrival of the Di Veroli family in Rome predates the ghetto by a generation or two. The name first appears in the city records in 1539 with the mention of a certain Jehuda Ben Moshè Ben Avraham de Veroli. "The last name comes from the period 1520–1538 and is probably the result of the family's trading contacts with the important commercial center of Veroli," according to historian Michael Tagliacozzo, a descendant of Jehuda's. Before coming to Rome, they were traders along the coast of North Africa who moved to Sicily sometime after 1200. After the order of expulsion of the Jews from Sicily in 1492, the Di Veroli ancestors headed north, perhaps stopping in the town of Veroli, near Rome, along the way.

"From their arrival in Rome all the Di Verolis were itinerant peddlers of textiles in the province around Rome," says Tagliacozzo. "Within the family there were no individuals of special note, only . . . simple . . . people strongly attached to their Jewish roots and dedicated to commerce."

Four and a half centuries after their arrival, the condition of the Di Verolis had changed little. All thirty-three members of the immediate family—the four Di Veroli brothers, their wives and children—lived on or near Via del Portico d'Ottavia. All of them were peddlers or shopkeepers like their ancestors from North Africa and Sicily.

For the members of the Di Veroli family who came of age between the two world wars, the ghetto was still a vivid memory. Their grandmother Sara was fourteen at the time of emancipation and lived well into the fascist era; she died in 1929 at age seventy-three.

"She told us things that sound absurd, like how you had to wear a yellow badge on your clothes to show you were Jewish, or how you'd get thrown into the river if you went into the Monte Testaccio area," recalls Michele Di Veroli, born in 1922, one of her twenty-five grandchildren. Because each of Sara's four grown sons (two others died in childhood) named a son after their father, he is one of four Michele Di Verolis born between 1919 and 1929. To avoid confusion, friends and relatives always call him Michele di Enrico (Enrico's son) to distinguish him from his cousins Michele di Giacomo, Michele di Umberto and Michele di Attilio. "Leaving the ghetto was always an adventure—you never knew if you were going to come back safe and sound. The papal cavalry had the nice habit of hitting you with their sword cases just for fun. It was enough to wear a priest's cassock to have the power of life or death over the Jews."

Most of Michele and Sara Di Veroli's grandchildren are serious, hardworking people not given to idle chatter or to dwelling on the past. They tend to be phlegmatic, diffident toward outsiders, frequently offering cautious, monosyllabic answers to questions. Michele di Enrico, by contrast, is loquacious and highly mercurial. One minute he is impulsively friendly, the next he lashes out in anger. One minute he adopts a cavalier pose of jocularity, the next he dissolves into tears. Like all of his relatives, he speaks Roman street dialect with a rough, gravelly accent, but his speech is sprinkled with unexpected references to psychology, literature and history; occasional English, French or Russian words; and sudden flights of flowery rhetoric. Similarly, he seems more interested in family history than do most of his siblings and cousins.

Many stories revolve around one of his grandmother's brothers, known simply as "Spaccamontagna"—Mountainbreaker—because of his prodigious strength. Like the legendary golem of the Prague ghetto, Spaccamontagna assumes the role of defender of the defenseless Jews.

"One day some papal soldiers at the bridge in front of the synagogue got drunk and started swearing at the Jews there and insulting them. Spaccamontagna disguised himself as a woman and went up to one of the soldiers and threw him in the river. A bunch of cowards is what they were! Another time, Spaccamontagna stole the sword from a papal guard—who must have gotten into a lot of trouble for losing his sword. These were the episodes she told us about before they broke down the walls of the ghetto."

* * *

With emancipation the papal guards disappeared, but the Di Verolis continued a hand-to-mouth existence as peddlers and seamstresses. Michele Di Veroli died young in 1892, leaving his wife Sara destitute with four small sons. "My father was eight years old, and out of necessity he began going around the city selling needles, thread, thimbles and buttons," says Michele di Enrico. As soon as they were able, Enrico's three younger brothers joined him. Their mother, like most women of the ghetto, was an expert seamstress and repaired everything from men's clothing to billiard table surfaces.

"My grandmother always wanted my father to study, because in that period there was terrible illiteracy—it reached almost ninety percent—especially in the ghetto," Michele Di Enrico explains. "It wasn't total illiteracy: people might know how to read a little Hebrew but not Italian. So my father would spend the days with his box of needles, thread and buttons, and in the evening he went to school."

When he was thirteen, Enrico Di Veroli went off by himself to Milan to sell postcards on the street. Three years later he launched his first major entrepreneurial venture. Having heard about the world exposition being organized in Paris to usher in the twentieth century, he produced a series of postcards to sell to tourists flocking there for the opening. "He had some photographs of Paris printed onto postcards here in Rome, on a machine that you worked with a pedal," says Michele of his father. "Then he went to Paris and found a place outside the exhibition hall on the night of December 31. A French guy came up and asked him, 'Are you Jewish?' He said yes, and the guy explained to him what to do, where to place himself, what price to sell at, and so on. In two days he sold everything he had, and he came back to Rome with a handkerchief full of gold coins." Michele starts to cry.

Soon all four Di Veroli brothers were traveling across Europe selling whatever merchandise they could get their hands on: Italian-made objects abroad and foreign goods at home. "My father spoke several languages with a certain ability—Yiddish, English, Spanish, German and French," Michele di Enrico says. "He went to Switzerland to sell binoculars to tourists there to see the Alps, to Spain to sell souvenirs of the Alhambra in Granada.

"Once he went as far as Astrakhan on the Trans-Siberian Express. He was in Vienna selling binoculars, and someone said to him: 'You know where you could sell a lot of binoculars? In Astrakhan, in Russia, where all the game hunters go.' At that time going to Astrakhan was like traveling to the moon. So he took the Trans-Siberian Express across Russia to the mouth of the Volga, and arrived at the Astrakhan station late at night with these heavy cases of binoculars. The Russians showed little regard for etiquette. He asked them where he could get a room for the night, and these Russians, who didn't give a damn, pointed in the distance and said, 'Go where those lights are.'

"So my father set out on foot toward the lights, but it was nighttime, the snow was three feet high and it was cold as hell, and the lights didn't seem to get any closer. And suddenly—honest truth, my father's words, and I believe him—just as he said to himself, 'I came all this way, just to kick the bucket!' he heard the bells of a troika. He took out a match and lit his newspaper to stop the sleigh. When it stopped, the man on it addressed him in Russian. My father didn't know a word of Russian so he asked the man if he spoke French. No. German? No. English? Italian? Yiddish? Nothing. My father, in despair, started to recite a prayer in Hebrew, Shema Yisrael. And then he heard the man finish the prayer in Hebrew.

"This guy brought my father to his house and the following day took him into the center of Astrakhan. He showed him a good place to sell, underneath a bridge out of the wind and snow, where merchants gathered to buy furs from the hunters. The hunters had never seen binoculars as good as my father's. What a bunch of simpletons! So he sold the binoculars for furs and then traded the furs for gold dust and came home with his pockets full of gold dust.

"He went all over Europe, especially Spain; in Granada he carved his initials on the flank of one of the lions at the entrance of the Alhambra. He had a great respect for German culture; he talked about Vienna and Cologne. During the war he said, 'After this war is over let's go to Cologne.' He traveled often with Uncle Umberto. They had a rather adventurous life, two good-looking young men. . . ." Michele winks, implying a life of romantic adventure and sexual conquest. Enrico Di Veroli has the reputation of having been the most handsome of the four brothers. "Uncle Enrico was tall and good-looking," says one of his nieces. "His sons don't resemble him at all." Michele and his brother, Gianni, are short and squat.

Enrico and Umberto were the most enterprising and successful of the four brothers; the latter was a veritable wizard of commerce. He came up with the ingenious idea of manufacturing little replicas of the Eiffel Tower in Naples, where they could be made cheaply, and selling them as souvenirs in Paris. He invented the name "Monsieur Macaroni" to give himself the air of an Italian entrepreneur in Paris. ("Monsieur" because "Mussiù" in the Roman dialect of the ghetto, while "Macaroni" was pronounced with a French accent.) Monsieur Macaroni became a legend of the ghetto, and even today his oldest son, Michele, is identified widely as "the son of Monsieur Macaroni."

" 'Monsieur Macaroni' practically became our family name," this Michele explains. "In the Jewish quarter in Rome, if you say 'Michele Di Veroli,' people will ask 'Which one?' because there are so many. But if you say 'Michele di Monsieur Macaroni,' they know right away who you mean. It was the tradition in Jewish families here to use the same names over and over, the names of grandparents." Not only did all four Di Veroli brothers each name a son after their father, they also each named one of their daughters Silvia, after another ancestor.

Michele, son of Umberto, could not be more different from his cousin Michele, son of Enrico. Where the latter is voluble and emotionally volatile, Michele di Monsieur Macaroni is laconic and phlegmatic in the extreme; while Michele di Enrico is a repository of family stories and facts, the other Michele does not pay much attention to them. He does not know, for example, when his brothers and sisters were born or when his parents were married. But this lack of interest in the past is not a lack of family feeling. Much of Michele di Umberto's life has been spent keeping faith with his ancestors. He keeps his father's old store on Via del Portico d'Ottavia, he lives in his parents' apartment above it, and he goes to the synagogue every morning. "He's rich as Croesus," says a friend. "He could live anywhere and do anything, but he prefers to stay right there, in the same store and the same apartment. He's like a king in his realm." Large, immobile, content with his lot, like a buddha, he holds court in his store in the ghetto, receiving clients, friends and relatives. He never married, but he insists on celebrating all the important Jewish holidays in his father's house. "Even if I have to be alone, I would rather celebrate by myself with tears in my eyes than go somewhere else."

Between one foreign voyage and another, the four sons of Michele and Sara Di Veroli started families in Rome. Enrico was the first to marry, in 1907, and Attilio, the youngest, married in 1922. Monsieur Macaroni, despite his constant travels, managed to father eleven children. As they started families and began to make a little money, their lives centered increasingly around Rome and their old neighborhood.

All the brothers except Attilio, who had lost the use of one eye in a childhood accident, fought in World War I—an experience that helped bring them into the mainstream of Italian life. Monsieur Macaroni became something of a hero for preventing King Vittorio Emanuele III from falling into the water when they were riding together on a river barge.

After the war both Enrico and Umberto, who had saved enough money during nearly two decades of crossing Europe, opened shops of their own in Rome. Enrico first had a store on Via delle Botteghe Oscure and later moved it to Via in Publicolis near Via del Portico d'Ottavia. As he had during his travels, Enrico sold all kinds of merchandise—printed postcards, antiques, Japanese objects, porcelain, toys, souvenirs of Rome.

Umberto opened a store on Via del Portico d'Ottavia, facing the synagogue. He specialized in work clothes of all varieties, everything from underwear to overalls, for everyone from farmers to firemen. With the habits he had learned on the road, he would try his hand at anything. "Uncle Umberto would buy everything," recalls his niece Rosa Di Veroli, who was born in 1923. "If he saw something he liked he would buy it and resell it—it didn't matter if it was shoes or ice cream. He made a nice fortune."

Rosa's own father, Attilio, never achieved the same degree of financial security, remaining a pushcart peddler. "My father had a cart from which he sold combs, all kinds of combs, big, small, at all different prices," says Rosa. He used to sell along Via Arenula, a main thoroughfare on the edge of the ghetto, not far from where Enrico had his store. Rosa's mother stayed at home, but one day a week she worked at the open-air market in Campo dei Fiori.

Giacomo, who had suffered a lung injury during the war and was less commercially minded than his brothers, took a job as a salesclerk. "Before the racial campaign my father worked many years for a big store that sold fabrics on Via Nazionale," says Giuditta Di Veroli. "He wasn't much for business; Enrico and Umberto had more money than we did. But my father, because he had to sell to rich people, was more refined."

"Uncle Giacomo was an extremely sensitive person," recalls Michele di Umberto. "The smallest thing would touch him emotionally. He was so good he would give you the shirt off his back. He was quite unusual that way."

From an early age the children of the new generation were introduced to the world of hard work and tough bargaining. "We were taught the instinct of commerce from the beginning," says Rosa Di Veroli. "From the time I was eight or nine, I worked in my uncle Umberto's store. I would go to school in the morning and then in the afternoon I would sew buttons on clothing. My mother said, 'At least this way she'll be good.' It was what they called a 'pass the lira' job: on Saturday my aunt would give me two lire for my work to keep me happy, I would give it to my mother, and she would give it back to my aunt. I caught on to the system and told my mother: 'But I really did sew on the buttons, so you have to keep the money.' Already I had learned the instinct of work and profit.' "

* * *

In this tight-knit world, revolving around family, work and synagogue, politics counted little.

"They were simple people," says Michele di Umberto of his parents' generation. "Everyone looked after his own family. No one looked more than a few inches in front of his own face." The ghetto—now that they were no longer forced to live there—was a warm and familiar cocoon, offering protection from the harsh and often unpredictable world outside.

"It was like a small village within a big city," says Giuditta, daughter of Giacomo. "It was very close. Cousins married cousins. Everyone was related to everyone else."

"There wasn't a single locked door in the whole neighborhood," says Rosa. "If someone was sick, you had only to shout out, 'Who has some broth?' And if people had some ready, they'd bring it. On Friday night each family would light the candles for the Sabbath and say the blessings.

"Relations with the outside world were good. There were Christians living in the neighborhood with us, and they were just like us. They even spoke like us—most of them had picked up the Roman Jewish dialect. There was a woman next door who said she was Christian—but no one believed her because she was always using Jewish expressions and oaths: 'I swear on the sepherim that I go to mass,' she used to say, 'I swear on a scroll of the Torah.' "

The advent of fascism in 1922 did little to change the lives of these peddlers and small shopkeepers of the ghetto, and it did not halt the slow ascent of the Di Verolis from poverty to a state of modest well-being. Largely indifferent to the abstract world of politics, the Jews of the ghetto were generally grateful to the new Italy (liberal or fascist) for allowing them to work, live and worship as they pleased. Only two generations away from the ghetto, many felt it was better to steer clear of politics, to give the authorities no reason to consider revoking their newfound freedoms.

Giacomo, Umberto and Attilio joined the Fascist Party, mainly because it was easier to work and raise a family with a party card than without one. "When there were parades on fascist holidays, my father would always put himself at the end and then at the first opportunity slip away down an alley and come home," says Giuditta. "He didn't care about politics."

The family was patriotic but not in an ideological way: Umberto was named after a king of Italy, and his wife, Elena, after a queen. In telling the story of how his father supposedly saved the king from drowning,

Michele di Umberto speaks of "His Majesty King Vittorio Emanuele III," reflecting in all likelihood his father's reverence for the monarch. During the fascist regime, Umberto enjoyed a position of honor by virtue of his having been decorated during World War I and having fathered eleven children. Convinced that a large population was a key to Italy's becoming a great power, Mussolini lavished special honors and financial rewards on big families. "We were what was then called 'a good Italian family,' " says Michele.

But Umberto was more interested in the affairs of Via del Portico d'Ottavia than those of Piazza Venezia, a few blocks away, where Mussolini had his office. Umberto's shop facing the synagogue was a gathering place for members of the community to take their problems. "They called him *lo sceriffo* [the sheriff], because when there were things to decide, disputes to settle, wrongs to repair, they went to Monsieur Macaroni. He tried to make peace," Michele says.

Only the oldest brother, Enrico, appears to have taken a strong interest in politics. "My father was the only one of the four brothers who refused to get a Fascist Party card," says his son Michele. "Having known freedom and traveled overseas, he was antifascist by nature." Enrico was a Freemason, and fiercely antimonarchical. When Mussolini came to power he outlawed Freemasonry, so that to be a member in secret was to be, by definition, antifascist. But Enrico was first and foremost a family man, with a wife, six children and a business to take care of. He kept his political opinions within the privacy of his own home.

Religion played a larger role than politics in the lives of the Di Verolis. All the brothers went faithfully to synagogue and observed the Sabbath. On Saturdays, Attilio not only put away his pushcart but also gave up his powerful addiction to cigarettes out of respect for Mosaic law. "Already by Friday he would begin trembling in anticipation of not being able to smoke on Saturday," recalls Michele di Umberto.

The sting of the racial campaign of 1938 at first was felt less acutely by the Jews within the ghetto than those outside. For middle-class professional Jews the laws were nothing short of catastrophic. Not only were they swept from their positions and deprived of their livelihood; they were stunned when suddenly the new Italy, in which they had believed so passionately, turned against them.

The shopkeepers, salesclerks and itinerant peddlers of the ghetto were largely ignored by the laws. Their psychological position was different too: not having risen so high on the social and economic ladder, they had a shorter distance to fall. They had cleaved closely to their community and religion, and had a rich collective life to fall back on. Through darker centuries, the solidarity of the ghetto had served as a buffer against persecution. Memories of past persecutions and humiliations were so vivid among the poorer Roman Jews that the fascist racial campaign may have seemed simply the latest in an endless series of storms to be weathered rather than a radical departure in history.

Unlike the thousands of professional Jews who left Italy after 1938, the Jews of the ghetto had neither the need nor the means to emigrate. "We were not bad off," says Michele di Umberto. "I had a bicycle, and in that period it was quite a privilege for a child to have a bicycle. There were people who needed one to go to work and didn't have it. When I came home from school I had a meal to eat. Dessert was a luxury; a banana was something you would eat only at a wedding. Sometimes we would hear ourselves insulted, called 'dirty Jews'; we couldn't go to the seaside. But we young people didn't pay much attention to it. Kids were not smart and well informed the way they are today."

The fascists "made a campaign against us that, luckily, not many people believed in, maybe twenty-five percent," says Olga, one of Enrico's four daughters. "There were a lot of people who didn't know what Jews were." Initially at least, the members of her generation didn't take the racial laws that seriously. "We young people didn't feel that sense of liberty you should feel when you're twenty, but we took the whole thing pretty lightly. The older people understood which way things were going."

Among the members of the older generation, the attitude was one of stoic resignation. "My father used to always say, 'Don't worry, it will pass for us, but for them it will never end,' " Gianni, Olga's younger brother, remembers. "He knew how to overcome these obstacles. The Jews gave their children courage."

But if the ghetto was spared the worst of the racial campaign of 1938, it was struck directly by a second wave of anti-Semitism that followed Italy's entry into war at the flank of Nazi Germany in June 1940. For reasons that are hard to justify as national security, the government now deprived Jewish street peddlers of their vending licenses, and thus took the bread from the tables of many ghetto families. The decree was as devastating to the ghetto as the ban on professional positions had been for the middle-class segment of the Jewish population. But unlike Jewish professionals, street peddlers had no financial cushion to fall back on. From one day to the next, they no longer had money to buy food. "Many of these families fell into the most squalid misery," says Michele di Umberto. "Most Jews in the neighborhood depended on vending licenses from the police department." Two of the Di Veroli brothers,

Giacomo and Attilio, were wiped out by this peculiarly spiteful decree.

Giacomo had taken up peddling again in 1938, when the fabric store he worked in was closed down as a result of the racial laws. Just as he had some forty years earlier, Giacomo took to the streets with needles, thread, pins, ribbons, buttons and thimbles—the instruments of the tailor's trade, on which the Jews of ghetto had depended for centuries. Then, in 1940, even this precarious livelihood was taken away.

"Because he was recognized as a wounded war veteran, my father was able to get the state to give him a job at TETI, the telephone company," says Giuditta, Giacomo's daughter. "He had to work an exhausting shift, from eleven at night until seven in the morning, for a low wage, but at least it was a job."

Attilio, who had to give up his comb pushcart, was not so lucky. He had not fought in World War I and had no patriotic qualifications he could parlay into a job. He took to wandering around Rome, going from church to church looking for odd jobs and discarded objects. He made repairs around churches for a few coins and took away any cast-off furniture, then fixed it and sold it.

To make up for their father's misfortune, Attilio's two oldest daughters were employed. Silvia worked as a seamstress in her uncle Umberto's shop, while Rosa found a job with a distant cousin, Renato Di Veroli, who had a clothing store in Vatican City.

In 1938 the teenaged Rosa had lost her job because of the racial campaign. "I worked in the most beautiful shop in Via del Tritone, and they let me go, saying, 'We're sorry, but you are Jewish.' I started working a bit for a woman with a stand on the street." Then her father found a permanent job for her with Renato. " 'I entrust my daughter to you,' he told me, because I was married," Renato recalls. "He was incredibly jealous," Rosa says. Because Attilio had no regular job, he would walk Rosa to work each morning. "And when I left in the evening, he would be waiting out on the sidewalk—I was so embarrassed!"

Enrico and Umberto, meanwhile, were able to keep their businesses and continue life more or less as before. Umberto, as a former member of the Fascist Party and a decorated war veteran, applied for and was granted discriminated status. Although the law had no specific provisions for shopkeepers, Umberto's son Michele insists that being *discriminati* was of great help to his family during this period.

From a business standpoint, Monsieur Macaroni's biggest problem was not the racial laws but the wartime rationing to which all Italian merchants were subject. "We worked on a point system; you could, for example, sell pants only to someone who had a card that authorized him to buy pants," Michele di Umberto says. "If someone didn't have the card, you couldn't sell anything to him. You couldn't order new merchandise unless you had already sold the old, so trade was limited. Because of his discriminated status my father was able to help a lot of people who couldn't buy merchandise. He bought goods that they would sell privately. But he couldn't stick his neck out too much. There were people who couldn't work because they were sent off to do forced labor, dig ditches. And they were lucky compared with those who were sent from their families into exile in the South. There was real poverty and hunger in the neighborhood then."

Michele di Enrico recalls the plight of unemployed peddlers during the war. "These poor bastards would come to my father, who had a store. And he would say, 'They are hardworking and enterprising men, we have to help them.' He told them, 'Take the merchandise you need, and you can pay me back later.' And so these people would go and try to sell things on the black market to make a little money. Some of them paid us back, others no."

In August 1942, with Italy already losing the war, there was an outbreak of resentment in some quarters against young Jews who sat at home while other Italians were off getting killed. To lessen this resentment, the regime ordered able-bodied Jewish men to do manual labor for practically no money. In many cities the order was largely ignored by local authorities, but in Rome it was widely enforced.

"My brother-in-law had to work the earth each day," says Olga, Enrico's daughter. "He had to go on foot, he wasn't allowed to take the bus. My cousin worked under Ponte Garibaldi by the river. They did useless work, hauling dirt from one place to another and then hauling it back. They had to work even on Yom Kippur, our most important holiday. All the men were hungry because they had to fast, and they were made to work even longer that day."

Olga's brother Gianni, only seventeen at the time, watched the work crews along the Tiber near the ghetto. "They made all these Jews—many of whom were doctors, lawyers and engineers—dig sand in order to degrade them, but I think it had the opposite effect. I remember—these things remain burned in the memory, you can't forget them—people walking on the bridges across the river, looking down at these men working. A lot of people made comments that fascism should be ashamed of itself, and watched with disgust. And these Jews forgot that they were professionals, and did their labor with great pride and dignity in order to show that we Jews have great strength of spirit."

Although the anti-Semitic propaganda fell on deaf ears among most Italians, small bands of fascists who wanted to show off, vent their violent impulses or simply steal would come into the ghetto looking for trouble. "Several times fascists would come along Via del Portico d'Ottavia and Via Arenula, punching people, drawing blood," Olga says. "I saw it myself once, from the windows of our house in Via [Santa Maria] del Pianto. There was nothing I could do."

"When they put on a uniform, Italians suddenly feel important, and whoever joined the Fascist Party never lacked a uniform," says Gianni. "The worst was the fascist militia, full of people who had been rejected by the army. When they marched, you'd see maybe one who was four-foot-ten, another who weighed three hundred pounds, a third who had one leg too short, another who didn't have all his marbles. They'd be limping along, singing 'Giovinezza.' They didn't have an inferiority complex, they *were* inferior—even mentally. Overseas it seemed like a comic opera, but here it was taken seriously. When these types put on a uniform they became dangerous, because they were stupid. To feel like they were doing something, they'd denounce some baker for selling an extra unrationed piece of bread, and maybe smash up his store. They would come into the ghetto, enter a store and take some piece of merchandise without paying for it. There was nothing you could do about it. These things were not very frequent, but they were demoralizing."

Olga remembers a client of her father's store trying to get her into trouble for complaining about spiraling prices: "I was talking with my mother in the store, and I mentioned that the price of stockings had gone up by fifty cents. A fascist client threatened to denounce me for spreading antifascist propaganda. I didn't think this customer could do anything, so I said—I was hotheaded then—'What do you want from me? I didn't kill anybody.' My mother was terrified they were going to come for me, and she kept me at home for fifteen days. So that's how we had to live, keeping our mouths shut."

But the Di Verolis were especially worried about their sons of military age, who were the most frequent objects of anti-Jewish feeling. "We were afraid to let the boys leave the house," says Olga. "We were afraid the police would stop them and ask why they weren't in uniform. So our parents would have ten or fifteen kids sitting around the house and would try to find a way to keep them amused."

"Youth for us was not what youth is today," her brother Gianni says. "The kids of my generation grew up in a hurry because they understood there were dangers everywhere. It was enough to look at a child of five and he would know automatically to shut his mouth. This was the climate we lived in for six years, and to a child, six years is a long time. I remember I was kicked off a public bus by a fascist who said, 'No Jews on the tram.' And even now, I remember it with a bitter taste in my mouth."

Gianni spent long days at home playing cards with his cousins. Although his family had dutifully brought their radio to the police to have it adjusted, he and his companions enjoyed the forbidden pleasure of listening to American records—which were banned in Italy. "The music of Glenn Miller seemed to us a music of freedom."

With a contemptuous wave of the hand, Michele di Enrico insists that his brother and sister exaggerate. "Gianni was the baby of the family, a little bit of a mama's boy, so he was timid. I didn't give a crap about the laws, and in a way neither did my father. He didn't give any weight to what people thought or said. There was a lot of discussion about what to do about this, what to do about that. We lived day to day, hour to hour, it wasn't like these English who take their tea at five!

"But let's not talk like victims," he says with a sudden flash of anger. "It's a mistaken psychology: Freud said that in his writings. Victims are only cowards toward themselves. We lived: I worked in the store, I went around town, I went to the movies. Some people knew I was Jewish but didn't say anything. We got by."

The weight of racial persecution was lifted suddenly when the news spread through Rome during the night of July 25, 1943, that the fascist Grand Council had voted Mussolini out of power. "We began to hear a big commotion on the street, and my father leaned out of the window and asked people on the street what was happening," Olga Di Veroli remembers. Fascism had fallen. "My father couldn't believe it."

"People came out of their houses, everybody was celebrating in the streets," recalls Giacomo's daughter Silvia, born in 1914.

"After that day, there were no more fascists; suddenly everyone was an antifascist," says Olga. "People spoke freely. But we were also more worried. My father said, 'I'm not sure it's a good thing. Who knows what will happen?' Having fought in World War I, he knew the Germans were treacherous."

But for most people the first forty-five days after the fall of fascism was a time of euphoria and, as it turned out, illusion. "We thought the war would finish at any moment," Gianni recalls. "The Allies had landed in Sicily and were roaring through Calabria. Maybe we were too optimistic. Unfortunately, things went differently."

September 8 appeared to bring the news that everyone was waiting for. The new prime minister, Marshal Pietro Badoglio, made a speech on the radio announcing that he had signed an armistice with the Allies. At the same time, American and British forces were launching a second major landing on the Italian peninsula.

Rome appeared safe for the moment. Six divisions of the Italian army were in or around the city. On the night of the eighth, the capital was deserted and peaceful. Families celebrated quietly in their homes.

The following morning, the thumping of artillery shells could be heard on the edge of town. Some said that it was the British fleet at Ostia, at the mouth of the Tiber. Others speculated that the Germans were blowing up their ammunition dumps before retreating north. Most preferred not to consider the possibility that it was the German army advancing toward the city. Rumors swirled wildly—the Americans had landed at Anzio, not even forty miles from Rome; Mussolini was dead; Badoglio had left to meet General Eisenhower; the king was in Sardinia.

There was widespread expectation that the city would be liberated at any hour. And yet there was a disturbing void at the center of power. No one seemed to know what was going on. Telephones weren't answered in government offices; the official news agency had no news. Badoglio and Vittorio Emanuele III had fled Rome hastily, and no one knew where they were.

Although the Badoglio government had signed the armistice secretly five days earlier, it had been caught off guard by its sudden announcement on September 8. Badoglio knew that the announcement and a second major Allied landing in Italy were planned for early September, but he did not know when or where the landing would take place. Fearful that some Italian fascist official might warn the Germans, the Allies were hesitant to reveal details of their invasion. The Italians begged that it be put off until September 12 at the earliest. On the night of September 6, General Maxwell Taylor sneaked into Rome to outline a bold plan to take the city immediately: he offered to land an entire division of American paratroopers if the Italian army agreed to hold the city's airports for four days. Although Italian forces in the area outnumbered the Germans, the chief Italian military commander, General Giacomo Carboni, balked at the commitment. Alarmed by the Italians' total lack of preparation and the speed with which the Germans were sending reinforcements into the country, the Allies refused to delay beyond September 8. They called off the paratrooper plan for Rome and limited themselves to a landing at Salerno, south of Naples. With even a small amount of courage and preparation, the Italian government might have prevented the German occupation of Rome entirely.

Despite the predictability of a German invasion of Italy, Badoglio had made few real arrangements for it. In his haste to leave Rome, he had left his generals no precise instructions. In a nationwide radio broadcast Badoglio stated vaguely that "Italian troops should respond to any eventual attacks from whatever direction they might come." Many Italian soldiers, as well as their commanders, were uncertain as to whose side they were on.

During the initial hours of battle outside Rome, most Italian troops in the field fought the Germans resolutely, but they received almost no support or guidance from the high command in the city. Astonishingly, with the fate of Italy hanging in the balance, General Carboni disappeared. (After several hours of frantic searching, he was discovered in civilian clothes, apparently about to flee Rome.) In his absence, during crucial hours of battle, the other commanders did not know what to tell the generals in the field. Finally, unnerved by Carboni's seeming desertion, they ordered a retreat—over the objections of many generals doing the fighting. Some units ignored the order, continued fighting, held their ground and inflicted heavy losses on the Germans. Others, however, fell back toward the city.

In the ghetto all the shops were closed. People were locked in their houses with the shutters drawn. Radios were on, but no news of the conflict was broadcast. People listened, instead, to the thumping of artillery coming closer. Occasionally telephones rang with the latest rumors from the street. The Germans were at Ponte Milvio, the Germans were in Piazza San Giovanni in La Feramo. There were reports of Italian soldiers running panicked through the streets of Rome, shedding their uniforms for civilian clothes.

At nightfall the city was still in Italian hands. On the morning of September 10, the radio announced that the Italian and German armies had agreed to a ceasefire. All fighting would stop so that the German army might move to points farther north. Suddenly it appeared that the day had been won. But by afternoon, street battles between German and Italian troops in the middle of the city put the lie to the report.

"Tutti a San Paolo! Tutti a San Paolo!" Rosa Di Veroli remembers the call from the streets of the ghetto for the men to assemble at the Gate of San Paolo, through which the Germans were entering the city. "Everybody was running all over the place. Some people went into hiding. Others went to fight. I remember people running from the ghetto carrying the Italian flag. A lot of people were killed."

One of those who left the ghetto for Porta San Paolo was Gianni Di Veroli. "They were handing out rifles with maybe three bullets," he says. When asked about his own role that day, he is somewhat coy. "I don't like to talk about myself, but I received the Bronze Medal at the age of nineteen. I am happy to have played a modest part fighting in the ranks of the partisan forces.

"Maybe if the Italian army had been led by officers with a little courage and spirit, the Germans would have left Rome entirely. But after three days of fighting the Italian forces surrendered to the Germans. At that point began the really black days."

Chapter Two

On the evening of September 10, it was announced that Rome was to remain an "open city." German troops, according to the radio broadcast, would occupy only three strategic points in the city: the German embassy, the main radio station and the German telephone plant. The idea of an "open city" sounded promising and seemed in keeping with Rome's special status as national capital, cradle of Latin civilization and center of the Catholic world. Perhaps, as everyone hoped, the Eternal City would be spared the atrocities the Germans were said to have perpetrated elsewhere in Europe.

The next day, however, German troops appeared to be everywhere. Tanks, armored cars and machine guns were positioned at practically every corner. The day's radio broadcast announced that it was forbidden for Italians to carry arms: any Italian with a gun would be sent to jail, and the penalty for firing on a German soldier was death. Otherwise the armistice was in force.

By evening, new orders from German Field Marshal Albert Kesselring were posted on walls throughout the city, declaring, among other things:

> The Italian territory under my command is declared to be war territory. It is subject to German martial law.

> Any crime committed in this territory against German armed forces will be punished according to German martial law. . . .
>
> Until further orders private correspondence is suspended. All telephone conversations should be as brief as possible, and they will be strictly supervised.
>
> The curfew will continue to be 9:30 P.M.

This, then, was the "open city."

All of Rome "seemed to divide into two halves, those who went into hiding and those who were helping them," Gianni Di Veroli recalls. "The population was very generous in giving civilian clothes to the Italian soldiers who were fleeing. People shut themselves up in their apartments. We understood that the situation was becoming more and more dangerous and dramatic. At home we tried to console each other and at the same time decide something."

Of the four Di Veroli brothers, only Umberto fled and went into hiding. "We left home almost immediately after the Germans arrived," says his son Michele. "My father listened often to Radio London. We didn't have a radio that could get London, but he had Catholic friends who lived in the country, at Ciampino, and he would go there and listen. London gave real news about the war and what was happening to the Jews. So he was better prepared than those who didn't listen. He stayed in Ciampino because he thought it would be liberated before Rome."

It was impossible for Umberto, his wife and their eleven children, some of whom by then had families of their own, to go into hiding together. "My father was afraid that as a big family we might be arrested all at once, so he gave a large sum of money to each of us children," says Michele. "Everyone was supposed to take his own road. My father gave me about fifteen or twenty thousand lire, which at that time was a fortune, like a couple hundred thousand dollars in your pocket now. You could get by on two or three lire a day back then." (Salaries in this period were often about 1,000 lire a month. So while not worth "a couple hundred thousand dollars," the 15,000 to 20,000 lire would have been a considerable amount: enough to support an entire family for more than a year.)

It was no accident that the first of the four brothers to go into hiding should be the one with the most money and the best information. People with more limited means forced themselves to be optimistic about staying in Rome. "We thought about fleeing, but quite frankly, we didn't have the money," says Attilio's daughter Rosa; her father had been jobless ever since the itinerant peddlers had lost their licenses. Likewise, Giacomo, living day to day with his job at the phone company, didn't have the money to rent rooms in a *pensione* or live for any extended period underground.

In the household of Enrico Di Veroli, who had a store and a little money, there was fierce debate about what to do. His older son, Michele, was in favor of fleeing to Switzerland. "A girl I knew then—I won't say exactly what the nature of our relationship was—worked in one of the embassies, and she said she could get me a passport. My mother said: 'But we have six kids. We can't all go. And the bones of our ancestors are here.' I said: 'I don't give a crap about the dead. Let's try to save the living!' That's my character."

But leaving home in the middle of the German occupation was not such an easy or safe proposition. The Germans had requisitioned all private automobiles and taxis and were monitoring the railways closely. They were already searching houses door to door for Italian soldiers who had refused to lay down their arms. "It was difficult to know where to go, so we remained at home," says Gianni, Michele's brother. "There were strict orders that people with guests living in their apartment had to inform the police."

The general climate of fear paralyzed the city, as the Italian journalist Paolo Monelli, who was in Rome at the time, described.

> It was forbidden to ride a bicycle, forbidden to walk along certain sidewalks, forbidden to cross certain streets, forbidden to stock up on food, forbidden to telegraph or telephone outside Rome, forbidden to enter or leave the city, forbidden to spend the night at friends' houses. It was dangerous to carry a package under your arm, to walk with a rapid gait, to have a beard grown too recently or to wear dark glasses. It was a mortal danger to hide a fugitive . . . or to listen to the [Allied] radio broadcasts from Bari or Palermo.

The shortage of food was becoming so severe that leaving home and livelihood seemed even more problematic. "The children in the neighborhood were crying because there was no milk for them," Gianni Di Veroli recalls. "This became the first priority. We would watch as our women went from one place to the next in search of food and returned home with their bags nearly empty and their heads down. And this got worse with each day."

The Allied forces had just landed in central Italy and most people expected them to reach Rome any day. Many Romans, particularly the Jews of the ghetto, had almost no real information about the course of the war, including the location of the Allied landing. Knowing almost nothing for certain, they were free to believe what they wanted.

"We kept hearing news: The Americans have landed here, the Americans have landed there, they have occupied this town, they have occupied that town," Gianni remembers. "They were all false rumors picked up who knows where. But they gave us a little hope, before we fell into hard reality. . . . We were afraid that sooner or later the Germans were going to make their presence felt. And some of us, the more pessimistic, managed to obtain false identity cards. We didn't trust the Germans because Radio London kept saying, Don't trust the Germans. I remember listening to the famous broadcasts of Colonel Stevenson and Fiorello La Guardia, who talked about what the Germans had done to the Jews in Yugoslavia and Czechoslovakia. But we still felt the Americans would arrive from one moment to the next."

Finally, also, there was the powerful, ineradicable belief among many that in Rome, the city where they had lived uninterrupted for two thousand years, the Jews would be safe and protected. "They were always hopeful," says Michele di Enrico of his relatives. "They used to say: 'But the pope . . . the Vatican . . . open city. Here they wouldn't dare touch anyone.' "

For a time such hopes seemed well founded. After the first days of terror—with shooting in the streets and looting in shops—the Germans restored order and normalcy to the city. On September 20, Field Marshal Kesselring paid a respectful visit to the pope. Three days later, Mussolini—who had been liberated by the Germans—announced that he would be forming a new fascist government, the Italian Social Republic. This too seemed a positive development to many Jews: perhaps Latin tolerance would continue to temper Teutonic hatred toward the Jews. After all, as long as Mussolini had been in power, the Germans had not dared harm a single Jew.

Little by little, a number of Jews who had gone into hiding on September 8 returned cautiously to their homes, reassured by the dead calm of the city. Often out of necessity, they went back to their jobs, reopened their shops and took their place in long food lines. It was not easy to continue imposing on Catholic friends who were having a hard enough time feeding themselves—let alone another family—when there did not appear to be any immediate danger.

In fact, the Germans seemed preoccupied with other, much more pressing problems: tracking down and disarming thousands of Italian soldiers, rounding up gangs of able-bodied men for work details. Surely the Germans were more worried about the possibility of another Allied landing than about the threat posed by a few thousand Jewish shopkeepers and street peddlers.

* * *

The uneasy calm in which the Di Verolis lived broke suddenly, early on September 27, when the phone rang at Enrico's house. "It was six in the morning and I answered the call," says Olga. "It was someone from the Jewish Community wanting to talk to my father. He went to the phone and then left home immediately, without saying a word. A couple of hours later he phoned my mother to tell her what had happened. 'The Germans want fifty kilos of gold [110 pounds], and if they don't get it they are going to take two hundred hostages.' I said, 'Fifty kilos of gold, where can we find that?' 'We'll see.' 'I'm coming too,' I told my father. He said, 'I won't tell you to come or not to come. You're old enough to decide for yourself, but you should know that it's a risk. The Germans might come at any moment and just shoot the whole lot of us.' I thought about my older sister, Silvia, with her three children, and said, 'We have to try to save as many as possible.' "

When Olga arrived at the offices of the Rome Jewish Community, inside the main synagogue, she learned the full story of the Germans' demand for gold. The previous evening, the head of the German SS in Rome, Major Herbert Kappler, had summoned the president of the Community, Ugo Foà, and the president of the Union of Italian Jewish Communities, Dante Almansi, to his office.

Kappler, according to an account written later by Foà, was a man "of medium build, blond, about forty years old, with a long scar across his cheek," who greeted his guests courteously and apologized for any inconvenience he may have caused them. But after a few minutes of polite, general conversation, Kappler's tone suddenly turned hard and menacing.

> "You and your fellow Jews are Italian citizens, but that matters little to me. We Germans consider you exclusively as Jews and therefore as our enemies. . . . And as such we must treat you. But it is not your lives or your children we will take, if you obey our requests. It is your gold we want, in order to get new arms for our country. Within thirty-six hours, you must turn over to me fifty kilos of gold. If not, we will take two hundred of your people and deport them to Germany or the Russian front."

Still living in the comparatively benign mental universe of the Italian racial laws, the two Jewish leaders naively asked whether this measure concerned only the Jews enrolled in the Jewish Community, or whether it applied also to people who were half Jewish or to Jews who had converted to Christianity. "I don't make any distinction between Jew and Jew," Kappler answered contemptuously. "Enrolled in the Community, baptized or mixed, all those who have Jewish blood are the same to me. They are all enemies."

When asked if it would be possible to give an equivalent amount of money instead of gold, Kappler dismissed the idea out of hand: "I wouldn't know what to do with your money. I can print as much of it as I need."

The idea of the gold ransom appears to have been Kappler's. The day before he called in the Jewish leaders, he had received a dispatch from the office of the chief of the SS, Heinrich Himmler:

> All Jews, regardless of nationality, age, sex and personal conditions must be transferred to Germany and liquidated. . . . The success of this undertaking will have to be ensured by a surprise action, and for that reason it is strictly necessary to suspend the application of any anti-Jewish measures of an individual nature likely to stir suspicion among the population of an imminent *Judenaktion*.

In his own defense after the war, Kappler insisted that the idea of extorting gold from the Jews of Rome was conceived as a means of preventing a full-scale deportation. By his own admission, Kappler was not moved by humanitarian considerations: as a career police official, he said, he considered mass deportations a waste of limited resources that might create fresh problems of popular resistance and disorder. By shipping fifty kilograms of gold back to Germany, Kappler said, he had hoped to show that stripping the Jews of their resources was preferable to killing them. Others have offered less charitable interpretations of his motives. Kappler knew that an earlier dispatch about deporting Jews from Rome had been leaked by a sympathetic German diplomat to sources in the Vatican; and some historians have suggested that he invented the gold ransom as a smokescreen to hide his real aim.

Whatever the case, if his intention had been to distract the Jews, rob them of the means to flee, and give them the illusion of being able to ward off the threat of deportation, Kappler could not have devised a better scheme.

After their encounter with Kappler, Foà and Almansi's first move was to appeal for help to the Italian government, which both men had served for most of their careers. Before the racial campaign, Foà had been a distinguished magistrate, while Almansi had been vice chief of police in Rome. After 1938 the two put their talents to work for the Jewish community, and their close ties in government had proved a valuable asset, softening some of the harsher aspects of the persecution and granting the Jews a greater margin of independence. Even in the darkest days of discrimination, Foà and Almansi had found their fascist interlocutors to be men of reason who bore no real ill will toward Jews. But when Foà called his friends in the Italian police on the evening of September 26, they demurred with apologies and kind words. "Evidently our Authorities," wrote Foà, with reverential capitalization, "could do nothing against the Teutonic power."

The next morning, after a brief debate, the leaders of the community decided they would do everything possible to meet Kappler's ultimatum.

The risks of disobeying the order seemed to outweigh by far those of obeying it. The 12,000 Jews in Rome were hardly prepared for mass flight or exodus. Many were too old, too sick or too poor to leave their homes and live in hiding for an indefinite period. The city was already crawling with German troops. Every building concierge was under strict orders to account for each person living there. German guards frequently went door to door looking for antifascists or fugitive Italian soldiers and routinely stopped suspicious characters on the street. Open defiance of the order might provoke the Germans to arrest many more than the two hundred they had threatened to deport, and would, in all likelihood, set off a citywide manhunt of ferocious intensity. Perhaps Major Kappler had meant exactly what he said: that the Germans wanted only their gold, not their lives. Certainly it was worth risking the gold, in the hope of preventing arrests and deportations.

The decision to pay was also consistent with the Jews' millennial experience as a small, threatened minority in the hands of a mighty, hostile power. This strange and barbaric demand for gold—something that seemed more likely to have sprung from the head of an Egyptian pharaoh than that of a twentieth-century bureaucrat—may have touched some deep, atavistic instinct among the Jews. Hundreds of times they had escaped attack or expulsion by paying tributes (often in gold) to ransom their people.

Defiance, by contrast, generally had led to unmitigated disaster. Some of the Jews of Rome owed their presence in Italy to one such failed rebellion: these were the descendants of the slaves Titus had dragged back from Jerusalem after smashing their revolt in A.D. 70 and thus wiping out Israel as a nation and condemning the Jews to nearly two thousand years of dispersion. Since then, countless rulers had risen and fallen, Rome had been invaded and sacked repeatedly, and the Jews of Rome had always kept their own tenuous foothold in the city through stoicism, flexibility and great self-control. They had been threatened and blackmailed by popes and princes and had always avoided disaster by at first accepting the most outrageous demands and then trying to reduce them through patient negotiation. Surely this time-honored strategy was preferable to some impulsive gesture that might bring about a second Masada.

"When I arrived in the Community offices, there were five or six members of the council discussing what to do," Olga Di Veroli recalls. "We had a list of names and began to telephone all the Jews to tell them we needed to collect these fifty kilos of gold. Some of the people we called wouldn't talk to us because they thought it might be just a trap."

In fact, during the first morning almost no one appeared. Many Jews were afraid that the SS might be lying in wait for them near the synagogue. After a few hours, during which only five kilograms were collected, panic set in. Two Jewish leaders, Adriano Ascarelli and Renzo Levi, rushed off to ask the Vatican for gold. Officials responded that the Vatican would lend the Jews whatever portion of the ransom they needed to meet the fifty-kilogram limit, to be paid back after the war. But when Ascarelli and Levi returned to the synagogue in the afternoon, they saw a miraculous sight: a throng of people outside the temple waiting to make contributions. It seemed that the whole of Rome—eager to express its disgust with the German occupation—had risen up in defense of the Jews.

Word of the ransom had spread quickly through the streets and brought Christians and Jews from all parts of the city to converge on the synagogue, carrying gold watches, earrings, pins, bracelets, cuff links, wedding rings, cigarette cases and coins. Those who had no gold brought money, and boys from the ghetto were soon running around with wads of cash and buying gold on the black market at two to four times the usual price.

With the sudden avalanche of contributions, the Jewish Community decided not to take the Vatican up on its offer of a loan; nonetheless, in the frenzied atmosphere around the synagogue, rumors swirled about a large gift of gold from the pope. With each telling the amount seemed to increase, and the excitement of the crowd and the air of impulsive generosity rose accordingly.

The collection took place in the council hall on the second floor of the synagogue. A jeweler, Angelo Anticoli, removed stones from the jewelry because the Germans wanted only pure gold, Olga Di Veroli recalls. She and other girls from the neighborhood sat around the U-shaped table taking donations and issuing receipts. The majority of the donors were the "little people" from the ghetto and Trastevere, who made contributions of less than an eighth of an ounce. But there were also large numbers of Christians, whose solidarity deeply moved the Jews. The Roman Jewish literary critic Giacomo Debenedetti described the trepidation of the Catholics entering the synagogue with their gifts:

> Cautiously, as if afraid of being refused, uncertain whether to offer gold to the rich Jews, some "Aryans" presented themselves. They entered the hall adjacent to the synagogue full of embarrassment, not knowing if they should take off their hats or keep their heads covered, according to Jewish custom. Almost humbly, they asked if they could—well, if it would be all right to . . . Unfortunately, they did not leave their names.

"I remember so many episodes," says Olga. "There was a Jew who brought four cigarette cases and four bracelets, each one a hundred grams of gold. He had four sons and he had given each of them a cigarette case, and a gold bracelet to each of his daughters-in-law. Then there was a lady with the blondest hair, slender, enchantingly beautiful—you could tell from her way of carrying herself that she was an aristocrat—who pulled out a handkerchief full of gold coins. 'Signora,' I said, 'what name do I put down?' 'Just write "Anonymous," ' she said. She went away without a receipt, so I told a couple of boys who were standing nearby, 'That woman just gave a lot of gold; follow her and see if you find out who she is.' But a big black limousine came and took her away. It didn't have any license plates. So we never found out who this woman was.

"Then there was the woman who used to sell candy to the children in front of the movie theater," Olga continues. "She removed her earrings and said, 'Take these.' I thought she wanted to sell them, so I asked the jeweler, 'How much should we give her?' The poor woman began crying and said, 'Look, Olga, the stones are fake. It's only a gram or two of gold, but it's all I have. My wedding ring I gave to the Fatherland on the Day of Faith. It's not much, but I want to give it.' I got up and embraced her. I felt terrible, because I had thought she wanted to sell them."

The day and a half spent collecting gold were hours of uninterrupted anxiety. "It was very dramatic," says Rosa Di Veroli. "All the women gave their wedding rings, and still it wasn't enough. Rich people giving their money. Telephone calls going back and forth, 'Help, help!' The line forming at the temple, the scales weighing every gram, everyone standing around watching and checking. People running around the piazza: 'How much more do we need?' 'How many kilos?' 'Are we there yet?' It was terrible."

On hearing about the Germans' extortion plan, Giacomo Di Veroli took his family into hiding. Nonetheless his wife, Angela, returned to the ghetto to make a contribution. The only gold she had left was half of her wedding ring. On the Day of Faith in 1935, when the married women of Italy were to give up their gold wedding rings for the Empire after the invasion of Ethiopia, she had shrewdly split hers in half, so that she could give some gold to the country and still keep some for herself. "My mother gave away her wedding ring twice, once for Ethiopia, once for the ransom of gold," says her daughter Giuditta.

While Enrico and Olga participated in the gathering of the gold, his son Michele—ever the family dissident—says he was unconvinced that the fifty kilos of gold would do any good.

"This gold business was a banal episode!" he says angrily. "That Almansi was a former police official who still believed in the good faith of the authorities. How can you believe in the good faith of a German officer? When the Nazis came to power, they said that treaties were meant to be torn up, that they weren't worth using as toilet paper! Nazi brutality was known all over the world. I said, 'It seems more like a warning. Let's get out of here and good night.' "

As he and his brother, Gianni, stood around the piazza watching the mayhem, they got into a conversation with some Italian antifascists who had come to the synagogue to show their solidarity. Michele favored forming a brigade of Jewish Resistance fighters who would join the remnants of the Italian army gathering in the hills outside Rome. But one of the partisan leaders advised against it. "He told us, 'Anytime anything happens, the Germans will blame it on you and will have your families here as hostages.' He had been with the army in Russia and had seen the Germans kill two or three hundred people an hour. He had seen it with his own eyes. But no one believed him."

By the time the synagogue was closed on the night of September 27, the Jewish community had collected forty-five kilograms of gold. Well before the noon deadline the following day, the Jews of Rome had, to their amazement, collected slightly more than fifty kilograms of gold, along with about 2 million lire in cash. (In the final hours, they were refusing cash donations and declining offers to buy gold.) Nonetheless, the Jewish leadership shrewdly decided to call the German embassy to ask for a few more hours. They were afraid that if it were known how successful they had been, the Germans might escalate their demands.

To avoid any dispute with the Germans, the Jews made sure that the gold was actually three hundred grams more than requested. Moreover, in carting it to the Germans, Foà and Almansi brought along an escort of Italian police as a guarantee against some last-minute trick. Their precautions proved well-founded, as Foà recounted in his diary.

> The gold was weighed by the German officials with a five-kilo sale. The weighings, in order to reach the fifty-kilo limit, would be ten. And ten they were. His Excellency Almansi on our part and a German official on the other took careful note of each weighing. Despite this, afterward the Germans, headed by a brutal and violent official, Captain Schultz (substituting for Major Kappler), claimed in an arrogant and threatening manner that five kilos of gold were missing, and insisted that the weighings had been nine and not ten. Schultz would not listen to the protests of the Jews who asked him to repeat the weighing. Only after prolonged discussion did he agree, and it turned out that the gold was above (by three hundred grams) rather than below the limit.

Adding insult to injury, Captain Schultz refused to give the Jewish leaders a receipt for the gold—something Foà noted with great indignation. This last small piece of bad faith might have put him on guard against treachery on a larger scale, but the former magistrate reacted as if he were living in a world in which receipts, rules and promises still counted for something. Foà and Almansi returned home as if an enormous weight had been lifted from their shoulders.

The threat had been averted, it seemed, and no one had been arrested. "Afterward we felt more secure," Rosa Di Veroli remembers.

But the next morning a cordon of SS men surrounded the synagogue, blocked all its exits and began to look for compromising documents. "And so," as Foà wrote later, "without any notification, and without showing any warrant or order from higher German Authorities . . . a group of German officials and soldiers, some of them experts in Hebrew, proceeded to search all the rooms of our office."

Even though he was writing at the end of the war, when the horrors of Auschwitz and Treblinka were fully known, Foà continued to express shock and outrage at the fact that the Germans would conduct a search without a warrant. Rational men of law and order, Foà and the other Jewish leaders seemed incapable of grasping the Nazis' murderous intentions.

Eventually the Germans filled a truck with documents and confiscated the 2 million lire in cash that had been collected along with the gold.

Despite this menacing development, there were fresh reasons for hope. On October 1, 1943, Allied troops marched into Naples in the wake of a popular uprising. Suddenly, with the liberating army less than two hundred miles from Rome, deliverance again appeared imminent.

That same day, however, a Gestapo officer expert in Semitic philology arrived at the Rome synagogue demanding to examine its incalculably valuable two-thousand-year-old collection of sacred texts and historic documents. A wonderful portrait of this emblematic figure appears in a memoir by Giacomo Debenedetti.

> A strange figure, all uniform, like the others . . . but while they begin to ransack the library of the rabbinical school, he, with cautious, meticulous hands like those of a lacemaker, touches, grazes and caresses manuscripts and rare editions, flips through membranous codices and palimpsests . . . written, for the most part, in remote alphabets. But at the opening of a volume, the eye of the official focuses and lights up and . . . in those aristocratic hands, the books, as if subject to an acute and subtle torture, spoke.

On October 13 the Germans rolled several railroad cars along streetcar tracks and parked them in front of the synagogue. They then spent several hours removing two thousand years of history of the Jews of Rome.

In the face of this outrage and the extortion weeks before, two of the four Di Veroli brothers and their families remained in the ghetto, along with most of their neighbors. They were alarmed, but they tried to console themselves with the fact that the Germans seemed more interested in the Jews' possessions—gold, documents, books—than in their persons. In fact, the Germans were busy rounding up other, non-Jewish Italians. On October 7, for instance, they arrested and disarmed much of the Rome police force. Two days later, they started picking up able-bodied Italian males and forcing them to participate in German work details. In Jewish as well as Gentile families, men kept off the streets and sometimes slept away from home. Women and children ventured out to do shopping and errands.

"On October 15, we worked normally," says Rosa Di Veroli. "We thought they wanted to take the men for work details, not for deportations."

"Everybody talked about the pope, about how in Rome the Germans would never do anything," says her cousin Silvia.

"The Jews here in Rome remained somewhat optimistic," Gianni Di Veroli says. "We didn't think they would persecute us to the point of eliminating us physically."

If the Jews of the ghetto had moments of uncertainty about whether to stay or to go, the continued presence of their leaders helped reassure them. Although religious services were canceled for Saturday, October 16, virtually all other community business continued as usual. Every morning Ugo Foà and his assistants arrived promptly at their offices in the synagogue. Foà and Dante Almansi tried hard not to alarm their flock. When the chief rabbi of Rome, Israel Zolli, convinced of an imminent German attack, fled and went into hiding, Foà let it be known that the rabbi was ill. The leaders have been heavily criticized for their stance, but they do not appear to have acted in self-interest. They continued to expose themselves to the same risks to which they subjected everyone else. Foà genuinely believed that by remaining calm the Jews would deprive the Germans of any pretext to attack them. As he wrote later, the Roman Jews

> felt the approach of terrible events, and yet because their own consciences were clear, supported by that high sense of civilization that comes from having grown up in our beautiful Italy, mother of morality and law that from eternal Rome has illuminated the whole world, they refused to believe that the thugs of Hitler would dare repeat the incredible barbarities they had committed in Poland, Germany, Holland and Belgium. Vain illusion!

Chapter Three

"It rained all night, and sometime after midnight there was the sound of gunshots," recalls Olga Di Veroli. She and the rest of Enrico's family were alarmed by the shooting, but it made them all the more inclined to remain snugly in their beds with their door bolted shut. When the gunfire died down, everyone fell, fully exhausted, back to sleep.

A few hours later, during the morning of October 16, they were awakened again, this time by the urgent ringing of the doorbell. "At about five a little girl who lived up on the fifth floor woke us," Olga says. "She rang the bell and said, 'Hurry, the Germans are coming!' My father looked out the window and saw armed soldiers and said: 'Let's get out of here!' "

Convinced that the Germans were coming to collect the men in the family for work details, Olga, her sister Flora and their mother wanted to remain behind. "But my two brothers [Michele and Gianni] said, 'No, we'll all go, maybe they want the women and children too.' My father said, 'We'll go to the store.' At that hour, no one would think to look in a store. My father went first and said, 'I'll give a signal. One whistle means the store is open, the second whistle means the coast is clear. Everybody go one at a time, walk slowly and calmly.' Mamma went first, then my brothers, then Flora, then me. I was in my nightgown, with a raincoat over it. It was still raining. As soon as I left the front door, I ran smack into this German soldier with a gun. He looked at me and I looked at him, and with his gun he made a sign as if to say, 'Run, escape.' I could hear my father—not seeing me come—whistling desperately. But I just stood there. I was afraid that if I went, the soldier would follow me and take our whole family. He repeated his signal, and then motioned that he would turn his back, and then, in fact, moved away about ten meters and motioned to me again to escape. And finally I ran off and joined my father and the others in the store. When I told my father what had happened, he asked me to describe the man's uniform, and he said to me: 'Olga, that wasn't a German soldier, it was surely an Austrian soldier.' " Stories of the "good Austrian soldier" were common among Italian Jews, many of whom simply refused to believe that a German soldier would save a Jew.

As soon as Enrico reached safety inside the store, he called his oldest daughter, thirty-four-year-old Silvia, who lived with her own family in Via del Portico d'Ottavia. But no one answered. Silvia, her husband, Romolo Calò, and their three children, aged ten, seven and three, had all been captured by the Germans.

Just a few blocks from Enrico, his youngest brother, Attilio, and his family were awakened by the sound of screaming.

"It began very early," says Rosa, Attilio's second daughter. "A woman named Elena—I bless her always—began to scream, 'Jews! Run! Run! The Germans!' She was one of the first to be rounded up. When we heard her, we ran to the window and looked out and saw them lining up Jews. We got dressed quickly, mother, father and five kids.

"When we were going down the stairs, we ran into a pregnant woman with a small child. My mother told her, 'Give me your little girl; in your state you may not be able to escape.' But the woman said: 'What are you talking about, "escape"? Are you kidding?' She was convinced the Germans wouldn't bother with women and children. A lot of people didn't believe it. We heard later that the Germans got that woman and all her family.

"Our building had two exits. So instead of going out into Via del Portico d'Ottavia, we went out the back near the Church of Sant'Angelo in Pescheria. Some good person told us, 'Escape this way because there's no one there.' And so we left the neighborhood and went toward San Paolo to the church in Via Filipine. Since my father used to go around collecting things from all the churches, he knew the priest there, Don Gregorini. He said to us, 'Come in, come in, we know everything.' We began telephoning all our friends and relatives, but no one was left at home."

* * *

On the morning of October 16, 1943, Giacomo Di Veroli and his family were safe in the apartment of his wife's sister in Trastevere, across the Tiber. "My aunt, Cesarina Solarino, had married a Sicilian," says Giuditta. Since she had a Catholic name, it was safer for the family to stay with her.

Umberto Di Veroli, Monsieur Macaroni, had already fled with his wife to the house of friends outside Rome. All but one of his eleven children had been able to flee. "We were scattered all over," says Michele, Umberto's oldest son. "My parents were with friends in Ciampino. My youngest brother, Enrico [who was ten at the time], was with a Catholic baby-sitter. Others of my brothers and sisters were with Catholic families, or in churches or convents." One sister, Esterina, thirty, did not follow her father's advice and was arrested at her home in Via del Portico d'Ottavia with her husband and two children (a seven-year-old and a nine-month-old).

* * *

The day's tally for the immediate families of the four Di Veroli brothers was: two daughters, two sons-in-law and five grandchildren. All in all, some forty-one Di Verolis were arrested in Rome that day.

There were dozens detained on the maternal sides as well. "My mother had a sister with thirteen children—all of them taken away," says Michele di Umberto. "A brother-in-law of my mother's was deported with his eleven children. One of them was pregnant and had her baby right there on the truck." None of the Di Veroli relatives arrested that day returned. But several Catholic eyewitnesses have left descriptions of the scene in the ghetto that morning.

> From a doorway in Via del Tempio several women with children are pushed brusquely toward the street. The children are crying. Everywhere you hear the heartbreaking cries and pleas of the victims while the thugs—some violent, some indifferent—perform their duty without any sign of human pity. One group of people, mostly women and children, are piled into a truck. Those being taken away yell what seem to me instructions to those remaining behind. It all seemed like a scene out of Purgatory. . . . I cannot understand what possible danger these innocent creatures could represent to Germany.

Other eyewitnesses and survivors have reported extraordinary scenes of escape and capture: entire families jumping out of windows; men running along rooftops; a mother tossing her infant to a stranger on the street while the Germans were not looking, before she herself was dragged off; another mother opening her blouse and squeezing her dry nipple in order to make a German soldier understand that her child needed food; a dying, half-paralyzed old woman being hoisted, wheelchair and all, onto a truck with other Jews.

Those who could not be taken away in the first transport were herded up and kept under guard in the remains of the old Roman amphitheatre, the Theater of Marcellus, next to the ghetto. A Roman who was walking in the area that morning described the families there.

> The men, some in jackets, some in overcoats, were sitting on the ancient rocks, or on suitcases, boxes or sacks. They were looking down at the ground, absently, without turning their heads. Perhaps they were saying good-bye to those familiar stones.
>
> The women, however, were still housewives, even in the open air, on the pavement and under the rain. With slow and somber gestures, in some ways hopeless but always with love, some of them were tidying the little clothes and coats of their children. . . . One of the women, with a baby at her breast, covered the head of the child with a shawl. Another put a kerchief on the head of her daughter, who was crying. She wiped the girl's tears and the drops of rain on her face, but always in silence. She had no words to comfort her. She could not even tell the child that Papà would know what to do; for he was there beside her, motionless, his blood turned cold with helplessness.

* * *

For the Germans it was a good morning's work. Using 365 German soldiers, the SS had arrested 1,259 people—about a tenth of the city's Jews—in only nine hours. The vast majority (896) were women and children. Many Jewish men, thinking the Germans were interested only in able-bodied males, had already gone into hiding or had fled to the roofs of their apartment buildings that morning, imagining that their families would be safe at home. (In their dragnet, the Germans had unintentionally arrested 252 non-Jews, and half-Jews, who were released the following day.)

That night the Gestapo command in Rome sent a triumphant report to headquarters in Berlin:

> *Judenaktion* initiated and carried out today according to plan . . . All available forces of the [German] security and police forces put to use. Participation of the Italian police, considering their unreliability in this affair, was not possible. We therefore carried out a series of arrests in rapid succession in twenty-six precincts. . . . The behavior of the Italian

> people was outright passive resistance, which in many individual cases amounted to active resistance. . . . As the German police were breaking into some homes, attempts to hide Jews in nearby apartments were observed, and it is believed that in many cases they were successful. The anti-Semitic part of the population was nowhere to be seen during the action, only a great mass of people who in some individual cases even tried to cut off the police from the Jews. In no case was it necessary to use firearms.

Escaping the initial roundup did not, of course, mean an end to danger.

Enrico Di Veroli, his wife and the four children with them, began a series of peregrinations that would take them to at least seven different hiding places during the nine months of the German occupation. "We waited in the store for a few hours and then went to Piazza Mazzini to see a salesman who had delivered merchandise to our store," Olga recalls. "We stayed for lunch, but unfortunately the custodian of the building had seen us come in and told our friends, 'Get those people out of here. If you don't, when the Germans come I will have to tell them that you're hiding Jews in your apartment.' "

After lunch the family again found itself on the streets, uncertain of where to go. "My father was desperate, mostly on account of my mother, who was very fearful," Olga recounts. "We walked awhile and finally my father said, 'Well, you know what we can do? Return to the store.' And in fact that's what we did." So on the first evening of clandestine life they were back in the heart of the ghetto, the now almost deserted neighborhood of their ancestors, from which several hundred people had been taken that morning.

The following day, October 17, the family paid a call on the local headquarters of the Red Cross to report the arrest of Silvia, her husband and their three children. "Signora Zingarelli, the head of the Italian Red Cross, brought food and blankets to the military school where my sister and all the others were being held prisoner," Michele di Enrico says.

After about two days of sleeping in the store, which had no food or running water, the Di Verolis went to see a Catholic relative who lived in Trastevere. "My mother remembered that this relative had told her that if we ever needed help we could come to her, and the address, Vicolo del Cinque 6 [Alley Five, number six], remained impressed in her mind. When we arrived, these people were overjoyed to see we were still alive; they'd been searching for us since they'd heard about the raid. They were incredibly poor: the husband was a street musician and the wife a laundress. But to show us how glad they were to have us with them, they cooked us a meal of potato gnocchi with pecorino cheese. In that period getting potatoes or cheese was unheard of; it wasn't really pecorino cheese—God only knows what it really was. But it was an enormous sacrifice for them. It tasted terrible, but we ate it all, to show them how grateful we were. The woman gave up her bed and put me and my sister in it. And the rest of our family slept in the laundry room. We were very happy there, no one bothered us. A lot of the people in the neighborhood knew we were Jews, and one person would bring us something to eat, another would bring something else, so that we didn't have to go out and risk being seen. After we'd been there a few days, I decided to take a chance and go to the vegetable market, and a woman there said to me quietly, 'Take this chicory, but get out of here. You can pay tomorrow, the day after or in six months, don't worry about it. But get going.' After we had been at these people's house for about four days, the wife came home and seemed to be having a kind of heart attack. Her face turned black and she had to lie down. My father said, 'She's ill, we have to call a doctor.' But then another woman who lived with them said, 'No, Signor Enrico, she's not ill. She just learned that someone from the neighborhood went to denounce you to the Germans. I'll take care of her and put her to bed, but you should leave.' And so we fled again. As we were leaving we could see the Germans arriving, but they didn't find us."

At the time of the raid Michele di Umberto was in a place of refuge—San Camillo Hospital. "The Germans had been picking up men for military service or work details, so I hid in the hospital, where I had an operation," he says. "The only problem was that my wound wouldn't heal. When October 16 came, people in the hospital told me about the roundup. I escaped from the hospital and went to the house of some Catholic friends. But my wound began to hemorrhage and I had to go back to the same hospital. For several days I hid in the morgue there. During the day I would go into an underground passageway, and at night I would come out and sleep among the dead. I was no longer afraid of the dead, I was afraid of the Germans. I was afraid when I heard noises—it could have been the Germans coming. But the dead don't make any noise."

During this period of convalescence Michele would receive occasional visits from his uncle Attilio, who was staying in the Church of San Benedetto. "Because he used to go around to all the churches and convents fixing things and taking away junk that he would resell, he knew all the priests, and he had gone to stay at the Church of San Benedetto, where Don Gregorini was. My father had left me all this money, and so my uncle came to help me but also to receive help. He would say, 'Michele, can I buy you something?' I would say no, thank you, and would give him a few lire. When my wound healed, he took me with him to the church."

"There were a lot of Jews there," recalls Rosa, Attilio's second daughter. "We tried to remain active. We cleaned, we taught the children. The nuns were good to us. The only problem was that they wanted us to go to mass, but we said we couldn't. But apart from that, Don Gregorini was a great good person."

In the two months after the big raid, relatively few Roman Jews were arrested. The special SS unit that had come from Germany to conduct the roundup in Rome had been sent north to carry out similar *Judenaktionen* in other Italian cities. Only three more Jews were arrested in the capital the second half of October; twenty-eight were captured in November. Mussolini's new government had not really taken shape, nor had it adopted a "Jewish policy." But on November 30 the new minister of the interior, Guido Buffarini Guidi, sent a dispatch to police precincts in Italy ordering the arrest of all Jews:

> The following order, to be executed immediately, has been sent to all police precincts throughout our territory: All Jews, even if "discriminated," and regardless of nationality, must be collected and sent to concentration camps.

When the order did not produce a noticeable rise in arrests, the Germans stepped up pressure and began to oversee Italian police operations. Rewards were posted for turning in Jews: 5,000 lire for men, 2,000 to 3,000 for women and children.

Since the October 16 raid, Giacomo and Angela Di Veroli and their three children had been living with Angela's widowed sister, Cesarina, in Trastevere. Because she had been married to a Catholic man, they felt safe: the neofascist government's arrest order specifically exempted members of mixed marriages. Out of sheer necessity and despite the fear of possible arrest, Giacomo and his daughter Giuditta continued to work.

Every night at eleven Giacomo took up his operator's job at TETI, the telephone company, just as he had since 1940. "The ration cards weren't enough to live on," Giuditta explains. "You might wait in line at the baker's, and when you got to the front of the line there was no more bread. Everybody worked clandestinely and bought food on the black market. I worked as a salesgirl in a shop on Via Appia. The store belonged to some Jews who had fled. The owner's brother and I kept it going."

On December 24, Giuditta went to work as usual, but she felt feverish. The custodian of the building where she worked gave her something to eat and invited her to spend the night. "But I said, 'No, I have to go home, because if my family doesn't see me come home, they'll go crazy thinking I've been taken.' We had no telephone."

That night, Christmas Eve, her father showed up for his shift at the phone company. When he left the next morning, the Germans were waiting outside to arrest him.

"Someone at the telephone company had turned him in," says Giacomo's older daughter, Silvia. "The Germans had come during the day shift looking for him. When he arrived that night, the phone company had him work his regular shift and no one warned him that the Germans had been there. When they arrested him, they threatened to take the foreman of the phone company hostage unless my father told them where our whole family was. Someone at TETI telephoned our old apartment. If only we had been there . . ." Instead, shortly after, at eight in the morning, the Gestapo arrived at the Trastevere apartment. "They knocked on the door and arrested us," Silvia remembers. "We were still in bed. When we went down, we saw my father with them in the car."

"They took us to Via Tasso [where Gestapo headquarters were located] and then transferred us to Regina Coeli," Giuditta says. "That was my father's birthday [he turned fifty-eight] and my aunt—with whom we had left our ration cards—brought us some food at the prison. We were there about two months."

Giuditta and Silvia, sorely tried by their wartime experiences, are characteristically laconic when discussing their time at Regina Coeli. "It was cold. It was boring. There was little to eat," says Giuditta. "There were quite a few people we knew. We could communicate with the people upstairs. They could bang on the floor and warn me: 'Giuditta, the Germans are coming to do a search.' And so I would hide all the things I had of value. But one day they found them anyway. Silvia was in a cell with Mamma."

"We were in the wing of the prison with the political prisoners," Silvia recalls. "There was a German woman, an English woman and the wife of an antifascist who worked at a bookstore. We talked, we read a little."

At one point the antifascists, who were allowed visitors, prepared a prison break. "The men who worked at the Croce bookstore had an escape plan," says Giuditta. "Someone would plant a bomb at the front door of Regina Coeli and then there would be a revolt inside."

"People told us that in a few days there would be a revolt," Silvia remembers. " 'We will come and open your cell,' they said. 'When you get out the front door, you will go down a narrow street, Via dei Riari. You will see a little bridge, take your mother across and look for a typographer's shop. Knock and they will let you in.' "

The escape plan never came off. Instead, on March 8, 1944, Giuditta and Silvia, together with their father, mother and brother were put on a train for Fossoli near Modena. Here, at a transit camp, Jewish prisoners waited until there was a sufficient number to fill a deportation train. Because the camp was only temporary, the Germans had not bothered to organize regular work details. Despite the cold and the lack of food, life was tolerable.

The only incidents of cruelty the two sisters recall occurred after a few prisoners attempted to escape from the camp. "The German woman I had been in the cell with in Rome escaped," Silvia says. "She was good—she got as far as Carpi [a nearby town]—but then they caught her. They executed two or three people who tried to escape."

"We didn't do much, we just sat around," says Giuditta of their period at the detention camp. "If only we had stayed at Fossoli!" When, in early April, the number of Jews at Fossoli reached 565, the Germans prepared a convoy for Auschwitz.

On April 4, the day before the family's departure, Giacomo managed to send a letter to his wife's sister in Rome.

> Dear Cesarina,
>
> Yesterday we received your letter, which gave us great pleasure to have news of you, when you receive this we will have gone from the camp of Fossoli, but we don't know where we're going. In any event, we hope for the best, I will try to keep you informed of everything. If you haven't already sent money or other stuff wait until you hear from us. Let all our friends and acquaintances know, with the hope of seeing one another again soon . . .
>
> Be calm, think of us . . .
>
> Kisses to all of you . . .

On the fifth of April, the family traveled by truck to Carpi and from there by train to Mantua and then Verona, where other deportation cars full of Jews were hitched onto theirs. It was a crowded train, with forty to fifty people in each car. In some there was not enough room for everyone to sit or lie down at once. People took turns standing and sleeping. Only once during the five-day trip were the prisoners given something to eat—a watery soup—and let out to go to the bathroom. They had to improvise a latrine in the train cars, and suffer the indignity and stench of performing their bodily functions in public.

Having survived more than three months since their arrest, the Di Verolis still believed they would come through their ordeal alive. "We were pessimistic but we thought we would be taken somewhere to work, because the Germans were at the front," says Silvia. But when they reached Auschwitz, with its crematoria working day and night, their mood changed completely.

"As soon as we arrived, right there at the end of the ramp was Mengele [Josef Mengele, the camp doctor] in his white uniform, with all his staff, the wretch, passing along and making the selections," Silvia says. "He even touched me. They began selecting the old and sick people, who were unable to work, and loading them onto a truck."

Giacomo, whose health had been damaged in World War I and further weakened by nearly four months of imprisonment, was selected immediately. And while they already suspected that meant nothing good, Silvia and Giuditta encouraged their mother to join their father; they felt instant death would be a merciful alternative to the slow torture of the camp.

" 'Go with them,' we said, and we pushed her toward the truck," Silvia recalls. "She could barely walk and would never have made it. So they put her on the truck with my father and another woman we knew."

* * *

Back in Rome, the circle was closing rapidly on Jews hiding throughout the city. The Italian puppet government installed a new chief of police, Pietro Caruso, who pursued the Jews with quickened vigor. In February 1944, his first month on the job, the number of Jews arrested in the city jumped from 29 to 141. And in March the number climbed further, to 163.

The hopes of an immediate Allied victory had faded. Although they were only some seventy-five miles from Rome, American troops were bogged down in the treacherous mountain country around Cassino; the standoff seemed to last forever.

With the Germans settling in for a long occupation, many Romans began reconsidering their options. Hunger was rampant in the city. Hard-line fascists crawled out from hiding and were on the ascendant; the temptation to make several thousand lire by selling Jews to the police became too much for some people.

Throughout those months the family of Enrico Di Veroli moved from house to house and convent to convent, always a step or two ahead of the Germans and the neofascists. Having narrowly escaped arrest while staying at their relatives' house in Trastevere, the family went to a convent near Ponte Rotto. "After about ten days we had to escape, because someone told the Germans we were there," Olga remembers. "In this convent, along with Jews, there were a number of soldiers and officers who had escaped from the Italian army. The people in the convent tried to help us as much as possible, but they had to send us away."

The family left the convent in the middle of the night and found refuge with some former clients of their store, who lived in Via di Porta Settimiana. "They opened their house to us, they gave us their bedrooms. There's no way around it: the people of Rome opened their hearts to us. Some did so out of self-interest, but a lot of them did it out of pure generosity. What little they had they shared with us. We were okay there; we stayed a few months. But then one day my father saw some people being arrested right under the windows of the house and he became afraid."

Olga recalls the period as an unbroken string of adventures, escapes and disasters. "After October 16, I began writing things down in my own fashion, and my father said to me: 'What do you want to write down? These are days you'll never forget as long as you live.' And so it has been."

After the arrests Enrico witnessed, the family decided to find a place in another convent or monastery. Olga's brothers, Michele and Gianni, did not like the idea of going into a monastery and instead left Rome to join the antifascist resistance. "I didn't want to die like a mouse in a trap," says Michele. "The Germans raided some of the convents and monasteries. If you have to die, better to die with rifle in hand. That's the way I am."

The two brothers joined a partisan group in the hills of Latium led by Giorgio Costanzo. Their main task was to recover parachutes dropped by Allied aircraft and give aid to American and British paratroopers. "Every day, a new episode," Michele recalls. "We were always on the move, trying to avoid a roundup." To Michele, fighting alongside his brother was not a source of comfort, but only made things worse. "It was a time of constant fear. To be with your own brother at war is the worst thing imaginable. What happens if he dies at your side? What do you do? Shoot yourself?"

Enrico and Grazia Di Veroli with their two younger daughters, Olga and Flora, found a place to stay in buildings connected to the Church of San Benedetto. There, they met up with Attilio and his family, as well as Michele di Umberto.

* * *

On March 3, not long after their reunion, the church was hit by an Allied bomb—one of the few that fell on Rome during the war. "I had gone out to get some bread, and when I was coming back I heard this explosion and a whole wing of the convent just collapsed," recalls Attilio's daughter Rosa. "Luckily, no one was killed. But we were told we had to leave."

Michele di Umberto was immediately able to find another place in a monastery, but his uncles, aunts and cousins were not so fortunate. "After the bombing, we wanted to stay in another convent but they wanted money, something like two hundred lire a day, which we didn't have," Rosa remembers. "Michele left, and we had to move from here to there to try to save ourselves."

With nowhere else to go, her family went with Enrico and his family to their store in the ghetto. Ten people now lived in the two-room store, with no kitchen, bathroom or running water. "At night a concierge from a building nearby on Via Arenula would bring us a bottle of water, which we had to use for all our needs, for drinking, cooking and washing," says Olga. "Some friends of ours who had a store nearby would let us know when it was okay to go out, and brought us things we needed."

But remaining in the ghetto for an extended period was impossible, and after four or five days, the families split up and left.

At the end of their resources, Attilio's family found itself back near the Theater of Marcellus, just next to the ghetto. "We sat there in the ruins the whole day, because we had nowhere else to go," Rosa remembers. "In the evening we would try to find a place to sleep, sometimes in the open air." One day Attilio ran into an acquaintance on the street and persuaded her to take in the family for a while. "We ate bread and lettuce, which we dressed with the salty liquid from anchovy cans." To collect a few lire a day, Attilio resumed his old itinerant life, making the rounds of churches, collecting used furniture, doing repairs, receiving an occasional handout. Because he was blind in one eye, he took his fifteen-year-old son, Michele, with him.

"One day we had an appointment to meet my father and brother at the Teatro di Marcello [the Theater of Marcellus], and when they didn't show up, we knew they had been taken," Rosa recalls. "It was March 18, 1944."

She and her family suspect they were turned in by the seamstress with whom they were staying at the time. "It's only an idea, we have no proof," says Rosa. "But I never had a good feeling about that place. One morning when my sister and I were in bed, we heard the woman's little boy playing with a German soldier. And the morning my father was arrested, the woman had told us, 'Don't all go out together.' So my mother and sisters and I went out alone, and we never saw my father and brother again; that's why we suspected her. That evening we were afraid to go back there. Luckily, we were able to find a place to stay in a convent near the Teatro di Marcello."

The next day was a national holiday, the feast of St. Joseph. "My sister Silvia and I went to Via Tasso [the site of Gestapo headquarters], and I said, 'I am an Italian citizen. You have arrested my father [and brother], and I want to bring [them] something.' 'Are you Jewish?' one of the men there asked. 'Yes,' I said. And they told me to go look in Regina Coeli. So we went there and brought them food. We were afraid, but we wanted to know, and at that point I didn't care. I was always the most reckless of the family."

Every day after the arrest, Rosa would appear at Regina Coeli with something to supplement Attilio's and Michele's meager prison rations. But when she arrived at the prison gates on the morning of March 24, the guards told her that her father and brother were no longer there; they had no idea where they had been taken.

Rosa, however, had her own suspicions. The previous day, a bomb had exploded in Via Rasella while a convoy of German soldiers was passing; thirty-two German soldiers were killed. The bomb had been set by partisans. Because the Germans were famous for their threat to kill ten Italians for every one German murdered, the city trembled at the prospect of a massive retaliation.

"The day of the attack at Via Rasella, we knew the Germans had taken some Jews," Rosa says. "We knew that for every German, ten people would be killed. But instead of killing 320, they killed more."

The story quickly circulated through the city that the Germans had taken a large group of Italians, mostly antifascists being held in Roman prisons, to the Ardeatine Caves just outside the city. Chained together in groups of three, they were led into the caves, made to kneel down and shot in the back of the head. When the killing was over—it took several hours—the Germans exploded dynamite at the cave entrance to hide the evidence of their crime.

No one knew the names of the people killed. Not long after the massacre, Rosa and Silvia ventured back into the ghetto area to get some bread. Although it was dangerous to return to the old Jewish quarter, the baker there knew them and made sure they got something to eat. As they were leaving, Rosa saw an old childhood friend, Celeste Di Porto, with whom she had gone to elementary school. Known as "Stella"—Star—because of her beauty, Celeste was from another large, old ghetto family. During the German Occupation, however, she had become one of the city's most lethal informants, turning in about fifty Jews from the ghetto to the Germans. Standing on the bridge between the ghetto and Trastevere, she would finger people as they walked by. In this period, the beautiful dark-haired Celeste earned a new nickname: "La Pantera Nera"—the Black Panther.

"I saw her and thought, *Mamma mia,* if they get us? It would have been enough for her to make a sign and they would have grabbed us. I got up my courage—and said: '*Ciao,* Celeste, how are you? You who know so much, do you know what's happened to my father and brother?' 'They're fine,' she said. 'They're with my cousin.' Silvia and I started walking off, when suddenly I heard her call my name. I said to myself: 'Oh God, she's going to get me.' 'Listen,' she told me, 'Rosa, stay out of sight for a few days.' And we went away."

To find out more about her father and brother, Rosa called her old employer (and distant cousin) Renato Di Veroli, who was hidden inside Vatican City. "He had been able to see a list of the victims and Attilio Di Veroli and Michele Di Veroli were on the list. He [Renato] had a brother named Attilio Di Veroli and thought it might be him. But I was sure it was my father.

"Celeste had said they were 'fine,' they were 'with her cousin,' and in fact, they were with her cousin—dead at the Ardeatine Caves. A couple of days after the massacre I went out there to look. I got a ride on a garbage truck. But I couldn't see a thing. It was dangerous to move around this way, but I had a certain strength that came from the fact that I didn't give a damn anymore. There were certain things that needed to be done."

Of the 335 men killed in the Ardeatine Caves, seventy-seven were Jews: all of them, like Attilio and Michele Di Veroli, nonpolitical Jews who simply happened to be in prison at the time of the ambush. They served to round out the number so that the Germans could maintain their ten-to-one quota. Twenty-six of the Jews who died in the massacre are believed to have been turned in by La Pantera Nera.

Lazzaro Anticoli, a young street peddler arrested the morning of the massacre, managed to scribble a note before being dragged off to the caves: "If I never see my family again, it is the fault of that sellout Celeste Di Porto. Avenge me." According to Italian historian Silvio Bertoldi, Anticoli's name was added at the last minute, replacing that of Celeste Di Porto's brother. Her own father was so deeply ashamed by his daughter's betrayal that he turned himself in to the Germans; he died in a concentration camp.

Among the Jews killed at the Ardeatine Caves was Aldo Finzi, former undersecretary of the interior and a member of the first fascist Grand

Council. Naturally, Finzi had been among the discriminated Jews, those granted exemptions for their patriotic contributions. But this counted for little with the Germans. The majority of the Jewish victims, however, were from the ghetto, with typically Roman last names—Di Consiglio, Di Veroli, Di Porto, Funaro.

The youngest victim was Rosa's little brother, Michele, who had celebrated his fifteenth birthday the month before his death.

"My mother continued to delude herself that they would come back, that there had been a mix-up, and maybe they had exchanged clothes and documents with other people," says Rosa. "She got this idea in her head."

* * *

Olga and Flora, together with their mother, Grazia, had moved into a convent of Philippine sisters on Via Cicerone. Despite the dangers of the German occupation, the women continued to move freely about the city during the day. They wanted especially to remain in contact with Enrico, who was now staying with friends. To stay locked in a room with no news of the family was more than they could bear.

Sometimes Enrico and his wife would walk arm in arm through the city. With spring warming the city and Allied troops inching closer and closer every day, the future was beginning to look brighter. On the afternoon of April 25, Enrico was walking Grazia back to the convent, when he heard someone call his name. "My mother, who was holding him by the arm, said she remembered feeling my father jump," Olga says. " 'Don't turn around,' my father said to her. 'Di Veroli, Di Veroli,' he heard again. Finally he turned around and said: 'My name is Nicola Rita'—that was the false name he was going by. The man who was calling him, who was with another guy, had been a client of our store. My father had loaned him a thousand lire. 'Enrico, don't play games with me. Don't you remember, you gave me a thousand lire of merchandise on credit. I'm supposed to pay you back one hundred lire a day. See, here's your signature on this receipt.' My father said, 'That's okay, it can wait until the end of the war.' But the man said, 'You have to come with us.' My father said, 'Don't hurt me, I have a family.' 'What hurt? We're just taking you in for questioning.' "

They dragged off Enrico, and in the fracas that followed, his wife Grazia was thrown to the ground and knocked unconscious, and lost several teeth. Luckily, several women who were watching came to her aid. Because the incident had occurred in front of the convent where she was staying, the women, not knowing where she lived, picked her up off the pavement and carried her to the convent.

Olga remembers that when she and Flora returned that evening, they found their mother in a strange state. "She was laughing and laughing. My sister said, 'Look how happy Mamma is. Maybe something has happened, maybe Silvia [their older sister] has been freed.' 'No,' I said, 'I don't think she's happy. She seems nervous.' We finally learned that my father had been arrested. We tried to shake Mamma a bit, but we couldn't get her to stop laughing. So we went up to a woman who was hiding in the convent whom we knew to be Jewish. We explained what had happened, and said, 'Our mother seems half crazy.' The woman came and gave my mother a hard slap across the face. Mamma stopped laughing and started crying.

"That evening the mother superior came up to me and said, 'Listen, Carmela'—that was the false name I went under—'you should have told me you were Jewish.' I said, 'If you want us to go, we'll leave immediately.' 'No, it's not that, we just need to know so that if they come for you, we can take you down a secret passageway.' The nuns were incredibly good and courteous to us. After that episode they even insisted on bringing us our meals in our room so that we would be seen as little as possible in public. They were afraid of informants."

After Enrico's arrest, Olga and her family developed contacts in the prison that allowed them to keep up a clandestine correspondence. "We had a system of communication, slipping notes inside clean laundry or packages of food," she remembers. "Using the same method, my father was able to send us back a couple of notes."

Particularly striking in Enrico Di Veroli's letters is the degree of concern for others at a time when he himself was in constant mortal danger.

May 15, 1944

Dear Grazina,

You cannot imagine how much pleasure I had receiving your letter of the 12th and in receiving good news and knowing that you all are well.

I beg you not to worry, that I am well and I feel strong and full of courage because I have hope that all will end soon and we will be able to embrace one another in perfect health.

Although full of spelling and punctuation mistakes, his letters are written in a shrewdly constructed code in order to avoid identifying friends and relatives. At one point Enrico wrote: "I hope that Signorine Michelina Rita and Gianna Rita study hard and never tire, succeed at their exams and listen to the advice of Professor Resciude." The young women he mentions "Signorine Michelina Rita and Gianna Rita"—are in fact his sons, Michele and Gianni; "Rita" is the false last name the family had been going under. "Professor Resciude" refers not to a person but to the word *resciudde* in Roman Jewish dialect, meaning "beat it" or "get lost": by urging his sons to "study hard" and "listen to the advice of Professor Resciude," Enrico was telling them to lie low and stay out of sight.

His letters offered practical advice—"Don't send cooked meat, it goes bad; send hard-boiled eggs instead"—as well as salutations to friends left behind—"Give my greetings to all those who ask of me." Enrico's strongest wish was that his family write him at once [adding a second "b" to the word "subito" (immediately) to stress its importance]: "I beg you to answer me immediately so that I can be at peace."

On May 20 the Allies broke the stalemate at Cassino and began the final offensive that would culminate in the liberation of Rome. But the day after Cassino fell, the Germans loaded 281 Jews onto a train headed for the detention camp at Fossoli. Prisoner 175 on the list was Enrico Di Veroli.

Two weeks later, on June 4, when Rome was liberated, Enrico was in Fossoli; that area of Italy would have to wait nearly another eleven months for the end of the war. On June 16, Enrico managed to get a letter from Fossoli to his wife, through a Catholic friend in Rome.

Written a few days before his deportation, this letter was much more forboding than those written in Rome: "Up till now I have been at Fossoli and we do not know what fate awaits us." Nonetheless, he took great pains to reassure his family and keep them from worrying: "I want you to know that I am well and that I am ready for whatever the future holds in store." At moments, his words express the stoic concern of a man trying to wrap up his affairs and take leave of the world. "I beg you all to be good, calm, and to always get along, and to take the best possible care of Mamma, to pick up the things from [Signor] Riso and those of all the others . . . so that when I return I will find all in good order, and if by some chance I should be delayed a bit, not to despair and to remain calm."

Even at this late date, Enrico does not appear to have grasped the full extent of the Germans' "final solution." He wrote hopefully of his oldest daughter, who had been arrested with her husband and children on October 16: "I have had news that Silvia and all the others are in Theresienstadt in Czechoslovakia and that we can write her through the International Red Cross."

One of Enrico's principal concerns was that the family would find ways of thanking and repaying the Catholic friends who had helped them in this time of calamity. He explained how one friend, a certain Gasparini, went all the way from Rome to Fossoli in order to give him a thousand lire. "Be sure," he urged his family, "never to forget as long as you should live the great and good action of this man. . . . In fact I beseech you as soon as you have received this letter to go and thank him and repay him all I owe him."

Ten days later, a convoy of more than a thousand Jews left Fossoli for Auschwitz. Only 275 were admitted to the camp to work as laborers; the other 750—including Enrico Di Veroli—were gassed immediately. Only thirty-two out of the entire group would return to Italy after the war.

* * *

Like his uncles Attilio and Enrico and their families, Michele was forced to find a new hiding place after the bombing of San Benedetto. He went to the Instituto Angelo Mai, a religious institute belonging to the Catholic Church, where about a hundred Jews were hiding. And from there, with help from Monsignor Tercole, a friend of his father's, he moved to the Lateran Palace, home of the seminary of the Basilica of San Giovanni in Laterano. It was not easy to get into the seminary, but Michele says, "Because my father had lots of Catholic friends I was always fortunate enough to be able to find hiding places in churches and convents. My Uncle Attilio had much more trouble.

"They needed to be certain about the people they let into Palazzo Lateranense. There were a lot of important Italian soldiers and antifascists there, people who became important political figures after the liberation. They even had a radio transmitter there, which broadcast war news to the Americans and the British. I sometimes had guard duty at night on the roof; they were constantly watching out for a raid by the Germans like the one at San Paolo." (The Germans had broken into the Basilica of Saint Paul's Outside the Walls and arrested numerous Jews and antifascists.)

Michele was posing as a Neapolitan student, with the name Michele Capuano, who had been stranded in Rome, behind the battle lines. "I had gotten false documents through friends who knew someone in one of the government ministries.

"I spent the days studying the Torah. I am very religious: I'm one of those Jews who goes to temple every day. I'm not a bigot but I'm religious. The people at the convent never tried to convert me. I can say only good things about them. They tried to help in every way possible. At night I slept on a table in the dining room, with a blanket. The seminary, which was for students of theology, had a movie theater. They let me work the projector. It seems like nothing, but it helped me pass the time."

* * *

In the convent in Via Cicerone, Olga, her sister and their mother spent the remaining days of the German occupation listening to the sounds of artillery coming closer to Rome and trying to avoid a last-minute capture.

One day Olga returned to the family store to retrieve something and found another family living there, one of the thousands of families displaced by the war. "I said to them, 'Listen, I've just come to get a few things I left here.' And they told me to get out. I said, 'I am the daughter of the owner.' And the wife said, 'So that means you're Jewish.' And she began to scream, 'Fascists, Germans—a Jew! Arrest her!' I got out of there in a hurry. Those people stole everything we had, our merchandise, our typewriter, everything."

Within the convent itself the family lived in fear of a fervent fascist woman and her daughter. "We tried to avoid all conversation about politics and so on, but the daughter of the fascist woman kept saying: 'This is the fault of the Jews, that is the fault of the Jews. If I knew where the Jews and the antifascists were hiding, I would go and denounce them.' And so I told her, 'If you want to know where Jews and Italian soldiers are hiding, I'll show you. But since it's curfew, we'll have to walk underneath the bridges of the Tiber.' One of the nuns called me aside and asked me what I was talking about. I said that I was going to take the fascist woman's daughter along the river, and when we reached a spot with strong currents, I was going to give her a good push into the river. The nun said: 'Listen, Carmela'—that was the name I was going under—'certain things you don't even talk about. Besides, the girl said she didn't know where the Jews and the antifascists were.' So I didn't do anything. I'm not capable of killing, but she had it coming to her."

By the first days of June, the Allies were fighting the Germans in the Alban Hills near Rome; the air was full of anticipation. On June 3, planes fought above the city and German armored cars and jeeps moved quickly through the streets. No one was certain whether the Germans were pulling out or preparing to make a last stand. On the morning of June 4, the capital seemed to come to a standstill: telephones went dead, electricity shut off, no newspapers appeared, bus and tram service came to a halt. Allied planes flew overhead, showering leaflets on the population. The "Special Message to the Citizens of Rome" from British Field Marshal Harold Alexander informed them that "the Allied Armies are nearing Rome. The liberation of the city will take place soon. The citizens of Rome must stand shoulder to shoulder to protect the city from destruction and to defeat our common enemies: the Germans and the Fascists."

In the center of town, curious Romans who strayed out of their houses witnessed a spectacle reminiscent of September 8, 1943, when the Italian army dissolved during the first days of the German occupation. But this time it was the Germans who were on the run. An American woman who published a memoir under the pseudonym "Jane Scrivener" described the scene in her diary entry of June 4:

> The Germans went on, wild-eyed, unshaven, unkempt, on foot, in stolen cars, in horse-drawn vehicles, even in carts belonging to the street cleaning department. There was no attempt at military formation. Some of them dragged small ambulances with wounded in them. They went, some with revolvers in their hands, some with rifles cocked. On Corso Umberto, when one of them stumbled, his rifle went off and caused a panic among the crowd: for a moment there was some indiscriminate shooting. Whereas last September they came with machine guns trained on the Romans, it was a different matter now. They were frightened. . . . Most of the Republicans [the followers of Mussolini's Italian Social Republic, based in Salò] were . . . looking anything but dignified in their anxiety to get away. Some Blackshirt soldiers . . . were desperately waving to occupants of German motor cars, begging for a lift. The latter, true to their custom . . . had no pity on them whom they had used as tools while despising them, and passed on, unheeding. The crowd showed a good deal of self-control in not lynching these remnants of the Fascist gangs.

In the middle of the day Allied planes began dive-bombing the departing German troops. The city shook with massive explosions as the Germans blew up supplies of arms and gasoline they could not carry with them, and destroyed a Fiat factory where armored cars and trucks were repaired. The news began to circulate that the Allies were at the outskirts of the city, but in the center all was quiet.

Most people were at home that evening in time for the normal curfew. The city was blacked out, as it had been throughout the German occupation. But many Romans sat at their windows in the temperate June air, looking for signs of the Allies' arrival. At about ten o'clock, the same American diarist wrote, those gazing out on the darkened city witnessed an extraordinary moment: Rome suddenly exploding in light.

> The electric light which had been cut off was turned on abruptly, and uncurtained windows flashed out brightly like a signal of liberation. . . . Suddenly, from the direction of Porta Pia, came a burst of wild cheering. The Allies had entered Rome. The sound of cheering followed the line

of Via Venti Settembre as far as Piazza Venezia. After that the whole town came to life. There was talk and laughter in all the streets, even in the narrowest ones; there was cheering and the sound of clapping everywhere.

Olga remained in the convent in Via Cicerone, outside the center. She heard the rumors of the Allies' arrival but was somewhat skeptical until she ventured forth the following morning. She and Flora's fiancé were arguing about whether the Allies had really arrived, when suddenly they saw what looked like an Allied soldier.

"I'm not much at physiognomy, but I'd swear he was Scottish; he looked just like those characters in the movies," she remembers. The soldier, who spoke Italian, overheard their conversation and came over to reassure them. "At that point, I burst out crying," Olga says. The soldier tried to comfort her and asked what he could do to help. "Bring back my father and sister!" she told him.

Full of the news that the Allies had arrived, Olga returned to the convent. One of the first people she saw was the fascist girl who had constantly hurled invective against the Jews. "She was eating a nice big sandwich—who knows where she would have gotten it in those days—and I took her by the hair and dragged her down the stairs; she had wanted to denounce us to the Germans. That day she and her mother went out saying they would be back at lunchtime, and they never came back. They left all their things. I think they had turned in a lot of people in their hometown and had a lot to get away from."

When Olga went to the center of town, she, along with the rest of Rome, was treated to the spectacle of a city transformed. Allied troops were everywhere, and the grim city of the Occupation was alive with flowers, banners and cheering crowds. Soldiers carried roses in the barrels of their guns and in the netting of their helmets, while ecstatic crowds applauded with the passing of every tank or jeep, even at the Allied planes overhead. Overnight, wrote Jane Scrivener, the population of Rome seemed to have doubled:

> Men who had been hiding for months, patriots, Italian soldiers, Allied prisoners of war who had escaped from their prison camps, young men of military age and persecuted Jews—were out and about. Bicycles appeared from their hiding places as if by magic. Rome had not seen such animation and laughter since the beginning of the war. . . . The Scots piped themselves down Via Nazionale to Piazza Venezia, where they gave a concert amid howls of enthusiasm. . . . The French paraded along Via dell' Impero to shouts of *"Vive le France!"* British units came up Via

> Ludovisi in triumph. American soldiers hoisted a big Italian flag on the balcony of Palazzo Venezia, the famous balcony whence Il Duce used to harangue the assembled multitudes. . . . Down the Corso men of the Fifth Army passed all day to the sound of ceaseless cheering. In reply they tossed American candy to sugar-starved children and cigarettes to men accustomed to a desperately meagre ration of tobacco.

Despite all the joy, Olga returned to the ghetto in the mood to settle a score. She walked straight into her father's store, still occupied by the family that had tried to have her arrested. "I was going to turn them in to the police," she says. "I've rarely fought in my life. But I beat that woman good. The husband, who knew what his wife had done, didn't lift a finger. But he said: 'Listen, don't send us away, we have a son who is sick.' We went together into the back room of the store, where they had put a bed. There was a boy about ten years old, pale and trembling with fever. 'Signora, don't send us away,' he said to me. 'I feel so sick.' I was moved and said, 'I won't send you away. I wouldn't send away a sick child.' And then he said, 'My name is Marco.' Strange coincidence, my nephew [Silvia's ten-year-old son, who had been taken away in October] was also named Marco. 'You're not bad like your mother.' "

The Rabbi, the Priest and the Aviator

A STORY OF RESCUE IN GENOA

PRECEDING PAGE–Rabbi Riccardo Pacifici with Jewish refugee children interned at Ferramonti Tarsia during the war.

TOP–Massimo Teglio in a hydroplane in the port of Genoa before the war. At the time, this was the only place in the city where planes could land and take off. BOTTOM RIGHT–Massimo Teglio with fascist leader and aviator Italo Balbo in Libya, where Balbo was governor of the Italian colony. Teglio is on the far right; Balbo is the man in the white uniform with the walking stick. BOTTOM LEFT–Massimo Teglio's wife, Graziella, and their daughter, Nicoletta.

LEFT–Rabbi Pacifici speaking to Jewish refugees interned at Ferramonti Tarsia. CENTER–Don Francesco Repetto in the ruins of the Archbishop's Palace shortly after the Allied bombing of May 19, 1944. The photograph was taken by Massimo Teglio. RIGHT–Don Francesco Repetto (later Monsignor), accepting an award after the war.

Chapter One

In the weeks following the German occupation of Italy on September 8, 1943, Massimo Teglio watched with increasing frustration and alarm as the doors of the Genoa synagogue remained open. Teglio, who lived directly opposite, saw the children of the synagogue's custodian playing carelessly in the square in front of the temple as if there were no danger hanging over their heads.

Since their arrival in Genoa, the Germans had shown no interest in the city's Jews. But Teglio believed it was only a matter of time. A Catholic friend of his had paid a private call on the German consul to find out the Nazis' intentions toward the Jews. "Tell your friend," the German consul said, "that at first the SS will have other problems to attend to, that he has a few weeks to wrap up his affairs, but then he should leave." With this advice in mind, Teglio remained in Genoa but began taking precautions. He kept his six-year-old daughter, Nicoletta, outside the city in Rapallo with his wife's parents, who were Catholic. For himself, he created a hiding place in his own building.

This refuge was the unexpected benefit of a recent bombing. One night an incendiary bomb landed in the living room of the apartment directly above his. Teglio, along with the custodian of the synagogue, Bino Polacco, ran upstairs to put out the flames, saving the furniture from being burned. When the upstairs neighbor, Angelo Costa, decided to remove his belongings from the apartment, Teglio asked if he could use the empty apartment to hide in. "I was more afraid of the Germans than of the bombs!" Teglio said later. Shrewdly, he moved his own furniture into the upper apartment: if the Nazis sought him in his own apartment, it would appear that he had left town.

Genoa is a long, thin strip of a city stretching for miles along the Italian Riviera around the wide semicircle of its harbor. Built on graduated levels into the Ligurian hills, the city is like an enormous ampitheater looking out over the Mediterranean—the stage on which its illustrious history has been played out. A powerful maritime republic from the twelfth to the eighteenth century, home to the great seamen Christopher Columbus and Andrea Doria, Genoa grew during the modern era into Italy's most active shipping port.

During World War II, however, the prominence of its port made Genoa, along with the industrial centers Turin and Milan, a favorite target of British and American bombers. Since the beginning of the war, the inhabitants of Genoa entered an entirely new kind of life: the city went dark at nine each night, and the daytime hours were punctuated by air-raid alarms. Streetlights were turned off or dimmed to a bare minimum; residents spent their evenings huddled behind windows sealed with cardboard and glue to keep light from attracting the attention of bombers. As one writer described the city during the period:

> In the moonless nights, one had the feeling of wandering through an immense aquarium where streets, palazzos and piazzas took on a new dimension, where distances seemed to expand enormously, silence grew heavier, and the shape of things and people blurred in an unreal atmosphere made of silence and tense expectation.

During the course of the war, bombs were dropped on Genoa eighty-six times, destroying 17,101 buildings. The people of Genoa spent 578 hours, 44 minutes waiting out air raids and another 300 hours in a state of pre-alarm. Those who took the precaution of going to underground air-raid shelters spent a total of more than thirty-six days underground. Within the first year of war, food became scarce and was rationed. Staples such as coffee, sugar and flour disappeared entirely, and as the war dragged on, bread was reduced to a few ounces a day per person. By 1943 the city even ran out of salt, and many Genoese were reduced to evaporating seawater to flavor their small rationed meals.

The war had also left Teglio, at the age of forty-two, a widower.

His wife, Graziella, who was Catholic, had been working as a Red

Cross nurse at one of the city's major hospitals. On the night of October 22, 1942, Genoa received one of the worst assaults of the entire war, with two hundred tons of explosives falling in a mere half-hour, gutting much of the old center of the city. Graziella escaped unhurt but the bombardment left her badly shaken and upset. The following day, after another, somewhat lighter bombing, she collapsed in the middle of lunch. Several of her colleagues from the hospital became sick from the same meal, but while the others simply vomited and recovered, Graziella fainted and never came to. Teglio believed that the shock of the bombardment, the food poisoning and a congenital heart condition combined to cause the heart attack that killed his twenty-eight-year-old wife.

Of her death, Teglio bore a last, surreal memory. When he went to the morgue in San Martino Hospital to have a final look at his young wife, he found her lying in a casket overflowing with flowers, dressed in her Red Cross uniform, looking as young and pretty as she had when he had first met her; the rest of the room was littered with countless naked, black bodies, their limbs strangely swollen and distorted.

"When I came into the room, I saw all these black bodies, and I thought: I never knew there were so many black people in Genoa," he recalled. Someone explained to him that these were not blacks but some of the 354 victims of that day's air raid. They had been killed not by the bombs but by a bomb shelter that had collapsed around them when the panicked crowd had run for cover. They had died of suffocation, and their bodies had swollen and turned black. "Compared with all these naked, black bodies, my wife in her uniform, in the casket surrounded with flowers, appeared to be almost privileged."

After the October 1942 bombings, the steady flow of people out of the city became a mass exodus. Genoa became a kind of commuter city, with much of its work force arriving by day and leaving by night. Businesses changed their hours so that all employees worked a single daytime shift in order to be able to join their families by evening. "In the late afternoon the city took on the appearance of an enormous train station," as historian Mauro Montarese noted. "People hurried onto trams crammed to the gills, the sidewalks were thronged, and merchant trucks and wagons were adapted with seats so that they might also carry passengers."

By late 1943, Teglio was the only member of his family left in Genoa. His brother, Mario—after an incendiary bomb landed in his living room but failed, miraculously, to explode—had moved to a country house near Siena with his pregnant wife and their son. Teglio's parents, with their oldest and youngest daughters, had taken refuge in a farmhouse they owned in the Piedmontese countryside. Teglio's middle sister, her husband and their two children had moved to the resort town of Montecatini in Tuscany.

That Massimo Teglio lingered behind in Genoa was due in no small measure to the fact that he no longer had a wife to worry about and could therefore yield to his own natural inclination to be at the center of the storm; he had been one of the first pilots in Genoa and was used to flying rickety single-engine planes without any instruments in all sorts of weather.

Before World War II, Genoa did not have an airport: the city relied on hydroplanes that took off and landed in the harbor. When a stiff *tramontana* wind blew in from the north, it was virtually impossible to take off. But Teglio was one of two pilots who were able to manage it, with a dangerous maneuver known as "jumping the dam." He would fly his small single-engine hydroplane straight toward the concrete dam in the harbor and wait until, at the last minute, the wind lifted the plane above the dam and into the air. From this he had learned that sometimes the best way to avoid danger was to fly directly toward it.

Concerned that Teglio was still in the city, Nello Mazzotti, a fellow pilot in the Genoa Aviation Club, came to see him. "You're insane to be running around the city this way," he told Teglio. At the very least, Mazzotti insisted, Teglio, as a Jew, should have false identification cards. Mazzotti, who held an important position at the port of Genoa, had managed to acquire authentic German identity papers for him, made out by the German navy itself. Anyone working in the port during the Occupation had to have special authorization from the German high command, but several workers had never appeared to pick up their documents. The papers were filled out, stamped and signed, and lacked only a photograph. One set of papers was made out to a carpenter; Teglio rejected them, afraid that his smooth hands would give him away too easily. Instead he took another card, made out to a certain Giobatta Triberti ("Giobatta" is a Genoese version of the name Giovanni Battista, John the Baptist), son of Carlo and Francesca Triberti, living in Via Pio Chiesa. Not only was Triberti's birthdate only a month before Teglio's own, but by making a small alteration Teglio was able to change Triberti's profession from sailor (*marittimo*) to shipping agent (*agente marittimo*)—something Teglio felt he could pass for without trouble.

"The strength of this document was that it was real and would hold up under scrutiny," he explained. "If I were stopped and someone checked with the Germans whether Giobatta Triberti, son of Carlo and

Francesca, was registered with the German command in the port of Genoa, the answer would be yes. Because it was true."

Teglio asked a non-Jewish friend to make discreet inquiries around Triberti's neighborhood, to find out as much as possible about the man whose identity he had assumed, in case he were ever questioned. Teglio learned that Triberti had not been seen in Genoa for some time, and that—conveniently enough—his parents were dead and he had no brothers or sisters. With his new identity and his hideout, Teglio felt safe enough to stay in Genoa.

By early October, Teglio began hearing rumors of German reprisals against the Jews. When he saw the temple doors still wide open, he went to the offices of the Genoa community to tell them to close the synagogue immediately. Neither the president, Luciano Morpurgo, nor the chief rabbi of Genoa, Riccardo Pacifici, was present. "I spoke with the secretary, Giorgio Baquis . . . and told him he had to shut the offices immediately." But Baquis insisted that he didn't have the authority. Teglio did convince him, however, to hide the list of names and addresses of Jews in Genoa; the Germans, Teglio understood already, must not get hold of the list. With the help of the temple custodian, Baquis stuffed the list in a bundle of clothes which he then hid in the basement of Teglio's apartment building. Teglio, a gregarious and extroverted man, was friends with a priest in a nearby church and arranged with him to find a more permanent hiding place. Baquis and the custodian promised to retrieve the list from Teglio's basement and take it to the priest at the earliest opportunity.

Teglio felt a certain bond with the Jewish community of Genoa: before the war his father had been its president. The Teglio family had only the faintest interest in formal religion. Even Teglio's grandfather, the most observant member of the family, expressed impatience with the length of Jewish religious services. "He used to say: 'All this ritual was fine when the Jews lived in the desert, where there wasn't much else to do, but in the modern world they've got to speed things up.' " Teglio shared his grandfather's irreverent sense of humor; an agnostic, he had caused a mild family scandal by marrying a Catholic woman. Nevertheless, he knew all the members of the Jewish community and was on excellent terms with them. Since he lived opposite the temple, whenever an extra person was needed to form a minyan—the ten people necessary to perform a religious service—someone would go to Teglio's to persuade him to join them. Out of good nature rather than devotion, he would agree.

In that same period, Teglio ran into Rabbi Riccardo Pacifici, with whom he had always been on friendly terms. Teglio urged the rabbi to close up the temple and its offices. But Pacifici argued that he didn't have the power to make the decision without authorization of the president of the Genoa Jewish Community, who was nowhere to be found. "Let the president of the Community come here!" Teglio replied hotly. Teglio was furious that Morpurgo had vanished while leaving the offices open. At the end of their conversation, Pacifici said something that stuck in Teglio's mind: "I am ready to die for the Jews but not for the Germans." He would take whatever precautions he could to prevent his own arrest but would continue to serve his community even if it meant risking his life.

* * *

The German occupation posed a particularly serious threat to the Jews of Genoa because of the high number of Eastern European refugees in the city. The port, then the largest in Italy, had long been a magnet for people seeking safe passage out of Europe. But many, especially during the war, had been stranded there.

Despite the heavy bombardments, Genoa acted throughout the war as the center of relief activity for Jewish refugees in Italy. One of the many contradictions in Italian fascism and its treatment of the Jews was that, except for one brief period, Mussolini's government allowed Jewish relief organizations to operate openly during the racial campaign, right up until the German occupation in September 1943. In 1933, with the rise of Hitler in Germany, Jews in Milan set up the Comitato di Assistenza agli Emigrati Ebrei (Committee to Assist Jewish Refugees), or Comasebit, for Jews fleeing Germany and Eastern Europe. After 1938, Comasebit also worked to help some 5,000 Italian Jews find homes abroad. Since in that year Mussolini had ordered all foreign-born Jews who had entered Italy after 1919 to leave the country within six months, Comasebit's activities were in fact consistent with the new policy of racial persecution. But because it was run in large part by recognized antifascists, among them Raffaele Cantoni, the government dissolved the assistance committee in 1939. It was almost immediately reconstituted under a new name, Delegazione Assistenza Emigranti Ebrei (Delegation for Assistance to Jewish Emigrants), or DELASEM, with new, politically acceptable leaders. Its director, Lelio Vittorio Valobra, a well-known Genoese Jewish lawyer, convinced the fascist government that DELASEM was a benefit to fascism since it would help relocate thousands of Jews no longer allowed to work in Italy, and would bring considerable amounts of foreign currency into the country. The group was funded heavily by the Joint Distribution Committee in the United States, which underwrote efforts to help European Jews escape persecution. The fascist government went out of its way to facilitate DELASEM's operations by giving the group a highly favorable foreign exchange rate, selling lire at fifteen percent below the inflated official rate. The organization was based in Genoa both because Valobra was Genoese and because it was a natural place from which to arrange departures to France, Spain, North Africa, and North and South America.

Valobra and his colleagues saved at least 5,000 Jews who would otherwise have remained trapped in Europe during the war. When legal emigration from Genoa became impossible in 1940, DELASEM engineered a number of illegal operations, renting boats to take refugees from Genoa at night to southern France, from where they would try to reach Spain. (Some 2,000 Jews were smuggled into Free French territories in North Africa.) After the United States entered the war and DELASEM could no longer receive American money directly, funds were channeled covertly through Switzerland.

Another consequence of the war was that the Italian government ordered the arrest of thousands of Jewish refugees living in Italy, treating them much as the United States treated Japanese-Americans during the war. Jews born outside of Italy were labeled enemy aliens, potential spies who had to be kept either in guarded camps or under close police surveillance. Although the policy was applied in a typically uneven fashion, about 3,500 refugees were sent to concentration camps in southern Italy. The largest camp, built at Ferramonti Tarsia, in a remote, malaria-ridden section of Calabria, held about 2,000 people. DELASEM was responsible for guaranteeing the well-being of the refugees in the camps and constantly petitioned the Italian government to maintain the minimal standards of decency to which it had committed itself. Another 5,000 refugees were assigned to live in a state of semiconfinement in small towns throughout Italy; they were required to remain within the city limits and register regularly with the local police.

Paradoxically, while the fascist government was mistreating refugees at home, it was rescuing them overseas. During the occupations of France and Yugoslavia, the Italian army steadfastly refused to give in to German demands that they hand over the Jews in their control. Italian diplomats in Yugoslavia distributed Italian passports to Jewish refugees in order to save them from deportation to Germany at a time when the official policy in Italy was to strip foreign-born Jews of their Italian citizenship.

Valobra and the other leaders of DELASEM participated fully in these rescue efforts and made frequent trips into Italian-occupied territory to bring Jews back into Italy—with the full cooperation of the fascist government. One of the most dramatic rescue operations occurred in 1942 in Italian-occupied Yugoslavia. Valobra learned that forty-two Jewish children were hiding in a castle at Lesno Brdno, in a no-man's-land between the Italian and German zones—territory in which Yugoslavian partisans were active. He obtained permission from the Italian government to travel to Yugoslavia and with the help of the Red Cross spirited the group out of the country. The children, who ranged in age from eleven to nineteen and had all lost their families to Nazi deportations, were brought to Italy with Red Cross identity cards. DELASEM acquired a villa in the town of Nonantola, near Modena, for the children; they all survived the war.

Some accounts of the Holocaust period have tended to blame Jews for failing to respond to the Nazi threat and for allowing themselves and their brethren to be led passively into the gas chambers. The story of DELASEM flatly contradicts that simplistic interpretation and shows clearly that in places where Jews had the freedom to organize and help themselves, they did so. The organizers of DELASEM worked tirelessly and selflessly on behalf of Jews from all over Europe and continued to do so even in the grip of the Nazi occupation.

After the armistice of September 1943, Valobra understood very clearly the danger that he and DELASEM's refugees were in. He realized he would have to dissolve the organization, and decided to ask the archbishop of Genoa if the Catholic Church would be willing to continue the group's work. The archbishop, Pietro Cardinal Boetto, had already demonstrated considerable sympathy for the plight of Jewish refugees stranded in Genoa and had even given some of them the money they needed to flee to safety.

In late September, when Valobra arrived at the Archbishop's Palace, adjacent to the medieval cathedral of San Lorenzo in Genoa, he was shown in to see the archbishop's personal secretary, Francesco Repetto. Valobra found himself in the presence of a slightly built, bookish, bespectacled young priest whose shy delicacy of manner belied his courageous conduct during the war.

Although his request was a risky one, Valobra decided to get right to the point. He asked whether the Archbishop's Office would take up the work of DELASEM, which, under Nazi rule, was patently illegal. Privately, Don Repetto was eager to accept, but he could only promise to speak with the archbishop. Many years later, in a 1982 speech, Repetto described the meeting in which he presented Valobra's request to Cardinal Boetto:

> When I went to talk to the Cardinal, the Archdiocese was already in a very difficult position. We had already taken on the burden of helping those who had lost their homes; and we had assumed the job of collect-

ing information about prisoners of war. Standing in front of the Cardinal's desk, I asked him, with studied indifference (because my position was only that of a lowly secretary), if we should accept or deny the request of DELASEM.

The Cardinal collected himself a moment, but didn't pause long to think: "They are innocents; they are in great danger; we must help them at whatever cost to ourselves." . . . In that moment we looked at one another like two old friends who understood each other well.

No doubt an important factor in the archbishop's decision was information he had received the previous year about ghastly atrocities being carried out by the Germans against the Jews of Eastern Europe. In April 1942 an Italian officer who had just returned from the Eastern front insisted on having an audience with the cardinal, to tell him of terrible things he had witnessed in Yugoslavia and Poland. Cardinal Boetto, visibly shaken by the account, immediately telegraphed the Vatican about what he had learned, and intensified his activities to help the Jews.

In agreeing to Valobra's request, Cardinal Boetto placed his young secretary in charge of the efforts to help the Jews.

Valobra explained to Don Repetto the structure of DELASEM, gave him the lists of its contacts around northern Italy, with hundreds of names, addresses and phone numbers. He also gave the priest 5 million lire, a considerable sum at the time, to distribute to the various groups feeding and hiding Jews. Valobra explained the system for channeling money into the country from Switzerland and told Repetto in which Italian banks it was kept.

Valobra was anxious that the DELASEM files—full of names and addresses—not fall into the hands of the Nazis. Don Repetto, without telling anyone, placed the papers inside the pipes of the organ at San Lorenzo and set about enlisting the aid of parish priests, monks and nuns across northern Italy who would be willing to hide Jews.

Clearly, for Don Repetto the challenge of the Nazi manhunt was a kind of apotheosis in which he fulfilled his own Christian mission. Everyone who had contact with Repetto in that period came away deeply impressed by his great sensitivity, courage and total commitment. Addressing a Jewish audience in 1984, Repetto—by then a monsignor—recalled with great emotion the condition of the refugees who appeared before him during the German occupation: "Along with the fear that gripped them, they suffered from the doubt that they were unwelcome because of the danger they brought with them. . . . But you seemed to us then, and you were, something sacred. As such we wanted to receive you and as such we were bound to treat you."

Unlike the small minority of priests who tried to convert the Jews living under their protection, Repetto emerged from the experience of the war with a profound interest in and respect for Judaism and with a deepened conviction in the links between that religion and his own.

* * *

Don Repetto was especially struck by the example of the chief rabbi of Genoa, Riccardo Pacifici, who, although only a man of thirty-nine, with a wife and two children, insisted on remaining in the city to help refugees trapped there during the Occupation.

"I always saw him dressed very properly in black," Repetto recalled. "His eye had a benevolent gaze, and he spoke with a gentle voice. . . . I had heard of the incomparable erudition of the rabbis and—despite the circumstances—I was flattered to meet him.

"I was in the early years of my ministry. With him, I immediately had the sensation that both of us were in the same service of the human soul, and because of this common goal and his gentle manner, it was easy for me to join with him in trust and goodness."

Rabbi Pacifici was not unaware of the danger he was in. Shortly after September 8, he had sent his wife, Wanda Abenheim, and their younger son, Raffaele, to stay with her family in Tuscany. (Their older son, Emanuele, who was in boarding school at the time, would soon join them.) Pacifici was faced with an agonizing existential dilemma: Should he flee with his family to safety or stay behind with the members of his flock who remained in Genoa? While the rabbis of most other cities could leave their posts justifiably, having told their followers to flee, Rabbi Pacifici had the added responsibility for the hundreds of refugees in and around Genoa. Italian Jews, if supplied with money and false identity cards, might melt into the local population, but the refugees, many of whom spoke only a few words of Italian, were easy targets for the SS and needed special care. In addition, throughout September and October 1943, hundreds more had streamed into the Genoa area after having fled southern France and crossed the Alps on foot.

Throughout his tenure in Genoa, Pacifici had felt a special commitment to the refugees. A Saturday never went by that a refugee family was not invited to share Sabbath dinner with his family, Emanuele Pacifici recalls. Despite the mounting difficulties in Genoa brought on by the war, Pacifici found the time to make three trips to Calabria to minister to the refugees in Ferramonti. Their plight made a lasting impression on him.

One of Italy's most learned rabbis—he had written several books of Jewish scholarship and history—Pacifici was an intensely active man who devoted himself to the innumerable practical concerns of the Jewish community under the racial laws. When Jewish children were prohibited from attending public school, he immediately began organizing a Jewish secondary school in the temple offices. For demoralized university students who could not continue their education, he offered classes as well. While he lived a rigorously Orthodox religious life, he was quite undogmatic and open-minded. "Better to close a temple than shut down a school," Emanuele remembers his father saying.

Each day at noon Rabbi Pacifici's synagogue was transformed into a makeshift cafeteria for indigent refugees. There were so many that they had to eat in two shifts. In the evenings Pacifici led study groups in the temple, with the lights dimmed in order to remain unseen by allied aircraft. On Sunday afternoons he took groups of young people out for walks in the countryside.

Augusto Segre, who worked with DELASEM in Genoa during the war, remembers Pacifici as a "whirlwind of activity" during this period. "With his quick step, his rapid gestures, Pacifici seemed to be in constant motion, involved without pause in thousands and thousands of things. . . . In his desire to reach all those who sought him out, he seemed . . . to be in a great hurry to finish as many things as possible." Despite all his responsibilities, Pacifici managed to keep up his scholarly activity. During the hectic war years he wrote two books of biblical commentary.

The sermons he delivered during this period have an apocalyptic urgency that reflects Pacifici's heightened sense of the impending tragedy and sacrifice awaiting the Jews. Pacifici could not speak openly because of fascist censorship, but through the discussion of biblical stories of exile, war and persecution, he managed to make clear parallels with the present. According to Augusto Segre, who heard many of those sermons, audiences during those years had keen antennae, finely tuned to pick up "references to current events in the tone or inflexion of the voice, in a brief, fleeting pause, a little gesture of the hand."

In the figure of Joseph sold by his brothers to be a slave in Egypt, Pacifici found a metaphor for the Jews living under the yoke of the racial laws. "Joseph is the first modern Jew, the first Jew who knows exile and hatred . . . the first Jew who experiences misery and prison, but who, as has happened so many times in the history of the Jews, also experiences sudden changes of fortune and moments of good fortune . . . a man who, despite all of the vicissitudes, the bitterness and disillusionment, remains true to himself."

In words that seem to prefigure the calamity of Italian Jews, Pacifici told his audience: "We feel that if Joseph, instead of rising to the honors that God had reserved for him, had faced even more bitter and difficult trials, even if he had been required to make a holocaust of his life, he would have accepted that supreme sacrifice with firmness and sealed his noble existence with dignity."

On October 1, in the third week of the German occupation, Rabbi Pacifici celebrated Rosh Hashanah, the Jewish New Year, in a nearly empty synagogue. "Perhaps on no other Rosh Hashanah has our temple been so deserted and abandoned as it is today . . . and yet, never as on this Rosh Hashanah have we entered here with our souls so full and impassioned with religious fervor, with the intense desire to be close to God . . . because for us the most serious and difficult hour of life has arrived, and never as when we find ourselves on the roughest shoals do we feel so near to God."

Pacifici was preparing himself internally for the choices he would soon have to make.

Shortly after giving his sermon that day, Rabbi Pacifici went to fetch his son Emanuele at school in Casale Monferrato, east of Turin.

* * *

For Emanuele Pacifici, only twelve years old, the German occupation was at first a relief: it meant that after four long years away, he would be coming home.

Ever since the family had moved to Genoa in 1936, Emanuele had had very little time with his father, who was thoroughly consumed by the larger problems of Genoa's Jewish community. When the rabbi was home, he was often locked up in his formidable study, walled with imposing shelves of sacred Hebrew texts, a room Emanuele knew instinctively not to enter.

Their years in Genoa had been a time of personal tragedy for the Pacificis as well as the Jewish community as a whole. Soon after they arrived, Emanuele's little sister, Miriam, died. One chilly autumn day, he and his mother went out to buy clothes for the coming winter. When they returned home, they found the housekeeper and Miriam lying unconscious on the kitchen floor. Against instructions, the housekeeper had lit a coal stove in the kitchen that had been malfunctioning; a toxic substance emitted by the stove had poisoned the two. The maid regained consciousness almost immediately, but Miriam did not. The image of his sister lying there, her eyes rolling white in their sockets, stayed with Emanuele for many years. After months of agony, she died in March 1937. The death cast such a pall over the family that they soon moved to another apartment.

The racial laws of 1938 brought other shadows and precipitated another family move. A strange, menacing individual seemed to be watching the rabbi's apartment; one night someone came to a window and threatened the family. After the Pacificis moved, the families in their new building shunned them; the other children would not play with Emanuele.

In 1938, Emanuele's childhood world came apart. When his brother, Raffaele, was born, Emanuele experienced violent feelings of jealousy and anger. In the fall, because of the racial laws, he was forced to leave public school and was sent to boarding school in Turin. In the seven-year-old's mind, these events—his brother's arrival, the racial laws, the banishment from home—were blurred together; he felt as if he had been supplanted in his parents' affection and exiled as a kind of personal punishment.

Life in the boarding school was indeed punitive. The children's hair was shaved close to their heads and the headmistress beat them for the smallest infraction of the school's many strict rules. Emanuele was not allowed to go home in the summer because the school felt it would increase his homesickness and make him more difficult to manage. Any letters home were closely censored by the headmistress.

When Emanuele first saw German soldiers in Casale Monferrato, where the school had moved during wartime, in September 1943, he went up and asked one of them if he could look through his binoculars. When he innocently told the headmistress about the incident, she gave him one of the ferocious beatings that were her educational trademark. The worn pages of the diary that Emanuele kept at the time reflect a child's perspective of the German occupation: the dramatic events of history alternate in striking contrast with the daily preoccupations of a twelve-year-old. "September 8, the last bulletin of the war . . . The headmistress gave me a beating. . . . I ate chestnuts for the first time. . . . September 30 is Rosh Hashanah, October 1 Rosh Hashanah." Because Rabbi Pacifici would not travel on the Jewish holy days, he arrived on Sunday, October 3, to collect his son.

When they returned to Genoa, Emanuele spent nearly two precious weeks alone with his father. Following him through his daily rounds, Emanuele was able to get a glimpse into the rabbi's life under Occupation. Pacifici moved furtively from appointment to appointment, meeting one person in a bar, another in a deserted back street, occasionally sneaking a visit to the synagogue or to the family's apartment in Via Antonio Crocco.

Emanuele remembers the rabbi's meeting with Raffaele Cantoni, a Milanese Jew who was one of the leaders of DELASEM. "My father had me sit outside the office so I couldn't hear what was being said, but at a certain point I heard Cantoni shout, 'We can't give up!' If my father had doubts about remaining behind, he certainly didn't after that."

Pacifici continued to walk around Genoa looking very much like a rabbi, with his somber black garb, beard and pince-nez spectacles. "Signor Rabbino," the superintendent of his building, Enrico Sergiani, implored him, "take off your dark clothes, shave your beard! At a time like this, there's no dishonor in that!" But the rabbi refused, and would say: "With the Torah under my arm, I can go safely anywhere." Next Sergiani tried to convince Pacifici to hide in a walled room in the building's basement, which the superintendent alone knew about. "To offer to hide—and feed—a person until the end of the war was an extraordinary commitment," Emanuele says. "This was a time in which food was rationed and a single ration was barely enough to keep one person alive, much less two!"

Rabbi Pacifici, although deeply moved by the offer, refused. Faced with a choice between fleeing and risking almost certain arrest, he elected a third course: he would try to ensure his own safety and meet his commitment to the Jews remaining in Genoa. His solution was to find a hiding place from which he could continue to minister to the refugees.

When he approached Don Repetto with the request, Pacifici meekly added that if it were possible he would like a place with a kitchen where he could prepare his food according to the kosher laws. "He waited for the answer in patient silence, like a poor man who had nothing left, and who could do nothing more for himself," the priest recalled. "I was able immediately to tell him yes, and he appeared happy and opened up even more and took me further into his confidence. . . . He assured me spontaneously he would tell no one the location of the hiding place, and he remained true to his word."

Emanuele Pacifici remembers that shortly after the Jewish holiday of Sukkoth—around October 19—which he celebrated alone with his father in his place of hiding, Carlo Abenheim, his mother's brother, came from Pisa to take him away. His father insisted on coming with them to the Principe train station, and as they stood on the platform, he placed his hands on his son's head and bestowed the priestly blessing: "Bless the Lord that he may keep you; may his countenance shine upon you, keep you in grace and grant you peace." "After blessing and kissing me, two large tears rolled down his cheek."

During the last days of October, Don Repetto accompanied Pacifici as he went about his rabbinical duties, as he described many years later.

> He asked me, always with great consideration and humility, if he might visit groups of foreign refugee Jews, who had been ariving secretly from

the hills in Piedmont to the area around Genoa, and were hidden in various religious institutions. I accompanied him at dusk; they gathered around him and he spoke to them in their language [presumably Hebrew]: in that moment, they opened up to him. It always ended in a prayer: his gaze raised toward the sky, their heads bowed. Then we would rush off with short, fast steps, our duty done.

I never noticed in him, although he was fully aware of being in danger, any nervous preoccupation about his own safety; not a single complaint about his own family, even though his heart was full of pain, memories and love for them!

His choice had been made. He wanted to honor that heroic choice. That choice involved complete forgetfulness of himself, and peace of mind. Peace in the middle of that tempest. And yet that's how I remember him: a figure totally at peace!

In the park, near the building where he was hiding, in that autumn with its long days of rain, he meditated in solitude, perhaps thinking to himself of the words he had said about the patriarch Joseph when he was taken prisoner: "If he were forced to make a holocaust of his life, he would have accepted that supreme sacrifice with firmness, and sealed his noble existence with dignity. . . ."

In his gentle manner he gave me one of his books . . . and he made it more precious with this dedication: "To the Reverend Monsignor Repetto (I was not a Monsignor, he was the first to give me this title; the Pope did so many years later), with the strongest sympathy and profound, heartfelt gratitude."

* * *

On the morning of November 2, Massimo Teglio returned to Genoa after spending several days in Rapallo with his daughter and in-laws. Because he was perhaps even better known in Rapallo than in Genoa, he felt it best not to stay long. He felt safer in the large, anonymous city than in the small seaside resort. By now he had heard reports that on October 16, more than a thousand Jews had been arrested in the area around the Rome synagogue.

When he arrived at his building in Passo Assarotti around noon, Teglio saw that the temple was still open. They're crazy, he said to himself, and went inside to eat lunch. His housekeeper, Eugenia, was living in his apartment; he would eat there and spend the rest of the time in the apartment upstairs. After lunch he decided to go across the street to the synagogue to warn whoever was inside to flee. There was an eerie calm around the temple; the custodian's two children were again playing outside. Teglio, terrified that what had happened in Rome would happen at any moment in Genoa, paused and then summoned his courage to enter the building. "I saw Linda Polacco, the wife of the custodian. 'Are you insane?' I said. 'Get out of here immediately! Don't you know what's happened in Rome?' They were Roman, and perhaps some of their own relatives had been taken. She said: 'As soon as my husband comes back, we'll leave.' While we were talking, the secretary of the Community, Baquis, arrived. I asked him if he had taken care of the lists [with the names and addresses of Jews in Genoa], and he said, 'We've taken care of them.' 'Good,' I told him. 'Then close this place and get out of here!' "

Teglio then went to the center of town and returned home at about seven in the evening. This time everything was closed, including the front door of his apartment building. He was somewhat suspicious: it was, after all, nearly two hours before the nine o'clock curfew imposed by the Nazis. He entered his building cautiously and found the superintendent in a state of great agitation and rage. "In Genoese dialect he yelled: 'What have I ever done to you?' 'What's happened?' I asked him." The Germans had arrived at the temple not long after Massimo had left that afternoon, and had arrested the custodian, Bino Polacco, his wife and their two children. Pointing machine guns at them, the Nazis threatened to kill Polacco's family unless he told them immediately where the lists of the Jewish community members were. Polacco and Baquis had not taken Teglio's warnings seriously and had left the lists in the basement of his building, where the Germans found them immediately. The Nazis had also questioned Teglio's superintendent, an old widower who in fact knew nothing about the lists. Luckily, Polacco had not mentioned Teglio's name, so that after finding the lists the Germans left instead of staying to wait for him.

As Teglio tried to calm the terrified superintendent, pretending to know nothing about how the lists ended up in the basement, the front doorbell rang loudly—the Germans had returned. They had gone through the lists, found Teglio's name, and now they had returned to take him away.

"I told the superintendent to wait a moment. I took the elevator to the second floor and left the door open so that it looked as if somebody had gotten off there. I walked up to my apartment on the third floor. The maid was there preparing dinner and had set the table for two. I told her to remove my place setting right away. Then I went upstairs to Angelo Costa's apartment, where I had moved my furniture. I locked the front door and opened the door to the terrace, which led to the roof; if necessary, there was a place up there behind the chimney where I could hide. It was already dark, so I figured I would be safe there. But the Germans never came up. They saw my apartment, saw the maid there alone with the single place setting, and the apartment empty of furniture except for her room. And she told them just what the superintendent had told them: 'After a bombing Signor Massimo left and took away all his furniture, and we haven't seen him since.' And so I was saved from the first strike."

Chapter Two

With a gun pointed at his head, Bino Polacco, custodian of the synagogue, began telephoning all the Jews of the city and telling them to come to the temple the following morning, November 3, 1943.

From his hiding place on the top floor of his building, Massimo Teglio heard an unusual movement of cars and trucks in the neighborhood during the night. In the morning his housekeeper came and told him that she had seen German soldiers enter the building next door.

Although he probably would have been safer had he stayed put, Teglio walked straight out of his building with as casual a manner as he could muster. He headed up a hill away from the center of the city, stopped in the first bar he saw, and began telephoning as many Jews as he could. He also called a Catholic friend, Angelo Oliva, and asked him to warn others.

From the terrace of her apartment near the synagogue, Romana Rossi-Serrotti watched the Germans prepare their trap. As the Jews began to enter the square she signaled to them with her hands to turn around and run. This was a special act of courage on her part: at the time she was hiding her own son who had deserted from the Italian army after the armistice. When several people got away, the Nazis spotted Rossi-Serrotti and arrested her.

True to his word, Rabbi Riccardo Pacifici had not told anyone, including the employees of the temple, the address of the hiding place given to him by the Archbishop's Office. He had arranged, however, to meet secretly on that very day with Bino Polacco, in an underpass in the center of town. When the rabbi appeared punctually at the appointment, several members of the Gestapo were lying in wait for him. They dragged him back to the temple, where they interrogated him, insulted and beat him. When they saw they were getting nothing from him, they took him to the Marassi prison. Signora Rossi-Serrotti saw him there, with blood on his face and a badly swollen eye. (She was not Jewish and was eventually released by the Germans, through the intervention of Esso–Standard Oil, for which her husband worked.)

* * *

Having escaped arrest two days in a row, Teglio decided to change apartments again. He had the keys to his Catholic in-laws' apartment, a block away from his own. It would take a while before the Germans would think to look for him there.

At his in-laws' Teglio typed a letter of warning to the rest of his family, which was scattered across northern Italy. His brother, Mario, was already safely in hiding with his wife and two children at a remote farmhouse in the Tuscan countryside near Siena. Teglio's parents, his youngest sister, Laura, and his oldest sister, Emma, with her husband and their two children, were in greater jeopardy. They were staying at a family house in Piedmont, where the Germans might well look for them. And Teglio's middle sister, Margherita, her husband and their two children were at a small hotel in Montecatini, whose address figured on the list the Germans had seized. Teglio drafted a quick letter, which said simply: "Rabbi arrested, custodian of the temple and his family arrested. Flee immediately."

Teglio had already thought up various systems for communicating with his family. Two carpenters who lived near him and who had done some work for the Teglios agreed to act as intermediaries between Massimo and Mario. "Their father had died recently," Teglio said, "so I asked if my brother could write to me using their father's name. 'That way,' I said, 'if my mother writes to your father, you will know it's for me and if by chance it should be opened, you can say you don't know anything about it.' "

To reach his parents in Piedmont, Teglio wrote to a Catholic friend in the area. And to communicate with Margherita, Massimo used two sailors who traveled back and forth from Genoa to Montecatini. Before giving the sailors his letter, he dropped it on the ground and smudged it; if they were questioned, the soldiers could say they had found the letter on the street.

Margherita and her family had already arranged for a hiding place with a Catholic friend with whom her husband had done business for many years. "When they got the message they were frightened and spent two days in hiding with friends," Teglio recounted. "On the third day they went back to the Pensione Morini to pack their suitcases."

Teglio had managed to warn several other Jews in Montecatini, who fled immediately. One of them spoke with Margherita before going into hiding, as Teglio learned after the war. " 'What are you doing here?' he said. 'Massimo is furious and says to go into hiding immediately. My sister said: 'We have ordered a taxi for tomorrow and, weather permitting, we will leave then.' "

Thinking that the Germans were interested only in men of military age, Achille Vitale did not sleep at the hotel on the night of November 5. When he returned in the morning, "he found his family gone and the room upside down," Teglio related. "The two maids at the *pensione* told him they had been taken to fascist headquarters, and he immediately went to join them. He did the right thing—I don't know what kind of a life he would have had after something like that.

"It's something that still burns in my heart," Teglio said, with an uncharacteristic bitterness and regret. "I still don't understand how they could have been so stupid. They waited three days. And they called a taxi—you don't call a taxi in Montecatini during wartime. There might have been two or three taxis in the whole town; if the Germans were looking for people, it would have been easy to trace them. You would just ask the taxi driver where he took them. They should have taken the train immediately—no one would have found them. And they had friends waiting to receive them."

* * *

His sister's arrest was the decisive event that pushed Teglio into staying in Genoa. "If she hadn't been arrested I probably would have escaped to Switzerland, but now I was determined to stay behind to find out what had become of Margherita and her family."

His search also led him to the Genoa archdiocese and to Don Francesco Repetto. "My life is full of strange angles and twists of fate," Teglio said. He had heard of Don Repetto quite by chance a few weeks earlier at a meeting with Lelio Valobra, the head of DELASEM. Although Teglio occupied no official position in the organization, he and Valobra had been friends since childhood and had attended school together. Because Teglio had a vast circle of acquaintances, in all walks of life and across the political spectrum, Valobra occasionally asked his old friend to use his contacts on behalf of DELASEM. Teglio, who was better at advancing the cause of others than pursuing his own self-interest, invariably accepted.

During the first weeks of the German occupation, Valobra had invited Teglio and his daughter to have lunch with him in Chiavari, a town on the Ligurian coast. Afterward the two men slipped off to pay a call on the bishop of Chiavari to enlist his aid in hiding Jews. "Valobra pulled out a letter from the Archbishop's Office in Genoa, which asked him to receive and help Valobra—it didn't use the word 'help,' it used one of those expressions that priests use, that doesn't seem to say anything but says it just the same. And the letter was signed by Francesco Repetto—the name somehow stayed in my head."

When Teglio appeared before the priest at the Archbishop's Palace in Genoa, Don Repetto, obviously suspicious, played dumb. "Va-lobra? I don't think I know him," Repetto said. Teglio then mentioned the names of several friends who he knew were active in the Catholic Church, including his upstairs neighbor Angelo Costa. "When I said 'Costa,' Don Repetto got up and excused himself. It turned out that Angelo Costa's brother was in the waiting room. And so he went and said to him, 'There's a man here named Massimo Teglio who says he knows you and your family.' And Costa said immediately, 'Yes, he's a good friend of Angelo's, and an excellent person.'

"Don Repetto then came back into the room and told me, 'If you come back tomorrow at around eleven, I may have some news about your sister and her family.' "

Teglio, stunned at receiving such a rapid response, replied, "It's a miracle!"

And then, very gravely, the priest said something that made a deep impression on Teglio: "The miracle will be if you ever see your loved ones again."

It was the first hint Teglio could recall of the German extermination program: "The priests knew much more than we did about what was going on."

* * *

On November 16, Pietro Cardinal Boetto, archbishop of Genoa, made an attempt to win the release of Rabbi Pacifici by writing to the head of the provincial government, Carlo Basile. He composed a cold, bureaucratic letter suggesting a legal loophole that would allow the authorities to let Pacifici go.

> Various good people have asked me to intercede with Your Excellency on behalf of the Rabbi of the Jews of Genoa, known as an exemplary and

> beneficent citizen who was imprisoned recently because of his race. . . . Today, having reread the law of June 24, 1929, I noticed that according to articles 3 and 4, religious leaders, if recognized and approved by the State (and such is the case until now of the Jewish religion), occupy a highly particular place with respect to the Law and have in certain occasions an official State function, as is made clear by article 7 of that law. This fact imposes on them the obligation of residence: if they were to leave they would fall short of their obligations as spelled out in the law of the Italian State. For this reason the Rabbi of Genoa should be released.

Many years later Don Repetto remarked: "This letter is without humanitarian appeal or indignant protest. When the ecclesiastical authorities find themselves in front of hostile civil authorities . . . then the Church must use cautious and conciliatory language."

The local Italian authorities, as the archbishop well knew, had virtually no power under the German occupation. Two days after writing, the cardinal received a reply.

> I have received Your Eminence's letter. . . . The position you have expounded is highly complex and deserves to be examined with the greatest attention. In any event I wish to inform Your Eminence that, if I should have the opportunity, I will make sure it receives the attention of the competent authorities.

"In this brief response," Don Repetto wrote later, "one can feel the humiliation, possibly sincere, of impotence and shame, also perhaps sincere, of complicity."

* * *

As he began visiting Don Repetto to find out more about his sister's fate, Massimo Teglio was quickly drawn into the clandestine world of DELASEM. His first job was to acquire ration cards for Jews in hiding. All food was strictly rationed at the time and ration cards were distributed directly by the police; it was almost impossible for Jews to buy food legally. At the same time, wandering the city to buy food on the black market was too risky for Jews who lived in hiding.

Teglio devised a system of buying ration cards using a Catholic charity as a cover. He figured that since non-Jews could buy food on the black market at little risk, some would be willing to sell their ration cards for a healthy profit. Don Repetto made him a lay member of the Company of St. Vincent, and Massimo (under the name Giobatta Triberti) went among the Catholic poor buying up ration cards for two or three times the official market value.

This system was, however, both expensive and cumbersome, and Teglio, who quickly showed a natural flair for clandestine work, soon devised a better solution. He decided to approach the police officer responsible for distributing ration cards, Colonel Orfeo Rossi. Teglio knew that as the exodus from the city continued with each month of war, the police were left with hundreds of unclaimed ration cards. " 'Every month that the ration cards expire,' I told Rossi, 'you send your men with the new ones and come back with a thousand left over. If you were to give me about a hundred, the city would still have nine hundred.' " Without even asking what Teglio needed them for, Rossi gave him the cards.

That Teglio should throw himself into clandestine work for DELASEM with such energy and commitment surprised some who knew him. Before the war he lived a gay and somewhat frivolous life, neglecting the family business in favor of his passion for aviation. Lighthearted, gregarious, quick with a joke, something of a ladies' man, he slept late and spent most of his afternoons gunning the motor of a hydroplane among the clouds above Geneva. He had little inclination for politics and had as many friends among Genoa's fascists as in the city's small Jewish community.

"Massimo was lazy," recalls his sister Laura, nine years younger. "He would sleep until noon. Many times we had to go and knock on his door to wake him for lunch. He would come down to eat in his pajamas. I would tremble while my father, who could be quite severe, scolded him. Massimo was always an original. He did only things that interested him. He was always very intelligent. He had a deep love of music. And of course there was his passion for flying. But he never had any interest in ordinary life or for business."

To Teglio, however, his life underground was a natural continuation of his career as a pilot, which he had pursued single-mindedly since the age of nine. His interest was kindled in 1909, when his father took him to Brescia to see one of the first exhibitions of flight in Italy. After a couple of aborted takeoffs, one of the planes managed a brief, two-hundred meter flight; and that brief spectacle of man gliding above the earth so captivated Teglio that from then on he was determined to be a pilot. As soon as he turned seventeen, he volunteered for the newly formed Italian air force. He was sent to flight school, but World War I ended before he had become a pilot.

When he returned home to Genoa after the war, he prepared for a career at Fratelli Teglio (Teglio Brothers), the dried-fish importing firm his Teglio grandfather had founded. Teglio went to business school but in typical fashion failed to get his degree because he didn't get around to finishing one of his courses. His mother wanted him to pursue a diplomatic career because of his charm and ability to get along with people, but nothing came of the idea. Instead he worked in a desultory fashion at Fratelli Teglio, while his real energy went into starting the Genoa Aviation Club. In fact, Teglio spent so much time in the air that eventually his father and brother kicked him out of the family business.

Many of the traits that made him ill-suited to the ordinary business world made him the perfect person in a crisis. The cool of the pilot and the daredevil attitude of the stuntman served him well in situations of extreme danger. He had made three solo trips from Genoa to Libya in tiny hydroplanes without instruments. He had flown in storms at sea, and in desert sandstorms in North Africa. He had crashed several times and survived.

His easygoing, social nature, which might have been a liability in business dealings, was a great asset during the war. His vast network of friendships, including the most powerful and the most humble people in Genoa, was invaluable. His open, undogmatic nature allowed him to move easily among different worlds—fascists and antifascists; rabbis and archbishops; soldiers, scholars and shopkeepers.

Through the aviation club he had come to know many of the wealthiest and most prominent men in Genoa, some of them with important positions in the Fascist Party. He had flown with Italo Balbo, who achieved the kind of heroic status in Italy that Charles Lindbergh enjoyed in the United States. Balbo had led an entire squadron of Italian pilots in a historic flight from Rome to Chicago in 1933. (Balbo Drive in Chicago commemorates the feat.) An early leader of the fascist revolution, Balbo was a member of the "quadrumvirate" that stood just below Mussolini in the hierarchy of fascist power. When Balbo's fame began to threaten that of Il Duce himself, he was shipped off to Tripoli as governor of the Italian colony of Libya.

Teglio flew to Tripoli three times to join Balbo in airplane races the colonial governor had organized. "Balbo liked me because I always told him exactly what I thought," Teglio recalled. "And he was a great friend of the Jews."

Teglio recalls the day in 1937 when Balbo flew from Tripoli to Genoa in order to dissuade Mussolini from a Rome–Berlin axis. "An alliance is a serious thing and it will lead to war," Balbo said to Teglio. The following year Balbo was one of the few fascist leaders who had the courage to oppose the racial laws openly.

The last time Balbo had visited Genoa was in 1939, in full racial campaign. Teglio, his wife, parents, brother and sisters turned out with the throng that greeted Balbo as he flew into the harbor by hydroplane. When the fascist leader came ashore he spotted Teglio in the crowd and motioned to him to come over. Balbo shook Teglio's hand warmly and asked, "Is there anyone else here from your family?" "They're all here!" Teglio answered. And in front of several hundred onlookers, Balbo made a point of greeting the family of his Jewish friend from Genoa first. "Afterward," Teglio remembered, "I asked Balbo's copilot, 'He knows I'm Jewish, doesn't he?' and the copilot replied, 'He did it intentionally.' " This close public association with Balbo did not hurt Teglio when he approached fascist officials for help during the German occupation.

The restrictions imposed by the racial laws had prepared Teglio for the life of subterfuge and bureaucratic legerdemain needed during the Occupation. By law the Teglio family was required to sell its business, but Massimo had helped dodge the laws by putting the ownership of the company in the name of his then three-year-old daughter, Nicoletta, who was half Jewish. "My father and brother kicked me out of the business, but when they needed help during the racial campaign, they came to me. But I've forgiven them." He also enlisted Giorgio Parodi, a leading Genoese businessman and friend from the aviation club, to act as the company's trustee.

In order to hide the Jewish ownership of the firm, its name was changed from Fratelli Teglio, to the anonymous-sounding Copeco. Although the name stood for "Preserved Fish Company" in Italian—Compagnia Pesce Conservato—*copeco* is also Italian for the Soviet currency, "kopeck." The subversive ring of the name and the fact that a Jewish company was being headed by his own three-year-old "Aryan" daughter appealed to Teglio's pranksterish sense of humor.

It was in a similar spirit that Teglio set about improving DELASEM's system of producing false identification cards. "I told Don Repetto, 'I don't think you want to become a forger, but I will give it a try.' " The organization had already acquired, at considerable expense, several hundred blank cards which needed to be authenticated with government stamps. Since the Allies had reached Naples by early October 1943, people looking to hide their identity would pretend to come from southern Italy because the Germans would have no way of checking the authenticity of their cards. So far DELASEM had procured the stamp of only one small town in Apulia, Troia. Teglio considered it the height of folly for hundreds of Jewish fugitives to be running around with identity cards from the same small Apulian town, especially one with such an eye-catching name—in Italian slang, *troia* means "whore." On seeing that, Teglio reflected, any Italian policeman would have broke out in laughter and said, 'Son of a whore.' It's a name they'd remember. Since it's such a small town, as soon as they'd seen two or three of them, they would know there was a trick."

On November 18, 1943, a leader of DELASEM, Enrico Luzzatto, and his wife were arrested by the Nazis; the couple had crudely forged identity cards. "Luzzatto was in many ways brave and intelligent, but he lacked both a certain imagination and a sense of humor," Teglio said. Not only was he carrying a Troia identity card, but he had changed the spelling of his name on it from "Luzzatto" to "Suzzatto," and put his real date of birth and address on the card. "Making the date and address the same [as his own] was bad enough—because he was supposed to be another person," Teglio said. "But simply to change an L into an S—which in script look similar—was sheer stupidity."

In order to create more convincing forgeries, Teglio obtained copies of official letterhead from various southern Italian towns. Through friends he found an engraver who would make rubber and metal stamps he could use to prepare documents with official-looking markings. The Archbishop's Office procured stamps for the corresponding church parishes, thus enabling Teglio to create baptismal certificates to go along with the identity cards. Before long he had assembled a whole workshop for manufacturing false documents; he kept the various tools hidden in several different apartments to minimize chances of detection.

In perfecting his forgeries, Teglio received unexpected help from another top fascist official, Commissioner Sbezzi of the Genoa police, whom he had gotten to know after the racial campaign began.

Because he had become too friendly with Jews and antifascists, Sbezzi had been transferred during the German occupation from the important "political department" to the lowly passport office. "One day, while riding on the tram, I was stopped by an agent who worked for Dottor Sbezzi. He said to me, 'Dottor Sbezzi told me to tell you that you shouldn't be riding on Via Venti Settembre at three in the afternoon.' " The agent also told him that Sbezzi wanted to invite Teglio to dinner at his house in Via Nizza.

Teglio had become friends with Sbezzi under circumstances that say much about the paradoxical nature of the Italian racial laws. After the declaration of war in June 1940, the government in Rome ordered the Genoa police to place ten antifascist Jews in house arrest outside Genoa. Sbezzi, then head of the police's "political office," responded that he knew of only one antifascist Jew in Genoa, Torquato Caffaz. The Ministry of the Interior nonetheless ordered him to come up with the list of ten Jews. Sbezzi decided that the only way to accomplish the task was to pick the remaining nine completely at random. Unfortunately for Teglio's sister Margherita and her husband, Achille Vitale, his was the second-to-last of the nine names chosen as Sbezzi moved from A to Z. (One of the nine selected turned out to be a heavily decorated hero of World War I; he was able to get out of the sentence. Vitale, however, was not so fortunate and spent nearly a year away from home in order to satisfy this bureaucratic caprice.) In efforts to free his brother-in-law, Teglio got to know Sbezzi; although he had Vitale arrested, the police official advised Teglio privately on how to win an early release.

When Teglio appeared at Sbezzi's house for dinner in November 1943, he received a tongue-lashing. Teglio later recalled: " 'You're crazy!' he told me. 'You belong in a straitjacket! You have a daughter who has already lost her mother. Now she'll lose her father!' I said, 'Listen, Doctor Sbezzi, I have perfectly authentic German documents. If they stop me with these, I'll be all right.' I showed him my papers. Then I showed him the false identity cards I was making, to see whether they would work. He told me, 'They're very well done, too well done. We don't do them as well. Change the writing in this way and that.' Then he turned one over, felt the underside and noticed that it was missing the imprimatur [a nearly visible seal embossed into the card]. 'Without that you'll be caught immediately.' "

Through another friend, Teglio was able to get the official printer for the Genoa police to put the imprimatur on his cards. The printer even refused to accept payment for the service. Hostility toward the German occupation and Mussolini's puppet government was so widespread that much of the legal apparatus was actively collaborating with the antifascist conspiracy.

* * *

Soon after Rabbi Pacifici's arrest on November 3, Don Repetto dispatched Gian Maria Rotondi—an exuberant young priest who rode a motorcycle—to give the rabbi's family the news and warn them to flee. Don Rotondi found Wanda Pacifici, with her mother, brother and two sons in her family's country house in the village of Calci, near Pisa.

Mrs. Pacifici's father, Umberto Abenheim, had been a prominent lawyer in Pisa and his family had spent their summers in Calci for thirty years. "People knew we were Jewish, but no one even knew what that meant," Emanuele Pacifici says. "We were known as the family of the Avvohado" (the Tuscan pronunciation of *avvocato*, lawyer). In a poor rural population where illiteracy was common, the title Avvohado, spoken with great respect, suggested a lofty peak of education and wealth. People would call on Emanuele's grandfather to seek his advice, and on every Friday he would distribute alms to the poorest members of the community.

The Abenheims' house was a center of social life during the summers: they were the only family in the village to own a record player—an early gramophone with a wind-up arm and a large horn. Some of Emanuele's fondest childhood memories are of summer evenings at Calci spent listening to famous arias of Italian opera with most of the village. "We would place the gramophone on the porch; I was in charge of winding the machine and cleaning the needle. The people of the town went mad with joy; many of them had literally never heard anything of the kind. My grandmother would finally say, 'All right, it's time for bed.' And the crowd would yell, 'Emanuele, put on one last record.' My grandmother would always relent."

But in November 1943 the family realized that even in Calci they were no longer safe. "There were people who wore the black shirt, and you couldn't be sure what they thought about the Jews," says Emanuele. "One morning we woke up early and saw a notice attached to a wall a few yards from our house, telling 'all Jews' to report immediately to the town hall. There were only about twenty-five families in the town and we were the only Jews, so it wasn't hard to imagine for whom that notice was meant." Since it would have been easy enough for an official to come and arrest them, Emanuele's family understood the notice as a friendly warning to the family to leave town quickly.

"As we were considering our next move, the priest, Gian Maria Rotondi, arrived with the terrible news about my father. Fearing that under torture he might reveal our whereabouts, Papà had advised us to flee. Don Rotondi gave us a letter from Cardinal Boetto to present to Cardinal Elia Della Costa, the archbishop of Florence.

"Around November 10 we fled to another small town near Calci, where my mother's childhood governess lived," Emanuele says. "But it was a very small town, and as strangers we would have stood out too much to remain hidden there long. We sneaked back to my grandparents' house in Pisa, which was right next to the police station. We stayed there for several days, locked up in the house until nighttime. Then we fled to Florence."

The family split up: Emanuel's mother, her two children and her brother traveled to Florence, while her parents went to a Tuscan village where they had friends.

"We arrived in Florence at about midnight," Emanuele recalls. "We had to stay in the train station because it was past curfew. The station was jammed, people were spread out everywhere. My uncle Carlo went to hide somewhere out near the train tracks. My mother was able to find a square of space in one of the waiting rooms, where we were able to stretch out. She lay down her fur coat for my little brother to sleep on; she sat up and I pretended to sleep in order not to worry her. At one point during the night, a group of young fascists, Italians, not more than eighteen years old, came crashing into the waiting room, their rifles pointed. They were looking for men who had evaded military service. Our identification cards had 'of the Jewish race' stamped on them, so if they had asked for our documents we would have been done for. My mother started fixing her face nervously, and I heard her saying under her breath the prayer: 'Hear, O Israel, the Lord is our God, the Lord God is one. . . .' Either because they took pity on us or because they had other things on their mind, they never asked for our papers and we were safe for the night. Whenever I celebrate Passover, and think of the image of the angel of death passing over the houses, I remember that night in Florence."

At eight the next morning, Carlo Abenheim joined his sister and nephews and took them to a priest whose name Don Repetto had given them, Leto Casini. "He gave us a list of convents, and the entire day we made the rounds, from convent to convent, knocking on doors, always hearing the same answer: 'We're full.' 'No room.' 'We're sorry.' Every time we heard a door close it was another moment of anguish. It was evening, about five or six, when we reached Santa Maria del Carmine." Because the convent there was restricted to women, the Carmelite nuns were prepared to take Wanda Pacifici but not her sons or brother. Under the circumstances, however, the mother superior agreed to make an exception for one night. "That evening my mother and little brother were allowed to sleep in a room upstairs, while I, as a boy of twelve, was made to sleep in the waiting room downstairs. It was Saturday, November 20."

The following day, Emanuele and Raffaele, who was five, were sent off to a Catholic boarding school for boys in Settignano, a town in the hills above Florence. They left their trunk full of clothing in the city; Wanda said she would bring it when she came for a visit the following Sunday.

"Mamma was supposed to come at about two-thirty," Emanuele recalls. "I placed myself in the window so I could watch her arrive." When he saw distant figures coming in the direction of the school, he would say to himself: Now she's coming, that's her! "As long as I breathe I will never forget those moments. But she never came, and finally a nun came and said, 'Emanuele, let's go to mass.' After a week, the nun told me with great delicacy: 'Your mother has met the same fate as your father.' "

Two nights before Wanda Pacifici was supposed to go see her sons in Settignano, the Germans made a surprise raid on the convent. Throughout the war in Italy, the Nazis were careful to respect Vatican property; the raid on Santa Maria del Carmine was a rare exception.

At about three in the morning, a troop of some thirty German SS and Italian militiamen arrived at the convent and rang the bell loudly. Before anyone inside could reach the door, they shot the lock and forced it open. At the same time, other soldiers scaled the garden wall and broke down a glass door leading into the convent. "Throughout the search [they] seemed to know exactly where to look—a clear indication of betrayal," noted the mother superior of the convent, Sister Esther Busnelli. Still reeling from the shock of the raid, Sister Esther prepared a report immediately afterward, written in the form of a diary entry.

> The Jewish women in the living room are captured immediately like mice in a trap. A soldier fires up at the balcony to force people to come down . . . only to discover no one there. One girl tries to escape out a window only to be run down by an SS soldier. . . .
>
> A German soldier demands to be taken to the telephone and with a big scissors cuts the telephone lines. Then, laughing with self-satisfaction, he takes out a candy and sucks on it.
>
> In the coatroom of the dormitory, a gun of one of the SS goes off by mistake, terrifying the poor women, and making us think that we may all be shot from one moment to the next.

For the next three days, the Germans kept their captives—some thirty women and children—under guard at the convent, before sending them to a concentration camp.

The state of mind of the women at the convent comes through strongly in a letter written on November 30 by Germana Ravenna, a woman from Ferrara who had arrived at Santa Maria del Carmine with her mother the day before the Germans.

> We are waiting for our fate to be decided, and we fear it will not be a happy one. Ask news of our last days here from Sister Emma Luisa, who, along with all the other nuns here, has been of angelic goodness toward us.
>
> I want you to know, my dears, that our every thought has been of you and that I have struggled these last months with all my strength to bring us to safety, and just when I believed I had succeeded, destiny has mocked us cruelly and everything has collapsed. . . .

Put some remembrance of Mamma and myself in the Ferrara cemetery near the tomb of our ancestors.

That same day the Germans told the women to prepare for "a very long trip" that evening. At lunch the nuns gave up a portion of their rationed meal to prepare food packages for the women to take on their trip. Sister Esther described the scene of the departure:

We tried to save two young brides with their babies. Vittoria, with two little ones, we put in bed, making believe she was ill. Anna, with her baby of thirteen months, we brought up into a room in the dormitory, hoping that in the confusion, among the crying and screaming, their absence might go unnoticed. . . .

The roll call began and they were loaded onto the truck like beasts to slaughter.

We gave each one the most affectionate sisterly embrace possible; it was a scene to make the stones cry, but those hearts hardened by hatred seemed to feel no pain. We kept hoping for the two women while the roll call continued. "Anna!" Silence. "Anna!" We answered: "She had to go to her room because of her child." "Get her." . . . Before I was able to open my mouth, she exclaimed radiantly, "Am I safe? Have they gone?" "No, Anna, they are still there and they are calling you." Courage!!!

She pulled the child from her breast and squeezed it in a frenzy. She grabbed her head with her hands and screamed like a wild animal: "It's impossible! What have we done wrong? I'm going crazy." She seemed in fact to suffer a wave of insanity. Then she got up and followed us in a kind of stupor, not hearing, as if unconscious. But when she reached the truck, she tried another route: "I have tuberculosis, I have a medical certificate." The official, responding with an ironic laugh, took the child, caressed and kissed it. He has a family and a child too. Then it's Vittoria's turn. She implores, yells that she is sick, begs for her children, but it's all in vain. . . .

Just and Merciful God, have pity on your chosen people. Dear Madonna, protect our unfortunate friends in life and for eternity. . . .

We heard later that they were taken to a fortress in Verona, and that Anna was showing signs of insanity . . . and then nothing more.

O Lord, how impenetrable are your ways!!!

* * *

The same day the trucks left Santa Maria del Carmine, Massimo Teglio went to the Archbishop's Palace in Genoa and to his surprise saw

Linda Polacco, the wife of the temple custodian who had been arrested at the beginning of the month.

While the Germans still held her husband in prison, they had released Signora Polacco and her two children, claiming that it was too much trouble to keep small children in jail. Having nowhere else to go, she took her children back to their old apartment at the synagogue—the place of their arrest. Teglio had kept his distance, believing that the Germans were using her as a lure to catch other Jews.

Teglio's housekeeper, Eugenia, had run into Signora Polacco in a local grocery store. Eugenia went to talk to her but was snubbed coldly. When the housekeeper complained to Teglio about her rudeness, he replied: "She wasn't being rude to you, she was being kind. It means she's being followed."

But when Teglio bumped into her on November 30, it was on safe territory, during one of his visits to see Don Repetto. Teglio knew from his own sources that the next day the first trainload of Jewish prisoners would be leaving Genoa to join a convoy to Germany. He warned Signora Polacco that if she returned to the temple that night the Germans would arrest her and the children and deport them the next day. She agreed to flee. "Her husband had told her that she should try to save herself and the children and that he would have a better chance on his own," Teglio recalled.

A recently widowed Catholic woman, Adele Castioni, who was at the archdiocese offices that morning, agreed to take the Polaccos to her apartment until evening, by which time, Teglio hoped, he would find another place for the family to sleep. Teglio arranged to meet Signora Polacco at six that evening in a bar in a somewhat disreputable part of town. To his astonishment, she entered dressed to the nines, with a fur, elaborate makeup and flashy earrings. "If I hadn't been expecting her I never would have recognized her. She was normally a plainly dressed woman who never used anything other than soap and water. And I thought to myself, What's gotten into her head, she looks like a streetwalker. Then she explained that the woman she was staying with had made her up this way so no one would recognize her. I started to have faith in this woman [Signora Castioni]. I told Signora Polacco, 'Go wash your face, get your kids, and come back to me here.' She then told me that she thought that if I were to speak with the widow she would let them spend the night. She had already put her kids to bed."

Teglio agreed but had Signora Polacco walk ahead without looking back, while he followed at a distance. The widow lived in the smaller of Genoa's two high-rise apartment buildings, which were known as the "little skyscraper" and the "big skyscraper." Teglio convinced the widow to let the Polaccos stay the night; the following morning Don Repetto would find a place for them to hide in a local religious institution.

That evening, however, the Nazis began to search for the Polacco family, aided by a foolish mistake on Linda Polacco's part. Knowing that she might never see her husband again, she had sent him a note that afternoon through an Italian soldier working at the prison. The Germans spotted Bino Polacco reading the letter, which included a number of clues as to his wife's whereabouts. The prison interpreter later recalled the letter as saying roughly:

> I went to the Archbishop's Palace and Don Repetto gave me 500 lire. Signor Massimo arrived: it must have been God who sent him, because he found a place for me to hide with a nice woman. I am in her house; the children have eaten and are playing. Her name is Castiglioni and she lives in the skyscraper. I am sending this through the soldier with the glasses.

For several hours, the Germans searched unsuccessfully: they were looking in the wrong "skyscraper," and the widow's name was Castioni not Castiglioni. But at about three in the morning they realized their mistake and tracked down the Polaccos in the "little skyscraper." As originally planned, the entire family left the next day on a train for Auschwitz, which contained the first hundred Jews arrested in Genoa.

Unable to do anything more for the Polaccos, Teglio sent a former employee of his family's business to the train station that day to note the serial numbers of the deportation trains. Then, through another friend with connections in the railroad, he was able to trace their progress through Italy and across the Brenner Pass on the way north.

One who avoided deportation that day was Enrico Luzzatto, the DELASEM leader who had been arrested with his wife two weeks earlier. Because Luzzatto spoke fluent German, the Germans decided to keep him at the Genoa prison as an interpreter. His wife, who was half Jewish, was allowed to leave the prison during the day but required to return there each night.

Teglio saw Signora Luzzatto's release as a chance to gain information regularly from within the prison, and he devised an ingenious system for meeting her without attracting the attention of the Germans. With DELASEM funds he had her hired by a friend of his whose office was in the same building as that of another friend. When Teglio wanted to meet with Signora Luzzatto he would visit the office of the second friend. "She would come up to me without leaving the building or being seen. I knew exactly what was happening in the prison. We could give information to relatives about people in prison. We knew when the deportation trains were leaving."

It was Mrs. Luzzatto, in fact, who told Teglio the story of the Polacco letter—so that at least Teglio knew that Linda Polacco had been arrested through her own mistake rather than through a betrayal on Adele Castioni's part.

* * *

Before leaving the convent in Florence, Wanda Pacifici had managed to scribble a furtive note to her brother, Carlo, addressed to the Catholic woman who had taken care of her during childhood. It is written in a kind of code—using the word "wounded" instead of "arrested," for instance—in order not to compromise her former governess. (Indeed, after receiving it, the woman vigorously crossed out her name and address.)

> I have been badly wounded and I don't know what fate awaits me. I am greatly troubled because I don't know if I will ever see my loved ones again. . . . Please tell my brother not to come here and that he should tend to his own great responsibilities.
>
> See if you can save me from this serious wound because I do not want to die. I was wounded rather brutally on the 26th of the month.

As her train left Verona, Wanda Pacifici dropped a second message from the railroad car headed to Auschwitz. Someone picked up the postcard and sent it on to its destination.

> December 7, 1943
>
> With heart afflicted I leave my homeland and head for distant lands alone. I try to keep my spirits up. Give a kiss to my brother and my dear mother, whom I will never forget. May they pray for me. I will do everything I can to send some news of myself. I am fine. Remind Carlo that those two [her sons] are not with me and that he should protect and help them as if they were his own. I hope we may be able to see one another again soon.

Adding an ironical and grotesquely tragic note to the message is the word VINCEREMO! ("We will win!") stamped on the card, as was common during the war years in Italy.

In Verona, Wanda Pacifici's train was hooked up to a train from Milan containing her husband. And so husband and wife, in separate cars and probably unaware of each other's presence, headed off together to Auschwitz. Of some six hundred on the train, three would return.

* * *

On the same train with Wanda and Riccardo Pacifici was Raffaele Cantoni, one of the leaders of DELASEM who had been arrested in Florence a few days earlier. When he spotted a loose plank in the wall of the railroad car, Cantoni smashed open a hole with the handle of his umbrella; as the train slowed down passing through Padua, he jumped out. The other passengers in the car, perhaps afraid they would be shot instantly if caught escaping, remained on board.

Throughout November, Cantoni and the old leadership of DELASEM had tried desperately to continue their work from underground. But one by one they had been wiped out. On November 18, Valobra's secretary, Luzzatto, had been arrested in Genoa. Then, on November 26, the Germans, aided by a spy who had infiltrated the group, burst in on a DELASEM meeting in Florence and arrested six people, including Nathan Cassutto, chief rabbi of Florence, and Don Leto Casini, the priest who had assumed a role in Florence similar to that of Don Repetto in Genoa. (The five Jews arrested were deported, while Casini was liberated after the intervention of the Vatican.) Three days later, Cantoni was captured with two other members of the group in Florence.

After jumping from the train, Cantoni managed to make his way back to Genoa to warn the remaining members of DELASEM. He had decided to flee to Switzerland; he realized that his presence had become more a danger than a help to the organization. Lelio Valobra had come to the same conclusion after the Germans discovered his hiding place near Genoa. When Cantoni arrived at the Archbishop's Palace in Genoa, he ran into Massimo Teglio. When he heard of the work Teglio had already undertaken, Cantoni designated him the head of DELASEM for northern Italy and entrusted him with the names and addresses of the group's contacts. Thus Teglio was invested officially with the role he had already begun to play informally.

Chapter Three

During the first months of the German occupation, DELASEM had begun sending groups of fugitives over the border into Switzerland near the town of Voldomino. But the system was risky and unpredictable: the organization had to rely on hired mountain guides and the goodwill of the Swiss government.

In early December, 1943, a group of approximately fifteen Jews led by the Genoese priest Gian Maria Rotondi was turned back by Swiss guards at the Italian border. When they returned to Voldomino, all but one—including Don Rotondi—were arrested in a fascist roundup. Through a stroke of good fortune, one young woman in the group who worked for DELASEM had stopped in a tavern to get something to eat. When the proprietress of the tavern saw armed men searching the town, she made the woman sit down and gave her some work to do. The soldiers entered to see if anyone was hiding in the tavern, but they found only the proprietress and her "niece," hard at work. The young woman returned to Genoa to alert DELASEM members about the arrests.

One of Massimo Teglio's first tasks on taking control of the group, then, was to establish a safe system for smuggling fugitives across the border into Switzerland. He sought out the aid of Leo Biaggi de Blasys, who was the representative of the International Red Cross for Italy and whose father was the Swiss consul in Genoa. Teglio, who wanted to coordinate the departures with de Blasys so that the fugitives would not be turned away by Swiss authorities, told him very frankly: "I don't want to fool you—along with the Jews there will also be Italians in danger."

De Blasys agreed to the arrangement and insisted only that the fugitives be furnished with plausible fake documents. They had to have two sets of documents: false for traveling within Italy, and real to show the Swiss that they were Jews in genuine need of asylum. At the same time, Italian citizens escaping military service, who were not allowed to enter Switzerland, had to be camouflaged as Jewish refugees. Teglio was turning Jews into Christians in Italy and Christians into Jews in Switzerland.

With the help of two Genoese lawyers, Ernesto Cuomo and Massimo Medina, Teglio found a safe place at which fugitives might cross the Swiss border. The two lawyers (both Catholics of Jewish ancestry) had a wealthy client with a large estate that overlapped the border. The client—whose name Teglio never knew—offered to let DELASEM use her land to bring people across the border to safety. She herself came to Genoa once a week and shepherded groups of refugees out of the country. Teglio arranged to move people out in small, inconspicuous groups, usually six people a week, never more than eight at a time. Because the woman traveled to Genoa with her maid, Teglio would have the two women split up and travel with three people each. They would leave the city from different train stations and sit in different compartments.

Thus, week by week, Teglio was able to move refugees hiding in various religious institutions from Italy to Switzerland. There Lelio Valobra, Raffaele Cantoni and other exiled leaders of DELASEM would be able to help them with funds that were still arriving from the Joint Distribution Committee in the United States.

As he became increasingly involved in clandestine activity, Teglio felt it was imperative to move his eight-year-old daughter to a more secure hiding place. Initially he had felt that, as a baptized Christian living with her Catholic grandparents, Nicoletta would be safe in Rapallo. Now he feared that if his role in DELASEM became known to the Germans, they might try to strike at him through the child. Moreover, Teglio learned from a friend that because Nicoletta's only living parent was Jewish the Germans would not hesitate to deport her.

"This convinced me that I had to act," he says. "I knew that my daughter was in mortal danger with her mother dead. Otherwise my in-laws would probably never have let the child go. I told them that if anything happened to her I would kill the both of them. I don't know if I would have done it, but I said it straight out. They couldn't protect her anymore."

Teglio asked Don Repetto to find a Catholic institution, and the priest placed Nicoletta with the Sisters of the Sacred Heart in Sturla, an outlying district of Genoa.

Having put his daughter in the convent, and unable to visit his in-laws for fear of being captured, Teglio was now alone in the world. He felt this even more acutely at the approach of Christmas, a holiday that he, although Jewish, was used to celebrating.

"As I was walking on Via Cairoli on Christmas Eve, I ran into the man who tended bar at the hydroplane station. 'Are you alone tomorrow?' he asked, and invited me to his bar on the other side of the city. It was a hangout for die-hard fascists. I said, 'You want me to be seen there?' And he answered, 'Don't worry, you'll be safer there than in your own bed. When I bring people there, no one bothers them.' In fact he was right, and I even gathered some useful information. I managed to find some kind of gift and I spent Christmas with him and his family."

* * *

In the Tuscan hill town of Settignano, Emanuele and Pacifici Raffaele lived at the boarding school pretending to be Catholic children. Going by the name Pallini, they attended mass each day but did not take Communion. Emanuele at one point asked if he could convert to Christianity. But the nuns were scrupulous in not wanting to exploit his desperate situation to make a convert. "The sister said to me, 'Let's wait until your parents return, and then you can.' "

The children knew that their parents had been arrested by the Germans, but they had only the dimmest idea of what might have happened to them. "It never even entered my head that they might have taken them to Germany," he says. "I was more afraid for my father than my mother, but I thought they would both be kept somewhere in Italy until the end of the war."

Although the nuns were kind, Emanuele's life in Settignano was not easy. The school went only up to fifth grade; Emanuele and another boy his age who were too old for the classes were put to work doing manual labor. They helped in the kitchen, watered the garden and cleaned the school. "We had to wax the corridor floors, and there was none of this liquid wax they have now. The floors had to shine like a mirror, and believe me, the nuns checked carefully."

But by far the most serious problem was hunger. "Black hunger," Emanuele remembers. "When this other boy and I peeled potatoes, we would peel them in such a way that some of the potato would remain on the peel. The nun told us, 'You've got to peel them more carefully,' and we would say, 'But sister, I can't.' These peels would be thrown into the garbage. We would fish them out of the trash and wash them, then go in the garden, light a little fire, and cook the peels and eat them with a little salt. That was hunger.

"Bread was impossible to find, although the nuns had it. One day I was near the kitchen and no one was around. I saw two pieces of bread and I grabbed them and put them into my pocket. Before I had managed to go a hundred yards, I ran right into a nun. The nun immediately said, 'Stop! What's in your pocket?' She put her hand into my pocket and took out two pieces of bread. Then she brought me in front of a class of the other children and put some hard kernels of corn on the floor and made me kneel down on them. As I shifted my weight from one knee to the other to avoid the pain, the kernels entered my flesh. And finally, when the nun saw the blood, she let me up. I still have the scars from that."

That punishment notwithstanding, Emanuele found the life at Settignano less painful than his experience at the Jewish boarding school in Piedmont, where he had spent four miserable years. "That was the only really bad incident at Settignano. The nuns were severe the way all boarding school teachers were at that time, but in Piedmont it was completely different. The headmistress there beat you all the time, for anything. And at Settignano I think the nun was admonished for the episode with the corn. I bear no hard feelings about the convent at Settignano. There were lots of difficulties, but for the most part they were the difficulties that everyone was suffering during the war."

* * *

By the end of 1943, the clandestine DELASEM network was running out of money. The German occupation had temporarily cut off the possibility of transferring money from Switzerland into Italy. But the leaders of the group had planned for this. An important collaborator named Shapira had a large textile business north of Milan. When Shapira fled to Switzerland he left the business in the hands of his Catholic partner, Tognella, and instructed him to forward money to Don Repetto; it would be repaid by DELASEM after the war.

Much of the old organization, run by Jews, had collapsed under the pressures of the Occupation. It survived, during its underground phase, as a loose patchwork of archdioceses, convents, monasteries and local parishes that hid and helped fugitive Jews. By design, Teglio wanted to keep the degree of organization to the absolute minimum. "The first thing I did was to put an end to all meetings. They were a danger to them and a danger to me," Teglio said. In some cases in such cities as Genoa and Florence, for example, DELASEM's efforts were coordinated by the local archbishops, but often there was a high degree of spontaneity and improvisation. Some individual parishes helped Jews, partisans, and escaped Allied prisoners of war and Italian soldiers without informing their superiors.

Because it was impossible for Don Repetto in Genoa to maintain regular contact with Rome, a separate, parallel network developed there. The head of DELASEM in the capital, Settimio Sorani, continued his work during the nine months of German occupation with the invaluable aid of a French Capuchin monk, Marie Benoit. They managed to obtain money from the United States through the American and British ambassadors to the Vatican. By the time Rome was liberated in June 1944, Benoit and Sorani were assisting some 4,000 Jews in more than a hundred religious institutions across the city.

Repetto and Teglio's network covered principally the northern regions of Piedmont, Lombardy, Emilia-Romagna, Tuscany, the Veneto and Trentino. They were in regular contact with the archdioceses—of Turin, of Milan, Florence, Bologna—mainly for the purposes of distributing money. They also collaborated directly with smaller parishes that required special help. Teglio traveled to Cuneo, in Piedmont, to help hide about 2,000 foreign Jewish refugees who had sneaked into Italy when the Italian army withdrew from France after the September 1943 armistice. Working closely with local parishes, Repetto was able to transfer many of the refugees slowly down to Genoa and then, a few at a time, to safety in Switzerland.

Having run through DELASEM's available funds, Teglio and Repetto decided to go to Busto Arsizio, the small town northwest of Milan where Shapira and Tognella's textile factory was located, to ask for an infusion of cash. Travel in the heavily bombed North was slow and cumbersome, and Teglio and Repetto planned to stop overnight in Milan. They had arranged to sleep in a building belonging to the Archdiocese of Milan, but when they arrived in the afternoon they found the place a shambles. The Germans had just been there, and had arrested a priest suspected of hiding Jews.

"Don Repetto was absolutely terrified," Teglio recounted. "But he was frightened mostly for me: 'What have I gotten you into!' he said. I had Catholic friends in Milan I could have stayed with, but I couldn't bring a priest with me because it would have looked suspicious. So he said, 'You go where you want, I'll find a place for myself.' I told him, 'Don Repetto, nothing has happened to us. Tonight we will sleep here: if they were here this afternoon, this is the last place the Germans will come tonight. And tomorrow we will continue on to Busto Arsizio.'

"Don Repetto was a funny character. He was fearful and yet he did courageous things. He used to say that he accomplished very little, that he hadn't risked his skin as others had. He thought himself small compared to me, and yet he put himself at risk constantly. He was very ceremonious and formal, and he spoke in that elaborate way that priests do, but he was very good, honest and sweet."

In Milan, Teglio and Repetto established contact with another priest, Giuseppe Bicchierai, chaplain at San Vittore, the chief prison of Milan. Don Bicchierai assumed an important diplomatic role mediating between the Catholic Church and the SS in Milan; he convinced the Germans to release both the Genoese priest Don Gian Maria Rotondi and a DELASEM collaborator, Harry Klein, who were imprisoned at San Vittore after their abortive trip to Switzerland. Miraculously, the SS had failed to discover that Klein was an Austrian Jew. On his arrest, he was found with false papers from the Apulian town of Troia; Klein spoke little Italian, but he had actually spent time in Apulia and had picked up some of the local dialect. (The other Jews in the refugee party, including a young girl about six years old, were deported and killed.)

In his position as chaplain at San Vittore, Don Bicchierai was privy to a great deal of information from prisoners, Italian guards and the Gestapo; he was thus invaluable to DELASEM. (Later in the war, Don Bicchierai became one of the chief mediators between the Allies and the Germans in negotiating the withdrawal of Nazi troops from northern Italy.) "I used to enjoy accompanying Don Bicchierai to San Vittore and saying good-bye to him in front of the prison," Teglio remembered.

While he was in Milan, Teglio also engaged the help of a highly resourceful double agent named Benuzzi, who had been an OVRA agent before the war. Because of his excellent knowledge of German, Benuzzi had offered his services to the SS at the start of the Occupation, but he began collaborating with antifascist forces at the same time. Through Don Bicchierai, Benuzzi gave DELASEM information about German plans in Milan.

After the first mass arrests of Jews in October and November 1943, it became much harder for the Germans to find people in hiding. In Genoa, they detained about a hundred people in November; it took them nearly a year and a half to catch another 124. Unable to arrest Jews in the more obvious places, the SS had to rely on betrayals, monetary rewards and difficult police work. Quite correctly, they figured that if they could find people hiding Jews it would be much easier than tracking Jews down one by one. Having gotten wind of Teglio's clandestine activities, the Germans placed a bounty of 1 million lire on his head and began dangling it in front of people who might know where to find him.

Teglio had lived in Genoa all his life and, highly sociable and open as he was, was known by hundreds, perhaps thousands of people. Flying was still an exotic and uncommon thing before World War II, and the free rides offered by the Genoa Aviation Club made Teglio even more visible: crowds would line up to fly in the backseat of his hydroplane. That Teglio could survive with a huge price on his head in a city where he was so well known is a testament to his great charm and sympathy as a person.

"I wasn't worried about betrayals—I had no enemies in Genoa, and many friends—but I was more afraid that someone might give me away unintentionally, out of nervousness or fear," he said. Indeed, this nearly happened soon after Teglio returned from Busto Arsizio. He was on a tram bringing clothes and a new identity card to Harry Klein, who had just been released from prison and was preparing for a second attempt to escape to Switzerland. Teglio spotted a female acquaintance and went over to speak with her. But when he said hello, the woman seemed confused and embarrassed and asked him how his son was. Since Teglio's only child was a girl—something this friend well knew—he was perplexed by her behavior. What he did not know was that a woman standing nearby watching them was an interpreter for the SS: the SS woman had approached Teglio's friend and offered her 200,000 lire as her cut of the million-lire reward for Teglio's capture. When the tram stopped near SS headquarters, both Teglio and the interpreter got off. The woman watched him suspiciously, but the naturalness of his gait threw her off the trail. Teglio, unaware of the extreme danger he was in, walked off to Klein's hiding place.

Eventually Teglio developed a series of strategies for settling into clandestine life. "I had a few basic principles. I tried to change my hours and my habits continuously. If I had to move around the city I tried to do it during the lunch and dinner hours—because even the Germans had to eat."

Moreover, he changed apartments frequently. "I had the keys to several apartments of friends who had left the city because of the bombardments; if I felt in any danger I would move. One apartment, belonging to a lawyer named Parodi, had two entrances, so if people were coming in one I could always go out the other." Teglio sometimes used his in-laws' apartment on Via Assarotti: they had two apartments in the same building, an office and a residence. Teglio removed the name plate from the door of the residence and put it on the door of the office; if the Germans came looking for him there, they would find a dust-filled apartment that had not been entered for months. The bathroom in the apartment he stayed in looked out over a back alley and Teglio installed a rope he could climb down from the bathroom if someone came to arrest him.

He even had a hiding place reserved for himself in the leper colony of a local hospital. The doctor told him there would always be a bed for him if he needed it: "The Germans will never enter, and as long as you leave them alone, the lepers aren't dangerous."

At a certain point, Teglio moved away from the center of town, to an apartment in a neighborhood where he thought he knew no one. "But after I had been there a few days I met a Red Cross nurse who had been a friend of my wife's. She knew who I was, and that I was Jewish. She asked me what I was doing there, and I told her that everyone in the center of town knew me. She said, 'There's one thing you have to be careful of: My brother is a fascist. I hope he doesn't remember you, but he might.' A few days later she told me, 'My brother knows you are here, and I think you'd better do something.' The brother was a stonemason, so I had him do work on the apartment I was staying in, which had been damaged in the bombings. He then offered to build me a hiding place in the wall. I accepted and paid him right away, and after that he was no trouble at all."

With his great resourcefulness and gift for improvisation Teglio often turned potentially dangerous situations to his own advantage. When he suddenly found himself face to face on a tram with the head of the Fascist Party in Genoa, Luigi San Germano, Teglio went straight toward him, just as he used to aim his hydroplane directly toward the concrete dam during rough storms.

"San Germano and I had been in elementary school together, but we hadn't seen one another for years. He got on the tram, and we saw one another. He said nothing and looked very nervous. I gave him a perfect fascist salute, and went right up to him and said, 'I'm very glad you're in this position. I hope I can count on your help if I need it.' He said, 'Yes,' rather brusquely. He was getting off at fascist headquarters and I was due to continue for two more stops. But I decided to get off with him, and I walked right to the entrance of the headquarters, where I gave him another crisp fascist salute right in front of all the fascist soldiers. And I thought to myself: These soldiers will never touch me for sure!" This was not an act of reckless bravado on Teglio's part: he felt certain that San Germano would not turn him in and that by appearing in public with the city's most powerful fascist, he created the illusion of being under his protection.

Teglio's precaution of putting his daughter into hiding soon proved well founded. In their efforts to capture him the Germans tracked down Teglio's in-laws at Rapallo. "My father-in-law, being Austrian, spoke fluent German and told them, 'We're Catholics and we have nothing to do with him.' He said that I had taken my daughter away and disappeared. They searched the house and eventually found a picture of me with my wife at our wedding." After the visit from the SS, his in-laws sent a message warning Teglio through his housekeeper, who had insisted on remaining in Genoa to help him. Eugenia's sister came to Genoa and said it was too dangerous for her to stay here. I said, 'No one is keeping her here. She is free to leave, but she's an adult and she can decide for herself.' She stayed."

Having learned that the Germans now had his photograph and knew who his in-laws were, Teglio changed not only houses but also his appearance. "I had a mustache and heavy eyebrows, so I shaved my mustache, trimmed back my eyebrows and began wearing glasses."

Laura Teglio was surprised and amused at seeing her brother when she sneaked into Genoa during that period: "If you didn't know him well, you wouldn't have recognized him." Laura had come to Genoa to get his help in dealing with the increasingly dangerous situation the family was facing in Piedmont. Laura, her parents, her sister Emma, and Emma's husband and their two children were all staying with a retired police marshal who had agreed to shelter them—for a price. Realizing the vulnerable position these fugitives were in, the man started pressing them for more and more money, indicating, not so subtly, that he would turn them in. "He would wake us up in the middle of the night and begin threatening us: 'You haven't given me enough money this month,' " Laura recalls. "So I decided to take him to see Massimo. I knew how to reach him through a certain office. And Massimo arranged a meeting, with another person hidden in an adjacent room who could listen to what was happening."

When the former police marshal adopted a menacing tone, Massimo Teglio fed him some of his own medicine. "He said to me, 'And if we went to the police station?' And so I told him; 'If you want, let's go to the police station. I'll walk out of there, and you'll be the one who stays behind. I'm protected by the Germans.' It was a bluff: I had some friends in the police, but I couldn't be too sure."

"Massimo treated him like a dog," his sister remembers. "And the man became really frightened, pale as chalk. I remember Massimo telling him, 'There are many in our family, and at least one of us will survive. If you touch my mother and father, we will make you pay! One of us will survive!' And so this marshal who came to Genoa acting like a lion went away as meek as a lamb. On the train ride back to Piedmont he kept saying, 'Quite a man, your brother! He must have important connections to move around Genoa so freely. A great person!' Massimo knew how to bluff."

Laura was struck by the transformation of her easygoing, good-natured brother into a tough, decisive man of action. "I marveled at his activity; he had always been rather lazy. But then again, I wasn't entirely surprised. When Massimo wanted to do something, like in aviation, he did it."

Ironically, while the Germans never had any success in catching Teglio, it was the Americans who came closest to killing him.

On the afternoon of May 19, 1944, Teglio was sitting in the offices of the Genoa archdiocese waiting for Don Repetto, when an air-raid alarm sounded. Everyone started for the bomb shelter, which was in the thick stone tower of San Lorenzo Cathedral. "Cardinal Boetto, who was passing through the hallway, saw me and asked, 'Signor Massimo'—they called me Signor Massimo in order to avoid using my last name—'aren't you coming to the shelter?' 'No, Your Eminence, I'll wait here,' I said. I felt I would be in much greater danger in the bomb shelter; anybody could have walked in there and recognized me. So I stayed behind and waited. I went out on the balcony and saw American bombers up in the sky. All of a sudden I heard the whistle of a bomb directly above me—luckily, the planes were very high. I raced to the stairs the cardinal had gone down. The bomb hit directly on the archdiocese offices. I made it down nine or ten steps, and the walls collapsed directly behind me. The roof caved in right behind me. I thought I was going to die then. I had had incendiary bombs dropped on my house. But this was one of those high-powered American bombs. The air around me just shook. I thought to myself: Now it's over. But I found myself all in one piece. I was barely scratched."

It was some time before he was able to make his way, in the dark, through the rubble into the church and then finally to the bell tower, where the cardinal and priests were hiding. Immediately after the bombing the priests had sent someone by another route to see what had happened; the person had found the room in which Teglio had been sitting nothing but a pile of bricks and plaster. Convinced that he was dead, the priests began discussing how they could give Teglio a proper burial without giving away the fact that he was Jewish. "They were planning on dressing up my corpse in priest's clothing. They were certain, they were. And then I walked in!" Teglio laughed with great pleasure at the memory. Covered from head to feet in the white plaster dust, he must have looked like a ghost. "You're alive—it's a miracle," the priests said. Teglio said simply: "I am the last person to have seen the frescoes of the Archbishop's Palace."

Because of the bombardment, the Archdiocese of Genoa was forced to move out of its offices and take up temporary residence at a nearby church. Although his health was failing, Cardinal Archbishop Boetto refused to leave the city, which was by now prostrate from the devastating bombings, growing hunger and the harsh restrictions of foreign occupation. Don Repetto continued energetically to help Jewish refugees; and when some priests felt he was going too far, the archbishop backed him completely.

"One evening two or three families of foreign Jews, about ten people in all, arrived at our office in Genoa," Don Repetto recalled. "I was alone in the office. The cardinal had left town for several days. The curfew had already fallen and it was impossible to take them to a safe refuge, so I put them in the remaining rooms of the Archbishop's Palace which had been vacated." Another priest, perhaps feeling that Repetto was exposing the Church to too much risk, complained about the incident to Cardinal Boetto. But the archbishop regretted only that the refugees had to endure such unwelcoming accommodations. "Poor people!" he told Repetto. "They must have hoped for a more secure place to spend the night. But you shouldn't be sorry."

In another instance, Cardinal Boetto agreed to break the rules of cloister in order to reunite a young Jewish couple. With the strict separation of the sexes in convents and monasteries, most Jewish families were split up. "The consequence, hard but necessary for everyone's safety, was that nobody could go out; each lived buried in a room," Don Repetto wrote after the war. The separation made one couple very anxious and I played postman, going back and forth between the husband and the wife. With silent looks and hesitant words, they asked me if they could see one another. When the cardinal heard about the situation, he repeated one of his favorite Latin maxims, *'Afflictis non est addenda afflictio'* [Let us not add afflictions to the afflicted]. He told me, 'Put them together,' and added a quotation from the Gospels: ' "Therefore what God has joined together, let not man separate." . . . Go to the mother superior and tell her I ask that she find a corner of the convent in which the man can stay.' In my heart I was very happy, but trying to be scrupulous, I said: 'But Your Eminence, the rules of cloister . . .' The cardinal looked up with a moment of irritation and said, 'The Holy Father has granted me special authority that applies also to the rules of cloister. Go and do as I say!' "

By the spring of 1944, the war in Italy had moved northward and increasingly had taken on the character of a civil war. Month by month the antifascist resistance in the North grew in size and force. What had started as small, poorly trained and poorly equipped bands had expanded into a force of about 100,000 men and women. Partisan groups roamed freely in the hills outside Genoa and frequently made bold incursions into the city. On May 15 a partisan bomb exploded in a movie theater used by the German army, killing five German soldiers. The Germans, determined to maintain their policy of killing ten partisans for every one of their soldiers assassinated, took a group of Jewish prisoners to Passo del Turchino, a mountain pass northwest of Genoa, and ordered them to dig an enormous ditch. The Jews were returned to prison and placed in a separate wing so that they could not tell anyone what they had done. The following day, the Germans took fifty-nine antifascists from prison, made them kneel by the ditch at Passo del Turchino, shot them and buried them in a mass grave.

When word of the massacre leaked out of the prison, Don Repetto went immediately to try to recover the bodies. The Germans held him under arrest briefly and then let him go. Having identified the shy young priest as an enemy of the Reich, the Germans began to investigate the charitable activities of the Genoa archdiocese.

In mid-June two strangers arrived at the archdiocese offices proposing to make a donation of 3 million lire for the assistance of Jews. Don Repetto and Massimo Teglio, who was posing as a lawyer for the Church, told them that there must be a mistake; they insisted that the Church had no special assistance for Jews, but was prepared to accept general donations for all the needy of Genoa. The next day Repetto received a phone call from a local bank saying that he was supposed to pick up a wire payment of 3 million lire. When he asked whom it was from, he was told simply that it had been sent from Verona—the headquarters of the Gestapo in Italy. Repetto understood this as an attempt to compromise the Church in its efforts to help the Jews, and he never showed up to accept the money.

About two weeks later Teglio learned that a pair of German agents were going around Genoa asking plenty of questions about Don Repetto. Teglio got a good description of the pair and told the priest to be on his guard. On July 4 the two men appeared at the archdiocese offices and asked to see Repetto. The priest, upon noting that their appearances corresponded to the descriptions given by Teglio, introduced himself by a false name and told them that Don Repetto was out and probably would not return that day. The two men demanded to see the archbishop. Repetto had them fill out a form for visitors: one of the men was from Genoa, the other from Verona. Repetto then took the form to Boetto, who told the priest to go out the back door of the building and flee immediately to a church on the outskirts of the city. When the agents asked the archbishop about Don Repetto, Boetto responded that he was not in Genoa. When they insisted on knowing where he had gone, they were told that he was doing Church business elsewhere and that they would be informed when he returned to Genoa.

The Germans went looking for another Genoese priest, Giacomo Lercaro (future cardinal archbishop of Bologna), who had been working closely with DELASEM. To help Lercaro escape, Teglio prepared false documents and offered to make up a false baptismal certificate for him. The priest looked at him scandalized. "But the archbishop himself has authorized me," Teglio responded. Lercaro assented, and he duly became a citizen of Naples, and member of a parish there that he knew well. Teglio loved the irony of a fugitive Jew manufacturing a false baptismal certificate for a priest.

While Lercaro and Repetto got away, the Germans arrested Don Giacomo Massa, chaplain at the Marassi prison in Genoa. A spy there had reported to the Germans that the priest had given a package of biscuits and 300 lire to a Jewish woman prisoner. It took extensive negotiations to win his release.

A week after Don Massa's arrest, the Germans rounded up most of the people working with the Archdiocese of Milan, including a Milanese lawyer, Giuseppe Sala; the director of the Brera Museum, Fernanda Wittgens; and several priests. At the end of July, Monsignor Vincenzo Barale, DELASEM's main contact in Turin, was arrested.

With his closest collaborators being apprehended in rapid succession, and Allied troops moving at a snail's pace up the peninsula, Teglio began to feel the tremendous weight of the underground life. "I remember hearing Churchill's speech on Radio London: It will still be a long time before the war ends . . . more blood, sweat and tears. It was a moment when I asked myself: Will I make it? I had all the enthusiasm possible, but I also had a brain that worked. Even with my constant moving I couldn't last forever without being caught. I no longer trusted anyone."

Despite the destruction of a large part of its secret network, the Catholic Church in Genoa did not let up its efforts to help the Jews. Cardinal Boetto immediately assigned Don Carlo Salvi to take up the work of Don Repetto, who spent the rest of the war in hiding.

Teglio received unexpected help in rebuilding DELASEM from an old friend, Achille Malcovati. A prominent Milan businessman, Malcovati ran the Centrale del Latte di Genova, the dairy association of Genoa, and had close ties to the Church in the city. Monsignor Giuseppe Siri (later cardinal archbishop of Genoa) had called on Malcovati as an important food distributor to help him feed the poor during the war.

"One day when I was at the archdiocese offices, I bumped into Malcovati, who was there seeing Monsignor Siri," Teglio recalled. "I was going out, he was going in, and he said to me: 'Even with those glasses you have on I can recognize you. You're crazy to be here. Come to Milan, I can use you there. You drive well, and I have several cars with German permits. That way you'll have a regular job that gives you a cover, and you can use it to do what you want.' " Teglio shifted his base from Genoa to Milan; he ate and slept at Malcovati's house.

As head of a large company, Malcovati had a fleet of trucks and cars at his disposal—indeed, with permits from the German government. And as he had suggested, working as a driver for him gave Teglio a perfect screen for maintaining the threads of the DELASEM network. "I traveled all over, picking up and delivering milk, butter and cheese and giving money to people hiding Jews."

Teglio had found a particularly fitting and competent protector. Malcovati was a man above all suspicion, one of the most heavily decorated Italian heroes of World War I; he had won five Silver and three Bronze Medals for military valor and had been wounded three times. When he walked around in fascist Italy with his chest full of medals, he was greeted instantly with great respect. "Because he had been wounded he was officially granted the privileges of a disabled war veteran—although he was hardly disabled," Teglio recalled. "He had the right to travel anywhere in Italy by train, first-class, for free—the sort of thing that happens only in Italy. And because he was 'disabled' he had a right to a caretaker, who could travel with him for free. He would tell me, 'Don't buy a ticket, you're my 'caretaker.' He was in some ways my maestro. I learned a lot of things from him: he would move around with enormous self-assurance, and as a result hardly anyone ever stopped him or questioned him. I followed his example."

As the military position of the Germans in Italy deteriorated, traveling became more difficult and dangerous. Train lines were constantly being destroyed by bombs, and Allied planes routinely strafed both trains and automobiles. "I would generally travel between eleven in the morning and two in the afternoon, when pilots were usually eating, and then again in the middle of the night," Teglio remembered. "Sometimes I'd have to leave the car at the side of the road, hide in the woods and come back for it later."

* * *

In late August 1944, Allied armies liberated Florence and German troops began withdrawing from Tuscany. One day Emanuele Pacifici went to fetch some water at a well near the school in Settignano. He saw a jeep and a soldier drinking. He was wearing a British army uniform but had a star of David sewn onto it—the mark of the Palestine Brigade, made up of Jews from the British protectorate in the Middle East. For more than a year Emanuele had been hiding his Jewish identity; his mother had instructed him to tell no one that he was Jewish, and the nuns at school had warned him never to speak with soldiers. He was torn between a burning desire to reveal his secret and fear about breaking his vow. Perhaps, he thought, this was a German soldier disguised as a British soldier. Finally, Emanuele devised a stratagem: he would recite a Hebrew prayer—only if the soldier were Jewish would he understand. Emanuele came up behind the soldier and began to recite Shema Ysrael, the prayer his mother had recited that night in the Florence train station when they had narrowly avoided arrest: "Hear, O Israel, the Lord is our God, the Lord is One. . . ." The soldier, hearing these familiar words, turned and looked at Emanuele, then embraced him.

The soldier, Eliau Dubinsky, was concerned that as an orphan Emanuele might lose contact with his Jewish heritage and become a Catholic. Although he spoke little Italian, Dubinsky went to the school and somehow communicated to one of the nuns his intention to take Emanuele and his brother to Rome, where he would find their surviving relatives. "The nun said, 'You're not taking anyone away,' " Emanuele recalls. " 'These children have been entrusted to us by their parents.' " The soldier went to the Jewish community of Florence, which had come out of hiding and was pulling itself back on its feet. The community interceded on Dubinsky's behalf. "He took my brother and me to Rome in a truck," Emanuele remembers. "While my brother slept, he said to me, 'I have to tell you something: It's possible that your relatives are no longer alive. Or that they won't want you to live with them. Or that they won't have room for you. But don't worry—if it doesn't work out, I will take you both as my sons to my kibbutz.' In a scene of wild joy, we found my aunts and uncles, and the soldier left. Before he went away he gave me a postcard with his address on it and told me, 'If at any moment in your life you need my help, I will always be near you.' "

* * *

Massimo Teglio, meanwhile, was stuck behind enemy lines and would have to wait another eight months for the arrival of Allied troops. The Germans formed a strong defensive front above Florence (the Gothic Line, as it was called), which the British and American forces were unable to break through during the winter of 1944.

But having moved to Milan, Teglio felt much safer than before. Nonetheless, he returned regularly to Genoa, and at Christmastime, managed to see his daughter. "I had my housekeeper pick Nicoletta up at the convent where she was staying," Teglio recalled. "I gave Eugenia instructions to get on the tram at a certain stop, I would get on at another, so no one would make the connection between us. Eugenia went to spend Christmas with her relatives, and I took Nicoletta to the house of my friend Angelo Oliva, who had a villa near there by the sea. Then I arranged to have her brought back to the convent, and I made my way to Genoa alone by car. On the way I saw a German officer looking for a ride. I picked him up. The German was all happy, and I felt that with him aboard no one would stop us. That was Christmas 1944."

In Milan, DELASEM had enlisted the help of the steel manufacturers Enrico and Giovanni Falck, who put the resources of their company at its disposal. The Falck company had a plant in Bolzano, a city in the Dolomite mountains near the Austrian border where the Germans had established a concentration camp. Disguised as a Falck employee, Teglio brought food and clothing to inmates at the camp through a local priest.

Achille Malcovati, Teglio's protector in Milan, had close contacts not only with the Germans but also with Mussolini's puppet government, which had its seat east of Milan at Salò. "Malcovati was friends with the man in charge of food rationing for the Republic of Salò, and got him all sorts of coupons for buying butter, sugar, chocolate, canned fruit—things that were impossible for most people to buy," Teglio recalled. "So whenever we needed a special favor from people, we could give them some of these coupons."

Malcovati used these privileges to win the friendship of a well-placed Nazi official at the German embassy in Milan. In taking over the city, the Nazis had requisitioned its most luxurious hotel, the Principe di Savoia for its embassy. Malcovati included the official in some lucrative black-market trading. "He had bought some fabric very cheaply and was afraid that if he shipped it by normal means it would be impounded. Malcovati offered to let the German official buy half of it at cost so that the Germans would provide the transportation." Malcovati used the same shipments of fabric to send guns and documents to Italian partisans; the surest way to avoid German checkpoints was to have the Germans themselves carry the material.

Teglio recalled a delivery he made with two Nazi officials. "We were supposed to take some fabric to Lodi and pick up a thousand kilos of salami for the Germans." Teglio and his companions arrived back in Milan in the middle of the night. Because of the late hour, Teglio decided to go to the German embassy rather than wake Malcovati and his wife. "I asked for a room for the night. The night porter answered that the hotel had been requisitioned by the German government. And

I said I was a friend of Herr So-and-so—the functionary we'd been dealing with. He wasn't in, but I knew that he had two rooms in the hotel. The night porter said he couldn't let me up to his room: 'I'd have to wake Major Schwartz, and it is very dangerous to wake him in the middle of the night. Why don't you sleep on a couch here in the lobby and then in the morning we can see about getting you a room? At a certain point the next morning, the air-raid alarm sounded. I knew that the Italian general Graziani [Rodolfo Graziani, defense minister of the Republic of Salò] was coming to see the German ambassador then, and with those important people around, there would certainly be a careful document check in the bomb shelter. If I hurried down to the shelter, I would get there before anyone began checking people. And in fact, I was there to welcome the German ambassador and Graziani. Imagine my satisfaction!

"At noon our embassy official returned. I made a bit of a fuss with him about the fact that the people in the embassy wouldn't give me a room and that I had to sleep on a sofa. He took me to the night porter and told him, 'Take a good look at this man, and the next time he asks for a room, let him go up and use mine.' So I had an absolutely secure refuge: the German embassy! In that period I would sometimes wake up in the middle of the night laughing about the strangeness of my life."

Teglio still made frequent trips back to Genoa, maintaining close ties with Cardinal Archbishop Boetto and his new assistant, Don Carlo Salvi. The war had had particularly drastic effects on the city: starvation was not unheard of among the civilian population. Through Malcovati's company, the Church in Genoa was operating its own food distribution, and Teglio often brought truckloads of food to the city. He also carried supplies of medicine for Boetto, who was suffering from a series of illnesses that would take his life a year after the end of the war. The cardinal, in turn, used Teglio as a courier for some of his more delicate operations. "Once the cardinal gave me secret documents about the German defense of Genoa to take to the Resistance in Milan," Teglio recalled. Although used to running risks, Teglio expressed some alarm at the danger of the mission. "Go, Signor Massimo, you have nothing to fear, my son," Boetto reassured him.

Throughout the war, Teglio had been careful to maintain his distance from the partisans. "Meeting with them would only bring danger to them and to me. But at a certain point, a lawyer connected with them contacted me and asked me to help them with false identity cards. Theirs lacked the fascist imprimatur and they asked to have some of mine."

By the end of the war, the Germans and the Italian neofascists had begun to crack down on typographers who were helping manufacture false documents. Teglio was an extremely gentle person by nature, but when it was necessary, he knew how to get tough. "I went to a typographer whom I used to pay very well to make false stamps. 'I don't want to have anything more to do with this business,' the man said. He was deaf as a post, so I wrote down on a piece of paper: 'These are the last ones I'll need. If you do them, I'll pay you such-and-such. If you don't, I'll denounce you to the police for the ones you've already done.' 'Oooohh, but they'd better be the last ones!' the man said. He told me to come at a certain time on a certain day. But instead of going on that day, I waited several days and came at a completely different hour. I figured that if he had decided to denounce me, there might have been someone there waiting for me at our appointment. Some people say I was a reckless fool, but I took the precautions that seemed really necessary."

On April 25, 1945, after two days of street fighting with Italian partisans, the Germans pulled out of Genoa. Cardinal Boetto and the archdiocese acted as mediators between the Germans and the partisans in negotiating the Nazi withdrawal.

"At the time of the surrender of Genoa, Malcovati was staying at my house in Genoa," Teglio remembered. "He drove to Milan to bring me the news. When he returned to Milan, he asked me if I would drive his wife to Pavia, where some of her relatives were. Malcovati's cars were all painted with the yellow and white colors of the Vatican. As we drove along, we were stopped by the Germans. They made us get out of the car and hold our hands high in the air. They wanted to take away our gasoline because it was scarce, but I took the hard line, *'Ich bin von dem Vatikan Diplomat'*—'I am a Vatican diplomat.' And I showed them Monsignor Siri's letter."

Once in Pavia, Teglio learned from Malcovati that the Germans had broken their agreement with Cardinal Boetto and had taken more than a dozen hostages from the Marassi prison when they withdrew from Genoa. The truckload of prisoners, riding with the German army as it retreated to Milan, had been hit in an Allied air attack. On his way back to Milan from Pavia, Teglio drove to the town of Bornasco to see what had become of the Genoese hostages. Four prisoners had been killed in the attack: they had been chained together in a truck and were unable to flee. Teglio recognized two of the corpses—they were acquaintances of his from Genoa, one an air force officer, the other a pharmacist.

After having negotiated his way through German checkpoints, Teglio now had to worry about getting through antifascist lines. "I drove slowly and honked the horn often. But we were stopped by the partisans. They saw the gasoline I was carrying and wanted to take it. I said, 'The Germans stopped me and tried to take my gas. I didn't give it to them, and I'm not going to give it to you.' They saw the documents that said I was a Vatican diplomat and let us through. When they heard we were heading to Milan, they told me to be careful. Partisans were looking for a white car there that had been used to carry out an assassination. And sure enough, when we arrived in Milan several young partisans with machine guns jumped out of a bush in front of us: 'Out of the car! Hands up! You have a white car.' I faced as much danger that day as at any time during the whole war. That was the last day of the war."

With the German surrender, the partisans immediately took control of Milan. And on April 28, Teglio went to the radio station to transmit news about the fate of the hostages taken from the prison in Genoa. While he was at the station, the word came that Mussolini, trying to escape to Switzerland disguised as a German soldier, had been captured by partisans near Lake Como. He and his mistress, Claretta Petacci, had been summarily shot. And the pair, along with other prominent fascists, were being strung up by their heels in Piazzale Loreto in Milan. "Someone said to me, 'You have a car, let's go see!' " Teglio recalled. But he had seen enough bloodshed and had no taste for vengeance or barbaric public spectacles. " 'Yes, I have a car,' I told him, 'but I have no interest in seeing anything of the kind.' "

Ferrara–Buchenwald–Ferrara

THE SCHÖNHEIT FAMILY

PRECEDING PAGE–Students in a play at the Jewish School in Ferrara during the racial campaign, when Jews were excluded from public schools. Second from left, in the top hat, is Franco Schönheit.

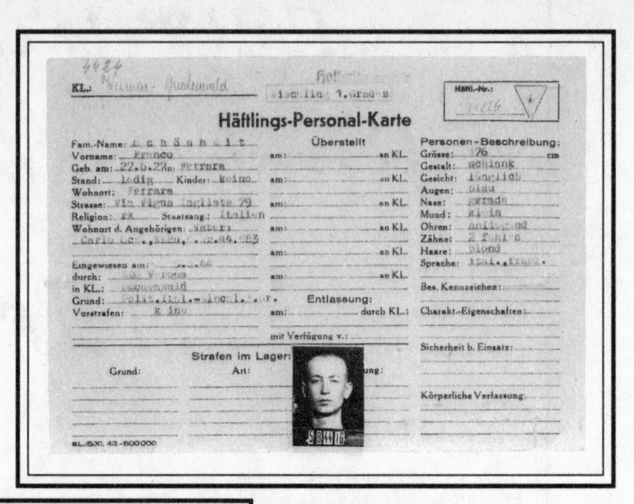

4424

KL.: Weimar-Buchenwald

Mischling 1. Grades

Häftl.-Nr.: 44816

Häftlings-Personal-Karte

Fam.-Name: Schönheit
Vorname: Franco
Geb. am: 27.6.24 in: Ferrara
Stand: ledig Kinder: keine
Wohnort: Ferrara
Strasse: Via Vigna Tagliata 79
Religion: rk Staatsang.: Italien
Wohnort d. Angehörigen: Vater: Carlo [illegible]
Eingewiesen am: [illegible]
durch: [illegible] Verona
in KL.: Buchenwald
Grund: Polit. [illegible]
Vorstrafen: keine

Überstellt
am: an KL.
am: an KL.
am: an KL.
am: an KL.
am: an KL.
am: an KL.

Entlassung:
am: durch KL.:
mit Verfügung v.:

Personen-Beschreibung:
Grösse: 176 cm
Gestalt: schlank
Gesicht: länglich
Augen: blau
Nase: gerade
Mund: klein
Ohren: anliegend
Zähne: 2 fehlen
Haare: blond
Sprache: [illegible]
Bes. Kennzeichen:
Charakt.-Eigenschaften:
Sicherheit b. Einsatz:
Körperliche Verfassung:

Strafen im Lager:
Grund: Art:

5 8 44 16

KL./5/XI. 43-500000

Franco Schönheit's personal file from Buchenwald. The photograph was taken upon his arrival, on August 5, 1944.

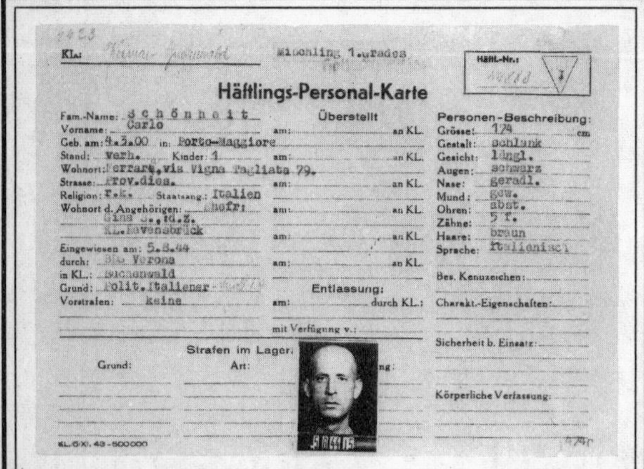

4423

KL.: Weimar-Buchenwald

Mischling 1. Grades

Häftl.-Nr.: 44818

Häftlings-Personal-Karte

Fam.-Name: Schönheit
Vorname: Carlo
Geb. am: 4.3.00 in: Porto-Maggiore
Stand: verh. Kinder: 1
Wohnort: Ferrara, via Vigna Tagliata 79.
Strasse: Prov.dies.
Religion: r.k. Staatsang.: Italien
Wohnort d. Angehörigen: Ehefr: Gina S., z.Z. KL. Ravensbrück
Eingewiesen am: 5.8.44
durch: BdS Verona
in KL.: Buchenwald
Grund: Polit. Italiener-[illegible]
Vorstrafen: keine

Überstellt
am: an KL.
am: an KL.
am: an KL.
am: an KL.
am: an KL.
am: an KL.

Entlassung:
am: durch KL.:
mit Verfügung v.:

Personen-Beschreibung:
Grösse: 174 cm
Gestalt: schlank
Gesicht: längl.
Augen: schwarz
Nase: geradl.
Mund: gew.
Ohren: abst.
Zähne: 5 f.
Haare: braun
Sprache: italienisch
Bes. Kennzeichen:
Charakt.-Eigenschaften:
Sicherheit b. Einsatz:
Körperliche Verfassung:

Strafen im Lager:
Grund: Art:

5 8 44 15

KL./5/XI. 43-500000

Carlo Schönheit's personal file from Buchenwald.

Gina and Carlo Schönheit with children from the summer camp they ran for many years after the war.

Chapter One

Ferrara

Sometime in the winter of 1943–1944, when he was sixteen, Franco Schönheit says, he stopped growing. At first it is not easy to understand what he means. Not only is Schönheit a tall, physically imposing man, well over six feet, but he seems a mature and fulfilled person as well: the head of a successful business in Milan, happily married, with two grown children. But when he talks about his experiences during the war, Schönheit's uncanny photographic recall of details makes it seem as if time had in fact stopped for him more than forty years ago.

One date stands out as the opening of that strange parenthesis in his life: November 15, 1943, the night Schönheit's father was arrested. "After that I grew emotionally several years in about six weeks," he says, "and then I stopped, and have never grown since."

* * *

That long November night is one virtually everybody in Ferrara past a certain age remembers well. On the afternoon of the fourteenth, the body of a local Fascist Party leader, Igino Ghisellini, was found by a roadside not far from the city, murdered in an ambush. Although it is unclear to this day whether he was killed by partisans or by rival fascists, the congress of the Fascist Party meeting in Verona demanded an immediate reprisal and dispatched squads of militia to Ferrara.

* * *

It was two in the morning when the Schönheit family was awakened by a violent banging on their front door. "They were ringing the bell and banging on the door with the butts of their rifles. My father didn't answer, but at one point he decided to turn on a light to see what time it was. The fascists saw the light and knew someone was home—in another minute they would have gone away. Because of that little bit of bad luck we were deported. After that evening, when they had arrested a certain number of people, the roundup ended. We would surely have fled after that night. Those who managed to avoid arrest fled, particularly those who had been sought out. Some people happened not to be at home that night; others didn't sleep at home because they sensed something was in the air. We hadn't left home that evening and hadn't heard the news about the death of the fascist leader."

Franco stayed in bed listening to the fascists ordering his father to come with them; he heard his mother yelling and his father trying to calm her. Only Carlo Schönheit was taken away. He did not take a suitcase or any clothing; nothing was said about how long he would be gone.

Franco and his mother learned the following morning the fascists had dragged seventy-four people from their homes during the night, about half of them suspected antifascists, the other half Jews, most of them, like Carlo Schönheit, with no record of political activism. They did not try to round up all the Jews of Ferrara; instead, they apprehended a certain number of heads of families to show the city that the new government meant business. Those arrested were held at Fascist Party headquarters with thirty-one antifascists who had been detained previously. In the small hours of the morning the fascists drank and argued about how many people to kill to avenge Ghisellini's death. At dawn they took eight of the prisoners, four of them Jews, stood them against the wall of the d'Este castle—the beautiful medieval fortress that is now one of Ferrara's main tourist attractions—and shot them. Later the fascists dragged the bodies of three other men they had killed through the streets to the castle, leaving a grisly total of eleven bodies on display as a clear message to the people of Ferrara.

On the morning of the fifteenth, Gina Schönheit went to the castle to see if her husband was among the dead. Although she did not see Carlo, she did recognize the bodies of two other Ferrarese Jews: Vittore and Mario Hanau, father and son, lay crumpled in the castle moat, clasping one another in a final embrace. The bodies were left all day so that everyone would see. In the late afternoon the eleven corpses were buried at the request of the archbishop of Ferrara, whose office window looked out on the castle.

* * *

One of the troubling questions of the Schönheits' story is why the family was still at home at such a late date, November 15, 1943. The Germans had invaded Italy more than two months earlier and a month had passed since the mass arrests of Jews in Rome.

"We heard about the October roundup in Rome the day after," Franco Schönheit says. "Trains carrying prisoners from Rome had passed through northern cities, and the people inside had thrown postcards and letters from the cars. But we were very incredulous. Italian Jews in general were very incredulous. German refugees who had escaped into Italy would take every opportunity to warn Italian Jews about what was happening to Jews in Germany, but we always said, 'What happened in Germany can never happen in Italy.' You heard that phrase constantly, up until the end."

Perhaps the incredulity of Ferrarese Jews is due at least in some measure to their history. In Ferrara in particular, an ancient bond of tolerance and affection tied the Jews to their city. From as early as the thirteenth century, it had distinguished itself among Italian city-states for its religious openness. Throughout the Renaissance the city and surrounding region were ruled by the d'Este family, whose brilliant court—based in the castle where the November 15 massacre occurred—attracted artists, writers and humanists of note, including the painter Cosmè Tura and the poet Ludovico Ariosto.

Jews may have settled in Ferrara as early as the eleventh century, but the first clear recognition of their presence is a decree written in 1275 by the *podestà*, or ruler, Obizzo d'Este, granting immunity and protection to the Jews because of their usefulness to the city. In 1461, Duke Borso d'Este, a self-proclaimed defender of the Jews, signed a letter of safe conduct for a Jewish banker of Ferrara in which he described him as "a noble man and most loved citizen of our city"; the duke urged his fellow potentates to treat the banker as "a dear relative, to give him free passage, to his retinue, his baggage, and to furnish him at his request with an escort."

Like many of the more liberal Renaissance princes, the Estensi had invited Jews to their territory in order to expand credit, stimulate commerce and help pay for extravagant building projects and wars of conquest. But while most other cities prevented Jews from doing any business other than banking, to avoid competition with local merchants, Ferrara granted them full rights. Consequently, the Jews of Ferrara contributed not only great bankers but also important geographers, architects, doctors, printers and scholars. In 1473 Ercole I d'Este opposed a papal suggestion to ban Jews from the city, and eight years later he approved their request to construct the synagogue that still stands on Via Mazzini in the center of Ferrara. In 1492 he welcomed Jews who had been expelled from Spain, and later his grandson Ercole II gave safe passage to Jews from Bohemia and to Marranos, Spanish and Portuguese Jews who had been forcibly converted to Christianity during the Inquisition. Under d'Este rule the Jewish population of Ferrara exceeded 2,000, and there were three different synagogues—Italian, German, and Spanish—in a city of 35,000 people.

During the Counter-Reformation, the Vatican slowly began to take Ferrara in its grip. In 1553 the d'Este family gave in to a Vatican request to have a rabbi engage in theological debate with a group of monks, and Alfonso II d'Este was forced to hand over three Marranos to the papal Inquisition in 1581.

Eventually the Vatican achieved total victory: taking advantage of the fact that there was no legitimate d'Este heir, it absorbed Ferrara into the Papal States in 1597. The Jews were eventually closed up in a ghetto, deprived of all civil rights and subject to the same humiliations and restrictions as the Jews of Rome. Within three years of the beginning of papal rule, a quarter of Ferrara's Jews, 500 people, left the city and moved into territory still controlled by the Estensi, who had transferred their court to Modena. By the time the Ferrara ghetto was eliminated in 1859, during the unification of Italy, the Jewish population had dwindled to 1,200.

Even after some two and a half centuries in the ghetto, the Jews reintegrated quickly into the larger society. The restrictions of the past had left them with a pent-up longing for assimilation. In some ways the Jews of Ferrara were more Ferrarese than their Catholic brethren. The dialect they spoke, which Franco recalls hearing throughout his childhood, was in great part simply Ferrarese dialect of the Renaissance. Because of their extreme isolation, the Jews emerged from the ghetto speaking essentially the same language their ancestors had spoken at the time they were first enclosed: they were like human time capsules, preserving the language of the d'Este era.

The coming of fascism in 1922 did not interrupt the integrating process that had begun with liberation. The principal fascist leader of Ferrara, Italo Balbo, was openly sympathetic to the Jews. His close friend Renzo Ravenna, a Jew, was mayor of the city throughout the fascist period until the enactment of the racial laws of 1938. Perhaps also because of this the Jews of Ferrara felt safer than most in Italy.

The novelist Giorgio Bassani has said frequently that he doesn't recall a single Jew when he was growing up in Ferrara who was not a fascist. Many of the Ferrarese Jews, Bassani says, were big landowners, and active supporters of fascism from its early days.

There were deep ties between fascism and the Jews of Ferrara, but Bassani's portrait is at best partial. Even among the city's wealthier Jews, there were a handful of courageous Jewish antifascists as well. Franco Schönheit's father-in-law, Renzo Bonfiglioli, a lawyer and landowner, was never allowed to practice law because he refused to join the Fascist Party; he was arrested and exiled for his beliefs.

The great mass of Ferrara's Jews, as Franco recalls, were neither especially rich nor particularly interested in politics. "The Jewish community of Ferrara before the war had a lot of poor people. Of the eight to nine hundred Jews of Ferrara, between a third and a half lived in the ghetto." The more prosperous Jews had moved out over the years, to more spacious and comfortable sections of town.

It was in the cramped, narrow streets of the old ghetto—formed by Via Mazzini and Via Vittoria, and including the three old synagogues, the Jewish school and a series of kosher shops—that Schönheit grew up, as his parents had before him. Neither of his parents had gone to college. Carlo Schönheit was a traveling salesman, dealing in underwear, pajamas and socks; Gina Schönheit, the only one of six children to finish high school, had obtained a teacher's license and taught elementary students at the little Jewish school in the ghetto.

Carlo Schönheit's grandfather had come to Italy in the mid–nineteenth century from Graz, Austria, while Gina's family, the Finzis, had lived in the city perhaps as long as there had been Jews in Ferrara. While Finzi is a famous Ferrarese Jewish name, belonging to prominent rabbis, scholars, businessmen, even a cabinet minister, the Finzis had their share of poor obscure ghetto dwellers as well.

The people of the ghetto were mainly shopkeepers and workers who wanted to be left alone to earn a living and take care of their families. Many of them, like Carlo Schönheit, joined the Fascist Party to avoid trouble in their jobs. Many Italians, Jews and non-Jews, joked that the initials of the party, PNF (Partito Nazionale Fascista), stood for *per necessità familiare*—"for family necessity."

"In general there was very little interest in politics among the Jews of Ferrara and in that they were exactly like other Italians," Franco Schönheit says. "They did what they had to in order to be left in peace: put their fascist uniform on the four or five fascist holidays when it was required, and that was it. Only a very small proportion was really active politically, either for or against fascism.

"The majority of Ferrarese Jews lived like ninety-eight percent of the Italians of that era. Some more convinced, some less so. Some wore the fascist uniform on holidays, others tried to avoid wearing it. Jews participated in the collection of gold during the Ethiopian war along with everyone else. For most Jews, the racial laws came like a bolt out of the blue—even though during 1938, after Hitler's trip to Rome, the newspapers began to refer to England and America as the Jewish-Masonic powers."

The Schönheits life centered more around Ferrara's tight-knit ghetto community than around the local political arena. Carlo, who had a beautiful tenor voice, was cantor in the synagogue. Although his job required almost constant traveling, he would always arrange to be home on the Sabbath and on the holy days in order to sing in the temple. Besides teaching in the Jewish school, Franco's mother ran a summer camp for poor Jewish children who could not afford to go away for the holidays. Naturally, Franco attended the camp each summer.

The racial laws disrupted the Schönheits' life less than most people's. As a simple salaried employee, Franco's father continued traveling the Italian countryside selling socks and underwear; his mother, because she taught in a private Jewish school, kept her job. Not surprisingly, the vast majority of the hundred or so Jews who emigrated from Ferrara during the racial campaign were professionals who had lost their jobs or businesses.

The racial campaign was probably more of a trauma for Franco than for his parents. He had to leave public junior high school and attend a private Jewish school. At the time, the local Jewish school ended after the first four years of primary school. In 1937, when Franco was ten, he had transferred to public school. It was a big adjustment to a completely new world: until then he had lived within the cocoon of Ferrara's small ghetto community. He attended a school where his mother taught, and he even had her as a teacher. On Saturdays he saw his classmates at the local temple and participated in outings and events organized by the synagogue. To have to switch back the year after making the adjustment was doubly traumatic.

"I had skipped fifth grade, so I was out of sync with my old classmates," he says. "I was always in a class that was at too high or too low a level. It was an awkward situation. But the teachers found an occasional fifteen extra minutes for me. And I was in a known and literally familiar environment. For those who were several years older than I, who were ready for university, the problem was much, much worse."

Because there were no higher grades at the Jewish school, they had to be invented. The many Jewish professionals and university and high school teachers put out of work by the racial laws provided an ample supply of excellent teachers. Among these new teachers was the young

Giorgio Bassani, who had just finished his university degree in literature.

"Practically until the arrival of the German troops, Jews who had remained in Italy led a fairly normal life, a life as second-class citizens, but bearable," Franco remembers. "We were not among those who were frightened enough to leave. My father continued to work, my mother continued to work. And after this single year in public school, I was able to return to a school and to classmates I already knew. I would to go to the soccer game every Sunday: I did before the racial laws and I did so afterward."

The period of seminormalcy ended with the arrival of the Germans in September 1943. It was then that most Jews fled the city. But the Schönheits stayed put. "Fleeing was not so simple—it required money," Franco says. Those who went to Switzerland needed money to pay guides to escort them across the Alps, to bribe border officials, to buy false documents and stay in hotels. Wealthier Jews tended to be more integrated into the wider Catholic society and had networks of friends to help them. They had country houses or friends and relatives with country houses where they could hide. "For us the idea of leaving the few things we had was very difficult," Franco says.

* * *

But perhaps the major reason the Schönheits did not flee—and a reason perhaps impossible for someone today to understand—is that they were facing a threat that was literally incomprehensible, totally beyond their frame of reference. "The term 'death camp' was not known," Franco says. "People talked about 'concentration camps.' But concentration camps had existed in Italy throughout the fascist period. Since the 1920s the regime had kept political dissidents in camps for periods of time, and generally they were released after a few years. We assumed that these concentration camps would be detention camps in Italy, run by Italians, where people would be kept until the end of the war."

The creation of the death camps was a grotesque monstrosity that docile, law-abiding Italian Jews simply could not grasp. Time and again, the Schönheits reacted to new threats as if they were safe, in their middle-class world in Ferrara.

The day after Carlo Schönheit's arrest, Franco and his mother went to the jail where he was being held. The scene came as quite a shock: nearly a hundred men crowded in an enormous cell guarded by fascist militia with machine guns. In the middle was Carlo Schönheit, the traveling salesman and synagogue cantor, looking disheveled and, to his wife's horror, not wearing a tie. "Where is your tie!" Franco's mother yelled. Her thundering voice astonished the guards and all the other families. "Have them give you your tie immediately! You're not a murderer!"

The incident, says Franco, was a pure expression of his mother's strong-willed, and even strident character. Gina Schönheit was famous with everyone who knew her for her loud, operatic voice and her impressive—if not intimidating—physical presence. She was a strapping woman, six feet tall and weighing nearly two hundred pounds. As a schoolteacher and summer camp director, she was used to giving orders. Her powerful voice had developed through years of keeping restless pupils bolt upright in their seats, alertly listening to her in terrorized silence.

There is, of course, something absurd in the incident, this desperate clinging to the appearances of normalcy—the tie—in the face of death and deportation. "Absurd" is a term Schönheit uses frequently when talking about his past. Absurdity, he says, was the essence of the concentration camp experience. Sometimes an absurd response was better than a rational one. In a number of situations, his mother's willingness to stand up to the Nazis and her ability to outshout them impressed her captors and surprised them into making unusual concessions.

In this instance her outburst might have been dangerous, for it was uncertain whether Carlo Schönheit and the other prisoners might still be put up against the castle wall. But her proud, stubborn refusal to change or bend also may have been a key to her survival.

* * *

After Carlo Schönheit was arrested, the problem for his wife and son was no longer whether or not to flee, but how to free him. Many families of the seventy-four who had been arrested on November 15 went into hiding, usually at the insistence of the family member who had been arrested. "Mamma and I didn't think for a second about leaving. We would never have abandoned Papà. In the days following the arrest, my mother immediately sprang into action."

She took advantage of one of the family's resources: the fact that they had Catholic relatives. Observant Jews who lived within the heart of the Jewish community, the Schönheits were in fact half Jewish. The mothers of both Gina and Carlo were Catholic. At the time, Franco's paternal grandmother, eighty years old, was gravely ill and in a Ferrara hospital. Even though her mother-in-law had lived in the ghetto for decades and had practically converted to Judaism during her marriage, Gina decided to use her condition to seek the intercession of the Church.

"My mother and I ceaselessly made the rounds from the police station to Fascist Party headquarters to the prefect's office, pleading the case of this man with his eighty-year-old Catholic mother ill in the hospital. Then I got the idea to involve a cousin of ours who was a priest in a village five miles outside Ferrara. He introduced my mother and me to the archbishop of Ferrara, of whom I have very fond memories. He received me each time I went to his office, and I spoke to him continuously about my father in jail and my Catholic grandmother in the hospital. On about the fifth of December, twenty days after the arrest, the archbishop obtained an extraordinary concession from the fascists. Every evening at five—I say 'evening' because it was already dark at five—an armed escort would accompany my father across the city on foot to the hospital, where he would be able to visit his mother and us in my grandmother's hospital room. The guard would stand outside the room and at the end of the hour accompany my father back to jail. By mid-January my grandmother's condition worsened, and the archbishop managed to obtain my father's release from prison."

But the release came with an important condition. The Ferrara police chief told Carlo Schönheit that he must under no condition leave the city; if he did, a reprisal would be made on all of his relatives. The family had numerous Catholic relatives in the vicinity who would be held hostage in the event of the family's flight. "It was a heavy threat and it most certainly would have been acted on. Because of that my father never thought of leaving Ferrara. The threat was too precise."

When his father was released from jail, Franco found him deeply changed. Normally easygoing and extroverted, a tall handsome man who loved to eat and talk, he returned in a state of total despair. "He was completely pessimistic. He saw we were going from bad to worse. He was totally without hope. Perhaps he was suffering from remorse, blaming himself for the situation we were in. He simply didn't think that we could . . . 'survive,' isn't the right word, it wasn't a word that even crossed our minds; we never thought we were being taken away to be killed.

"My mother and I were decidedly more optimistic. Having managed to free him from prison, we felt we could face anything."

The frantic period of trying to win his father's release had changed Franco too. Although tall for his age, Franco had been a boy of fragile health; he was more than a little spoiled by his adoring parents. "He was the classic only child," his wife, Dory Bonfiglioli Schönheit, says. The two have known one another since childhood: their families were friends, and both attended the Jewish school and had Franco's mother as a teacher. In class Gina treated Franco with the same iron rigor she used on all the students, but outside of school she softened completely:

it was he and not she who commanded. "She called him her 'little lord,' " Franco's wife reveals with a laugh.

Franco toughened considerably during the German occupation and his father's imprisonment, acquiring a kind of street savvy that would later serve him well. "Astuteness, that is what I learned," he says. "Knowing who was the right person to approach at the right time in a given situation. The education we received from November 15 to February 25, when we were finally arrested, may have given us the psychological preparation that saved us. I grew up so fast in those weeks that I just stopped. I've remained at that point."

For more than a month after Carlo Schönheit's release, the family waited at home for their arrest. By now virtually everyone they knew had either fled or been captured. "Some remained in the area around Ferrara, but many were turned in by people informing on them. We stayed at home because my father had to go to present himself at the police station once a week.

"So many of us, my family included, allowed ourselves to be arrested at home. We waited for them, we knew they would come the day it was decided that Jews could not remain freely at home but would have to be held in 'detention camps,' as they called them."

Finally, on February 25, 1944, the Italian police came and brought the Schönheits and other Jews to the old synagogue, which had been built under Este rulers and badly destroyed by fascist thugs in 1941. They slept amid the broken furniture of the temple where they had gone every Saturday and where Carlo Schönheit had sung the Jewish liturgy for much of his life.

Chapter Two

Fossoli

When the Schönheits left Ferrara on February 26, they acted and felt like people heading on a long, difficult journey, not like people being sent to German concentration camps. They were encouraged by the Italian authorities to take suitcases full of clothes, and books, and even the mattresses off their beds. They were sent by train to a camp at Fossoli di Carpi, just north of Modena. No mention had been made of Germany.

"The arrival at Fossoli was a shock especially for me and my mother," Franco says. "We looked out of the window and saw the uniforms of the SS. The Germans were in charge. Until then we had dealt only with Italians, Italian police, Italian soldiers. And we fully expected to go to an Italian concentration camp."

The Germans did not wait long before letting the Schönheits know that their lives had changed drastically. As the Schönheits were unloading their belongings from the train, the Germans, through their Italian interpreters, ordered Franco to carry his mattress on his back. When he stumbled and fell under its weight, the commandant of the camp, Sergeant Major Hans Haage screamed at him in German, "Work, boy!" "My mother, indignant, responded immediately with her thundering voice: 'One moment—we're not animals!' She didn't say it, she shouted it. The commandant turned to the Italian interpreter, who most certainly gave a different translation of what she'd said. She didn't understand that we were already animals."

The camp of Fossoli had been used for British prisoners of war but was adapted in September 1943 as a gathering point for Italian Jews and political prisoners. The two groups were kept separate in a rectangular area two kilometers long and one kilometer wide. To Franco it looked like an ordinary military camp, a long series of barracks with a large central hall where everyone ate. Every barracks was divided into about thirty semiprivate cells, with two sets of bunk beds in each. When the Schönheits arrived, the camp was nearly empty. Only four days earlier, on February 22, all the Jews in the camp had been deported to Auschwitz.

Soon after they descended from the train, Franco remembers, a fellow prisoner gave them a piece of advice that almost certainly saved their lives. "A Signor Levi from Milan came right up to us and asked, 'Where are you from? Do you have any relatives who are not Jews?' When we told him we did, he said, 'You must tell the Germans immediately that you are part Catholic.' " At Fossoli, the man explained, the Germans made a strict distinction between pure Jews and Jews of "mixed blood." While the pure Jews were sent off in cattle cars to Auschwitz at the end of each month, the mixed-blood Jews remained behind to work as the administrators of the camp, preparing the deportations.

"My father asked, 'But won't they ask us whether we were married in the temple in Ferrara?' And the man said, 'They won't ask. The Germans care only about race, not religion. They will want to know whether you have any 'pure blood' and whether you have some documentation that can prove it.' Sure enough, he was right. We wrote away to a Catholic cousin of my father's, a fireman, who arrived in his fireman's uniform with the baptismal certificates of my two grandmothers in hand."

So the Schönheits were selected for positions of responsibility among the half-Jews who helped administer the camp. "Every month the camp would fill with Jews gathered in roundups from all over Italy. Mixed Jews, Jews married to non-Jews, and the children of mixed marriages all remained behind to organize the departure of the others and to maintain the structure of the camp. Month in, month out, we would watch as these people streamed in and headed out for Auschwitz."

Waiting until early August, unsure of whether they too would be deported, the Schönheits established a degree of normalcy in a highly abnormal situation. Conditions at the camp were rough—they suffered from the cold, and food was scarce—but life was tolerable. Prisoners were allowed limited contact with the outside world. They could occasionally write letters to and receive packages of food and clothing from friends and relatives. People with money were able to buy food from outside the camp. And although most things were rationed at the time, peasants from the surrounding countryside usually had something to sell them to supplement the inadequate camp diet. Because most of the inmates waited there only a few weeks before deportation, there were not the regular, back-breaking work details that existed in the German camps.

The prisoners were not in a daily struggle for survival, and thus were friendly and generous with one another. "At Fossoli there was still a certain amount of solidarity among the inmates," Franco remembers. "We lived as if in a low-level *pensione*. In the evening we played cards to pass the time; we exchanged books and read. I had brought an English grammar book, a dictionary and a notebook with me, and I would study."

While it might seem like denial and self-delusion, Franco believes it was essential to maintain this air of normalcy. "It was very important, for sanity, to focus on the little problems of everyday life—procuring food from the outside, arranging the work at the camp. About the bigger problem—where all these people were going—it was better not to think of that.

"The turning of the screws was gradual, so we weren't really frightened. First my father's arrest and his release under rather precarious conditions; next our arrest and the arrival at Fossoli; then our remaining there while all the others were deported, and the slow worsening of conditions. With each new change we created a new normalcy."

Over time the Germans took increased control of the camp. Before the Schönheits arrived, Italian police had been in charge of Fossoli; the SS began to move in only in mid-February. "As long as there were Italians in the camp it wasn't so difficult. During the first few months it was hard because of the cold and the hunger. The Italian policemen helped a great deal. One Italian guard would call my father to his guard tower in the evening and give him little bags full of bread—not sell, give. And this was at a time when bread was rationed in Italy, almost impossible to get."

At Fossoli the SS tightened its grip, but not so quickly that the inmates would become frightened and rebel. Rations were slowly reduced; in June 1944 women and men were separated for the first time in order to break up families. Discipline grew sharper. Franco remembers that at one point the head of the camp, Major Haage, gave the prisoners a little lesson in obedience. The Jewish inmates were called over to the barbed wire separating them from the political prisoners to watch the punishment of a man who had tried to escape. They watched and listened in silence as Haage literally beat the man to death with a stick.

"The Germans never hesitated to tell us, when something was wrong, that Fossoli was an earthly paradise compared with what awaited us in Germany. And they were right. They would say it to the Italian interpreters whenever there were complaints about the food.

"The difference between the behavior of the Germans and that of the Italians was enormous. One of the most dramatic episodes at Fossoli occurred when they decided to let us out of the camp to work, to clear up the rubble caused by an Allied bombardment. Normally the Germans used Italian interpreters when they organized work teams, but in this case there was a new arrival from Germany, with no interpreter. So the German SS soldier shouted an order in German to a Jew from Rome, who obviously didn't understand it and went in the wrong direction. The German pulled out his pistol and shot him on the spot. He aimed right for his head and split it open. The Italian Jews in the camp were shocked by the incident, while the foreign Jews who had been arrested in Italy did not seem surprised at all. We thought, It's an isolated incident: it's a new guard who wasn't following orders."

Later in the spring Franco gained an even better glimpse of the Nazi system. "It was May 20, there was a transport of five hundred people; a Jewish woman from Florence who was at least ninety was supposed to be in the transport. At the roll call for the departure, this woman's name was called and no one responded. The SS official told the Italian interpreter, who called me—as one of the assistants in the camp—to find the woman and bring her right away. I found her immediately, in her bed, unconscious. It was clear that she was in the last moments of life. So I returned to the courtyard and told the interpreter: 'This woman is dying; she is in no condition to be put into a truck and then to ride on a train.' The interpreter, who knew the Germans, did not even translate my words but simply told me that if I didn't want all hell to break loose I should get someone to help me bring the woman at once. I returned to the barracks with three other people, and we wrapped the woman in a blanket and carried her into a truck. She weighed practically nothing, no more than seventy-five or eighty pounds. The Germans, without batting an eyelash, watched this dying woman being carried onto a truck to be transported hundreds of miles, as if this were a normal occurrence. For them it was a purely administrative problem: the woman's name was on the list and so she had to be taken. If she had died a minute earlier, her name could have been crossed off the list, but as long as she was breathing she had to be transported, even though she certainly did not arrive at her destination. The interpreter performed an act of humanity toward me; if he had translated what I said, the Germans would have lashed out at me. I probably would have been beaten or shot."

From late February to the beginning of August 1944, Franco saw about a third of the 6,746 Italian Jews captured by the Nazis pass through this way station between life and death. Some of them were family friends and acquaintances from Ferrara. Among them was his future wife's grandmother.

Dory Bonfiglioli and her family had escaped to Switzerland, but her maternal grandmother was captured trying to make the crossing. "We fled right after September 8 because my father had already been in trouble for political reasons," Dory explains. "We decided to cross the Swiss border. One of my aunts, who was recovering from an operation, was unable to make the trip with us. So my grandmother, who was my mother's mother and not the mother of this aunt, volunteered to stay behind and take her across the next day. When they were almost at the border, my aunt, who was lagging somewhat behind, heard the guide yell, 'The Germans!' The guide fled, and then my aunt heard my grandmother talking to the Nazis in German, saying that she was alone. My aunt hid behind a boulder and was saved. My grandmother was sent to Auschwitz, where she was probably killed instantly because of her age."

Franco had the shock of seeing the arrival and departure of an aunt and uncle and two cousins, as well as the uncle's elderly parents. Because the uncle's side of the family was completely Jewish, they were not able to qualify as mixed-blood Jews. "So the whole family of six, including a boy of fifteen, a girl of five, and their two grandparents in their eighties, was sent to Auschwitz. Nothing was heard of them again. We saw them leave on the transport of April 5. It was a terrible shock, but none of us had any idea they were being taken off to be killed. We knew that a family taken to a concentration camp in Germany was facing an extremely difficult life, probably with terrible sanitary conditions and poor food. We knew that there was a risk that they might die, but of natural causes, not through some organized extermination: the notion that the Germans would ship thousands of people hundreds of miles just to kill them seemed inconceivable. It was from this lack of comprehension that our hope sprang."

As the summer progressed and the Germans continued retreating throughout Europe, the SS actually talked about releasing the Schönheits and the other mixed-blood Jews at Fossoli. "In mid-July they asked us questions about where we lived, whether we had a place to return to, and what our economic conditions were. Then came the assassination attempt against Hitler on July 20. Immediately, the whole atmosphere changed. On August 2, the camp was evacuated. We were the last people deported.

"We were taken to Verona by truck because the train tracks between Fossoli and Verona had been bombed out, and there we were separated. For mysterious reasons different people were slated for different directions: my father, myself, and twenty-one other Italian men were headed to Buchenwald, my mother and the women to Ravensbrück, the foreigners to Bergen-Belsen and the others to Auschwitz. These names—Buchenwald, Bergen-Belsen, Auschwitz—were all the same to us. It was only after the war that we learned what the distinctions among them were.

"In Verona we made a desperate attempt to bribe our way out of the situation. I had the feeling, and I still do, that if we had had some gold we might have been able to bribe some Italian officials—not German, Italian—into letting us escape. My mother was the one who tried it. And the officials were ready to listen, but when they learned that we would have to return to Ferrara for the money, they immediately lost interest. The separation from my mother in Verona was most difficult for me. I was seventeen at that point, I was optimistic. But in Verona I had a sudden moment of weakness and wanted to throw myself at the Germans and try anything—a stupid attempt that would have accomplished nothing. My mother, who never lost her head, responded like a good schoolteacher, *'Franco, non fare lo stupido!*—'Don't be stupid!' And she succeeded in comforting me, saying, 'You've got to go with Papà; we must live so that we can all see one another again.' "

They traveled in separate cars but along the same tracks as far as Nuremburg. Franco recalls the growing sense of despair as he watched out of the slats of the cattle car: the Italian names on the stations ticked away bringing them closer to the Austrian border. "As long as we were in Italy, there was a degree of hope. In Italy we would hear news of the war. The Americans were about to arrive; they kept climbing up the peninsula. It seemed as if the war would end soon. We understood very well when we had crossed the border. We waited a long time in the station at Brennero."

In Nuremburg the Schönheits were allowed to leave the train for a few minutes to say good-bye—an unusual concession made by Major Haage himself. Afterward, Franco and his father boarded a train car for Buchenwald, and his mother one for Ravensbrück; the cars were placed on separate tracks and headed off in different directions.

Chapter Three

Buchenwald

It was one in the morning when the train arrived at the entrance to Buchenwald. "Of the twenty-four hours of the day, they couldn't have picked a more depressing hour to arrive in a place like that," Franco Schönheit says. He remembers the forbidding metal gate of the camp with the macabre inscription worked into the wrought iron: JEDEM DAS SEINE, "To Each His Own." There is a perverse genius in using a motto in homage to the individual as the inscription for a slave-labor camp designed to reduce its prisoners to numbers before eliminating them physically.

The Nazis' penchant for this kind of "theater of cruelty" was widespread: the motto of Auschwitz was *Arbeit Macht Frei*, "In Work There Is Freedom." In a sense, however, the inscription at Buchenwald truthfully announced the Nazis' precise intentions: to destroy any possibility for solidarity, friendship and trust among prisoners by pitting them in a vicious struggle for survival. At Buchenwald the prisoner was indeed on "his own."

To the new arrivals, the inscription had the chilling effect of the words above the entrance to Dante's Hell: "Abandon all hope, you who enter here." "Many people gave up hope that very night, and for them there was nothing more to do," Franco says. "As hopeless as the situation really was, the only thing to do was to hope, to attempt a miracle."

After the Schönheits entered the camp, the Nazis, in good bureaucratic style, photographed them and made them fill out cards with their biographical data. "After our liberation I remembered these photographs, and one of my desires before leaving the camp was to get hold of them. I managed to convince an American guard to let me have these documents. I still have them." Schönheit opens a small box with a few yellowing, tattered documents. "I have never shown them to anyone before, not even my wife." In the photographs father and son look remarkably similar, like versions of one another twenty-five years apart. But their expressions are very different. The father, although older, looks smaller and more vulnerable, his face dark and frightened. "These were taken right after our arrival. My father looks terrified. I look cold and hard, like someone steeling himself to face the impossible. My father understood much better than I did that the odds of our surviving were practically nil. From a logical point of view he was absolutely right. But to survive you had to hope; it required the courage of ignorance. I had that largely because of my age. I was seventeen when I entered the camp."

After being photographed, Franco, his father and the other twenty-one Italian men were made to undress and stand naked for hours. Then they were inspected, showered, disinfected and issued camp uniforms.

From that process, Franco remembers a small but meaningful detail. As the two undressed, his father turned and asked his son to excuse him. Even at the mouth of hell, Carlo Schoñheit felt ashamed that his son should have to see him naked. Franco, reacting to his father's vulnerability and despair, said, "Don't worry—we're naked now and they're clothed, but one day we will be clothed and they will be naked."

* * *

Buchenwald had been built in 1937 as a camp for political prisoners. Some of its most veteran inmates were German communists and socialists who had been in various Nazi camps since 1933, when Hitler took power. As the regime widened its policy of state terror it began placing people from suspect groups—doctors, lawyers, Seventh-day Adventists—in the camp. The regime also dumped the refuse of its prison system—thieves, murderers, rapists and other common criminals—into the camp both to relieve its crowded jails and to increase the sense of terror at Buchenwald. By the time the Schönheits arrived, with the addition of resistance fighters from nineteen countries across Europe, the camp's population had grown from several thousand to about 30,000.

Buchenwald was not designed as a death camp in the way Auschwitz and Treblinka were. In the death camps, most of the inmates—those too young, old or sick to provide productive labor—were gassed immediately upon arrival. The others were "selected" later for the gas chambers as day by day they outlived their usefulness. At Buchenwald, labor was the first priority, death the second. Factories connected to the camp produced the V-1 buzz bombs and V-2 rockets that were dropped on London during the blitz, along with other weapons and war materiel. "Elimination" was achieved more gradually as prisoners were worn down under a system of hard labor, malnourishment and physical punishment. There is little question, however, that the Nazis considered the crematorium a prisoner's final destination: when the inmates arrived the SS performed a meticulous inventory of their dental work so that silver and gold fillings could be extracted easily before the bodies were burned. The camp's crematorium, with its thirty-five-foot-high smokestack, was kept busy day and night spewing out the mortal remains of the 150 to 200 people who died in the course of an average day.

In one sense, Franco and his father were lucky to have been deported so late in the war: they would have to endure Buchenwald only for a short period. But in some ways their timing could not have been worse. The last months of Buchenwald were by all accounts the most hellish. As the end of the war neared, the Nazis frantically became more concerned with eliminating the prisoners than with exploiting their labor.

Moreover, the late arrivals were at the bottom of a well-developed pecking order that had evolved at the camp during the previous six years. The German political prisoners were the camp elite, and had survived so many years by securing positions of privilege from the German guards. Next came the German common criminals, who were frequently recruited as *Kapos,* or bosses, and generally lent themselves to the task with a ferocious zeal that exceeded even that of the SS. Then there were Soviet prisoners of war—by 1944 the largest single group at Buchenwald—who by their very numbers had a power base in the camp. The same was true to a lesser extent for the Poles, Hungarians and Czechs. The many partisans who were shipped to Buchenwald found protection among the ranks of the political prisoners. The Schönheits, as Italians and Jews, had no group in which they could seek protection. There were relatively few Jews, and even fewer Italians. Jews had no real place in the camp (most of those there had been arrested for political reasons), and so virtually no one knew the Schönheits were Jewish. On their uniforms they wore the red triangle of the political prisoners with the initials IT, for "Italian," in the center. "No one could figure out what we were doing there," Franco says. The Italian prisoners were a small, disliked minority. The other inmates, regarding them as the allies of Hitler, called them "Mussolini"; the SS, considering them traitors who had withdrawn from the war, called them "Badoglio."

The Italians were separated from the other prisoners also by a language barrier that often proved fatal. "Most Italians knew only Italian," Franco says. "If they studied a language at school it was French or English. And this fact cost many of them their lives. The Russians and the Slavs either knew some German or were able to pick it up fairly quickly. For many Italians, as for the French, this language sounded hard, impenetrable and incomprehensible, and they were lost. Not to understand an order was a mortal danger, and it was even more dangerous to understand it incorrectly. I had been to school and knew a little bit of English and French, and having been exposed to some foreign languages helped. My father had never studied any language and found German impossible. I knew immediately that it was absolutely vital to learn those three or four hundred German words in order to understand orders. There was no way of faking it. Even at Fossoli I knew that, so I learned the hundred German words that got us through the first days at Buchenwald; then I learned probably a thousand more in our time there. The Germans never repeated an order; it had to be understood right away. Failure to understand gave an excuse to the Germans and the other prisoners to torture a person."

The first day at the camp, the Schönheits were given their numbers. And for hours and hours that day, Franco and Carlo repeated the five digits over and over in German until they could say them in their sleep. "You had to know these five numbers perfectly. The numbers would be called out quickly in a long list and you had to be able to pick them out immediately. You would not have a second chance. I made my father repeat his number in German until he got it right. There were people like my father who simply couldn't understand it. Many of them died just because of that. Imagine what it was like for an Italian just arrived in Germany to have to distinguish five numbers shouted rapidly in German." Franco Schönheit takes out his pipe and utters a garbled mouthful of guttural German consonants. He then says the number in Italian: 44,826. "It was absolutely necessary to understand that right away, to know when to get your piece of bread or take a shower. If I have to say my number in Italian, I have to think about it, but it comes to me right away in German. Because we also had to be able to repeat our own number, not just recognize it. Even though it was written right on our uniform, they made us say it."

The behavior of the SS at Fossoli, the occasional flashes of violence, had given the Schönheits a foretaste of Germany, but at Buchenwald violence was the stuff of every hour of every day. "It was like the difference between day and night. The Germans at Fossoli were right when they told us that it was an earthly paradise compared with what awaited us in Germany."

Each day began and ended with a long roll call; every one of the 30,000 prisoners in the camp would be counted and recounted. They rose at four in the morning, went to work at six, stopped working twelve hours later and frequently had to stand at roll call until nine at night. Virtually every memoir of Buchenwald dwells at length on the procedure, known in the camp as the *Appell.* While a roll call may seem little more than a time-consuming nuisance, at Buchenwald it was refined into an instrument of torture and physical annihilation that resulted in the deaths of thousands.

"The SS could have counted us much more quickly, but they insisted that the prisoners count themselves," Franco says. Row by row, barracks by barracks, throughout the camp the prisoners counted, with the prisoner at the end of each row shouting out the number in German. Franco soon learned to try to avoid being one of those in the front row who had to shout the number. There were usually about three hundred people in every barracks, and they lined up in thirty rows of ten. "The person in the front row had to count out the number in German, and there would be trouble if he got it wrong. Every evening there was a battle not to be first in line. We tried to place Germans in the front row, but some barracks were composed almost entirely of Poles. A couple of times, I got stuck in the front row. You had to prepare yourself mentally. You had to strain your ear listening for the voice behind you, which belonged to a person who probably wasn't German and who may not have understood the person behind him, and then say the right number. And if you said 'twenty' instead of 'twenty-one' you were in real trouble. I never allowed my father to be in the front row. The danger was enormous. They would punish you by making you stay an extra hour in the *Appellplatz* [assembly square] counting and recounting. These were the little acts of sadism that occurred all day long and made every moment full of anguish and worry."

In winter it was common for twenty people to die during each roll-call. Buchenwald was built on a hill, and the sharp wind that cut across it made the winters glacial and made fall and spring seem like winter. Experienced veterans learned to swing from side to side, so as to brush up against their neighbors and increase their body heat. If there was a miscount or a prisoner was missing, the *Appell* could last five or six hours and kill off a hundred people at a time. As this small city of prisoners stood there at attention, someone would eventually find the reason for the delay—some poor soul who had fallen asleep from cold or hunger, or frozen to death in a corner of the camp.

As the SS guards moved in their fur-collared coats among these blue-faced, shivering prisoners, they would bark orders to the inmates to stand more erect and straighten out their ragged columns. If a line was not straight enough for the SS man's satisfaction, he might pull out a pistol and shoot whoever had stepped out of formation.

When the count was completed, the block leader would report to the SS guard and give him the count of his men, and of those who had died during the roll call. The guard would then make his own count and kick each corpse to make sure it was really dead. With the precision of a stock clerk receiving a new order of merchandise, he would hand the barracks leader a receipt.

Rebellion and even sabotage were virtually impossible and were brutally crushed when they occurred. The Nazis would punish everyone for one individual's act of rebellion, so that prisoners would resent rather than applaud acts of courage. In one instance, when the SS discovered that a single prisoner had slashed the belt of an assembly line where he was working, for example, they killed all 200 prisoners working in the vicinity.

When inmates left the camp, they were accompanied by SS guards with attack dogs. The dogs were trained specially to tear out a prisoner's throat, and some accounts of life at Buchenwald report that when a new dog was brought in, it would be tried out on some prisoner chosen at random.

Three heavy layers of electrically charged barbed-wire fencing surrounded the camp; some prisoners tried to commit suicide by throwing themselves against it. But even the freedom of taking their own lives was denied: guards usually shot prisoners before they could reach the fence.

* * *

Every day of the eight and a half months they spent together at Buchenwald, Franco Schönheit and his father had the same conversation. "We'll never get out of here alive," the father would say. "We're going to get out of here alive," his teenage son would answer. They repeated this ritual every day.

Carlo's pessimism developed into what Franco affectionately calls "the Russian complex." "He felt that even if by some miracle we did manage to survive and the Germans were suddenly forced to flee the camp, the Russians would kill us. I would say, 'Let's concentrate on getting through this period, and then we'll worry about the Russians.' "

At times Franco cannot keep from laughing when he remembers himself and his father at Buchenwald, and indeed, they must have seemed like characters from a black comedy of Samuel Beckett: two gaunt scarecrow figures with shaved heads, drab prison clothing and clogs, seesawing between hope and despair with the void for a background.

Objectively, Carlo and Franco Schönheit were unlikely candidates for survival at Buchenwald: a frail high school student and a forty-four-year-old traveling salesman and synagogue cantor. Neither knew much German; neither had ever been outside of Italy; neither had a valuable skill—(such as engineering, mechanics, medicine, carpentry, masonry) that would have given him bargaining power within the camp; neither belonged to any group that might offer protection.

Their only real asset was each other. But this was exceptionally valuable: in a Babel of prisoners from nineteen different countries it was often difficult to communicate with other people, let alone trust them. During their imprisonment at Buchenwald they managed never to be separated, except when they worked. In this hostile, menacing environment, having a person nearby whom one could count on absolutely was an immeasurable psychological advantage that contributed to their survival. The Schönheits were among the very few who were not alone in a place dedicated to the idea "to each his own." Without his son Carlo Schönheit almost certainly would have perished, and it is difficult to predict what the effect on Franco might have been if he had lost his father.

The situation of father and son at Buchenwald was so unusual that most other inmates didn't understand it at all, Franco says. "In the moments of rest, our walking around the camp together, sometimes arm in arm, was mistaken for something quite different from a father-son relationship. A father and son together at Buchenwald were so anomalous that we were often thought to be a homosexual couple. People would smile or snicker when I tried to explain in my broken German that we were father and son."

Instead of being dangerous, this misunderstanding actually provided Franco useful protection from real predators. "Homosexuality was rampant at Buchenwald. I realized only many years later, after reading books, what the role was of these young boys who cleaned the barracks and had light jobs working for the barracks leaders. So this misunderstanding may have spared me unpleasant encounters with dangerous people. I was seventeen when I arrived there, and the very young were much in demand at Buchenwald."

Father and son, with the same tall, thin build, the same chiseled features, could not have had more different characters. Carlo was constantly worried; Franco had the reckless confidence of his age. In their particular symbiotic relationship, with Franco's optimism and youthful will tempered by his father's realism and experience, they were a highly effective team.

While being together was a great advantage, it brought with it many new worries. Wanting to remain together created an enormous dilemma most prisoners didn't have to face. "The problems of a couple are greater than that of one person alone," Franco says. While they were allowed to share a bunk, he and his father were almost always sent out on different work details. Each day was filled with the anxiety that the other might not be there in the evening. "Seeing each other after work was the most important moment of every day."

The days at Buchenwald were long but so filled with incidents that required judgment and reaction that they often passed quickly, Franco says. "You lived from hour to hour, confronting a whole range of little problems that changed from one hour to the next: problems of work, problems of food, problems of avoiding unpleasant encounters, problems of behaving or carrying yourself at work, of knowing at every moment the right thing to do at the right time. Many died precisely because they didn't know.

"To come out alive from a German concentration camp required the convergence of an infinite number of favorable circumstances. Every day you had to be lucky several times, and some days you needed a stroke of luck every hour.

"They woke us up at four in the morning, and then we took a cold shower. You were supposed to wash yourself with cold water in the middle of the winter. That's when the first compromises began. You had to try to wash yourself without removing your shirt. The water was freezing and our bodies were badly emaciated. Then they distributed that little wisp of bread they served. You had to try to get into a group of honest people so that they would cut the bread fairly into even pieces. Then when they dished out this dark liquid they called coffee, you had to try to get the bottom part of the pot, where the liquid was thicker. Then during the roll call you had to hope the numbers were right, and had to try not to be on the outside row, so that the wind would blow less hard against you. When you went off to work you had to try to get one of the lighter jobs, working out of the wind, behind a wall, or—if you were clearing rubble and moving stones—lifting the smaller pieces. The entire day was composed of thousands of little strategies to work as little as possible and to get your hands on as much food as possible."

As they lived through this grinding daily routine, the Schönheits felt themselves to be living in a human atmosphere that was usually indifferent, often hostile and sometimes violently dangerous. "We had friends in the camp, but real solidarity didn't exist," Franco says. "It couldn't exist, because any little advantage you won could not be divided into ten. In fact, you had to try to hide it from the other nine people or it was no longer an advantage but a problem. You hid what little things you were able to obtain. I remember once for several weeks my father had the good fortune to be assigned to work in a warehouse where they stored cans of lentils. At risk of death he was able to hide a can of lentils and bring them back for me. We boiled some in water, and a French prisoner saw us and started complaining, saying that we were stealing lentils meant for the prisoners' soup. My father, of course, didn't understand what he was saying, but I did. When I told him, my father asked me to explain to him that this food was not meant for the inmates but had been stolen from the SS. When had he ever seen lentils in our soup? We told the Frenchman we were sorry we couldn't share the soup with twenty other people, and he would have to eat something else. It was important to explain this, or it might have been dangerous."

In their division of labor Franco was the translator, while Carlo provided practical know-how. "My father used to say, 'You're the brain and I'm the arm.' In the morning when the alarm sounded, he would leap out of our bunk and run to the next room, where our things were. Theft was not allowed but it happened continuously. And you had to be constantly on guard not to be robbed. In the evening you were required to leave your jacket and clogs in an adjacent room. So my father would arrive first in the morning, to grab our jackets and shoes before the other 350 people in the barracks arrived and before someone exchanged his jacket with mine. Because if someone noticed that my jacket was in better condition than his, he would switch them."

The lack of solidarity among prisoners was one of the most demoralizing elements of camp life. Especially painful were the frequent episodes of violence visited on prisoners by other prisoners. "The violence of the SS was not justifiable but was somehow more understandable," Franco says. "The violence of one inmate to another seemed so senseless. It was extremely common."

The psychologist Bruno Bettelheim was so struck by the same phenomenon when he was imprisoned at Buchenwald in 1938 that he wrote at length about the psychological dynamics of the camp. The more veteran prisoners were almost always cool and suspicious of the new arrivals, when not actually hostile toward them, he noted in his essay "Individual and Mass Behavior in Extreme Situations": "Newcomers presented the old prisoners with difficult problems. Their complaints about the unbearable life in camp added new strain to the life in the barracks, as did their inability to adjust to it. Bad behavior in the labor gang endangered the whole group." But aside from these more understandable reactions, Bettelheim observed that many of the older prisoners, even those with developed antifascist political ideas, unconsciously absorbed the views of their captors and imitated their brutality. They shared the SS contempt for the "unfit" prisoners and helped the Nazis select them. Some even tried to imitate the dress of the Nazis by picking up scraps of SS uniforms and adding them to their prison garb, even though this practice, if observed, would be punished.

"The identification with their torturers went so far as copying their leisure-time activities," Bettelheim wrote. "One of the games played by the guards was to find out who could stand to be hit longest without uttering a complaint. This game was copied by some of the old prisoners, as though they had not been hit often and long enough not to need to repeat this experience by inflicting pain on fellow prisoners."

The most painful and humiliating experience that Franco can recall of Buchenwald was having to watch a show of violence without being able to intervene. "I remember one incident in particular: It was Christmas Day, 1944, the only Christmas we spent at Buchenwald. Even though we were Jewish, we were all looking forward to the holiday, thinking that perhaps this day of festivity might be a little different from the others. Instead, that day, probably intentionally, the Germans reduced the bread ration. The little piece of bread we got now had to be divided among twelve prisoners instead of eight. That day, passing in front of a barracks that was not our own, we came upon a group of 'green triangles,' common criminals, who were starting to punish another prisoner who had stolen a piece of bread. Stealing bread was of course a serious crime at Buchenwald, but a piece of bread is still only a piece of bread. We could not turn back because a group of SS officials sat nearby, smoking cigarettes and watching. And so we had to just stand there and look on as this young man, about twenty-five or thirty, was kicked to death. Try to imagine what it takes to kick a person to death!"

Violence was often a means of survival, Franco says. "By beating up another prisoner, an inmate would attract the attention of the SS." The SS needed especially violent people, and this violence was rewarded with supervisory positions, better food, indoor work, cigarettes, even access to the Buchenwald whorehouse, set up for the prisoners with female concentration camp victims. With a delicacy his father would have appreciated, Schönheit refers to this with the rather elegant nineteenth-century euphemism *casa di tolleranza* (literally, "house of tolerance").

But camp violence was not without its perils. "The *Kapos* ran their own risk of becoming too powerful and then being eliminated by the SS, at a certain point at Buchenwald. They had become dangerous because they were too much like the SS. So even the *Kapos* had to play their own balancing game."

Other survivors of Buchenwald, for the most part political prisoners, have painted a far more positive picture of cooperation and solidarity among the prisoners. Some have recalled incidents in which prisoners shared food with each other and took care of a group of children who were briefly interned in the camp.

There was in fact a highly developed underground among the political prisoners, which provided some measure of mutual support. A hidden radio allowed them to listen to war broadcasts and spread accurate news about the progress of the war to other prisoners. The organization may also have had a role in assigning jobs, eliminating particularly violent *Kapos* and stealing tools and food from camp warehouses. They had even assembled a small cache of arms that were hidden for the day when the Germans might try to impose the final solution on Buchenwald.

"You couldn't survive long at Buchenwald without some organization," Franco says. "There were political prisoners who had been there for years; you couldn't last six months without organization. Those who were unable to organize, that mass of people psychologically stunned by their arrival in camp, ate only what was given them and waited to die."

Although the Schönheits relied mainly on each other, they received vital help from a powerful German political prisoner named Ludwig Weisbeck, who became their guardian angel. A German doctor whom the Schönheits suspected was Jewish, Weisbeck held key positions as both an infirmary doctor and a translator for the SS. Franco and his father called him Ludovico (Italian for "Ludwig") because the doctor, a superb linguist, spoke Italian along with about eight other languages. "Perhaps the situation of this father and son together, Jews who had not done anything to be arrested, pained him. For whatever reason, he became our friend."

Weisbeck helped Franco obtain a medical exemption from work for six weeks. "There was the hospital game: There was a kind of infirmary with doctors but practically no medicine. What good was it? At times it was helpful to go there with an imaginary illness, but it was a big risk. Imaginary illnesses at Buchenwald were punished by death. So you had to fake it, but up to a point. I was able to get out of work for five weeks during the winter; I faked having a swollen knee, with Ludovico's help. I had fallen and after the first week certainly could have gone back to work, but instead I got an exemption from work week after week, five extremely important weeks in the middle of winter. While the others were out in the cold working, I could return to the barracks, where at least there was a little stove. But then Ludovico warned me not to come back the next week because they were onto me."

Weisbeck also played a determining role in keeping the Schönheits from being separated when prisoners were suddenly assigned to other camps. Although nominally only a translator for the SS, he often had the power of life and death in his hands. "Whenever there were transfers, he would be there as translator. The one time he wasn't there, I ran and got him."

In one instance father and son were in line for transfer, and by chance Carlo Schönheit was forced into line in front of Franco. Normally Franco would go first so he could speak to the SS for the both of them. Once a sequence in line had been established, it was impossible to change it—part of the German mania for order. "Our doctor friend, Ludovico, explained to us that it was important that my father be able to say, in German, to the SS colonel who was doing the transfer that we were father and son and had to remain together. 'It is important that he should be able to say a few things in German and then I will intervene,' he said. So in the few minutes that remained as we stood in line I taught my father the simplest German phrase I could think of: 'Father and son, always together.' " Terrified, Carlo blurted out this phrase in his nonexistent German and the perplexed SS colonel looked at the translator. Weisbeck explained that they were father and son and must always be together, whether they were transferred or remained at the camp. "Then Ludovico, shrugging as if it didn't matter at all to him, said, 'Let's leave them here.' " And so they again escaped both separation and transfer.

The Schönheits were terrified of being moved to one of the many small satellite camps that surrounded Buchenwald, where conditions were even more hellish. Buchenwald, Franco says, was in effect a city of 30,000 prisoners: "It was possible to hide in the crowd. The satellite camps were dangerous especially because of their size. If you were working at a quarry with, say, one or two hundred people, each of you would be under constant scrutiny." And under the command of a common criminal—and the SS frequently put criminals in such positions of responsibility—a prisoner could find himself the constant target of a vicious psychopath.

One of the paradoxes of life at Buchenwald was that a prisoner had to avoid calling attention to himself but at the same time retain his individuality. "You had to blend into the crowd, but not *become* the crowd," Franco says. "This was very important: to be able to distinguish yourself in some tiny way, through some little nothing, through . . . through a hat, yes. I got a hat from a Russian prisoner in order to have a hat that was different from everyone else's. A beautiful red Russian hat with a fur border. I had to pay a half-portion of bread for it, but it served me well."

Surprisingly, in a place dominated by a struggle for survival on its most basic level, appearances were very important. "The SS demanded that our clothes be in good condition and that we be neat. The sleeves had to be the right length and maybe even with a crease. The beds had to be made perfectly. They asked you to do things without giving you the means to do them, but they had to be done. If a button was missing from your jacket it had to be repaired—even though, officially, there was no thread, and no needles. But you had to find them, trade bread or cigarettes, if there were any, for thread."

Those who became dirty and disheveled, who became the crowd of faceless masses waiting to die, were referred to contemptuously as "musselmen." "I remember people who, out of fatigue and weakness from lack of food, no longer had the desire to wash themselves and walked around the camp looking dirty. And within days they were gone, eliminated. I saw many Italians like that. I remember a copy editor from Mondadori [a Milan publishing house] who suddenly became very rundown. He didn't wash or change his clothes, people began to avoid him, and then he was gone, from one day to the next—never heard from again. It was very important not to be run-down beyond a certain point; you were already so badly degraded that if you gave in, that was the beginning of the end. You had to remain a man. You had to maintain the respect of both the guards and the other prisoners."

Despite the brutality of the camp there was a well-developed social code that was largely respected by the prisoners. While stealing clothing and belongings was rampant, stealing food from inmates hardly ever occurred; when it did it was punished by death, carried out on the spot by inmates. The prohibition was so strong that the prisoners could store food in open lockers in the barracks, even with starving men walking by every day. The one time the Schönheits attempted stealing, the taboo against it foiled their efforts.

"We never stole anything from other inmates," Franco recalls. "But my father once tried. He was working in the storeroom with the lentils, and on the same work detail was another French prisoner who left the same piece of bread in his locker for more than a week. The locker was right next to my father's, and every day he would see this same piece of bread just sitting there and it started driving him crazy. My father said, 'He must have forgotten, or he doesn't want it, but if I ask him for it he won't give it to me.' So one day he stole it. He brought it back, and we took this stale piece of bread, hard as marble, divided it in two and ate it, avidly, with great pleasure. And then immediately my father began to say, 'And if this guy notices? And if he denounces me to the *kapo*?' And I said, 'It's impossible; there are twenty people working in there. How will he ever know it was you?' He kept saying, 'But . . . well . . . I don't know.' And the next morning he said, 'Franco, I'm sick over this. I haven't slept at all. We've got to put the bread back. Maybe they'll kill us.' So we took our fresh bread of that day and cut a piece identical to the hard piece we had eaten the night before, and my father put it back into the French prisoner's locker. Several days went by, and my father continued to look at this piece of bread as it started to get hard. He would tell me, 'He still hasn't touched it!' Then one day he said it was gone. I thought, Finally the episode of the bread is over. Apparently this fellow liked hard bread. That was my father's only attempt at theft: exchanging a good piece of fresh bread for a piece of stale bread."

* * *

One day, a few months after their arrival at Buchenwald, a small miracle occurred: Franco and his father received a letter from his mother at Ravensbrück. They were stunned; the idea had never occurred to them that prisoners in two different pockets of hell could correspond with one another. "My mother had seen more quickly than we had that the German prisoners, and only the German prisoners, were allowed to write a letter a month to their relatives at home or in other camps," Franco says. "So she, mocking the Nazis with her German-sounding name, managed to get ahold of these letter forms and wrote us three or four letters. Naturally, the letters had to be in German, so she had someone help her with them. Because they had to pass through the camp censors, she limited herself just to letting us know that she was alive. We succeeded in writing to her using the same system, and so for several months we conducted a correspondence."

Franco has managed to keep all her letters. The letters bear their concentration camp numbers and a note in German that the contents have been checked by the camp censors. "With great joy I received your letter of November 5," he says, translating one of the letters. "I am happy to know that you are all right and want you to know that I am well. And," he explains, "there is something about an Italian prisoner was able to receive a package, and she asks whether someone in Italy might be contacted to send us something. In another letter, to my father, she wrote: My dear husband, my health is good. I hope the same is true for you and for our dear son. I think constantly of you both and I hope we will all see one another again. I kiss you." Franco, who always maintains an upright posture and an almost military bearing, becomes highly emotional and passionate when reading his mother's letters.

The first letter from Gina arrived in late October 1944 and the last in early March 1945; the letters stopped as communications within Germany broke down under the Allied invasion. Those last months, the winter of 1944–1945, were by universal consensus the worse in Buchenwald's seven-year history. "October 1944 began what was to be the nightmare within the nightmare," wrote Eugene Weinstock, a Hungarian partisan who spent three years at Buchenwald, in a memoir of his experience immediately after the war, *Beyond the Last Path.* With the steady retreat of German forces on both eastern and western fronts, conditions in the camps worsened. As they pulled back, the German troops dismantled the death camps in Poland and forced the remaining prisoners to undertake death marches to camps inside Germany. Built to house 25,000 to 30,000, Buchenwald suddenly held 82,000 prisoners who fought over the same meager resources 30,000 men had had to share.

"During that terrible winter," Weinstock recounted, "the SS committed at least 40,000 murders in Buchenwald. The figure is so gigantic that it is almost meaningless, but every murder involved a man, an anti-fascist, who bled and suffered agonies in one of the weirdest bursts of mass sadism in the world's entire history. Other concentration camps in the path of Allied armies were closed or dismantled, or fell before conquering troops. . . . Transport followed transport. There was no place to put prisoners, no food to give them . . . no work. There could be only one solution to this problem from the Nazi point of view. That solution was death."

Weinstock described the fate of 900 Hungarian partisans who arrived at the camp in early December, the survivors of a group of 5,000 that had departed Hungary two months earlier on a nonstop march that had killed off more than 4,000 of the men. When they arrived at Buchenwald they were so exhausted that forty more died from the cold showers inmates were given at their induction into the camp. "The new prisoners were housed in the Small Lager where all sanitary precautions had broken down and an epidemic of dysentery raged. There was no medicine or doctors and it is doubtful whether either would have been any use. At the end of December only four of the 900 Hungarians were alive.

"As the number of prisoners in the camp increased, the food decreased proportionately," Weinstock wrote of those final months. "Our individual rations dwindled to a few crumbs. There was plenty of food in the warehouses but now the Nazis were husbanding these stores because the food situation throughout Germany was desperate. . . . December, January and February passed in the same fashion but the tempo of the torture increased. More tension, less bread, a growing feeling of uncertainty. Death had never before been so omnipresent in the vast graveyard of Buchenwald."

As one of the last Nazi concentration camps, Buchenwald was gradually transformed from work camp into death camp. From this final period, Franco Schönheit recalls the first mass "selection" at Buchenwald. "Each barracks was divided in half, section A and section B, and we were made to gather in the two halves. Then two or three SS officials began dividing up the prisoners into two groups. The most run-down, sickest, oldest and weakest were directed toward section A. My father and I both managed to make it to section B. We never saw any of the others again."

In mid-March the Nazis began trying to evacuate Buchenwald, although there were few other camps to which prisoners could be transferred. "This was just another form of elimination," Franco says. "Making completely malnourished people walk for miles without food could have no other purpose. As soon as people stopped or lagged behind, the SS would shoot on sight. We understood this immediately, and the camp underground spread the word to resist being taken outside the camp at all cost."

All trappings of order began to break down. While the Germans continued the usual *Appell* to gather and count the prisoners, the inmates now refused. The Nazis no longer had the troop strength to round up all the inmates and force them to leave. Instead, groups of SS would enter the camp with motorcycles and machine guns and surround a particular section of it—while the prisoners, in a deadly game of musical chairs, struggled to move to some other part of the camp.

"Every morning from late March on, the SS would enter the camp in force, seal off a part of it and force the inmates into the central square," Franco recalls. "Once the prisoners were in the central square, surrounded by machine guns, it was easy to get them all to line up and march out of the camp. Many began long marches to other camps but few arrived, because of their physical condition. So for fifteen days the daily problem was not to be where the roundup would take place. Two or three times we were able to escape from the blocks before the SS arrived.

"Then on April 9 they surrounded the block where we had taken refuge, and we were forced to line up in the central square. There was total confusion, however. The entire center of the courtyard was littered with dead bodies. As the structure of the camp had begun to collapse no one bothered to remove the dead anymore. So all of us who were supposed to be forming into lines were moving around these dead bodies strewn everywhere."

The SS, as usual, made use of the *Kapos* to help them herd everyone into formation, but by now the SS were so reduced that they recruited additional personnel to help out. These people were given white cloth to wrap around their arms to distinguish them from other prisoners. "I told my father: 'We are absolutely in no condition to go on this march, not even for five kilometers. Let's make an effort to sneak back into the camp'—even though we were already in the assembly area. My father asked me, 'What can we do?' I said, 'Let's start by putting a white rag around our arms and pretending we are *Kapos*. We don't have to beat anybody or force anyone out of the camp.' We put handkerchiefs around our arms and suddenly all the other prisoners started moving away from us. We noticed that there was a path between two barracks that led to the road back into the camp, but to reach the road you had to turn a corner at the foot of a guard tower where two SS guards were keeping watch with a machine gun. The only way back into the camp was to pass this tower. I told my father, 'Let's go down this road and we'll try to turn the corner.' He said, 'They'll shoot us as soon as they see us. They're not going to let us back into the camp just because we have some rag on our arms.' I said, 'Let's try it anyway, because we certainly are not about to march. Dying on the road or dying here is the same thing.' We said good-bye to one another and headed together down the road. When we reached the tower the guards saw us and lowered their machine gun toward us. I looked at my father one last time, and at that precise instant an air-raid alarm sounded. The SS looked up to see the incoming planes, and we turned the corner back into the camp."

Two days later Buchenwald was liberated. During the last two days, some prisoners who were part of the camp underground dug up guns they had managed to conceal for months. Had they attempted to use these few weapons before, they would have only provoked a mass bloodbath, but now, with Nazi manpower greatly depleted, the camp's resistance helped prevent further evacuation and death. From their hiding place, Franco and Carlo saw the incredible sight of prisoners carrying guns, running and firing. The pounding of artillery signaled that American troops were only a few miles away. A few hours before their arrival, the Nazis abandoned the camp. Then, in the tense silence that followed, a jeep carrying four American soldiers pulled into Buchenwald. Almost immediately the soldiers left, in pursuit of the retreating German army; the prisoners remained in charge until the Americans returned the next day.

The camp by now was a field of corpses. Of the 80,000 or so prisoners who had been at Buchenwald in early March, only 23,000 remained: the rest had been taken off either on forced marches or died in the camp. "The bodies remained there for a week," Franco says. "The Americans did something I thought was very beautiful and very important. They brought Germans from the surrounding area to see the camp. There were hundreds and hundreds of people, some who came by bus from Weimar, some who walked six or seven kilometers from nearby towns; they looked without speaking. I remember one American official, a black man, tall and strong, who must have weighed two hundred pounds, came with a camera to photograph the camp three days after the liberation. I watched him as he entered the crematorium: I can still see him now. I was right near the crematorium. Behind the oven was an enormous pile of naked, rotting corpses, thirty feet long, fifteen feet high, ten feet wide. These were the last corpses, the ones the Germans hadn't had time to burn. I saw the soldier lift his camera and then lower it suddenly and then grab onto a wall for support. He couldn't do it. This was not a boy; he was a fighting soldier, who had already seen it all, who had fought and fired a gun, killed and seen men die next to him. But this was not a heap of soldiers killed in battle, dressed in their uniforms: this was a pile of naked men stacked neatly like cords of wood. This last sight was just too much for him. These young soldiers liberated the camps, but they had no idea what was in them. After a week we buried the dead because the risk of an epidemic was too great."

Epilogue

The Ovazzas of Turin

During their exile in New York City, Vittorio Ovazza and his family threw themselves into Jewish life in a way they never had in Turin. They joined a synagogue and volunteered for various Jewish charitable organizations, anxious to move out of the shadow cast by Ettore. "We were branded," says Franca Piperno, Vittorio's older daughter. "The name Ovazza equaled *La Nostra Bandiera,* which equaled fascism. People didn't bother to look to see if we were different, if my father was different from my uncle. We were the Ovazza family. That's why I started working for these Jewish organizations when I got to the States: so that people would know that we were different."

After Franca began working for the World Jewish Congress, the U.S. State Department asked the organization to prepare a report on the Italian Jewish community in anticipation of the Allied invasion of Italy. "We were asked to compile lists of names of Jews who were fascists and Jews who could be trusted. I was charged with making inquiries, and I put down my uncle's name in the list of fascists. At one point they said to me, 'We have to discuss fascism among Jewish groups in Italy. Would you kindly leave the room?' I hid in the bathroom and cried. And then one of the men brought me back to the room and took me by the hand and said, 'If each one of us had been working for five years, doing all the dirty work, without ever asking anything in return, then we might be able to point a finger at her. But at this moment we should fully apologize to her for what we just did.' So they all shook hands with me."

Back in Italy after the war, the remaining Ovazzas started to piece together the story of their relatives' fate. They received a vague account of the death of Ettore and his family, as well as of another cousin, Virginia Montalcini, who had been hiding in a sanatorium in northern Italy when one of the doctors there turned her in to the Germans.

"During the summer of 1948, I went to Gressoney on vacation, and there I met a former Italian air force pilot who had been wounded and sent to a sanatorium near Milan," Franca recalls. "He heard my name and came up to me and said, 'You are a cousin of Virginia Montalcini, aren't you? She and I were very good friends, and I was at the clinic when they took her away.' And then the village doctor [Raggi] heard my name, and he came to me and said, 'I was here when your uncle and his family were taken away.' It was the strangest thing: at the same time and in the same place, I heard what happened to my cousin and to my uncle and his family. The doctor told me, 'If you'd like, I can take you to the hotel where your uncle was staying when he was taken by the Germans; the owner is still alive.' I called my father and said, 'Let me go with this doctor; we can put the hotelkeeper against a wall and get him to spit out all he stole from the family.' My father told me I shouldn't go."

For the next several years, the family worked to bring the perpetrators to justice. Witnesses identified the lieutenant who commanded the SS unit that killed the Ovazzas as Gottfried Meir, a schoolteacher from Austria.

In 1953 an Austrian court tried Meir and acquitted him, on the grounds of insufficient evidence. They blamed the crime on two SS officers under Meir's command who had died (conveniently) later in the war. But in 1955 an Italian court, unable to win Meir's extradition from Austria, placed him on trial in absentia. The trial, held in Turin, shed light on some of the more obscure aspects of the Ovazza case.

One witness, Bruno Henke, who had acted as an interpreter for the SS, testified that he had seen Riccardo Ovazza before he was killed.

> I was in the girls' school at Intra [where the SS unit had set up headquarters]. In the corner of the room, with his face turned to the wall, I saw a young man in hiking clothes, about twenty years old. I asked a German soldier present who he was, and he told me it was a Jewish student who had been arrested by the German police. From a letter written in German I saw sitting on the table in the office, I learned the exact status of the young man: he was a young student named Ovazza whom the German police had arrested in the mountains with numerous

> letters of recommendation written by his father for the Swiss authorities and with about 5,000 Swiss francs and a certain quantity of gold. I spoke to Ovazza in Italian and he seemed very happy to talk with me, and he confirmed what was written in the police report and asked that I help him. I tried to keep his spirits up and promised him I would speak to the commander of the SS. In that moment Commandant Meir entered the office and, seeing that I was speaking with the young man, began screaming at him, calling him a "Jewish pig," and lifted a chair over his head and said: "I'll break your head, turn to the wall!" I intervened and prevented Meir from going further.

When asked what would become of the young man, Henke was told he would be sent to a German concentration camp. But the next day someone at the SS compound told him that Riccardo Ovazza had been killed "in the basement of the school at about five o'clock, and burned in the furnace."

If Henke's story is true, it would help explain another mysterious event at the school in Intra. The custodian, Ida Rusconi, testified in her deposition that the Nazis had killed a British prisoner a few days before the Ovazza family. No other trace of a British prisoner of war was found. Rusconi had not spoken with the prisoner and had assumed from his khaki-colored clothes that he was an Allied prisoner. The court ruled that this person was, in all likelihood, Riccardo Ovazza.

As for Gottfried Meir's responsibility, the court did not have much doubt. "Everything occurred in the defendant's [Meir's] office, where he was omnipotent, from which he granted safe-conducts, issued passports, requisitioned hotels, schools, cars. . . . How can one imagine that he was in the dark? In what army (and note that here we are dealing with the German army . . .) could the commandant of a company not be aware of what was happening in his own office?"

The court, citing Meir's "limitless infamy," sentenced him to life imprisonment. On a practical level, however, the sentence was meaningless: Meir lived out his days peacefully in the Austrian town of Ponfeld, working as a schoolteacher until his death in 1970.

The keeper of the hotel where the Ovazzas were arrested, Arnaldo Cochis, was never tried for any crime. He never accounted for the large stash of money and jewelry that Ettore Ovazza had deposited in his hotel safe. Another guest at the Lyskamm, a Signora Pellegrino, testified after the war that she had seen Cochis ostentatiously displaying a handsome ring that may have belonged to Ovazza. She described a reception Cochis gave during the German occupation to celebrate his own appointment as local police commissioner: "He showed off his fine clothes and his elegance and told everyone to look closely at the things he wore in order to prevent some malicious soul from later spreading the rumor that he had enriched himself through his position as police commissioner. . . . He wore a new suit and had a gold ring with a precious stone, probably that of *Commendatore* Ovazza."

Despite the opprobrium that still clung to the Bandiera movement, the Ovazzas remained closely tied to the Turin Jewish Community. Both Alfredo and Vittorio moved back to their native city, where most of their descendants continue to live.

The younger generations have had the difficult task of repudiating their family's fascism while remaining true to the family itself, which is still a tight-knit clan. Carla Ovazza, although married, continues to use the Ovazza name and has sacrificed to keep the Villa Ovazza, despite the fact that it is much larger than her needs, and a drain on her resources.

The life of Ettore Ovazza remains for the surviving members of his family a hard, undigested, almost incomprehensible piece of the past. "Looking back, I don't understand how we could have accepted such a thing, a Jew attacking another Jew," says Carla. "*La Nostra Bandiera* was a filthy thing, and it was extremely damaging, a black page in the history of Italian Judiasm. But I find Uncle Ettore's life sad because he died for his ideals. He believed, up until the end. I am ashamed, but I respect him. He didn't do it out of malice or out of personal interest. He didn't want anyone to get in the way of his love for fascism."

The Foas of Turin

The Foa family, scattered by the racial laws, remains geographically disparate but emotionally close. Vittorio lives in Rome, Anna in Boston, and Beppe in Bethesda, Maryland. Their parents lived in Turin until their deaths.

For Beppe and Anna, the decision to stay in the United States was partially a practical one: they had worked hard to rebuild their lives and were not anxious to uproot themselves a second time. But there may have been psychological reasons as well.

When Beppe returned to Turin for the first time after the war, on assignment for the U.S. Army as an aeronautics expert, he was overcome by a terrible wave of anxiety. "As soon as I reached Turin I felt exactly the way I had in the days before I left Italy, right before the war, when I was trying desperately to get a passport. I felt the same awful terror, as if I were caught in a trap. I knew very well that I could leave, I was an official in the American army, but I again felt as if I couldn't leave. Being back in that same atmosphere—Turin never changes; in two hundred years it will be exactly the same—brought back this feeling of terror and claustrophobia."

Like many refugees, Beppe returned to America and placed an enormous distance between himself and Italy. He is married to an American woman and has lived a highly Americanized life. He changed his name from Giuseppe to Joseph. Until quite recently, he had never brought his four daughters to Italy. He has had a very successful career as an aeronautical engineer in both private industry and university teaching. In 1990, at the age of eighty-one, he was still active at George Washington University in Washington, D.C.

Anna and Davide Jona stayed in Boston. They Americanized their last name to Yona to fit English pronunciation, and he dropped the final *e* from his first name. But they remained much more attached to Italy than Beppe. Since both husband and wife were Italian, they continued to speak Italian at home, and since their two daughters had been born in Italy, they spoke it as well. Vittorio says he likes visiting Anna's house because it reminds him of being in Turin: Anna has kept much of the antique Italian furniture their parents had at home.

The difficulties of persecution, war and exile have left Anna a much stronger person than the timid young woman she was in Turin during the 1930s. She recalls that while growing up she was so frightened of her father that if she had something to ask him she would put a note under his pillow. As if to make up for her childhood, she became extremely forthright and strong-willed, with passionately held opinions. In 1948 she lost the radio job she had, for advocating the presidential candidacy of Henry Wallace over the air. While her father never allowed her to complete her education, Anna has ended up as a teacher of Italian at the New England Conservatory of Music. David died in 1972, but Anna, at age eighty-two, was invited back to teach for the 1990–1991 school year.

Fifty-eight years after his youthful decision to join Giustizia e Libertà, Vittorio Foa remains passionately involved in political life.

At the end of World War II, the antifascists who had been outcasts suddenly became the leaders of the new democratic Italy. Vittorio and a number of his former co-conspirators were elected to parliament as members of the newly formed Partito d'Azione, the successor of Giustizia e Libertà. But the Italy of the antifascist resistance was short-lived. Much to the disillusionment of Vittorio and his friends, Italy underwent no socialist transformation. The Partito d'Azione proved a short-lived experiment. Composed mainly of intellectuals with little mass following, it was, in the words of one member, "an army with all generals and no infantry." Nonetheless Vittorio became a leader in Italy's labor movement and for a time, headed the country's principal union confederation.

Politically, Vittorio has been a dissident, generally favoring the underdog in a series of losing battles. After the dissolution of the Partito d'Azione, he became a socialist during a period (the 1950s and 1960s) when it was overshadowed by Italy's larger and more radical Communist Party. He left the Socialist Party in the 1970s as it grew simultaneously more conservative and more powerful. Recently, even despite its being in danger of disintegration, Vittorio gravitated toward the Communist Party as it began to abandon communism. When it officially changed its name in 1991 to the Democratic Party of the Left, he became a member of the party, which, at age eighty, he represents in the Italian Senate.

To some, Vittorio might appear a quixotic supporter of lost causes. But he has the serenity of one who has simply been ahead of his time. Often his views have prevailed in other people's hands. Giustizia e Libertà was crushed in the 1930s, but its opposition to fascism was later shared by the majority of Italians. The democratic socialism of the Partito d'Azione was too moderate to be successful in the highly polarized battles of the cold war, but gradually its position has been adopted by much of the Italian left. In fact, when the Italian Communist Party debated changing its name in 1990–1991, both "Giustizia e Libertà" and "Partito d'Azione" were considered.

As in childhood, of the three siblings Vittorio appears to be the most removed from his Jewish roots. "I always considered the racial campaign, which I felt very strongly while I was in prison, as a violation of the Italian national tradition, as a blot on its history of democracy and civility, but not as a reason to reject assimilation. There were many Jews in the Resistance with me, but I always felt their commitment was not so much an expression of their Jewishness as a sign of their integration. We viewed the racial campaign as a shameful stain on Italy that we were trying to wipe out in order to return the country to its traditions of democracy and tolerance."

Despite his increased detachment, Judaism has made a curious revival within Vittorio's own family. Although the child of a mixed marriage and not officially Jewish, his oldest daughter, Anna, became increasingly fascinated with the Jewish side of her family and undertook the arduous process of conversion to Judaism. "There is a great revival of interest in Judaism among the younger generation," Vittorio says. "I have arguments about it all the time with Anna. And when I tell her I don't understand what she's doing, she says to me, 'How can you, you're assimilated.' " Anna Foa studies the history of the Marranos, who lived secretly as Jews after their forced conversion in Spain—something of a metaphor for her own experience of rediscovering the Judaism in her own family that has been submerged since the death of Rabbi Giuseppe Foa in 1916.

* * *

The news of Pitigrilli's spying activity did not become public until the end of the war. When antifascists occupied the police station in Turin, they uncovered the numerous spy reports written by agent 373, many of which were later published in Giustizia e Libertà's newspaper, *L'Italia Libera.* Pitigrilli flouted the charges against him but remained safely in Switzerland, where he had fled in 1943.

From abroad, Pitigrilli began a long, slow campaign of self-rehabilitation. At the center of his efforts was a much-publicized conversion to Catholicism. His seemingly convenient conversion was greeted by much cynicism and ridicule ("Pitigrilli the Catholic is the funniest character created by Pitigrilli," one critic wrote). Nonetheless, he was warmly received by the Church, which began working openly and behind the scenes to enable him to return to Italy.

Pitigrilli's public conversion was accompanied by a series of violent diatribes against his Jewish relatives and Jews in general. In 1948 he published one of the oddest Holocaust novels ever written, *Mosè e il Cavalier Levi* (Moses and Cavalier Levi). A strange piece of fictional schizophrenia, the book deplores the injustice of the Italian racial campaign while essentially blaming it on the Jews. "Anti-Semitism is a disease that explodes from time to time," says the novel's hero, "but between one explosion and another, the Jews succeed in keeping it alive."

The book's heroine makes a declaration that appears to be a justification of Pitigrilli's own conversion. "If it were possible to turn a switch and cease being a Jew, cease ever having been a Jew, cease having a Jewish name . . . and a nasal voice . . . on condition that no one would know you had turned the switch . . . there wouldn't be one Jew left on the face of the earth."

Pitigrilli accepted an invitation to lecture in South America and eventually settled in Buenos Aires, where he wrote for the daily *La Razón.* He is said to have enjoyed the protection of dictator Juan Perón and is even rumored to have ghost-written an autobiography of Evita Perón. But according to his wife, Avvocatessa Lina Furlan, Pitigrilli felt stifled in Argentina, and in 1958 he moved with her and their son, Pier Maria, to Paris. Later the Avvocatessa returned to Turin so that Pier Maria could receive an Italian education; Pitigrilli himself began making furtive occasional visits back to Italy.

In exile, railing against the injustices of fate, he watched his reputation sink as rapidly as it had risen. Meanwhile, many of the people whose fates he had controlled as a spy—Carlo Levi, Natalia Ginzburg,

Cesare Pavese, Alberto Moravia—joined the ranks of Italy's most respected writers and intellectuals. Although Pitigrilli wrote and published prolifically, he was never able to regain his former popularity. The "new," converted Pitigrilli denounced his early books as immoral and refused to have them reprinted. But with his rejection of the superficial, cynical posing of those works his writing became didactic and sententious. In his later books he committed the one literary sin the young Pitigrilli would not have tolerated: dullness.

In the mid-1960s, after the scandal had died down, Pitigrilli quietly settled again his native Turin. For a man who had thrived on being the center of controversy, he must have been disappointed by the silence that accompanied his return. In virtual obscurity, he wrote for a small church newspaper, *Il Giornale di Sant'Antonio.* By the time he died in 1975, virtually all of his more than twenty books were out of print. In a fate worse than being tried and sentenced, Pitigrilli was simply ignored and forgotten.

Nonetheless, Pitigrilli enjoys a strange form of immortality. He met with great success in Poland in the 1920s and 1930s, and gave a series of lectures in Warsaw in 1930. His notoriety was such that the adjective *pitigrilli,* referring to something suspect, vaguely obscene or morally ambiguous, survives in Polish. Although his novels are now forgotten, Pitigrilli has metamorphosed for posterity into a Polish insult.

The Di Verolis of Rome

After decades of hard work the Di Verolis, for the most part, have been able to reconstruct their lives. To a remarkable degree, that life resembles the one they led before the war, the life led by their ancestors for centuries.

After the liberation of Rome, Umberto Di Veroli (Monsieur Macaroni) and his family had to start over, forced back into peddling their wares on the street. Both their shop and their apartment on Via del Portico d'Ottavia had been occupied by families who had lost their homes during the war.

"We slept in the store with the people who had moved in," says Michele di Umberto. "My father had walled up all our merchandise and capital, but the Germans found it and stole everything. So we had to begin again from zero, doing all kinds of jobs. I went around town selling postcards and souvenirs, and fruit on the street corners. One of my brothers sold chocolates and other things on the black market, another one worked as a shoeshine boy for the American soldiers, who really liked to have their boots clean. Since there was no possibility of cooking at home, I continued to go back to the Lateran seminary for my meals. As soon as the Jews moved out of there at the time of the liberation, the Germans moved in. They sought the protection of the Church and the Church opened its doors to them. They asked me to give my blanket and pillows to the Germans, and I rebelled. 'You're being a Jew and not a Catholic,' they said. 'When you needed help, we took you in; now they need help.' I said, 'But these people stole everything from me and took away my sister.' 'You can't live with resentment,' they said to me. 'In fact, not only should you give them your bed and your blankets, but if there's anything else you have, you should help these people.' And so I gave everything I had: my blanket, my pillow, my razor."

As the only one of the four not to lose its father, Umberto Di Veroli's family had the easiest time starting over. Monsieur Macaroni reopened his shop with his old entrepreneurial zeal, and when he died in 1962, he left a considerable inheritance to his eleven children. His four sons divided up the business; Michele, the oldest, kept the original store at Via del Portico d'Ottavia, while his two brothers used their share of the inheritance to open stores of their own. All three have shops in the ghetto today.

Some of Umberto's daughters have followed similar paths. "Rita has a knitting shop," Michele explains, "Settimia, a clothing shop; Vimma, a shop of used objects. Emilia, her husband drives a taxi. Elia's husband had a gift shop. Maria's husband used to work as a salesman for a textile company.

"We all had a great desire to start over," Michele says. "If we had sat around and thought about what we had lost, and felt resentful, we just would have lost work. What happened, happened. The only thing you can do for the dead is weep. It's over."

The children of Enrico Di Veroli, perhaps because they had lost their father, did not have as easy a time letting go of the past. Knowing that the men who betrayed him were former clients of their store, still living in Rome, filled them with a desire for justice.

In 1947 a trial was held for a number of the most active Nazi informants, including the two men who had turned in Enrico. But the family felt that justice was stacked against them. "The judges were still all fascists," says Gianni Di Veroli bitterly. The judges challenged the validity of their mother's identification of the pair, who were acquitted because of "lack of evidence."

At one point during the trial, Michele di Enrico got close enough to the defendants to begin punching one of them in the face. "I was arrested, and for a while it looked like I was the one who would go to prison," he said.

"The two were finally sentenced to thirty years in prison," said Gianni. "But not for the crime of turning in my father, for other crimes.

But then they were let out with a general amnesty. For all I know, they're still alive."

Consumed with the trial, Enrico's family was not particularly successful in rebuilding its business. "My father had created an empire," Michele said, with a characteristic touch of hyperbole. "But without his creative capacity, things went differently after the war."

All of Enrico's children worked at the store, says his cousin Michele di Umberto. "But without the father, the head of the family, it was like a ship that had lost its captain, and the ship began to sink. There were too many commanders." The two sons, Gianni and Michele, jumped ship. Olga hung onto the shop as long as she could. But when business went from bad to worse, she sold the store and went to work in an office.

Gianni became a salesman. Michele moved about restlessly from one profession to another. Doing "a thousand different things," as he said, selling a little of this and a little of that, he eked out a modest living. After just as unsettled a personal life, he married in 1961, when he was almost forty. But as Michele readily acknowledges, it was a practical marriage, born of necessity on both sides.

"It was almost an arranged marriage. There is almost a fifteen years' difference between us. She was still a child when I was a grown man. An aunt of mine said to me, 'Look, as a bachelor you'll have no future. Now there's your mother, but later if you need a clean shirt, who are you going to ask? Go and see this girl.' I saw her. She had a very serious face. She had been through a lot in the war: they took her father away when she was seven and he died when she was eleven; her brother was half paralyzed from fear of the Germans. She worked hard for a few lire a month. Her situation moved me. She was very serious, while I had always been attracted by, let's say, more effervescent, more superficial girls. The poor thing showed that she was up to the situation. We have four children."

An air of tragedy hangs over Enrico's family. With the failure of the shop, his children went their own separate ways, each under precarious financial conditions. Olga, the only one to remain in the ghetto, always maintained that she never married because she had made a vow to keep the family together. But while she presided alone over the family store and the old family apartment in Via in Publicolis, there was no more family to hold together. In 1987, Olga, took ill and died at age sixty-nine, and Gianni, sixty-two, was struck down by a cerebral hemorrhage and confined to a hospital, where, barely conscious, he clings to life. "He doesn't live, he vegetates," said Michele. Gianni's wife died the same year he became ill, leaving their two children entirely on their own. Fernanda and Flora led their own lives with their families.

Looking back, in 1988 Michele di Enrico oscillated between remorse and defiant anger. "There are still things that disturb me after forty-five years," he said. "Imagine those who were in the camps, with what they've seen. They murdered my father, my sister and my uncles, but I don't want to get mileage out of that to gain pity. People who play victim are cowards toward themselves. For a long time, I felt guilt at having survived. But I don't want to sit around weeping about it. Cowards only make people sick. But let's not talk about all this foolishness, we have more important things to discuss."

Caught painfully between conflicting impulses, Enrico's older son insisted that he does not like to dwell on the past, but could not keep himself from doing so. He mocked those who cry and complain, yet he could not talk about his family's experiences without breaking down. He died in 1990 of heart failure.

For Rosa Di Veroli and her family, liberation meant an opportunity to find out finally what happened to her father and brother.

A major operation was undertaken to dig up and identify the bodies of the victims of the Ardeatine Caves massacre. Rosa went to the site with her uncle Umberto and his son Michele. "I recognized my cousin Michele [Attilio's son] because he was wearing a raincoat I had given him," says Michele di Umberto. "My uncle Attilio we recognized because of a ring he had on. There was another cousin of mine, from my mother's family. We recognized him by some jewels he had hidden in his pants."

As they dug up the bodies, the Di Verolis studied their positions to decipher something about the way their relatives had died. "My brother was killed first, then my father—you could tell by the way the bodies were placed," Rosa says. "So my father must have had to watch his son die. The bodies were well preserved even though months had passed. I recognized them right away—and not only because of the clothes and the objects found on them. In Michele's case, the only thing missing were the eyes." Rosa repeats her sentence softly, matter-of-factly, with just a touch of wonder: "The only thing missing were the eyes."

After the war Rosa succeeded in building a new life on the foundation of the old. She works in the same shop where she was a salesgirl as a teenager. But now she moves about with the proud, contented air of an owner.

Needing a job at war's end, Rosa turned to her old boss, Renato Di Veroli. Not only had Renato's business been wiped out, but he had lost his entire family, his wife and their three children, in the October 16, 1943, roundup. Like so many Jews who were convinced that the Germans would arrest only able-bodied men, Renato had spent the night of October 15 hiding in a basement while his family remained at home. The next day he ran back to his apartment only to find the typed sheet of paper the Germans had handed his wife when they arrived, which bore chilling words: "Together with your family and with any other Jews belonging to this household you must be transferred."

Renato's wife and children never returned, his store was looted, and after the war he was in a situation similar to Rosa's. "He wanted to reopen the store, and I had no work," Rosa relates. "Initially we opened the store only half a day because we had no merchandise. Since Renato is an honest man, known by our suppliers, they gave him things on credit, telling him to take the merchandise and repay them when he could.

"It took a long time to get back, five or six years. At first we had no real desire to work. Renato was consumed with trying to find any news about his family. He kept hoping they might return. He would sit at home after dinner and just cry. Then, bit by bit . . ." In 1949, Rosa and Renato, both of whom had lost so much in the war, married and started a new family of their own. They now have two grown children.

As far as her wartime experiences, Rosa appears to have achieved an equilibrium: she is neither paralyzed by the past nor forgetful of it. She had the satisfaction of seeing the Italian who is thought to have turned in her father and brother sent to jail. Moreover, Herbert Kappler, the head of the SS in Rome, was condemned to life in prison for his role in the Ardeatine Caves massacre. Kappler was imprisoned at Gaeta, between Rome and Naples, but in 1977, after bribing Italian prison guards, he escaped and returned to Germany. The West German government turned down Italian requests for extradition, and Kappler, who was already sick when he fled Italy, died peacefully in his bed in 1978.

Rosa's old school friend, Celeste Di Porto, La Pantera Nera (The Black Panther), got off much more lightly. "Right after the liberation, the wife of a man whom Celeste had turned in and who had been killed at the Ardeatine Caves tried to kill her," Rosa says, "but people prevented her." Di Porto was eventually sent to prison but was released after only seven years in a general amnesty in 1954. "She converted to Catholicism and was going to become a nun, but then she got married," Rosa says. Her relatives stayed in the old ghetto and reopened their shops, and they remain active members of the Rome Jewish community.

Rosa has a mixed view of the behavior of the leaders of the Rome community during the war. "They continued to believe, even though they knew what had happened in Poland. What I don't understand is how they could let the Germans get ahold of the lists with all our names and addresses on them." (The question of whether or not the Germans used the lists of the Jewish community or whether they relied on similar lists they obtained from the Italian government has been a matter of great debate.)

Slowly Rosa began to reacquire the sense of being Italian she says had been taken from her in 1938 at the time of the racial laws. "Mussolini had made us feel Italian. I can't tell you how many times I cried seeing the Italian flag but not being able to salute it." In 1946 a referendum election was held on whether to keep or eliminate the Savoy monarchy. Because the king had gone along with Mussolini for more than twenty years, a majority of Italians voted to get rid of the monarchy. "In the referendum, all the Jews voted for the republic against the monarchy," Rosa says.

But she realized in 1967, during the Six-Day War between Israel and Egypt, how strongly she felt about being Italian as well as Jewish. There was a backlash in Italy against both Israel and Italian Jews. "One of our clients said to me, 'Why don't you go live in Israel?' And I said, 'I'm Italian, I'm Roman.' "

The surviving members of the family of Giacomo Di Veroli were the last to resurface.

The first news of their arrest came to Michele di Umberto in the form of a watch. "My cousin Michele, Silvia and Guiditta's brother, had been wearing a wristwatch I had loaned him. Thinking he was going to be deported, he wanted to return it. He found a soldier he trusted and asked him to bring it back to me. And this person—I don't remember if it was before or after the liberation—came and found me. And so I knew the family had fallen into the hands of the Germans. I still have that watch, somewhere."

In the summer of 1945, almost a year after the liberation of Rome and a few months after the Nazi surrender, a message arrived from Giuditta, Giacomo's younger daughter. An Italian prisoner of war wrote saying that he had seen her in Germany at the end of the war; she had asked the soldier to tell her family that she was alive, but alone; she knew nothing about her father, mother, brother or sister.

Shortly after Giuditta's message arrived, her sister, Silvia, appeared in the doorway of Monsieur Macaroni's store in the ghetto. "We were expecting Giuditta, because this soldier had written saying that Giuditta had been liberated and would come to Rome as soon as she could find a military transport—but then Silvia showed up," Olga Di Veroli recounted. "And she said Giuditta was dead."

For a brief period the two sisters had been together at Auschwitz, but as soon as the Germans realized they were related, they were placed in separate barracks. The sisters managed, for a time, to see one another at roll calls and moments of repose. Then Giuditta, who was growing sicker and sicker, was brought to the camp infirmary—frequently the waiting room for the gas chambers at Auschwitz.

One day when Silvia went to visit the infirmary, Giuditta was gone. Silvia assumed that her sister, like so many who were judged unfit for work, had been gassed. When she returned to Rome, Silvia told her relatives unequivocally: Giuditta is dead. The family assumed that the soldier who sent the message must have met Silvia and not Giuditta and then confused the two names.

But Giuditta had survived the Auschwitz infirmary. "I was terribly sick," she recalls. "As happens when you're in the mountains it would be incredibly hot during the day and then suddenly very cold. We stood for hours during roll calls in the rain. I got a terrible sore throat. I got typhus. My feet swelled up, my whole body swelled, my lungs were full of something. They put me in the hospital. It was very dangerous to be sick in the camp, because they usually selected you for the gas chambers. I took beatings. I had dysentery and was so weak I crapped on myself like a hen. I was really about to die, but I kept telling myself, I have to get back, I have to go home.

"We were taken away on a march to Bergen-Belsen, but we never arrived because of bombardments. We walked all night. They took us into a wooded area. I was with a woman from Fiume who understood German. She heard them say they were taking us to the woods to shoot us. There was a bombardment. The Germans ran away and we were left there. There were lots of dead all over the ground. We were liberated on April 1, 1945. The Americans gave us everything they had."

Silvia, meanwhile, was liberated at Theresienstadt, where she had been transferred in the last days of the war to work in a weapons factory. Completely unaware of one another's fate, the two sisters entered Italy at almost the same date but at different points, Silvia at Treviso, Giuditta at Como.

When Giuditta reached Rome a few days after Silvia, she first ran into Olga's sister Flora. "My sister called and said that Giuditta had arrived," Olga Di Veroli remembered. "So I said to Silvia, 'Come with me to Flora's—Giuditta has arrived!' Silvia told me: 'Don't bother me, Giuditta is dead.' And she refused to speak to her over the phone. Giuditta then told me over the phone: 'Tell Silvia that if she doesn't get over here immediately, she'll never see me again.' I told Silvia this, and used swear words I wouldn't use now at my age. We took a taxi in a great hurry. I was afraid that they might both die of a heart attack; Silvia has a weak heart. We arrived at Flora's and at first Giuditta and Silvia didn't even embrace or anything. One sat in the dining room and the other in the living room, and they would look at each other without saying anything. And then finally they embraced."

Of the nucleus of thirty-three family members—the four brothers, their wives and their children—ten were either deported to Auschwitz or killed at the Ardeatine Caves. Giuditta and Silvia were the only two to return. There were 353 Di Verolis listed in the 1938 census; 77 were deported during the German occupation, 8 returned. Not included in this total are the five grandchildren and the two sons-in-law who were also arrested and deported. Nor does it include the dozens of other aunts, uncles, and first and second cousins, on the maternal side of the family. The Di Verolis, however, were in no way exceptional. Out of the estimated 12,000 Jews present in Rome at the moment of the German occupation, about a sixth were captured. Of the 2,094 arrested, 1,739 were deported, of whom 114 survived. Another 75 were killed in the Ardeatine Caves. Although more than half were captured by the Germans, the Italian police and various Italian neofascist bands bear principal responsibility for the approximately 800 arrests after October 16.

The overall picture for Italy was fairly similar. There were an estimated 39,357 Jews in the central-north parts of Italy occupied by the Germans after September 8, 1943. Some 5,500 managed to flee to Switzerland, while another 500 made it past German lines to safety in the south of Italy. Of the 33,357 Jews who lived out the German occupation in Italy, 6,746 were deported to concentration camps. Another 303 were killed on Italian territory.

After their reunion, Giuditta and Silvia Di Veroli never separated again. They live and work together today.

Giuditta, the younger, a handsome, dark-haired woman in her seventies, seems to have had an easier time readjusting. She married a man who had lost much of his family in the war; they have children and grandchildren. "Giuditta is more at peace; Silvia never really recovered," says their cousin Rosa.

Thirty years old when the war ended, Silvia never married. She became a kind of adoptive mother to a girl who had lost her parents to the deportations. "When I returned to Rome, I saw this girl, she was thirteen, yelling, 'Mamma, Mamma.' From that day she became like my daughter. Even after she married. I was like an idol to her, but unfortunately . . . she died at thirty-three."

As the family had lost what little they had during the war, Silvia took the only job available—her father's old position at the phone company. (In Italy, where work is often hard to find, jobs are almost like birthrights, held for years and passed on to relatives.) Silvia found herself where her father had been arrested on his fifty-eighth birthday. "I never felt comfortable, because I knew someone there had turned my father in, but I was never able to figure out who it was," Silvia says. "People there knew when he went to work that evening that the Germans had been looking for him, and no one warned him. I always used to throw that in people's faces there. I was never happy in that office."

Silvia and Giuditta were pained by the initial reception they received from the Rome Jewish community. "They didn't treat us too well," Giuditta recalls. "They acted as if we must have done something bad to have survived. The Catholics all said, 'You poor things, how you must have suffered,' but a lot of the Jews acted as if we had been used as whores by the Germans. I once heard a conversation in which one man asked, 'Would you marry a woman who had been deported?' 'No,' another answered. 'Neither would I,' the first one said. That kind of thing hurt us a lot."

Giuditta's husband, however, was different. "He said to me, 'I'm in love with you and I want to marry you. If anything happened to you in the camps, it won't make a difference. But tell me now, and we'll never discuss it again. I said, 'Nothing happened.' And he never mentioned it again."

After several years of working hard and saving, the two sisters had enough money to start a store of their own. By choice, they live and work far from the center of the city and the old neighborhood. "We were tired of being the 'poor people' of the ghetto," says Giuditta. "The houses were old and broken down and we wanted something new. We didn't want to hear 'ghetto' anymore. In fact, when we go back to the old neighborhood, we say 'piazza' instead of 'ghetto.' We say: 'I'll meet you in the piazza.' "

Silvia and Giuditta remain, however, strongly attached to the Jewish community, and they return often to the street where they grew up. The sisters work selling mattresses—a trade that was at one time the special domain of the Jews in Rome. (Centuries ago, they had a commission from the Vatican to make mattresses for the Vatican army.)

And although many of the Jews from Via del Portico d'Ottavia are now spread out all over the city, they migrate back with predictable regularity. In the evenings and on weekends, they stroll by the kosher shops and bars behind the synagogue. They set up folding chairs and card tables on the sidewalk and spend time catching up with former neighbors, relatives and old friends, gossiping, arguing or playing cards.

"The war decimated the neighborhood, and a lot of people left their old houses," says Michele di Umberto, who has not moved a millimeter from his parents' store and apartment. "The new parts of the city offered new facilities. And people were tired of feeling like mice in a mouse hole. But a lot of them feel the call of the old neighborhood; as soon as they have a day off, they're back here. And then it's still like a small village in a big city."

Massimo Teglio and Emanuele Pacifici

The liberation of Italy did not immediately end Massimo Teglio's career as a forger of documents and protector of fugitives. With the German surrender, a period of violent retribution against more than twenty years of fascism began. Those who had collaborated with the Nazis were rounded up, tried quickly in "people's tribunals" and shot. Even as Teglio welcomed the new antifascist order, he found himself helping several people hunted as war criminals.

Teglio had never been a political ideologue, and he tended to have a natural sympathy for people in trouble. Moreover, in his own experience of the Occupation, the line between fascists and antifascists had become quite blurred. Many people who were officially part of the fascist government had gone out of their way to help Teglio or at least had turned a blind eye to his activities.

In May 1945, Teglio recalled, "the functionary at the German embassy in Milan with whom we had worked came to Achille Malcovati's house to find me; he was going to be put on trial. I told him, 'You come to me, a Jew?' He said, 'I've heard your story and I'd like to learn something from you.' His wife was in Switzerland and he wanted to get there. I told him if he came back in a few days and brought a photo I could make him a false identity card. I appreciated the help he had given us, even though he was unaware of having given it. That was the second-to-last false document I made."

Back in Genoa, Teglio went to the aid of fascist officials such as Luigi San Germano, the head of the Fascist Party there during the Occupation; he told partisan leaders that San Germano had used his power leniently. Teglio also helped save Benuzzi, the former OVRA official who had worked for both the SS and DELASEM.

"Don Bicchierai told me that I should write to Lelio Valobra in Switzerland and tell him that Benuzzi hadn't done anything bad and had helped us. I wrote the letter, and at the end I noted: 'Of my sister, who has the name of a flower [*margherita* means "daisy" in Italian], we have no news.' In this way, Valobra would know that the letter from me was genuine and written spontaneously. Valobra took the letter to Zurich and Benuzzi was released."

Finally, Teglio tried to save Enrico Luzzatto, the imprisoned former DELASEM official who in order to avoid deportation had acted as an interpreter for the Germans until liberation.

Before the Occupation, Luzzatto had been one of DELASEM's most dedicated and courageous leaders, putting his own life at risk numerous times. He had smuggled Jewish refugees into France illegally and been arrested more than once. He had traveled to Yugoslavia and worked to save Jews from brutal Croatian fascists. After the Germans occupied Italy, he refused to flee and continued traveling through the country distributing DELASEM money.

But after his arrest Luzzatto found himself in the ambiguous role of interpreter for his captors. Out of fear of the Germans he adopted a brusque, unpleasant manner with the prisoners; secretly, he saved some inmates from the concentration camps by omitting their names from deportation lists, having them transferred from the prison to the hospital or getting them menial jobs in the prison.

"A terrible atmosphere surrounded Luzzatto at that time: the other Jews had been deported, and he had saved himself working," Teglio recalled. "He had had food to eat while they had had little. And the Germans allowed him to sleep with his wife in the prison. He hadn't done anything really wrong, but he had adopted a tough attitude with the other prisoners: if he had cigarettes, for example, he wouldn't give any to the other inmates. So he had come to be regarded as a traitor. But he had also tried to do some things in favor of other inmates, and through his wife, who was allowed to leave the prison, Luzzatto had given me useful information about what was going on in the prison."

After liberation, Teglio advised Luzzatto to go into hiding for a while until the heat of those seeking retribution cooled down. "I made him a false document—the last false identity card I made—and offered to take him to Milan. But he wanted to turn himself over to the Allies, insisting he had done nothing wrong. I talked privately with an American officer, who advised me not to have him go to the Allies. But Luzzatto was hardheaded and turned himself in to the Americans, who immediately delivered him to the Italians. A special tribunal was in session and many people wanted the death penalty for him. I went to the prosecutor and said I wanted to testify on behalf of Luzzatto. I told him Luzzatto may have done some things wrong but not so wrong as to warrant the death penalty. The prosecutor said, 'We need an example.' And I said, 'You're right, we need an example, but make an example out of someone who has done something really bad.' I went to the trial and testified, and the people in the crowd began whistling, shouting, calling me all sorts of names; there were communists, and some Jews. But I said loud and clear exactly what I knew, offering names and dates and facts. I explained that Luzzatto's wife had given me all kinds of information from within the prison. In the end the prosecutor relented and asked only for life in prison." After several years in prison, Luzzatto was granted clemency.

Gradually the demand for Teglio's rather unusual skills of wartime survival diminished. During the first Arab–Israeli war, Ada Sereni, a leading Italian Zionist pioneer in Israel, came to Italy for help, and Teglio used his connections in the world of aviation to help obtain planes for the new Israeli air force.

But besides that, Teglio returned to being what he had been before World War II: a charming, popular, impractical man. He tried his hand at various business ventures, none of which went especially well. "I let myself be tricked sometimes. I don't like to distrust people," Teglio said, laughing, without a tinge of regret. "My daughter often says to me, 'I can't believe that at your age you still believe people.' She is much sharper than I am."

Teglio had a naive, open face and the amused, boyish air of a prankster rather than the grave countenance of a hero or a saint. Short and delicately built, but with great physical vitality, until soon before his death in January 1990, Teglio moved about the hilly streets of Genoa with a light, buoyant step; he could be seen hopping on and off buses in crowded streets like a mountain goat. When he was tested in 1988, at age eighty-eight, he still had the vision and reflexes of a pilot; the City of Genoa had no choice but to renew his driver's license.

Teglio had a tougher, more serious side to him, of course, and his commitment to the "Jewish underground" ran deeper than his puckish sense of fun. His decision to work for the underground was a direct result of the arrest and deportation of his own sister Margherita and her family—something he never got over. "It still burns in my heart," Teglio said with uncharacteristic bitterness and regret. "I saved so many people whom I didn't even know; I was happy to do it and would do it again immediately. But is it possible I wasn't able to save my sister?"

While the antifascist resistance in Italy has been glorified to mythic proportions, little attention has been paid to the Jewish underground. Leaders of the Resistance were covered with medals and lauded in government ceremonies, but the contribution of Teglio and those who worked closely with him went unnoticed for the most part. If nothing else, the government of Israel recognized the achievements of the valiant Catholic priests who helped Jews in Italy. In Israel's "Avenue of the Righteous" areas were planted for each of the "righteous Gentiles" who saved Jews from the Holocaust.

Don Francesco Repetto did not receive his gold medal of valor until 1982, in part because he never bothered to collect the documentation necessary to receive the award. But according to his three sisters, when he lay dying in Genoa in the summer of 1984, a thought tormented him: "If we only could have saved more!"

Teglio himself received only a small token of thanks. In 1979 the Genoa newspaper *Il Secolo XIX* printed an article about his career during the war, calling him "the Scarlet Pimpernel" of the Jewish underground. A group of Israeli students whom Teglio helped when they were studying in Genoa had the article translated into Hebrew and brought it to the attention of Israeli government officials. "The Israelis contacted me and asked if I could provide them with a list of the people I'd saved, with addresses, preferably in Israel," Teglio recalled. "But I kept no lists; I didn't even know the names of most of the people I'd helped. Then Don Repetto told me he had some notes from that period, and he compiled a list of more than four hundred names, which we brought to Israel when they had the commemoration for him. The government of Israel gave me a letter of thanks."

There are trees in the Avenue of the Righteous for Francesco Repetto, Carlo Salvi, Gian Maria Rotondi and many of the other courageous priests who worked with DELASEM. But there were no awards, in Italy or Israel, for those who like Teglio saved their fellow Jews. "They said if I saved people, it was my duty as a Jew," Teglio observed. But the lack of public recognition doesn't seem to have bothered him much. He learned to be skeptical of the vagaries of public opinion. "If I had been caught and killed, people would have said I was a reckless fool; because I survived, I'm a hero."

* * *

If Massimo Teglio emerged virtually unscathed by the war years, the same cannot be said of Emanuele Pacifici.

A thick, knotted red scar marks the spot on his throat where one of his vocal cords was removed. A medical brace that looks like a bulletproof vest, worn under his shirt, keeps his torso straight, serving the function of the stomach muscles he lost to a bomb. Pacifici's injuries came not during World War II but on an ordinary autumn day in 1982. He was walking out of the Rome synagogue when an Arab terrorist tossed a bomb into the crowd, to protest the Israeli invasion of Lebanon. The explosion killed a small boy and wounded about forty others. Pacifici, initially taken for dead, was among the most seriously injured.

But it is the distant past, the years of the war, that have marked him in much deeper ways. From 1938, when the racial laws began, until his marriage in 1958, his life was an almost uninterrupted string of misfortunes. The agonizing years in boarding school were followed by the German occupation, which began with the terror of living on the run and culminated with the arrests of his parents. After the war he and his brother, Raffaele, were raised by different sets of aunts and uncles; he thus was separated from the only remaining member of his immediate family. When still a teenager he attempted to emigrate to the new state of Israel, but he was diagnosed as having tuberculosis and spent three years in a sanatorium in a distant province of northern Italy.

After that terrible start Pacifici recovered the equilibrium of his life to a remarkable degree. In 1958 he married a woman named, appropriately enough, Gioia, Joy. "I began to recover my own serenity, finding a marvelous woman and creating a family. . . . When I married, my wife said she wanted my brother to come live with us, and so it was really only then that I got to know my own brother." Working as a salesman in the clothing business of one of his uncles, Pacifici began to scratch out a decent living and a modest prosperity for his family.

In contrast with his visible scars, Pacifici's character is highly animated; he is talkative and sociable. True son of his father, he sprinkles his conversation with Hebrew, and he recalls events and dates around the holy days of the Jewish calendar. His household is lively and welcoming. The seder Pacifici hosts each year is legendary in the Roman Jewish community, with sometimes as many as fifty guests, Christians as well as Jews, crammed into his not very large apartment.

While having avoided the potentially crippling effects of his own experiences, Pacifici has a powerful interest in the past. His living room is lined from floor to ceiling with bookshelves filled two rows deep with some 2,500 volumes on Jewish art, religion and history; World War II and the Holocaust; and anti-Semitism. On the wall is a copy of the infamous papal bull *Cum nimis absurdum* with which Pope Paul IV banished the Jews of Rome to the ghetto in 1555. Pacifici has an archive of documents and photographs from the war and a vast collection of Jewish religious music.

Before the 1982 bombing, he traveled around Italy and recorded the prayers and songs of aging synagogue cantors, in order to preserve the liturgy of his father's generation from complete extinction. (He has what may be the only recording of the Ferrara cantor Carlo Schönheit.) He has organized numerous tours to various Italian cities and towns, including Sermoneta, Fondi and Pitigliano, that once had flourishing Jewish communities.

It would seem as if through his years of collecting Pacifici has been patiently reconstructing the past he lost in November 1943 when his parents were taken away. Filling his shelves and closets with books, recordings and photographs, he has waged a private battle of memory against the forces of oblivion.

Pacifici has been very active in promoting good relations between Jews and Christians in Italy, and he often speaks to schoolchildren and church groups. He does not downplay his continuing moral outrage over the racial laws and their disastrous consequences for Italian Jews, but he has a deep appreciation for the courage of many Italians in saving Jews, himself included. It is undoubtedly this, despite his own family's bitter experience, that allows Pacifici to continue living in Italy. While his family was subjected to terrible tragedy, he has experienced a few small miracles too.

To illustrate this point, Pacifici relates the story of his father's library. Before the war Rabbi Pacifici had built a superb collection of scholarly books and sacred texts; these remained in his apartment in Genoa during the German occupation. The superintendent of the Pacificis' building, Enrico Sergiani, although unable to save the rabbi, did save his books. Sergiani was a simple workingman, and a Catholic at that; however, he knew that this great library was sacred to the rabbi. Sergiani transferred the books to the same secret chamber in the basement where he had offered to hide Rabbi Pacifici. Working during the night in order to avoid charges that they were helping Jews, Sergiani and his wife moved the 3,000 volumes by hand to the basement and sealed them into the wall. After the war Sergiani found Emanuele Pacifici and returned the library.

Because the Jewish community of Rome had been stripped of many of its books by the invading German army, Emanuele donated his father's collection to the rabbinical college of Rome. "I'm not at a high enough level for those books," he says; "they are above me." Although he is a passionate collector and walking encyclopedia of Italian Judaica, Emanuele insists he is a sock salesman and not a scholar. Through

Sergiani's courageous and compassionate action, the learned spirit of the rabbi of Genoa survives in the library of Italy's chief rabbinical school.

Emanuele has still not entirely absorbed his parents' deportation. For many years he held out a desperate hope that they might someday return. "In Rome there was an information center for deportees and anyone who returned would give whatever information he had about other deportees. One prisoner from Auschwitz said he had seen my father heading toward the gas chamber, but it is still a 'presumed death.' With every year that passed, I would say to myself: my parents aren't coming. Even today I don't say the Kaddish [the Jewish prayer for the dead] for my parents, although I know perfectly well that they are dead. I recite it for my brother [who died several years ago], my sister and other relatives, but I don't recite it for my parents."

Pacifici is concerned that as the Holocaust recedes in time, it will simply take its place in history in the endless chain of atrocities. He perceives a disturbing resurgence of anti-Semitism among his fellow Italians—more than in the fascist period, he says. All the time of the Israeli invasion of Lebanon in 1982, much of the protest in Italy was directed against the tiny population of 35,000 Jews. The marble plaque in Genoa honoring his father was defiled with a swastika. Demonstrations started in front of the Israeli embassy in Rome and wound up in front of the synagogue with crowds shouting anti-Semitic slogans. The backlash culminated in the bombing that nearly killed Pacifici.

Nonetheless, he continues collecting books and material on the Holocaust, speaking in schools, fighting what he sees as an uphill battle against historical amnesia. "The kids of my son's generation know nothing about the Holocaust and the war. Already, to them it has become what the Great War was to the people of my generation. Something that old men sit around talking about, ancient history, like Caporetto, Garibaldi, the Risorgimento."

The Schönheits of Ferrara

Although the camp of Buchenwald was liberated on April 11, 1945, Franco and Carlo Schönheit lived there for another two months. Europe was in complete chaos. Train tracks all over Germany were torn up. Gasoline was scarce. And as the British, Americans and Russians began to struggle for control of Central Europe, relief efforts to sort out and help displaced millions were slow in coming. Franco and his father tired of waiting for a much-promised train that was supposed to come from Italy and, along with a group of Italian prisoners, set off on their own. On the morning of June 20 they gathered in the central courtyard of the camp to board an eleven-o'clock train that would take them to Weimar, where they would try to find another train. But Franco, to his alarm, could not find his father. "Then I got an idea. I ran over to the crematorium. And there he was, standing alone, with his inmate's cap on his head, loudly reciting a special prayer for the dead, the Kaddish. He had been cantor in the synagogue; he loved to sing and had a beautiful voice. I said, 'It's late.' And he said, 'I had to say at least one prayer for them before leaving.' In fact, when I didn't see him I had the feeling that he had gone somewhere to pray. We had not been able to pray the entire time we had been at the camp, except mentally. That day he prayed loudly."

After a week of hopping rides on different trains and trucks, Franco and his father reached Ferrara. Despite some bombardments, the city was surprisingly the same. Even now it looks much as it did when the d'Este family ruled from the central castle. If you didn't know to look for the nicks in the castle walls, you would have no idea of what happened there at dawn on November 15, 1943.

In one of his *Ferrarese Stories,* Giorgio Bassani describes the sense of dislocation experienced by a young Ferrarese Jew who returns home from Buchenwald after the war, supposedly the only deportee from the city to survive the camps. He is both amused and dismayed to find his name on a plaque outside the main synagogue commemorating the Ferrarese Jews killed by the Nazis. His return, as if from the dead, rather than a cause for celebration becomes a source of discomfort for the Jews of Ferrara, who are forced not only to change their commemorative plaque but to confront the reality of a fate that they escaped.

Bassani's story is fiction: five of the eighty-seven Jews deported from Ferrara returned. But there is a grain of truth in the Bassani story, Franco says. "Because nearly everyone was dead, we were like 'white flies.' It was so unusual for anyone to return that those who had been in hiding in Italy didn't know what to make of us. Why had these people survived? How had they survived? What had they done to survive? Bassani's story 'A Plaque on Via Mazzini' is based loosely on what happened to Eugenio Ravenna, now dead, who was deported to Auschwitz. After the war he cut himself off completely from the Jewish community and wanted nothing to do with anything."

Franco's own reintegration was not quite as difficult. While the young man in the story, like the real-life Eugenio Ravenna, had lost his entire family, Franco returned with his father and had strong hopes, reinforced by her letters, that his mother was still alive. "Even though I worried about my mother, after the camp everything seemed like a breeze; life seemed such a marvelous thing. I immediately started studying for my high school diploma, to make up for all that lost time."

Franco and his father returned to their old apartment above the Jewish school. They had practically nothing, but the archbishop of Ferrara, who had helped in Carlo Schönheit's release from prison a year and a half before, gave them each 5,000 lire, at that time a considerable sum of money, worth a few hundred dollars today.

A month after their return, Franco's future wife, Dory, and her family came back to Ferrara from Switzerland. She was now fourteen and he eighteen. "Even though they had been liberated more than two months earlier, they were in pretty bad shape," Dory remembers. "They were still very, very thin. Franco seemed much more mature than other boys his age. Very serious. We had an extra apartment above our house, and since they really had nothing, my father asked them to stay there."

During their return trip, Dory and her family had picked up news of Gina Schönheit, while searching for information about a grandmother who had also been deported. "We listened to the radio for the lists of survivors but heard nothing of my grandmother, and then we met a woman who had been deported to Ravensbrück. My mother asked if she had seen my grandmother, and she said, 'The only woman I saw from Ferrara was a schoolteacher, tall and thin. The night before the camp's liberation, I saw her when everyone was starting one of those forced marches. She was still alive.' My mother was very uncertain whether or not to tell Franco and his father, for fear of getting their hopes up too much: many people never returned from those marches. In the end, when they came to see us, my mother did tell them."

On the evening of August 20, while Franco was studying at the house of a science tutor, the phone rang. "It was my father asking the tutor if I could leave early. I raced back home on my bicycle. My mother was there. She was badly, badly reduced, just skin and bones, much worse than we. She had been liberated on May 2, but was in such bad shape she was put in a hospital in Lübeck." Franco is generally matter-of-fact and candid in his descriptions, but when asked about the day his mother returned, he says simply, but with strong emotion, "It was a very particular moment."

As reduced as she was physically—she had gone from nearly two hundred pounds to about half that—Gina's character remained as indomitable as ever. "She was helped by her great self-discipline and sense of order. She always managed to be in the right place at the right time. She was severely beaten a few times at Ravensbrück, but with her great precision, she always removed her glasses first so they wouldn't be broken. She kept herself very clean and neat, which was important. She even traded bread for soap, to keep clean; almost everyone did the opposite, trading soap for bread. But when people allowed themselves to become dirty, they became 'musselmen,' and were eliminated."

In Ravensbrück she had worked in the tailor's shop. Here, Franco says, "Each day she had to sew seven buttons on a hundred pairs of pants belonging to the SS. That's seven hundred buttons a day. Nonetheless, she found time to commit little acts of sabotage: she would take lice from her own clothing and put in the pants pockets. I asked her, 'Aside from the risk, surely they disinfected these pants before giving them to the SS?' She said, 'You never know, one of them may have lived, and I gave it to them with my compliments.' "

The family was now able to resume their lives where they had left off before the war. Carlo once again traveled the countryside selling underwear, socks and lingerie. He left each week, suitcase in hand. He kept up this routine until the end of his life; he died in 1978, at the age of seventy-seven. "He always took trains because my mother wouldn't let him drive." Gina resumed teaching at the Jewish school and directing summer camp, terrifying and educating her young pupils with her powerful voice and strict ways.

Franco devoted himself to his studies and entered university in the fall of 1945, as he would have had he completed the final two years of high school normally. "They basically gave me my diploma," he says. "I remember my English exam; the teacher would ask me questions in English and I would answer in German. She would say 'Answer in whatever language you want,' and then she passed me. They rewarded me for the effort: I had tried to cram two years into two months."

While many survivors returned to find their families decimated, their lives shattered, the Schönheits could literally resume the same life they had led before, as if the deportations had never happened. "Because all of them came back, it's as if that period were a hole in time," Dory Schönheit says.

Franco's childhood friendship with Dory was unbroken. After the war they lived under the same roof, and became sweethearts and eventually husband and wife. In a typically united Italian family, Franco's parents lived with Dory's family for the rest of their lives.

Franco studied chemistry at the University of Ferrara and then found a job in Milan at a company that makes adhesive stickers; now he is director of the company. Dory, who interrupted her university studies in order to marry, is a housewife. During their thirty-five years of marriage, she says, they have talked about his wartime experiences for perhaps a total of an hour. "He has never discussed it with our children, but they understand, and have learned about it on their own."

Primo Levi, the great Italian Jewish writer who survived Auschwitz but committed suicide in 1987, said that Holocaust survivors generally belong to one of two categories: those who talk and those who don't. While Levi belonged to the first group, Franco clearly is a member of the second.

"I admire those who, like Levi, have succeeded in articulating their experiences, but I am not able to," he says. "I remember when we returned, my father said something that I thought hit the nail on the head. In fact, it's something that Levi said too, in his last book, *The Drowned and the Saved*: Even if we did get out of there no one will believe us; it's impossible to give anyone an idea of what it was like. Even though I can talk about it here now, a person who didn't go through that experience can't imagine what deportation was like. I cannot explain to you what it meant to be in the hospital at Buchenwald, what it meant to visit my father, who was suffering from bronchitis in the Buchenwald infirmary, because you will think of the Polyclinic in

Milan or a hospital in Rome. Buchenwald was outside the normal sphere of life. I can't give you an idea of the strangeness of that place, the strangeness of that life.

"Stalin's purges, what happened in Vietnam, Argentina, Chile, Cambodia are all terrible, tragic experiences. But this was different. This science of organized extermination was unique. And because it was unique, it is untellable and unexplainable. Carrying a ninety-year-old woman on a train in order to kill her six hundred kilometers away, even though she is going to die on the trip anyway—this belongs to a dimension of the absurd.

"The Germans succeeded in creating a world of organized absurdity, with all the contradictions of life in a single hour. Of having no water to clean your shoes but having to keep your shoes clean. Of having to replace missing buttons, maybe even sew the cuff on your pants, without thread or needle. Imprisonment does not have to be absurd. Punishment does not have to be absurd. Imagine a man who has to take thirty lashes across the back—often enough to kill him—and who is forced by another man to count each lash in German, a language he doesn't even know, and if he makes a mistake in the counting, it has to be done over. And the man is not tied down, but has to remain still through the beating, counting.

"Certainly these are experiences, but always absurd experiences. How can you learn something from an experience of this kind? That's part of the reason I never talk with my children about it; those experiences teach nothing. They belong to a world of the impossible, totally outside the sphere of ordinary humanity.

"Part of what kept me going was that it bothered me to have to die for nothing, for nothing. . . . A politician or someone working for a cause might sacrifice himself, but what was I supposed to die for? For a faith? It wasn't a question of that. Anyone in the camp would have made an ideological compromise to get out. It wasn't that. To die for something, to give life to another person, yes. But how to accept dying for nothing? It wasn't even like a car accident.

"That part of my life remains separate, a closed chapter. It is a tragic experience and is to be considered by itself. My character has surely been influenced in some way, even if I would prefer to think it hasn't. Episodes of violence, even small, casual violence, appear in a different light to one who has lived with violence. My memories of that time are as strong as ever, but not my desire to talk about them."

Franco never intended to discuss his deportation experience or write about it. He spoke with me out of politeness, simply because I, a complete stranger, called him up and asked him. But when he did so, in a long conversation on the evening of July 25, 1986, it took on particular meaning for him. That evening, as I learned when I spoke with him nearly a year later, his mother, age eighty-five, died of a sudden heart attack. "It was a death that we should all be so lucky to have, instant, without suffering," he said. She was watching television with Dory's mother and, feeling tired, excused herself and went upstairs and never awoke. Although Schönheit did not believe there was any causal relationship between our conversation and her death, he was deeply struck by the coincidence. "She was very old, but it is a very curious coincidence. I had never spoken about this with anyone, never shown anyone those photographs or those letters we exchanged in the camps, and while we were talking, suddenly, three hundred kilometers away in Ferrara, she left me."

Franco's usual silence does not indicate an attempt to minimize the importance of that strange parenthesis in his life. It still seems to hold the powers of life and death and the ultimate meaning to the strong bond between him and his parents. At each of their funerals, the incidents he chose to discuss related to their deportation. In his father's death, he described the scene at their arrival at Buchenwald when the two were shaved and stripped naked and Carlo Schönheit asked his son to excuse him for his nakedness. That moment of bashfulness—even in the face of mortal danger—always struck Franco as emblematic of his father's shy and gentle character. Throughout his time at Buchenwald, Carlo never lost his delicacy of feeling or the simple decency of his provincial Italian Jewish middle-class upbringing. Franco also recalled his father's repeating again and again the German phrase "Father and son, always together," in order to avoid being separated from Franco. And finally he remembered his father's temporary disappearance on the day of their departure from Buchenwald to say a prayer for the dead.

"Of my mother I chose three rather hard episodes," Franco says of his mother's funeral. All of them commemorate her formidable character and thundering voice: One was the incident of her yelling about her husband's not having a tie on when she visited him in the Ferrara prison. Next, her challenging the SS commandant at Fossoli, who had screamed an order at Franco. "Wait a second!" she had yelled back. "We're not animals."

In a number of situations, his mother's willingness to stand up to the Nazis and her ability to outshout them impressed her captors and surprised them into making unusual concessions. She was always true to her own strict principles of life. Gina Schönheit walked out of the camp at Ravensbrück eighty-five pounds thinner than when she walked in, but inside she was the same person.

Finally, he remembered the moment of their separation, when he and his mother were being placed on different trains. Franco had wanted to try something desperate, perhaps grab a German soldier's gun and try to escape. But Gina Schönheit did not favor useless acts of defiance: she had stopped him with her curt manner, "Don't be stupid!" and then said firmly and softly: "We must go that we can all live to see one another again.' That sentence always stayed in my head during the time at Buchenwald."

Franco's sense of his place in the world has been deeply altered by his experiences. He no longer feels any emotional tie to either Italy or Ferrara. "Most Ferrarese I know, Jews as well as non-Jews, dream of nothing but returning to Ferrara when they retire. That doesn't interest me at all. Certainly the situation of Italian and French Jews is nothing like that of German or Polish Jews, almost none of whom returned to their countries. In Italy there were a lot of people who helped the Jews, but let's not forget that fascist Italy initiated the racial campaign. How were the Germans able to catch all these Jews in Italy? It wouldn't have been possible if they hadn't been organized into communities, if there hadn't been lists, if the fascists hadn't stamped 'Jewish' on their identity cards. In Poland, the Jews lived in shtetls—all they had to do was surround them. In Italy, if they hadn't kept all these lists, with addresses and telephone numbers, or if they had thought to destroy these things, it would have been almost impossible for the Germans to tell who was Jewish. Instead, our only identity card had 'Jewish' stamped on it, and with that stamp, what Italian hotel could I have hidden in? No Italian Jew went to an Italian hotel unless he was sufficiently resourceful or lucky to have false papers—with all the risk that that entailed. Most hid in convents precisely because they didn't need an identity card there.

"Even though I returned to Italy, I no longer identify myself with the country. It no longer says anything to me. I would happily live elsewhere and change one set of habits for another. The Jews who feel that way and are the most coherent go to live in Israel, but I have no desire to live there. I took two trips to Israel and to tell the truth I felt no particular emotion at all." Franco lost any nationalism during the war, and his sense of belonging is more fragile, to a time, a place, a feeling. "When I went to the United States, as the plane began its descent I suddenly saw again the American jeep that drove into Buchenwald on April 11 with four soldiers in it. I saw those four soldiers tossed in the air in a blanket with joy by a large group of prisoners. I remember those young soldiers as they bounced in the air, astounded at what they saw. My father and I just watched because we no longer had the strength to lift our arms."

Source Notes

Fatherland, Faith and Family: The Ovazzas of Turin

The principal sources for information on Ettore Ovazza are his own published writings and unpublished personal papers, interviews with remaining members of the Ovazza family, and material in the Archivio Centrale dello Stato (ACS), the Italian state archives, and the Archivi dell' Unione delle Comunità Israelitiche Italiane (ACUII), both in Rome. Ovazza's personal papers are in the Fondo Ettore Ovazza at the Archivio del Centro di Documentazione Ebraica Contemporanea (ACDEC) in Milan.

Of great importance were interviews with Carla Ovazza, Franca Ovazza Piperno, Giorgio Ovazza, Maria Ovazza-Momigliano, Mario Pavia, Vittorio Segre and Sion Segre Amar.

Chapter One

Pages 19–20 The accounts of the birth of Ettore Ovazza's son and the death of his father are from *Diario per mio figlio*, pp. 20–26, 185.
20 The number of Jews who were awarded a certificate for having participated in the March on Rome comes from Renzo De Felice's *Storia degli ebrei italini sotto il fascismo*, p. 90. De Felice lists 227 Italian Jews and three non-Italian Jews as having received the award. It should be noted that many people, like Ettore Ovazza, were given the certificate for their overall contribution to the fascist revolution and not necessarily for any specific actions they may have taken during the insurrection of October 1922, which brought fascism to power.
20 The quotation from Ovazza is from his *Diario per mio figlio,* p. 36.
21 The quotation on religion is from the same source, p. 86.
21–22 The development of Ettore Ovazza's political career can be traced through his various books and articles. His published works include the following: *L'Uomo e i*

fantocci (Milan, 1921); *Ghirlande: liriche* (Milan, 1922); *In Margine alla storia* (Turin, 1925); *Diario per mio figlio* (Turin, 1928); *Lettere dal campo, 1917–1919* (Turin, 1932); *Politica fascista* (Turin, 1933); *Sionismo bifronte* (Rome, 1935); *L'inghilterra e il mandato in palestina* (Rome, 1937); *Sita: Poema indiano* (Turin, 1937); *Il problema ebraico* (Rome, 1937). Virtually all the issues of Ovazza's newspaper, *La Nostra Bandiera*, can be found at the ACDEC.

22 For the Jewish population of Italy, see De Felice pp. 6–9. The 1938 official census placed their exact number at 47, 252. There were another 10, 173 foreign-born Jews in Italy, many of whom had been living in the country for a number of years.

22 For the fascist party affiliation of Italian Jews, see De Felice, p. 90. He counts 10,125 Jews as party members, out of a total of 32, 289 Jews over the age of 21.

22 Mussolini's famous phrase about "the delirium of race" is from Emil Ludwig's *Talks with Mussolini*, and is quoted in Meir Michaelis' *Mussolini and the Jews: German-Italian Relations and the Jewish Question in Italy 1922–1945*, p. 25. The quotation from Hitler on "kosher fascism" is from Michaelis, p. 95. The first chapters of Michaelis' book describe the early tensions between Italian fascism and German Nazism.

22 For the number of Jews in ancient Rome, see Attilio Milano, *Il ghetto di Roma,* p. 15. For the origins of the Italian Jewish community, see Attilio Milano, *Storia degli ebrei in Italia,* and Cecil Roth, *The History of the Jews of Italy*.

23 A discussion of the origin of the *ghetto* is in Riccardo Calimani, *Storia del ghetto di Venezia*, pp. 69–75.

23–44 For the history of the Jews of Piedmont, and an account of the role of the Jews during the period of the Italian Risorgimento, see Salvatore Foa, *Gli ebrei nel Risorgimento*; Milano, *Storia*; and Roth.

24–26 Information on the history of the Ovazza family comes from interviews with relatives, in particular Carla Ovazza and Franca Ovazza Piperno.

24 The story that the Turinese Jews painted the *aron kodesh* black at the death of Carlo Alberto comes from the vice-president of the Turin Jewish community, Anna Vitale.

24 On the liturgy at the Turin synagogue, see Sion Segre-Amar, *Il mio ghetto*, and Vittorio Segre, *Memoirs of a Fortunate Jew*. Information came also from interviews with Carla Ovazza and Franca Ovazza Piperno.

24 On the literacy rate of Italian Jews, see Zuccotti p. 16.

25 On the high degree of acceptance of Italian Jews, see Roth and the second chapter of Susan Zuccotti, *The Italians and the Holocaust*, pp. 16–27.

26 The quotations from Vittorio Segre are from his autobiography, *Memoirs of a Fortunate Jew* (pp. 39–40 of Italian edition, pp. 17–18 American edition).

28 The de Chirico quotation comes from Rita Montalcini Levi, *Elogio dell' imperfezione,* p. 18.

30 On the patriotic contributions of the Italian Jews during World War I, see Zuccotti, pp. 16–26.

Chapter Two

Page 31 Ernesto Ovazza's letter of July 19, 1907, is in Fondo Ovazza, ACDEC.

32 Ettore Ovazza's poem is from *Ghirlande,* p. 18.

32 Alfredo Ovazza's letter, dated Jan. 1, 1916, is in the Fondo Ovazza, ACDEC.

32 Ettore Ovazza's poem of July 25, 1916, is from *Ghirlande,* pp. 93–94.

33 Alfredo Ovazza's letter of July 26, 1917, is from the Fondo Ovazza, ACDEC.

33 Ettore Ovazza's war letters are found in *Lettere dal campo, 1917–1919.* This one appears on p. 198.

33 Ettore Ovazza's description of his mother during wartime is from *Diario per mio figlio,* p. 152.

33–34 The apocalyptic description of Caporetto is from *Diario per mio figlio,* pp. 66–74.
34–35 Ettore Ovazza's comments about discipline are from *Diario per mio figlio,* p. 166.
35 The quotation from Pietro Nenni is from Alastair Hamilton, *The Appeal of Fascism* (London, 1971), pp. 22–23.
36–37 Descriptions of Ettore Ovazza's experience of the "Red scare" and the rise of fascism are from *In margine alla storia.*
38 The description of the performance of Ovazza's play is from *In margine alla storia.*
38–39 Ettore Ovazza's dramatization of the March on Rome is in *Diario per mio figlio,* pp. 133–37.

Chapter Three

Pages 40–42 The description of the Ovazza family comes from interviews with Carla Ovazza and Franca Ovazza Piperno.
44–45 The quotes on Mussolini's early statements about the Jews are from Michaelis, *Mussolini and the Jews,* p. 13. Michaelis and De Felice are the principal sources for the history of Italian-German relations and their influence on Mussolini's policy toward the Jews. Additional information is in Ludwig, Denis Mack Smith, *Mussolini,* Paolo Monelli, *Mussolini, piccolo borghese* and Luigi Salvatorelli and Giovanni Mira's *Storia d'Italia nel periodo fascista.*
45 Ernesto Ovazza's letter rejecting Zionism out of a sense of loyalty to fascism was reprinted in *La Nostra Bandiera,* May 1, 1934.
46 Ettore Ovazza's quotation about his daily life in the 1920s is from *Diario per mio figlio*, p. 112.
46–47 His description of his walk with his son, Riccardo, is from *Diario*, pp. 115–19.
47 Ovazza's account of his first meeting with Mussolini is in *Politica fascista.*

Chapter Four

Page 48 The Mussolini quotation is from *Il popolo d'Italia,* August 22, 1933.
48 The interview with Emil Ludwig is in *Talks with Mussolini.*
49 The "several thousand German refugees" are referred to in Settimio Sorani, *L'Assistenza ai profughi ebrei in Italia, 1933–1947*, pp. 40–42.
49 Accounts of the first anti-Semitic attacks in the Fascist press appear in both De Felice and Michaelis.
50 Ettore Ovazza's telegram and those of several other prominent Jewish leaders are in the files of the Presidenza del Consiglio dei Ministri, 1934 '36/ 1.6.4/936, in the ACS. They are cited in the graduate thesis of Celeste Pavoncello, "*Gli italiani di religione Ebraica: Il gruppo de* La Nostra Bandiera, 1934–1938," University of Rome, 1981.
51 The account of Farinacci's attack is from *Il regime Fascista.* April 10, 1934.
51 The response of the editors of *Israel* is from the April 12, 1934, issue.
52–53 The Mussolini quotation and the quotations from Ettore Ovazza's editorial are from *La Nostra Bandiera,* May 1, 1934, and are reprinted in Ovazza's *Sionismo bifronte.*
53 The circulation figures are from a letter Ovazza wrote to the Italian government, now in envelope 130 of the Ministero di Cultura Popolare file "La Nostra Bandiera," in the ACS. (Because of a reorganization of the state archives, this file is being reclassified and is currently not available to the public.)
53–54 A copy of Rabbi Bolaffio's sermon can be found among Ettore Ovazza's papers in the ACDEC.
54 On the elections in the Turin community, see Pavoncello.
54–55 For an account of the disastrous first meeting between Mussolini and Hitler, see Mack Smith, *Mussolini,* and Monelli.

55–56 Mussolini's invective against Hitler and his courtship of the Zionist movement are well described in Michaelis, pp. 67–70. Goldman's account of his 1934 meeting with Mussolini is reprinted in full in the appendix of De Felice, pp. 609–21.
56 Ettore Ovazza's attempt to avoid closure of *La Nostra Bandiera* is documented in envelope 130 of the Ministero di Cultura file for the paper at the ACS.

Chapter Five

Pages 57–58 Sermons delivered on the Day of Faith come from the archives of the Unione delle Comunità Israelitiche Italiane (AUCII).
58 The Hitler quotation comes from Michaelis, p. 95.
59 The quotation about anti-Semitism from the magazine *Marc'Aurelio* is from *La Nostra Bandiera,* January 31, 1936.
59 The account of Lattes's trip to London is from Michaelis, pp. 84–85.
60 The letter of the insulted Jewish woman is from *La Nostra Bandiera,* May 31, 1936.
61 A copy of Liuzzi's pamphlet can be found among Ettore Ovazza's papers in the ACDEC.
61 Ravenna's response is in the AUCII.
62 The letter of the Italian government to the prefect of Turin is in envelope 130 of the Ministero di Cultura Popolare files at the ACS.
62 Il regime fascista, September 12, 1936, quoted in De Felice, pp. 250–51.
63 On Ovazza's rank in the Italian army. During the war, he held the rank of lieutenant of the artillery. But in his curriculum vitae of 1938, he refers to himself as captain. Because he served for an extra year after the end of World War I, he was presumably promoted during this period.
63 Mention of the various recognitions Ovazza received from the regime and the royal family is made in his papers at the ACDEC.
63 References to the nickname "Platinum Head" are in Segre-Amar, p. 132, and from interviews with him.
65–66 For the controversy around Orano's book, see Paolo Orano, *Gli ebrei in Italia;* Ettore Ovazza's response, *Il problema ebraico;* and Abramo Levi, *Noi ebrei.* See also the accounts in De Felice and Michaelis.
66 Orano's letters to Ovazza are in the Fondo Ovazza at the ACDEC.
67–68 Quotes from Ovazza's *Il problema ebraica* are from pp. 49, 109, 124 and 135.
68 The observations of the British diplomat McClure are from Michaelis, p. 6.
68 The quotation from Vittorio Segre is from his autobiography, p. 62.
69 Jesi is mentioned also in Augusto Segre, *Memoire di vita ebraica.*
70 The *"Manifesto degli scienziati razzisti"* ("The Manifesto of the Racist Scientists") is reprinted in De Felice, pp. 660–62.

Chapter Six

Pages 72–73 Ovazza letter to Mussolini from ACS, *Segreteria Particolare del Duce, Conteggio Ordinario,* N. 211–398.
73–74 The account of the meeting of the Turinese Jewish Community in the wake of the racial laws is from Segre-Amar, pp. 129–33.
74 Letter of the Florentine Jews is quoted in a circular of the Unione delle Comunitá Israelitiche Italiane, dated Dec. 19, 1938, from the AUCII.
74–75 The fascist racial legislation is detailed in De Felice.
75–77 The description of Ovazza's proposed raid on Israel is from Vittorio Segre's memoirs, pp. 79–80. Brief mention of it is made by De Felice.
78 On Starace's response to death of Formiggini, see Antonio Spinosa, *Starace* (Milan, 1981).

78 On conversions and traffic in Aryanization certificates, see De Felice and Zuccotti.
78 The Minutes of the December 21, 1938, meeting of the Turin Community are in the archives of the Unione. They include references to Ettore's letter of resignation and to the withdrawal of a number of people from the Community.
80–81 Orano's letters are in the Fondo Ovazza at the ACDEC.
81–82 The letter to Gallo is in the Fondo Ovazza at the ACDEC.
82–83 Ovazza's requests during the racial campaign and the government responses are documented in his personal file in the ACS P.S., A1 1942, envelope 86.
83 The account of Ovazza's telegram after the fall of fascism is from Maria Ovazza-Momigliano, his sister-in-law.
84 The description of Ovazza's behavior in the first days of the German occupation comes from a cousin, Mario Pavia, who saw him during that period.
84–89 Documents relating the final days of Ettore Ovazza and his family are in the Fondo Ovazza at the ACDEC. Testimony was gathered during the investigation into their deaths.
88–89 On the murder of the Ovazzas, see Mario Lombardo, "Meir, il carnefice di Intra," *Storia Illustrata,* n. 186, 1973.

Commitment and Betrayal: The Foas of Turin

Chapter One

Pages 93–94 The police department description of Vittorio Foa made at the time of his arrest is in his personal file at the ACS (Ministero dell'Interno. Direzione Generale Pubblica Sicurezza, Casellario Politico Centrale, envelope 2095).
94–98 The principal sources for the history of the Foa family are Anna, Giuseppe and Vittorio Foa. Also extremely helpful were Natalia Ginzburg, Giorgina Lattes Herlitzka, Anna Maria Levi, Primo Levi, Piero Luzzatti and Sion Segre Amar.
98–99 For a description of the Turinese antifascist milieu, see Natalia Ginzburg, *Lessico familiare,* Family Sayings, New York, 1967, and Sion Segre Amar, *Il mio ghetto;* and Barbara Allason, *Memorie di un antifascista* (Florence, 1946); Michele Giua, "*Ricordi di un ex–detenuto politico, 1935–1943* (Turin, 1945); and Giancarlo Pajetta, *Ragazzo rosso* (Milan, 1983).
98 For information on Italian fascism in 1933, I relied heavily on Paolo Monelli, *Mussolini, piccolo borghese;* Antonio Spinosa, *Starace;* Tracy Toon, *Believe, Fight, Obey,* is an excellent documentation of the militarization of Italian life through the public education system.
100 The account of the arrests is from *La Stampa,* March 31, 1934. For an account by Sion Segre, who publishes under the name Segre Amar, "Sopra alcune inesattezze storiche alle passate vicende degli ebrei in Italia," in *Rassegna mensile di Israel,* May 1961; and "Sui 'fatti' di torino del 1934," in *Gli ebrei in italia durante il fascismo,* vol. 2.
101 The response of the anti-Semitic newspaper *Il Tevere* is quoted in De Felice, p. 179.
102–3 Interesting light on the GL conspiracy in Turin is shed in the catalogue for an exhibition of drawings of Carlo Levi organized by the state archives, titled "Carlo Levi: Disegni dal carcere 1934: Materiali per una storia." Of special interest are the essays by Giovanni De Luna, "Una cospirazione alla luce del sole," and Vittorio Foa, "Carlo Levi: Uomo Politico."

Chapter Two

Page 104 The Mussolini quotation can be found in Mussolini's *Opera Omnia* and in Monelli, p. 156.

105 The memorandum on the March 13 arrests, along with virtually all the confidential police reports on GL, are from the files on the Turin branch of GL in the ACS, in particular: Ministero dell'Interno, Direzione Generale della Pubblica Sicurezza, Divisione Polizia Politica, K. 7/15, envelopes 117 and 118. Some letters, which I was unable to find in the ACS in Rome, are reprinted in D. Zucarò, *Lettere di una spia* (Milan, 1947, 1977). Zucarò based his work on letters released immediately after the war by the "Questura" or police of Turin.

105 The proofs of the identity between "the well-known informant 373" and Pitigrilli are so many as to put the matter beyond any shadow of doubt. From the nature of their interrogations in prison, some members of GL, such as Vittorio Foa and Michele Giua, realized that the only person who could have furnished the police with the information they had was Pitigrilli. This view was confirmed widely when the letters were discovered at the end of the war. Numerous people written about in the letters—including Vittorio Foa, Massimo Mila, Aldo Garosci, Carlo Levi, Emilio Lussu, Sion Segre, Mario Levi, Natalia Ginzburg, Anna Foa, Michele Giua—instantly recognized conversations and encounters with Pitigrilli carefully recorded.

Moreover, in their efforts to prevent the rehabilitation of Pitigrilli after the war, Vittorio Foa, Aldo Garosci, Michele Giua and Emilio Lussu—all members of the Italian parliament at the time—asked the government officially to acknowledge Pitigrilli's role as an OVRA informant. Vittorio Foa kindly provided me with a copy of this statement by the Italian Presidenza del Consiglio, Ufficio Sanzioni Contro il Fascismo, dated October 13, 1947, addressed to the commission examining activities of OVRA informants. The commission ruled that Pitigrilli's guilt was proved "irrefutably": "While it is true that all the official papers . . . always mention agent 373 and not Pitigrilli . . . nonetheless even the least doubt has been swept away by the unequivocal and categorical testimony of the above-mentioned members of parliament about encounters and confidential conversations that took place exclusively in the company of Pitigrilli, whom they took in good faith to be a fellow antifascist." *("Ora è vero che tutti gli atti ufficiali . . . menzionano sempre il fiduciario 373 e non Pitigrilli . . . tuttavia il benchè minimo dubbio al riguardo non avrebbe più ragione d'essere dopo le inequivocabili e categoriche attestazioni dei predetti onorevoli sugli incontri avuti e le confidenze fatte esclusivamente al Pitigrilli, da essi ritenuto in buona fede un compagno di lotta.")*

If all this were not enough, there is massive internal evidence that makes clear that agent 373 is none other than Pitigrilli. Although the agent's letters are unsigned, numerous references make his identity quite obvious: mention of his address on Corso Pescara in Turin, for example, of his being put on trial in 1928, and of his career as a writer. A letter dated March 13, 1936, from one of the heads of OVRA to agent 373, deals with the problem of the government censoring agent 373's books and refers to one titled *V. a 18K,* clearly a reference to Pitigrilli's novel *La Virgine a 18 Carati,* which had run afoul of Italian censors.

106–17 For the portrait of Pitigrilli I have relied primarily on the letters to OVRA in the ACS, signed letters by Pitigrilli to Mussolini also in the ACS, interviews with his widow, Lina Furlan, his first son Giovanni Segre, his cousin, Sion Segre, as well as his many published works. Ones that I have relied on particularly are:

Mammiferi di lusso (Milan, 1920). *La cintura di castità* (Milan, 1920).
Cocaina (Milan, 1921). *Oltraggio al pudore* (Milan, 1921).
L'Esperimento di Pott (Milan, 1930). *La dolicocefala bionda* (Milan, 1936).
Mosè e il cavalier Levi (Milan, 1948). *La piscina di Siloe* (Milan, 1948).
La meravigliosa avventura (Milan, 1948). *Pitigrilli parla di Pitigrilli* (Milan, 1949).

106 The aphorisms of Pitigrilli quoted here are from the story "Il pessimista sereno," in his collection *La cintura di castitá,* p. 223.

106 The comment by Mussolini is from an essay by Umberto Eco, which appeared as the introduction to a recent reprint of *L'esperimento di Pott,* p. viii.
106 Pitigrilli, *La cintura di castitá,* p. 211.
107 The passages on the childhood of Pitigrilli come from his autobiographical volume, *La piscina di Siloe,* pp. 15–17.
109 Pitigrilli, *La cintura di castitá,* pp. 215, 222.
109 The telegram of praise to Mussolini is in ACS, S.P.D., C.O. 532.422.
109–10 Information on Pitigrilli-Brandimarte-Guglielminetti case can be found in Pitigrilli's police file in ACS, P.S. A1, 1929, envelope 25.
110–11 The letter on his first visit to the Levi household is in Zucarò, pp. 22–25, from the first edition of 1947.
111 Pitigrilli, *La cintura di castitá,* p. 221.
111–12 The comment of Lussu about Pitigrilli as the prototype of the fascist opportunist is taken from the introduction he wrote to the first edition of Zucarò, pp. ix–xii.
112 Pitigrilli, *La cintura di castitá,* p. 221.
112 Pitigrilli's joke is contained in a report to OVRA dated June 10, 1934, in ACS, Pol., envelope 117.
113 The quotation about "incorruptible" people is from *L'esperimento di Pott,* p. 228.
113 The letter dated June 1, 1934, is in ACS, Pol. Pol., envelope 117.
114 The letter dated June 21, 1934, is in ACS, Pol. Pol., envelope 117.
114 The letter dated October 16, 1934, is in Zucarò, p. 78.
115 The letter dated May 24, 1934, is in ACS, Pol. Pol., envelope 117.
115–16 The letter on the Segre-Ginzburg trial is in ACS, Pol. Pol., envelope 114.
116 The letter dated February 20, 1935, is in ACS, Pol. Pol., envelope 117.
116 The letter that mentions Beppe Foa is in ACS, Pol. Pol, envelope 117.
117 The police report of May 6, 1935, is in ACS, Pol. Pol., envelope 117.

Chapter Three

Pages 118–19 The description of the arrests of May 15, 1935, are primarily from interviews with Anna Foa Yona, Vittorio Foa and Giuseppe Foa. I have also relied on the written, unpublished memoirs of Anna Yona, and of her husband David Yona, with which she kindly provided me.
119–20 The OVRA dispatches about the May 1935 arrests are in Pol. Pol. file 117.
122–33 Copies of the interrogations of Leo Levi and Giulio Muggia as well as the plea for clemency by Levi are in the same file at the ACS in Rome.
125 Quotes from David Yona come from his unpublished memoirs provided to me courtesy of Anna Yona.

Chapter Four

Page 132 Letter dated June 8, 1935, is in file 117 of Pol. Pol. in the ACS.
133 Letter about proposed staged arrest is in Zucarò, pp. 129–32.
134 Letter dated Jan. 2, 1936 (in the file it is misdated 1935), comes from file 118 of the Polizia Politica files in the ACS.
134–35 The letters about Signora Olivetti and the "young Malvano" are from the same file.
135–36 The letter about Signora Valabrega is from the same file.
136 The quote from De Felice is from his *Storia degli ebrei italiani sotto il fascismo,* p. 229.
137 The Mussolini speech from June 1935 is from his *Opera Omnia.*
137 The Mussolini speech of Oct. 2, 1935, is also in *Opera Omnia.*

139 The Mussolini quote on giving the middle a "kick in the shins" is from Monelli's biography, p. 165.
140 On the role of the Orano book see Michaelis and De Felice.
140–41 The Mussolini quote to Generoso Pope is reprinted in De Felice, p. 238.
141 The letter of Beppe Foa of August 1938 is in his file (number 2095) in the Casellario Politico Centrale of the ACS.
143–45 The letters of Vittorio Foa from prison were kindly provided to me by their author.

Chapter Five

Page 150 Pitigrilli's letters to Mussolini are in file N. 532,422 in the Segreteria Particolare del Duce, Carteggio Ordinario of the ACS.
151 The information about Pitigrilli's firing is from Zucarò, p. 140.
152 The information on Pitigrilli's period of detention is in ACS, PS A5G, II G.M., envelope 303.
152–53 The description of Pitigrilli's experiences with the medium are from *La piscina di Siloe.*
153–54 The Nov. 8, 1941, and Feb. 9, 1942, OVRA dispatches are reprinted in Zucarò, pp. 146–51.
154–55 The March 1942 and 1943 letters from Pitigrilli to Mussolini are in ACS, SPD, CO, envelope 532.422.
162–65 The description of the life of Ettore and Lelia Foa during the German occupation comes from their children as well as from their letters written during that period provided to me by Anna Yona.

A Family of the Ghetto: The Di Verolis of Rome

Chapter One

Page 171 The quote from Flavius Josephus comes from Robert Katz's *Black Sabbath,* p. 8.
171–73 Material on the history of the Rome ghetto comes from Cecil Roth and from Attilio Milano, especially the latter's *Il ghetto di Roma.*
171 The estimate of the population of the ghetto comes from A. Milano, p. 15.
172 The estimate about half of the Jewish population of Rome living either within or nearby the ghetto comes from Katz, pp. 10–11.
173 The information about the history of the Di Veroli family comes from a letter to me from Michael Tagliacozzo.
174–87 The vast bulk of the Di Veroli section comes from interviews with various members of the Di Veroli family: Three children of Enrico and Grazia Astrologo Di Veroli, Michele, Gianni and Olga. The eldest son of Umberto and Elena Frascati Di Veroli, Michele. The daughters of Giacomo and Angela Funaro Di Veroli, Silvia and Giuditta. The middle daughter of Attilio and Costanza Funaro Di Veroli, Rosa.
185–87 For descriptions of the political and military events between July 25 and Sept. 8, 1943, see Monelli's *Roma, 1943,* pp. 197–233.

Chapter Two

Pages 188–89 The Kesselring order is reported in Jane Scrivener's *Inside Rome with the Germans,* p. 10.

190 The quote from Monelli is from his *Roma, 1943,* p. 386.
192–98 The principal sources for the account of the German extortion of the gold of Rome are: *Ottobre 1943: Cronaca di un' infamia* published by the Comunità Israelitica di Roma, 1961, which contains the diaries of Ugo Foà, president of the Jewish Community of Rome and Rosina Sorani, who worked in the community offices at the time; Katz's *Black Sabbath;* Michael Tagliacozzo's "La comunità di roma sotto l'incubo della svastica: La grande razzia del 16 Ottobre 1943," published in vol. 3 of the ACDEC's *Gli ebrei in Italia durante il fascismo;* Liliana Picciotto Fargion's *L'Occupazione tedesca e gli ebrei di Roma;* and Giacomo Debenedetti's *16 Ottobre. Otto Ebrei.*

There are also good synthetic accounts of the raid in Zuccotti and Mayda.
192 The quotes attributed to Kappler are from Ugo Foà's account in "Ottobre 1943," pp. 12–13.
193 The telegram to Kappler is from Tagliacozzo's essay "La persecuzione degli ebrei a Roma," in Picciotto Fargion's "L'Occupazione tedesca e gli ebrei di Roma," p. 152.
194 Quotation about the impotence of Italian "Authorities" is from Foà, p. 14.
196 Debenedetti's description of the collection of the gold is from his memoir *16 Ottobre,* p. 36.
198 The quotations from Foà on the weighing of the gold and the search of the Jewish Community's offices are from his "Ottobre 1943," pp. 16–17.
199 Debenedetti's description of the SS appropriation of the Jewish archive is from *16 Ottobre,* p. 40.
200 The final quotation from Foà is from his memoir, p. 24.

Chapter Three

Page 203 The description of the Roman bystander comes from the Tagliacozzo essay in Picciotto Fargion, pp. 156–57.
204 The other description of a Roman bystander is from Morpurgo's *Caccia all'uomo,* p. 141, reprinted in Katz, *Black Sabbath,* p. 185.
204–5 The German dispatch describing the round-up is from Picciotto Fargion, p. 19.
205–6 For Olga Di Veroli's account of the German occupation, I have used along with my own interview with her in 1986 two other interviews she gave: one for the television program called *Memoria presente* and the other in Nicola Caracciolo's *Gli ebrei e l'Italia durante la guerra 1940–45,* pp. 102–11.
207 The Buffarini Guidi dispatch is reprinted in Picciotto Fargion, p. 24.
208 The April 4, 1944, letter of Giacomo Di Veroli is reprinted in Picciotto Fargion, p. 121.
210 The figures on arrests in Rome in 1944 are from Picciotto Fargion, p. 22.
214 The quote from Lazzaro Anticoli is from Silvio Bertoldi's "*I tedeschi in Italia,*" pp. 120–21.
214–15 Accounts of the Ardeatine Caves massacre can be found in all the principal accounts of the German occupation of Rome. Specifically on the "caves" see: Attilio Ascarelli, *Le fosse ardeatine.*
216–18 The letters of Enrico Di Veroli are reprinted in Picciotto Fargion.
218 On the numbers of the convoys and survivors see Picciotto Fargion and the ACDEC publication: *Ebrei in Italia: Deportazione, resistenza.*
220–22 The three descriptions of the liberation of Rome are from Scrivener, pp. 194, 195 and 199.

The Rabbi, the Priest and the Aviator: A Story of Rescue in Genoa

Chapter One

The most important single sources for these chapters were Massimo Teglio and Emanuele Pacifici. Of great help were also Teglio's brother and sister, Mario and Laura Teglio, as well as Umberto Jacchia, Laura Cavaglione and Bernard Grosser. The best single work on the Jews of Genoa is Carlo Brizzolari's *Gli ebrei nella storia di Genova.* Briefer but important accounts are: Salvatore Jona, *La persecuzione degli ebrei di Genova,* Genoa, April 1965; Aldo Luzzatto, *La deportazione degli ebrei di Genova,* Quaderni del Centro di Studi sulla Deportazione e l'Internamento, n. 8, Rome, 1969–71. Emanuele Pacifici, *Testimonianza sulla deportazione di Riccardo Pacifici,* in Quaderni del Centro di Studi sulla Deportazione e l'Internamento, n. 4, 1967. See also Augusto Segre, *Memorie di vita ebraica* and Paini, *Sentieri della speranza.*
227 The statistics on the bombing of Genoa are from Montarese *Genova bruciata* (Genoa, 1971), p. 308.
227 The quotation on the daily evacuation of Genoa is from Montarese, p. 111.
230–33 For the history of DELASEM see Paini, *Sentieri della speranza* and Sorani, *L'assistenza ai profughi ebrei in Italia (1933–1947).*
231 For more information on the camp of Ferramonti, see Carlo Spartaco Capogreco, *Ferramonti,* Florence, 1987, and Francesco Folino, *Ebrei destinazione Calabria (1940–1943),* Palermo, 1988.
232–33 The quotation from Don Repetto comes from the speech he made on April 20, 1982, when he was awarded the medal of honor from Yad Vashem in Jerusalem. His sister, Teresa Repetto, kindly provided me with a copy.
233–34 This quotation from Repetto and the one that follows it come from a speech made on June 13, 1984. It has been reprinted in a volume published privately by Emanuele Pacifici, *Commemorazione di Riccardo Pacifici,* Rome, 1985, pp. 20–21.
235 The quotations from Augusto Segre come from his introduction to the collection of Rabbi Pacifici's sermons, *Riccardo Pacifici, Discorsi sulla Tora,* Rome, 1968, pp. xv–xvi.
235–36 Pacifici, *Discorsi sulla Tora,* pp. 60–61.
236 Pacifici's sermon of October 1, 1943, is contained in an anthology of his writings published in his honor by the Jewish Community of Genoa, *In perpetua ricordanza di Riccardo Pacifici,* Genoa, 1967, p. 43.
237 The excerpt from the diary of Emanuele Pacifici was given to me by its author.
238–39 The quotations from Repetto are from his 1984 speech.

Chapter Two

Pages 242–43 Along with interviews with Massimo Teglio and Emanuele Pacifici, there are numerous accounts of the raid on the Genoa synagogue. Among the ones I consulted were the file on Rabbi Riccardo Pacifici at the ACDEC in Milan. Files on individuals during the war are in the archive on "Vicissitudini dei singoli," archive 5-H-b, which is arranged alphabetically. See files on Riccardo Pacifici and his wife, Wanda Abenheim. I consulted the ACDEC files organized by city, archive 9/1, Genoa.

There are also full accounts in Salvatore Jona's article, *La persecuzione degli ebrei a Genova,* Genoa, April 1965, and in Brizzolari's *Gli ebrei nella storia di Genova,* as well as shorter accounts in Mayda's *Gli ebrei sotto Salò* and Zuccotti's *The Italians and the Holocaust.*

There are two conflicting versions of Pacifici's arrest. According to some (including Teglio and Repetto, which both Brizzolari and Zuccotti have followed), Pacifici had made an appointment to meet the custodian of the temple, Bino Polacco, in the Galleria

Mazzini, where the SS ambushed him. According to others (Aldo Luzzatti, rabbi of Genoa after the war and Emanuele Pacifici), Rabbi Pacifici called the temple the morning of the Nazi raid and the custodian told him to come to the synagogue. Unfortunately, none of these sources were eyewitnesses of the event. However, Don Repetto was able to visit Rabbi Pacifici while he was in prison in Genoa and presumably based his account of the arrest on the basis of their discussions. For this reason, I have chosen to follow his version.
245–46 The letter from Cardinal Boetto and the response of Carlo Basile are contained in Don Repetto's speech of June 13, 1984, in *Commemorazione di Riccardo Pacifici,* pp. 23–24.
254 The diary/report on the raid of the convent at Santa Maria del Carmine in Florence was given to me by the convent. The report is unsigned but is believed to have been written by the mother superior during the war, Sister Ester Busnelli.
254–55 The letter of Germana Ravenna is in the ACDEC, *Vicissitudini dei singoli,* archive 5-H-b.
255 The description of the departure from the convent is from the diary of Ester Busnelli.
257 The content of the letter of Linda Polacco was referred to Massimo Teglio by the Italian interpreter of the prison, Enrico Luzzatto. Teglio repeated it in a report he made on January 19, 1965, which can be found in ACDEC, archive 9/1, file on Genoa. It is also cited in Brizzolari, pp. 310–311.
258 The two letters of Wanda Pacifici were kindly provided to me by her son, Emanuele Pacifici.
259 On the arrests of Nathan Cassutto, Leto Casini and Raffaele Cantoni, see Paini, *Sentieri della speranza,* pp. 149–62.
260–61 On the DELASEM underground railroad, see both Paini and Brizzolari.
264 On the Rome operation of DELASEM, see De Felice and Settimio Sorani, *L'Assistenza ai profughi ebrei in Italia, 1933–1947.*
264 For more on the foreign Jews hiding in and around Cuneo, see Alberto Cavaglion, *Nella notte straniera.*
265 For more on the arrest and escape of Klein, see Paini.

Chapter Three

Page 269 The date of the bombing of the archbishop's office is confirmed in Brizzolari, p. 272.
270 Don Repetto's account of hiding the family in the ruined archbishopric is in his 1982 speech, as is his anecdote about Cardinal Boetto breaking the cloister rules.
270 Paul Ginsborg, *A History of Contemporary Italy: Society and Politics 1943–1988* (London, 1990), p. 65, puts the number of partisans at the end of the war at about 100,000.
271 The account of the May 15, 1955, partisan bombing is from Brizzolari, pp. 338–39.
271 The calling card of the German officers, with the date July 4, 1944, is reproduced in Brizzolari, p. 272.

Ferrara-Buchenwald-Ferrara: The Schönheit Family

Chapter One

Pages 281–82 For the account of the murder of Ghisellini and the round-up of Nov. 15, 1943, I relied on Mayda's *Gli ebrei sotto Salò,* on the article by Bruno Traversari, "Ferrara quella feroce notte del '43," *Storia illustrata,* November 1983, and also Giorgio

Bassani's story, "Una Notte nel '43," in his collection *Cinque storie ferraresi* (Turin, 1956). See also Renzo Bonfiglioli, *Gli ebrei a Ferrara dal fascismo alla liberazione,* in Competizione Democratica, April 25, 1955.
283–84 For notes on the history of the Jews of Ferrara I consulted a speech given by Matilde Finzi Bassani, "Cenni storici sulla comunità di Ferrara," dated Dec. 16, 1975, kept in the ACDEC, archive 9/1, Ferrara.
284 On Renzo Ravenna, mayor of Ferrara, see De Felice. I also relied on an interview with Paolo Ravenna, the mayor's son.
284–85 For Bassani's comment on the Jews of Ferrara I relied on an interview with Bassani as well as a speech by Lia Cases, "Gli ebrei antifascisti di Ferrara," dated 12/16/75 in the Ferrara file in the ACDEC.

Chapter Two

Pages 291–96 For accounts of Fossoli, aside from the tale of Franco Schönheit, I also consulted Zuccotti, Mayda and Primo Levi's *Se quest' è un uomo.* See also Picciotto Fargion, *Il libro della memoria.*
295 The most recent and authoritative data on the number of Jews arrested and deported is Liliana Picciotto Fargion, *Il libro della memoria.* Her data places the number of Jews arrested at 7,013. Of these, 2,489 were arrested by the Germans, 1,898 by Italians, and 312 by Germans and Italians together, while the identity of those who arrested the remaining 2,314 is still unknown. Of the 6,746 deported, Picciotti Fargion says that 2,445 were first interned at the Fossoli camp.

Chapter Three

For other accounts of life at Buchenwald I also consulted Bruno Bettelheim's *Surviving* (New York, 1979); Eugene Weinstock, *Beyond the Last Path* (New York, 1947); and Davide Rousset, *Les jours de notre mort* (Paris, 1947). Because Rousset and the Schönheits were both in "Block 14" during their final weeks at Buchenwald, the last chapters of *Les jours de notre mort* dovetail closely with the Schönheits' experience.
305–6 The quotations of Bettelheim are from the collection of essays *Surviving,* pp. 78–80.
311 The quotations of Weinstock are from *Beyond the Last Path,* pp. 243–46.

Epilogue

Page 318–20 For the material on the investigation into the death of the family of Ettore Ovazza and the trial of Gottfried Meir, see the Fondo Ovazza, ACDEC, and "Meir, il carnefice di Intra," *Storia Illustrata,* n. 186, 1973.

The Pitigrilli quotations on Jews and anti-Semitism are from *Mosè e il cavalier Levi,* pp. 52 and 54.
333 Renato Di Veroli kindly provided me with a copy of the typed orders he found in his home on October 16, 1943. Because it was a standard form, a virtually identical version can be found reprinted in Picciotto Fargion, *L'Occupazione tedesca e gli ebrei di Roma,* p. 159.
330 For the fate of Celeste di Porto after the war, see Bertoldi, pp. 120–21.
333 On the number of Di Verolis deported I made calculations based on the lists in Picciotto Fargion, *L'Occupazione tedesca e gli ebrei di Roma.* Her figures on the numbers of Roman Jews arrested and deported are on pp. 41–42. The figures on the numbers for Italy as a whole come from Picciotto Fargion, *Il libro della memoria,* pp. 30–32.
344 The Bassani story on the sole survivor of Ferrara is "Una lapide in Via Mazzini" ("A Plaque on Via Mazzini") in *Cinque storie ferraresi.*

Selected Bibliography

The most authoritative general histories of the Jews of Italy are Attilio Milano, *Storia degli ebrei in Italia* (Turin, 1963); and Cecil Roth, *The History of the Jews of Italy* (Philadelphia, 1946). A less detailed and more popular account is Luciano Tas, *Storia degli ebrei italiani* (Rome, 1987).

On the history of Italian Jews during the fascist period, there are various books, on different aspects. Perhaps the central work remains Renzo De Felice, *Storia degli ebrei italiani sotto il fascismo* (Turin, 1961, 1972), which includes extensive documentary material. Especially valuable information on the diplomatic relations between Mussolini and Hitler and their effects on fascist racial policy is found in Meir Michaelis, *Mussolini and the Jews: German–Italian Relations and the Jewish Question in Italy 1922–1945* (Oxford, 1978; in Italian, *Mussolini e la questione ebraica*, Milan, 1982). Giuseppe Mayda's *Ebrei sotto Salò* (Milan, 1978) is a good basic account of the principal events of the roundup of Jews during the German occupation. Susan Zuccotti's *The Italians and the Holocaust* (New York, 1987) takes advantage of the existing Italian literature and adds archival material to provide what is probably the most accessible general introduction to the subject in Italian or English.

A number of books touch on specific elements of the topic:

H. Stuart Hughes's *Prisoners of Hope: The Silver Age of the Italian Jews, 1924–1974* (Cambridge, 1983; in Italian, *Prigionieri della speranza*, Bologna, 1983) is an analysis of the Italian Jewish literary tradition.

The richly documented and illustrated catalogue produced by the Jewish Museum in New York for its 1989 show Gardens and Ghettos, edited by Vivian Mann, Berkeley, 1989, covers some 2,000 years of Italian Jewish culture.

The three volumes of *Quaderni*, edited and published by the Archivo del Centro di Documentazione Ebraica Contemporanea in Milan (ACDEC) under the title *Gli ebrei in Italia durante il Fascismo*, contains a number of useful essays and personal reminiscences.

Liliana Picciotto Fargion's *L'Occupazione tedesca e gli ebrei di Roma* (Rome and Milan, 1979), is another publication of ACDEC. This collection includes historical essays by different authors on the German occupation of Rome; documents; and a complete list of names and dates for all Jews deported from Rome. Picciotto Fargion has also recently published a book on the deportations throughout Italy, *Il libro della memoria: gli ebrei deportati dall'Italia* (Milan, 1991), which came out after I had finished my research. It contains a brief biographical account of each of the 6,746 Jews deported from Italy during the war as well as a detailed explanation of the modalities of all the deportations.

Ebrei in Italia: deportazione, resistenza (Milan and Florence, 1975) is an ACDEC booklet with data about the various deportation convoys from Italy to Germany during the war.

Robert Katz's *Black Sabbath: A Journey Through a Crime Against Humanity* (Toronto, 1967; in Italian, *Sabato nero*, Milan, 1973) is a highly readable, if polemical account of the Jews of Rome during the German occupation.

Fausto Coen's *Italiani ed ebrei: come eravamo* (Genoa, 1988) deals with the enactment and repercussions of the Italian racial laws.

Ugo Caffaz's *L'Antisemitismo italiano sotto il fascismo* (Florence, 1975) focuses on the facist racial legislation.

Rosa Paini's *I Sentieri della Speranza: Profughi ebrei, Italia fascista e la Delasem* (Milan, 1988) is a good account of the activities of the principal assistance organization to Jewish refugees in Italy.

Settimio Sorani's *L'Assistenza ai profughi ebrei in Italia, 1933–1947* (Rome, 1983) covers the same subject from the point of view of one of the group's principal leaders.

Also useful on this topic is Massimo Leone, *Le organizzazioni di soccorso ebraiche in età fascista, 1943–1947* (Rome, 1983).

Alberto Cavaglion's *Nella notte straniera: Gli ebrei di S. Martin de Vësubie e il campo di Borgo San Dalmazzo* (Cuneo, 1981) is a good account of the predicament of Jewish refugees in a small northern Italian town during the German occupation.

Nicola Caracciolo's *Gli ebrei e l'Italia durante la guerra 1940–45* (Rome, 1986) contains interviews made for a television documentary about the Italians' treatment of the Jews during the war.

The history of Jews in specific Italian cities is covered by the following: Carlo Brizzolari, *Gli ebrei nella storia di Genova* (Genoa, 1971); Riccardo Calimani, *The Ghetto of Venice* (New York, 1987; in Italian, *Storia del ghetto di Venezia,* Milan, 1985); Attilio Milano, *Il ghetto di Roma* (Rome, 1988); Sam Waagennaar, "*Il ghetto sul tevere* (Milan, 1972); Luciana Finelli, Italo Insolera, and Ada Francesca Marcianò, *Il ghetto* (Rome, 1986); Salvatore Foa, *Gli ebrei nel Risorgimento* (Rome, 1978).

Among the many autobiographical accounts I made use of are: Galeazzo Ciano, *Ciano's Hidden Diary, 1937–38* (New York, 1953); Giacomo Debenedetti's *16 Ottobre: otto ebrei* (Rome, 1978); Natalia Ginzburg, *Lessico familiare* (Turin, 1963); Primo Levi, *Se questo è un uomo* (Turin, 1947); Rita Levi-Montalcini, *Elogio dell'imperfezione* (Milan, 1987); Piero Modigliani, *I nazisti a Roma: Dal diario di un ebreo* (Rome, 1984); Luciano Morpurgo, *Caccia all'uomo* (Rome, 1946); Jane Scrivener, *Inside Rome with the Germans* (New York, 1945); Augusto Segre, *Memorie di vita ebraica* (Rome, 1979); Sion Segre Amar, *Il mio ghetto,* (Milan, 1987); Vittorio Segre, *Memoirs of a Fortunate Jew* (Bethesda, MD, 1987; in Italian, *Storia di un ebreo fortunato,* Milan, 1985); Elio Toaff, *Perfidi ebrei, fratelli maggiori* (Milan, 1987).

The following books provide general orientation: Attilio Ascarelli, *Le Fosse Ardeatine* (Bologna, 1965); Giorgio Bassani, *Il giardino dei finzi-contini* (Turin, 1962) and *Cinque storie Ferraresi* (Turin, 1956); Silvio Bertoldi, *Salò: Vita e morte della Repubblica Sociale Italiana* (Milan, 1976) and *I Tedeschi in Italia* (Milan, 1964); Giorgio Bocca, *La repubblica di Mussolini* (Rome and Bari, 1977); Giampiero Carocci, *Storia d'Italia dall'unità ad oggi* (Milan, 1975); Alastair Hamilton, *The Appeal of Fascism* (London, 1971); Abramo Levi, *Noi ebrei* (Roma, 1937); Emil Ludwig, *Talks with Mussolini* (Boston, 1933; in Italian, *Colloqui con Mussolini,* Milan, 1933); Denis Mack Smith, *Italy: A Modern History,*" (Ann Arbor, MI, 1959), as well as his biography *Mussolini* (London, 1981) and his book on fascist foreign policy, *Mussolini's Roman Empire* (London, 1976); Paolo Monelli, *Mussolini, piccolo borghese* (Milan, 1950) and *Roma, 1943* (Milan, 1963); Benito Mussolini, *Opera Omnia* (Florence, 1951–1981); Paolo Orano, *Gli ebrei in Italia* (Rome, 1937); Luigi Salvatorelli and Giovanni Mira, *Storia d'Italia nel periodo fascista,* (Turin, 1956, 1961); Raleigh Trevelyan, *Rome '44: The Battle for the Eternal City* (in Italian, *Roma '44,* Milan, 1983).